The Malmedy Massacre

The War Crimes Trial Controversy

STEVEN P. REMY

Harvard University Press

Cambridge, Massachusetts & London, England

2017

Printed in the United States of America

First printing

Library of Congress Cataloging-in-Publication Data

Names: Remy, Steven P., author.
Title: The Malmedy Massacre : the war crimes trial controversy / Steven P. Remy.
Description: Cambridge, Massachusetts : Harvard University Press, 2017. |
Includes bibliographical references and index.
Identifiers: LCCN 2016040444 | ISBN 9780674971950 (hardcover : alk. paper)
Subjects: LCSH: Malmedy Massacre, 1944–1945. | Malmedy Trial, Dachau,
Germany, 1946. | War crime trials—Public opinion.
Classification: LCC D804.G3 R46 2017 | DDC 341.6/90268—dc23
LC record available at https://lccn.loc.gov/2016040444

For April

Contents

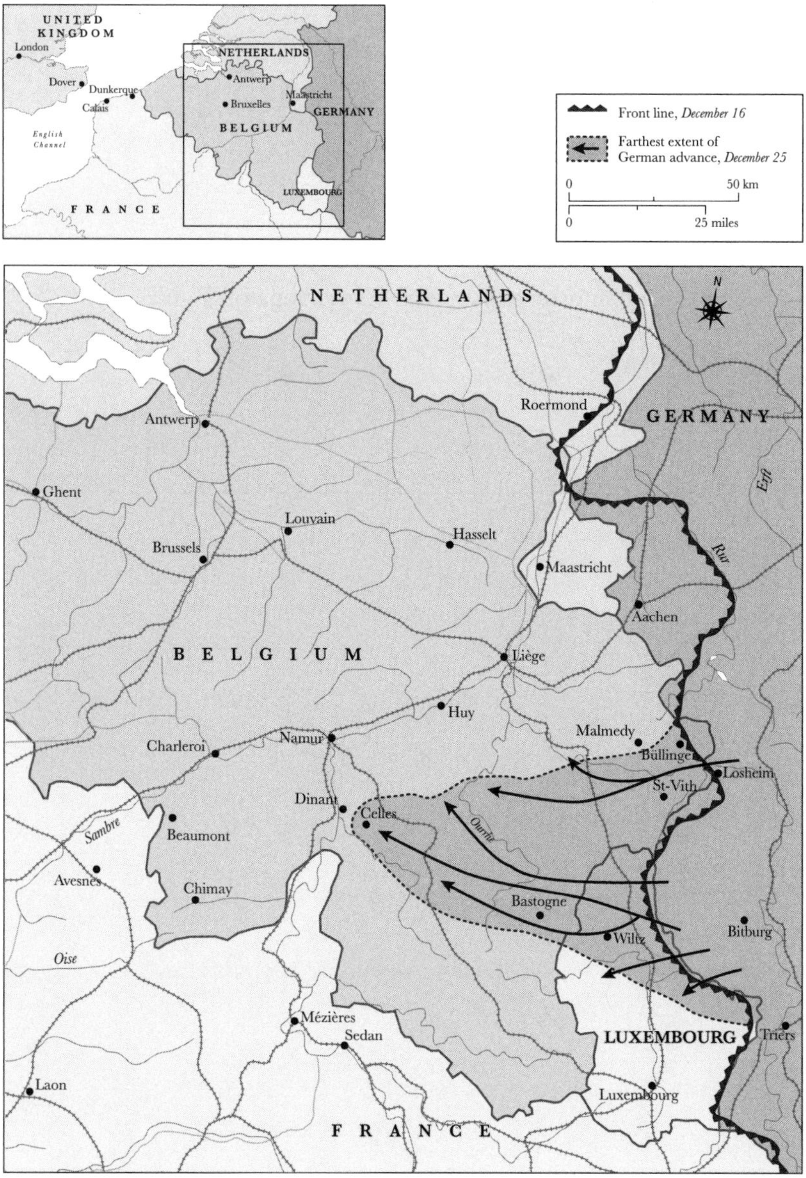

The Battle of the Bulge: December 16–25, 1944

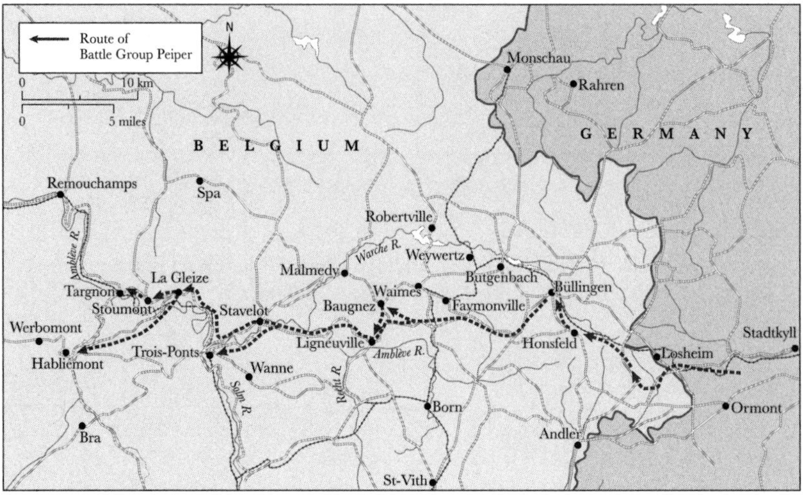

Advance of Battle Group Peiper: December 17–24, 1944

Introduction

An American Courtroom in Dachau

Beginning in 1936, Germans taken into "protective custody" in the Dachau concentration camp entered the expansive prisoner enclosure through an iron gate. Constructed by other prisoners, the gate bore the words "Arbeit Macht Frei" ("Work Makes One Free"), a perverse lie. After the camp became a national memorial site in 1965, visitors passed through the very same gate until the section of it bearing the infamous inscription was stolen in late 2014. Most visitors were unaware that the thirty-seven-acre prisoners' compound made up less than one quarter of the entire Dachau complex. The bulk of it comprised a largely self-contained facility for socializing men and women in the culture of the Schutzstaffel (SS) and preparing them to administer what would become a vast domain of conquest, exploitation, and genocide.[1]

By 1946, Dachau, its name now synonymous with terror and lawlessness, had been transformed into an important site of judicial reckoning with the crimes of the Nazi regime. The U.S. Army's Counter Intelligence Corps (CIC) had converted the complex into "War Crimes Enclosure No. 1," with suspects—most of them members of the SS—held in the former prisoners' and SS compounds. A new division of the War Department dedicated to prosecuting suspected war criminals then built makeshift courtrooms in some of the intact buildings. For nearly three years, army judges conducted trials of hundreds of German concentration camp personnel and those suspected of murdering American prisoners of war and civilians of Allied nations. The first of the army's trials was, appropriately enough, the trial of the camp's former personnel.[2]

Sitting in the dock in one of these courtrooms on May 16, 1946, were seventy-four former members of the Waffen SS. They were accused of killing hundreds of Americans prisoners of war and Belgian civilians in December 1944 and January 1945. The most notorious of such crimes had taken place on December 17, the second day of a surprise German counterattack in the Ardennes region of Belgium that resulted in the Battle of the Bulge. At a crossroads village near the town of Malmedy, a Waffen SS combat group executed eighty-four captured American soldiers. The incident quickly became known in the United States as the "Malmedy massacre." It would be the single deadliest of such encounters involving American and German forces in the European theater. The trial of the suspected perpetrators would be the highest-visibility case prosecuted by the army at Dachau.

Three months later, the court convicted all the defendants, sentencing forty-three to death and twenty-two to life terms. What followed was a decade-long transatlantic controversy surrounding accusations that American interrogators had tortured the defendants, forcing them to sign false confessions and thus sealing their fates at the trial. A loosely interconnected network of Americans and Germans sought to overturn the verdicts and, more broadly, discredit all Allied war crimes trials. The critics claimed to have exposed the army's most important case as a sham and considered the investigators, prosecutors, and judges to be no better than the camp's former overseers. As a result of the controversy generated by these accusations, which would test the limits of the early U.S.–West German relationship, none of the death sentences was ever carried out and every convicted perpetrator was freed by 1957.

Historians have been no kinder in their assessments of the army's conduct before, during, and after the trial. To a remarkable extent, they have adopted the arguments made by critics of the investigation in the late 1940s and early 1950s. A consensus holds that the U.S. Army, outraged by the discovery of the victims' remains in January 1945, tracked down the alleged perpetrators, forced them to confess to crimes they did not in fact commit, and put them on trial before a court that was nothing more than a vehicle to exact victor's justice. Echoing an argument made by defense lawyers in the Dachau courtroom, the most influential accounts of the massacre conclude that it resulted not from orders or from a mode of warfare particular to the Waffen SS, but from heat of battle circumstances that could affect any group of soldiers in any war. Historians who have written about this and other Allied war crimes trials have also emphasized the importance of a Cold War climate that ultimately made it impossible for the governments of the United States, Great Britain, and France to keep convicted German war criminals in prison.[3]

In this book, I suggest another way of looking at the most controversial war crimes trial in American history. Contrary to the claims of its veterans and their sympathizers, the Waffen SS was an integral part of the SS and, along with the Wehrmacht, an instrument of the regime's war of genocidal conquest. In the Ardennes, the Waffen SS waged a terror war, just as it had done elsewhere in Europe. It sought a reputation as a fearsome fighting force by making no distinction between armed combatants, prisoners of war, and civilians. SS soldiers considered themselves not "ordinary"—and hence law-abiding—but modern-day Mongol warriors and the spearhead of Nazi Germany's race war. American investigators came to understand this in the course of a lengthy investigation and produced a damning case against seventy-four former SS officers and enlisted men. That the principal interrogator in the investigation was one of thousands of German-born Jewish émigrés serving in the U.S. Army would become of central importance to the posttrial controversy.

The claims that American interrogators tortured the suspects were fictitious. They originated with an attempt by Americans sympathetic to the accused, the accused themselves, and Germans seeking amnesty for convicted war criminals to discredit the investigation and trial. With great determination and considerable long-term success, a German-American network of trial critics promoted a story of a blameless SS, an investigation corrupted by vengeance-seeking Jews, and victor's justice dressed up as a war crimes trial. The critics implied or simply stated outright that there really was no difference between the U.S. Army in Europe and the Waffen SS. They insisted that both were comprised of ordinary soldiers who, when placed under enormous pressure, occasionally overstepped the boundaries of law and civilized behavior. The Cold War's realignment of allies and enemies would act as an accelerant in this campaign to deny or relativize the significance of crimes committed by the Waffen SS.

Revisiting the entire Malmedy massacre affair now is important for several reasons. We are at risk of drawing the wrong lessons from it at a time when a historically informed discussion of interrogation methods and military courts is compelling. For one thing, attempts to link the pretrial investigation to the use of systematic torture by the U.S. military and the Central Intelligence Agency (CIA) after 9/11 are misguided and unhelpful. For another, the suggestion made by Americans and Germans that the army's Dachau courts were "un-American" distorted the historical record, as military courts were—and remain—very much a part of the American legal tradition. As the rules and procedures of these courts are now a topic of intense interest and significance, it is necessary to have an accurate understanding of how they operated in the past.

My purpose in writing this book was not to make policy recommendations. Like any historian, of course, I would be more than happy if it was read by those who bear the burden of pursuing terrorists and war criminals. At its heart, *The Malmedy Massacre* contributes to an ongoing sea change in how historians and the wider public have understood the relationship between Nazi Germany and the postwar Germanys. Often in the face of considerable resistance, scholars on both sides of the Atlantic have spent several decades studying the most significant segments of German society and have revealed the extent to which former National Socialists and their apologists have shaped our knowledge of the Nazi dictatorship, the war, and the Holocaust since 1945.[4]

The Malmedy affair—and the historiography that emerged out of it—shows us that Germans seeking to interpret the past to suit their interests had plenty of help from influential Americans. In their efforts to explain the intense controversies generated by war crimes trials in occupied Germany, historians have overlooked the importance of the symbiotic relationship that developed between American and German amnesty advocates.[5] A close look at how that relationship fueled a long controversy over the Malmedy massacre investigation and trial reminds us that postwar Atlanticism was built on more than a shared commitment to democracy and antitotalitarianism. Conspiratorial anti-Semitism, a willingness among political leaders, diplomats, and military officials to believe that Nazi Germany fought to defend Western civilization against "bolshevism," and Anglo-American fascination with alleged German military prowess were also important features of this partnership. That its construction came at the cost of a more substantial measure of justice for Nazi Germany's victims should be acknowledged as one of the darker legacies of World War II and the Cold War.

ONE

The Commitments of a Bad Reputation

Terror War in the Ardennes

On December 16, 1944, several hundred bored American soldiers occupied the Belgian village of Honsfeld, just a few miles west of the German border in the northeastern reaches of the Ardennes. With nearly all residents having been evacuated, Honsfeld was serving as a rest center for the men of the Ninety-Ninth Infantry Division and other units. The twenty-mile stretch of the front held by the division had been quiet since Anglo-American armies drove German forces out of Belgium three months earlier. Along this "ghost front," as one British Army veteran characterized it, trench foot claimed more casualties than combat. Preparing for an appearance by Marlene Dietrich and the United Service Organizations scheduled for the following day had been the most pressing concern of the officer in charge.

The calm was broken after midnight as American vehicles moving away from what appeared to be a German counterattack began streaming through the town. Honsfeld's commander cancelled Dietrich's performance and ordered makeshift defensive positions to be deployed later that morning. As more vehicles moved through, most GIs bedded down in requisitioned houses along the main street. In the predawn dark, German tanks and armored vehicles rolled in undetected behind American jeeps. A brief firefight ensued as paratroopers and Waffen SS soldiers of a First SS Panzer Division "Leibstandarte SS Adolf Hitler" ("Personal Standard SS Adolf Hitler") battle group swarmed the village. Taken by surprise and overwhelmed by the speed and stealth of the enemy's appearance, American soldiers began surrendering.[1]

Charles Huttoe, a twenty-three-year-old private, watched an officer bearing the white flag of surrender lead a group of twelve men of the 612th Tank Destroyer Battalion out of the house in which he and about twenty other GIs had been hiding. Waffen SS soldiers opened fire on the group, killing most of them. The Germans then accepted the surrender of the remaining Americans—eventually totaling around two hundred—and ordered them to march out of town past the column of vehicles advancing in the opposite direction. As they walked, some shot at their captives. Sergeant John Dluski of the 612th heard one shout out "Hey you!" in English before shooting Corporal Johnnie Stegle in the forehead with an American revolver, killing him instantly. The shooting, seemingly random, sent frightened GIs scrambling into a roadside ditch. A few who played dead were able to recount their ordeal at the 612th's headquarters a day later.[2]

As the Americans had already evacuated most of Honsfeld's residents and those of surrounding villages, few civilians in this area were harmed. But in a string of towns further west, Belgian men, women, and children would soon endure not only fierce fighting between Americans and Germans, but also the brutality of the Waffen SS. Between December 17 and 25, the men of the battle group that captured Honsfeld murdered hundreds of American prisoners and Belgian civilians between that town and La Gleize, roughly thirty miles west of Honsfeld. The incident that would become known as the Malmedy massacre was only one of these encounters, albeit most likely the single deadliest.

Our Strength Lies in Our Speed and Brutality

Assessing what happened between Honsfeld and La Gleize in the last weeks of December requires a close look at the Ardennes counteroffensive and the special role of the Waffen SS as an instrument of terror war, a mode of warfare in which the boundaries between lawful combatants, prisoners of war, and civilians were erased and fear deployed as a weapon. Honsfeld's capture took place on the second day of a surprise operation aimed at seizing the port of Antwerp. Following the liberation of northern France, Belgium, and Luxembourg in August and September 1944, Allied forces pushed toward the

German border along a five-hundred-mile front stretching from the Scheldt estuary in the north to the tri-border junction of France, Germany, and Switzerland in the south. Tenacious resistance demonstrated that the German army was not at the verge of total collapse here nor in Italy nor on the Eastern Front. A poorly conceived and executed Anglo-American attempt to open a drive across the north German plain by capturing bridges over the Meuse, Waal, and Lower Rhine Rivers failed in September. Manpower and supply shortages, worsening weather, and the demands of feeding newly liberated populations further hindered rapid Allied advance, dimming hopes of ending the war in 1944.[3]

Despite massive German losses on all fronts in the summer and fall, the threat of Allied armies storming across Germany's western borders was therefore not an immediate one. In late July, Hitler sensed that the moment was arriving to gamble his dwindling resources on an all-or-nothing counteroffensive in the west. He ordered an attack to strike across one hundred miles of Belgium with the objective of seizing Antwerp. The drive to the port city would separate American and British armies. New German weapons then in production would work their intended "miracles," and the resulting disruptions would force the Americans and British to seek a separate peace with Germany. Hitler would be free to concentrate on holding off Soviet forces in the east.[4]

The plan was fantastical for several reasons. Not least was the fact that German forces did not have near enough fuel and other resources to reach and hold the crucial channel port. And while Hitler understood that the Red Army would have to be fought to the end, he dismissed the depth of the American and British commitment to Germany's unconditional surrender. His faith in the infallibility of his own judgment was, as always, unshakable. In a meeting with his commanders at his East Prussian headquarters on September 16, Hitler settled on the Ardennes region as the attack's focal point. He had already ordered the attack for November, counting on bad weather to keep Allied air forces grounded, but clear skies and manpower and equipment shortages forced him to postpone until December.

The army's High Command spent the next two months planning the offensive in strictest secrecy. Codenamed "Watch on the Rhine" and later renamed "Autumn Mist," three armies with rebuilt or newly constituted reserves would attack across the weakly defended Ardennes front. Heavily wooded and scored with rivers, streams, and narrow roads, the Ardennes was unsuitable for the rapid movement of tanks and armored vehicles, especially in winter. Yet surprise and speed were essential conditions for success, and any hope of capturing Antwerp depended on the seizure of bridges spanning the Meuse River before the Americans could destroy them. Hitler ordered four Waffen SS armored divisions of General Josef "Sepp" Dietrich's Sixth Panzer Army to spearhead the offensive. Its northern shoulder, which offered the shortest route to the Meuse and then to Antwerp, was assigned to the Twelfth and First SS Panzer Divisions, joined by elements of Volksgrenadier and Luftwaffe paratrooper divisions. The First SS Panzer Division would be subdivided into four battle groups of the Personal Standard SS Adolf Hitler.

The Waffen SS was the armed forces division of the SS. It was formed from a small bodyguard detachment established by Hitler in 1933 and assorted local units of armed SS men. By the late 1930s, Hitler and SS chief Heinrich Himmler had created the basis of a consolidated fighting force. These "SS disposition troops"—later designated "Waffen SS"—were to serve under Hitler's direct command. "Neither a part of the Wehrmacht, nor of the police," as he put it in August 1938, they were to form "a standing armed unit, at my exclusive disposal."[5] During the war, Himmler expanded the Waffen SS into a nearly one-million-strong force of thirty-eight divisions and other field units, some comprised substantially of non-German volunteers and conscripts. A special unit, the Death's Head, supplied guard detachments to concentration camps and later formed its own combat division.[6]

For decades after the war, Waffen SS veterans and their sympathizers worked tirelessly to shape the memory of the organization's purpose and record in wartime Europe. The Waffen SS, they claimed, was strictly an elite military force comprised of nonetheless ordinary soldiers who fought honorably for their country—and for all of Europe—against "Bolshevism." With the exception of the Death's Head division, which was associated indelibly with the concentration camps, apologists insisted that Waffen SS field units had little or nothing to do with the larger SS, the camps, war crimes, or the Holocaust. Their efforts not only influenced political and public opinion in West Germany, Britain, and the United States, but also informed the first scholarly histories of the Waffen SS, which portrayed a traditional military fighting force for which the commission of war crimes was incidental or a fiction concocted by vengeful Allied prosecutors.[7]

Recent research has challenged this consensus by disentangling the Waffen SS's wartime record from the distortions of postwar apologetics. The Waffen SS was an integral part of the SS and a principal weapon of its campaigns of conquest and genocide. Placed under the tactical command of the Wehrmacht, the two forces spent most of the war fighting side by side. And while some Wehrmacht officers and enlisted men eventually expressed grudging admiration for the bravery and skill of the much-derided Waffen SS "asphalt soldiers," many also disdained their unprofessionalism, recklessness, and criminality. Given the Wehrmacht's deep complicity in the war's worst crimes, including the Holocaust, distinctions between it and the Waffen SS must not be overstated. Nevertheless, wherever Waffen SS field units were deployed, they demonstrated a greater willingness relative to their counterparts in the Wehrmacht to fight fanatically, even suicidally, and murder prisoners of war and civilians.[8]

The Waffen SS was created to wage precisely this kind of warfare. The guiding spirit was Genghis Khan. The Mongol warlord fascinated Hitler and Himmler. While they considered Mongols to be members of an inferior race, Genghis Khan's successes as a conqueror of an enormous empire could not be denied. Their conception of him was shaped by a characterization of his fearsome reputation formulated in two quasi-factual books written in the mid-1930s by Michael Charol, an obscure Russian émigré writer who wrote as Michael Prawdin. In Prawdin's histories, Genghis practiced an early form of "war of annihilation" by destroying whole towns and slaughtering or enslaving enemy warriors and civilians without hesitation. Prawdin's accounts so impressed Himmler that he authorized a one-volume edition of both books to be published and distributed to every SS officer.[9]

Hitler and Himmler imagined the Wehrmacht and the SS, including the Waffen SS, as forming a modern, "Aryan" version of the Mongol "hordes." Victories against larger forces would be assured—as they were for Genghis Khan—by mobility, speed, and utter ruthlessness. For Hitler, armed SS units would form the spearhead of terror war. A week before a million German soldiers poured across the Polish border on September 1, 1939, he laid out to his generals his vision of this kind of war and the special role of the Waffen SS in it: "Our strength lies in our speed and brutality. Genghis Khan hunted millions of women and children to their deaths, consciously and with a joyous heart. . . . The aim of the war lies not in reaching particular lines but in the physical annihilation of the enemy."[10] Hitler and Himmler recognized that this mode of warfare would earn the Waffen SS a reputation which itself would become a kind of weapon.

Between the invasion of Poland and the Ardennes offensive, Hitler deployed armed SS units and the Waffen SS as instruments of terror war from one end of German-controlled Europe to the other. In Poland and the Soviet Union, SS mobile execution squads (Einsatzgruppen), battalions of SS Order Police, and Waffen SS divisions murdered over a million civilians and prisoners of war. All across the Eastern Front and in the Balkans, Waffen SS cavalry brigades, tank divisions, and motorized infantry led assaults, counterattacks, and rear-area "pacification" operations in which the distinction between combatants and civilians was erased. In the late summer of 1941, Waffen SS forces operating in southern Belarus under Himmler's direct command were the first SS units to expand the murder of Jews to include women and children. There, Himmler had deployed the Waffen SS as the spearhead of the Holocaust.[11]

In Western Europe, the Waffen SS became both the principal perpetrator of war crimes and a frequent target of retaliatory executions by Allied soldiers.[12] On May 27, 1940, elements of a Personal Standard division massacred eighty British and French prisoners of war in Wormhoudt near Dunkirk. The same day, a Death's Head division company executed ninety-seven surrendered British soldiers at Le Paradis. Civilians were also targeted—long before the formation of organized armed resistance to the Germans. Over the course of three days that May, Death's Head regiments murdered 164 civilians in northwestern France. Reports of these incidents led Wehrmacht general Erich Höpner to threaten those who executed prisoners of war with trial by military courts on charges of murder. Yet the Wehrmacht's hands were hardly clean in the few weeks it took to conquer France: both Wehrmacht (especially its strongly indoctrinated "Greater Germany" division) and units of the SS Death's Head division massacred at least fifteen hundred captured African soldiers then serving in the French Army.[13]

In Italy in 1943 and 1944, both Waffen SS and Wehrmacht forces killed thousands of civilians in putative "antipartisan" campaigns or in retaliation for partisan attacks on German forces. The Waffen SS carried out the worst of these massacres. In about three hours on August 12, 1944, elements of the Sixteenth SS Panzergrenadier Division "Reichsführer" slaughtered nearly the entire population of the Tuscan village of Sant'Anna di Stazzema. Two months later members of a reconnaissance battalion of the same Panzergrenadier division killed nearly eight hundred civilians around the village of Marzabotto, near Bologna.[14]

The Waffen SS was also responsible for nearly all of the deadliest massacres of prisoners of war and civilians in France before and after D-Day. On April 1, 1944, men of the Twelfth SS Panzer Division "Hitler Youth" executed eighty-six French men outside Lille. A battalion of the same division—trained and led by former Personal Standard officers—executed 155 Canadian soldiers in Normandy from June 7 to 12, 1944. On the night of June 11 and 12, soldiers of the Seventeenth SS Panzergrenadier Division Götz von Berlichingen left no survivors in the Norman village of Graignes when they murdered perhaps twenty wounded American paratroopers, the two French priests who had been caring for them, and two women before burning much of the village. Two months later, a battalion of the same division murdered 124 residents of the Loire Valley village of Maille. On June 9, elements of the Second SS Panzer Division "Das Reich" killed around 120 men in the Limousin village of Tulle. A day later some seventy miles northwest of Tulle, soldiers of the same division slaughtered nearly every inhabitant of Oradour-sur-Glane—642 people—in retaliation for alleged resistance activity in the area. Soldiers of various Waffen SS field divisions were also responsible for multiple atrocities against Belgian civilians during the German retreat from Belgium in September.[15]

These were neither isolated incidents nor the result of frightened and angry young soldiers lashing out at civilians in the immediate aftermath of attacks by partisans. Waffen SS forces were applying what one colonel called their "Russian education" to the Western Front.[16] With few exceptions, the perpetrators of these massacres would never stand before Allied or civilian courts.

One of Our Best Weapons

In the course of a long speech to his generals three days before the launch of Autumn Mist, Hitler demanded that the offensive's Waffen SS spearhead "spread fear and panic" and show no mercy to enemy combatants, prisoners of war, and civilians alike.[17] The commanders and officers of the First SS

Panzer Division Personal Standard battle group were well prepared to oblige the order. The unit that captured Honsfeld was known informally as "Battle Group Peiper" after its twenty-nine-year-old commander, Lieutenant Colonel Joachim Peiper. The arrogant, handsome Peiper personified the SS ideal of the ruthless practitioner of terror war. His name associated indelibly with the Malmedy massacre, he and many of his former comrades spent decades after 1945 cultivating a very different image—that of a daring but still ordinary soldier defamed by Allied war crimes prosecutors.

Most daring but ordinary soldiers, of course, do not sacrifice men and material heedlessly, and the soldiers under Peiper's commands bore the brunt of his recklessness repeatedly. Nor do most daring but ordinary soldiers commit serial war crimes, and Peiper was, without question, a war criminal. The Personal Standard, like other Waffen SS field divisions, sought and earned a reputation among Allied armies, civilian populations, and the German army for brutality toward prisoners of war and civilians. Peiper was proud of this reputation and, like Himmler, believed that ongoing demonstrations of terror were necessary to maintain it. "A bad reputation," he became fond of remarking, "has its commitments."[18]

Peiper was as pure a product of the SS as one might imagine. He claimed the example of his father—an Imperial Prussian Army officer and veteran of German colonial wars in Africa, World War I, and Free Corps campaigns in Silesia—inspired his desire to become an army officer. Rather than pursue the traditional route to officer candidacy, the eighteen-year-old Joachim joined an SS cavalry unit in October 1933. He was most likely drawn to the SS because of its elite status within the Nazi Party, believing that it represented the "guard of the new Germany," as Himmler described it in 1931. By early 1935, allegedly at Himmler's personal encouragement, he began a training course for future Personal Standard leaders.[19]

Peiper belonged to a generational cohort trained in SS leadership academies *(Junkerschule)*. The academies produced officers for Waffen SS field divisions and functionaries for other arms of the SS, including the Security Service (Sicherheitsdienst), Gestapo, and the Death's Head division. Candidates, having met rigorous physical and hereditary standards, were to be cultivated as the racial-political elite of a new Germany.

The academies provided military training by experienced, if not necessarily distinguished, army officers and intensive indoctrination in the racial-imperial worldview of the SS. This indoctrination sought to shape all aspects of the candidates' lives, from the superficial to the most intimate. Hence, they were instructed to master the intricacies of an etiquette manual ("champagne glasses to be parallel to the third tunic button, arm extended at forty-five degrees") and to otherwise mimic the manners of the British aristocracy.[20] Off duty a more egalitarian ethos prevailed, as officers and cadets socialized and addressed each other informally. Less superficially, their wives were expected to be as committed to Hitler and National Socialism as their husbands. And while Himmler would not tolerate atheists, candidates were admonished to reject the Christian churches. "For a member of the 'black corps,'" an officer lectured cadets in April 1936, "Adolf Hitler and not the Pope in Rome is the highest authority."[21]

Peiper began his training in an SS leader candidate course near Berlin at Jütebog, where his principal instructors were two fanatical National Socialists, Gustav Lombard and Emil Sator. Having been recommended to the Braunschweig leadership academy in April 1935, he was commissioned as an SS leader at the rank of second lieutenant a year later. His immersion in the culture of the SS deepened considerably when he was promoted to Himmler's personal staff in 1938. As part of the inner circle, Peiper came to idolize his boss, even embracing the quasi-mystical, occultist "religion" that obsessed the increasingly powerful SS chief. In 1939 he married one of Himmler's staff secretaries. That year, Peiper began serving as Himmler's first adjutant. In this capacity, he accompanied Himmler on inspection tours around Germany and Europe, visits that included concentration camps, asylums, and Jewish ghettos in Poland and Ukraine, where he witnessed gassings. Peiper was fully informed of Hitler's order to murder Poland's intellectual and cultural elites and, later, of the mass shootings of Jews in the Soviet Union by SS Einsatzgruppen.[22]

Despite his proximity to the center of political power in Nazi Germany, Peiper still wanted to be a soldier. In May 1940, he left Himmler's staff temporarily to serve as a platoon leader in France, where he commanded a company in the fighting around Dunkirk and was subsequently promoted to captain and awarded two Iron Crosses. It would be in Russia, however, that his style of command evolved fully, cementing the "bad reputation" that would prompt Sepp Dietrich to entrust him with leading the spearhead of Autumn Mist's northern shoulder. Peiper's battle groups would stage rapid

The recently decorated Joachim Peiper (far right) stands behind Heinrich Himmler as Himmler converses with Höhere SS- und Polizeiführer for Saar-Lothringen, SS-Gruppenführer Ernst Berkelmann, in France, September 1940 (NARA).

armored attacks or counterattacks without regard for flanks or material and manpower losses. The murder of prisoners of war and civilians was central to this mode of warfare. "Even old Genghis Khan would gladly have hired us as assistants," he wrote Himmler's mistress in March 1943, and bragged that "our reputation precedes us as a wave of terror and is one of our best weapons."[23]

Following brief reassignment to Himmler's staff, Peiper returned to the war in the late summer of 1941 and was given command of a Personal Standard company in Ukraine. Here he led the spearhead of an assault on Rostov and shocked the company's wounded former commander with his recklessness and the casualties his men suffered as a result. After a brief interlude in France, during which he was given command of a battalion, he was transferred back to Ukraine at the beginning of 1943. In the aftermath of the German Sixth Army's encirclement at Stalingrad, the Red Army pushed westward, capturing Kharkov and surrounding cities. Field Marshal Erich von Manstein ordered a counterattack against overextended Russian forces and recaptured the city, the Soviet Union's third largest. Manstein's forces had been bolstered by an infusion of Wehrmacht troops from Western Europe and three Waffen SS divisions, including the Personal Standard. Peiper commanded one of the motorized infantry battalions that charged straight into the city on March 9. After vicious house-to-house fighting, Kharkov fell back under German control.[24]

The counterattack marked the highpoint of the Personal Standard's—and Peiper's—battlefield victories. The recapture of Kharkov allowed the Wehrmacht to stabilize the front in Ukraine, at least temporarily. Peiper and other Personal Standard officers were showered with decorations—Peiper was awarded the regime's highest military honor, the Knight's Cross of the Iron Cross—and regime propagandists celebrated their boldness and tenacity. The newspaper of the Waffen SS, *Das Schwarze Korps (The Black Corps),* described Peiper's decisions as "bold and unorthodox" and issued "not from clever deliberation, but rather from a personality whose heart, brain, and hands are the same."[25]

The article also noted that Peiper could be "hard if necessary." "Hard" was a reference to the willingness of Waffen SS divisions to fight fanatically and without regard for material and manpower losses. The cost to the Personal Standard of Kharkov's recapture was indeed enormous: over eleven thousand casualties, among them hundreds of experienced officers. "Hard" also referred to terror war. It was in the fighting around Kharkov that Peiper's battalion adopted the nickname "Blowtorch." Fire, one Personal Standard infantryman recalled, terrified everyone, especially the Russians.[26] Paul Zwigart, a Personal Standard sergeant and former Death's Head concentration camp guard who served under Peiper in Russia and Belgium, described the battalion's operations to American investigators: "In Russia generally, we did not take any prisoners at all. . . . On various occasions we burned down whole villages with our blow-torches." During the Battle of Kursk in the summer of 1943, Zwigart received a regimental order from Peiper ordering the burning of an entire village and the murder of its inhabitants in the Belgorod sector around Kursk: "I saw clearly . . . [how] women with children among them came running out of the burning houses . . . were mowed down by our men."[27] After the war, Peiper claimed that blowtorches were used merely to heat engine blocks and boil water for cooking. "In action our armored personnel carriers were in the habit of going into the attack at full speed and with all guns blazing," he told one of many credulous postwar admirers: "As the Russian houses mostly had thatched roofs, it was inevitable that they would catch fire during the battle."[28]

Like other Waffen SS battalions, Peiper's would apply these methods in Western Europe. As Mussolini's regime disintegrated in the summer of 1943, Peiper's battalion was transferred there to assist the Wehrmacht in securing the country's north. Italian soldiers, now considered prisoners of war, were to be disarmed and transported to Germany where they would be deployed as slave labor. Rumors of the transports unnerved civilians and led to brief exchanges of fire between small, uncoordinated groups of Italian soldiers and German forces. After one of Peiper's men was shot and two taken prisoner when Italian soldiers caught them stealing spare vehicle parts from an army depot, Peiper sent a detachment of around eighty men into the Piedmontese village of Boves where they burned homes and killed twenty-four civilians ranging from sixteen to eighty-seven years of age. It was the first massacre of civilians by the Waffen SS in Italy.[29]

"Securing" northern Italy also entailed the murder and systematic roundup of Italian Jews, the vast majority of whom fell under German control in 1943. Hitler dispatched Waffen SS general Karl Wolff to oversee their roundup and deportation. In late September, Peiper's men arrested several hundred Italian and European Jews in and around the city of Cuneo. They were held in a makeshift camp in Borgo San Dalmazzo, where one of Peiper's officers, Georg Preuss, served briefly as commandant, and then deported. They were among the roughly ten thousand Jews in Italy transported to Auschwitz, where the vast majority would die.[30]

Peiper returned once more to Ukraine in November as commander of the Personal Standard's First SS Panzer Regiment, now fighting with Army Group South to contain the Red Army's winter offensives. His battle group again spearheaded armored counterattacks straight through Soviet lines, and again burned villages and executed Soviet prisoners. In the spring of 1944, the badly battered Personal Standard was withdrawn from the Eastern Front for the last time to be reformed in Belgium in preparation for the expected Allied invasion of France. To toughen up untried and undisciplined replacements, Peiper ordered the execution of four young SS recruits court-martialed for robbing Belgian civilians.[31] Following the Allied invasion of Normandy in June, the Personal Standard was deployed south of Caen and in the intense fighting for the Falaise Gap in July, Peiper was relieved as an SS Panzer regimental commander following what may have been a nervous breakdown or drug-induced collapse.[32] By the end of August, the Personal Standard had, yet again, been nearly wiped out.

This Is the Customary Way to Shoot People

While Peiper recovered, the refitted battle group was tasked with leading the attack along Autumn Mist's northern shoulder. Like Sepp Dietrich and other officers, Peiper claimed after the war to have had grave misgivings about this "highly defective" undertaking.[33] Like Hitler's generals in December 1944, however, he did everything he could to realize the leader's objective. Peiper's experience and that of the officers under his command were suited perfectly to the attack plan: a rapid armor-led advance deep into enemy territory without regard for flanks or manpower and material losses. The refitted battle group was comprised of 3,000 men and equipped with around 120 tanks, over 100 armored personnel carriers, and various support vehicles. Peiper estimated that the battle group would form a convoy stretching twenty-five kilometers. He would establish his command around the midway point, though preferred to ride with the lead elements.

In December 1944, most of the battle group's enlisted men were hastily trained young conscripts with little or no combat experience. The Personal Standard's commander, Colonel Wilhelm Mohnke, hoped that intensified doses of political instruction would turn them into "fanatical fighters." Conscripts were told, for instance, that the Personal Standard had "brought the greatest sacrifices in blood and life, [and] always stands, by the will of the Führer."[34] Its battlefield successes were celebrated and the American soldier demonized. A desire for revenge against American forces and Belgian civilians was likely intensified by the memory of the humiliating retreat from France and Belgium in summer and early fall. After the war, Peiper claimed that a British bombing raid on the Rhineland town of Düren on November 16, the cleanup of which his men participated in, fueled vengeful urges during Autumn Mist.[35]

Of greater importance to the battle group's record in the Ardennes than last-minute admonitions to "stand by the will of the Führer" was continuity among its officers. Most who had been given command of tank and armored personnel carrier (Schützenpanzerwagen, or SPW) battalions had been

Stormtroopers and Nazi Party members since 1933 or were leadership academy graduates. All had served under Peiper in Russia, Italy, or Normandy. Of the seventy-four members of the battle group tried by the U.S. Army, over half were officers or noncommissioned officers (NCOs), and among them ten or more had combat experience on the Eastern Front or service with the Death's Head division in one or more concentration camps. Twenty-five had joined the Waffen SS before 1939. Though Hitler had demanded that Waffen SS forces "spread fear and panic" and show no mercy to enemy combatants and civilians, Dietrich, Peiper, and other officers did not need to be told this. Their familiarity with terror war required no explicit verbal or written orders regarding the treatment of prisoners and civilians. Nonetheless, versions of the order to "spread fear and panic" were passed down through the battle group's battalions, regiments, and companies in the days before the attack.

The battle group rolled out of its staging area near the town of Blankenheim toward the Belgian border on the afternoon of December 16. Though the Sixth Panzer Army's orders called for "ruthless and rapid penetration," Peiper hoped to avoid engaging the enemy where possible, believing that the offensive's surprise and speed would cause American forces to dissipate and flee. He intended to pass south of the town of Malmedy, skimming just under American lines, race through four other towns, and reach the Meuse by dawn of December 18. But rough terrain, disrupted lines of communication, minefields, disabled vehicles, and pockets of unexpectedly strong American resistance slowed its advance from the start.[36]

After securing Honsfeld, Peiper ordered his lead elements to nearby Büllingen where they would seize an American fuel depot. Still possessing the element of surprise, the battle group encountered little resistance there and captured several hundred more American soldiers. After ordering some of them to assist in the refueling of its vehicles, he ordered the prisoners marched out of the town toward the German border. An unknown number were shot upon surrender or abused as they trudged past the advancing German column. Battle group soldiers also executed two civilians they had ordered to accompany the captured Americans.[37]

Peiper's next immediate objective was to reach the north-south roadway connecting Malmedy and Ligneuville. From there the battle group would drive west toward Werbomont, beyond which lay more open terrain stretching twenty-five miles to the Meuse River town of Huy. In the early afternoon, however, the lead elements encountered a convoy of the American 285th Field Artillery Observation Battalion, Battery B, as it was snaking south on the roadway through the crossroads village of Baugnez, about three miles south of Malmedy.

The convoy was en route to St. Vith, where it was to assist in the defense of that beleaguered town. Consisting of around 140 men in trucks and jeeps and tasked with sighting enemy artillery positions, the men of Battery B had little or no direct combat experience and were lightly armed. As it passed through the crossroads around 1 p.m. the convoy came under fire from the battle group's lead elements, which were at that time advancing toward the juncture from the southeast along a parallel road. Taken by surprise, a few men in the American convoy returned fire. Most took cover in a roadside ditch before surrendering. A handful at its head fled into a nearby wooded area while several others hid in a café at the juncture.[38]

Members of the battle group began looting the abandoned and damaged American vehicles, disarming the prisoners and stealing personal possessions. The result was even more delay. German soldiers then moved their captives to a field alongside the main road connecting Baugnez and Ligneuville, where they stood for perhaps an hour. Several GIs recalled noticing that some of the Germans manning tank- and halftrack-mounted machine guns were piling up ammunition and loading the weapons. Both American and German eyewitnesses would recall the same sequence of events that followed: one or more German soldiers fired pistol shots into the group of American prisoners, then machine guns opened fire. German soldiers in passing vehicles also fired into the mass of fallen bodies.

As the rest of the battle group moved south past the field, now strewn with dead and wounded GIs, several groups of men walked into the field to kill the survivors. American medical examiners estimated that more than half of the victims had probably been killed by coups de grace administered by bullet, bayonet, or blunt instrument. The forensic evidence revealed that four victims had their eyes gouged out while they were still alive. The clinical, detached language of the autopsy reports does not mask the terror experienced by many of the wounded men in their last moments: "The appearance of the body with the position of the hands over his face seems to indicate that the soldier covered his face as a means of protection from a close range shot."[39] Murdering prisoners of war in this manner was not new to Waffen SS battle groups. The massacre of British soldiers in Le Paradis in 1940 by members of a Death Head battalion was carried out in almost the same manner: surrendered soldiers were first shot with machine guns and any survivors were administered coups de grace or stabbed with bayonets.

When the Germans guarding the prisoners began firing, some of the Americans ran for the cover of a wooded area behind the field. Others played dead in the field itself. Those hiding by the crossroads café were shot after German soldiers flushed them out, killing the proprietor in the process. In all, perhaps fifty American soldiers escaped the encounter with Battle Group Peiper wounded or unharmed; eighty-four were killed.[40] Its members murdered more American prisoners and civilians—perhaps several hundred—during its advance and retreat between December 17 and 25. The questions of where and how many would become two of the many points of contention during and after the trial.

The evidence collected by American investigators implicated either Peiper or the battle group's tank commander, SS Major Werner Poetschke, as having given the order to shoot the captured Americans. Frustrated by the mounting delays, Poetschke, who had a reputation among the men under his command for brutality toward them and the enemy, may have ordered the execution. He was killed near the war's end, and American officials would come to suspect that surviving former battle group members under investigation for the Baugnez massacre were scapegoating their dead comrade to deflect blame from themselves and Peiper. Yet other accounts identified Peiper as having given the order, possibly when he communicated with Poetschke briefly before speeding off toward Ligneuville.[41]

Peiper did not witness the massacre, claiming after the war to have been informed of it hours later or perhaps the following day. He had been driven past the field where the prisoners were standing toward Ligneuville, where an American general had his headquarters and might be captured. Brigadier General Edward W. Timberlake had in fact already abandoned the town, and the battle group rolled through following a brief firefight with soldiers of the U.S. Ninth Armored Division. Paul Ochmann, a sergeant of the First Battalion, admitted to American investigators that he and another soldier ordered seven captured GIs in Ligneuville to dig graves for dead German soldiers before executing the Americans with shots to the backs of their heads. "I [knew] from my service with the Death's Head [unit]," Ochmann asserted, that this is the customary way to shoot people." Belgian witnesses recalled that he was preparing to murder a group of civilians when a sixty-nine-year-old German-born resident distracted him with wine and cognac.[42] Around the same time, a battle group reconnaissance battalion operating in nearby Wereth captured and murdered eleven black American soldiers.

By the evening of December 17 the battle group halted for the night outside Stavelot, where Peiper assumed he would meet considerable American resistance. Its defenders—"those whom we thought invincible," a local inhabitant recalled—had in fact largely abandoned the town earlier that day.[43] The following morning the battle group moved through almost unopposed, capturing an Ambleve River bridge connecting the town's southern and northern halves. Yet Peiper had not really secured Stavelot. He had simply charged through it without regard for the flanks of his battle group's long tail. He had also lost the element of surprise. Detachments of the U.S. 117th Infantry and the 118th Field Artillery Battalion quickly recaptured the town's northern half and engineers destroyed a series of bridges in and around nearby Trois Ponts. A Fourteenth Cavalry Group force prevented the remainder of the battle group from reaching its lead units with reinforcements and fuel.

American forces continued to cut off the battle group's avenues of advance and resupply, and over the next three days boxed it in along a six-mile stretch of the twisting Ambleve River between Stavelot and Stoumont. To make matters worse for Peiper, clearing skies allowed American pilots to hit battle group positions from Cheneux through La Gleize and back to Stavelot, slowing but not halting its advance and killing several Belgian civilians.[44]

The murder of civilians intensified in and around Stavelot, Trois Ponts, and La Gleize. In Stavelot and nearby hamlets, Belgian investigators estimated that battle group soldiers murdered around 130 civilians. Perhaps thirty Belgians were killed in the fight for Stavelot, though Peiper's men had been shooting civilians in that town even before American resistance stiffened. They sprayed houses with machine gun fire at random, killing a fourteen-year-old boy. Other civilians were executed in the street or in their homes. Twenty-two were massacred outside the home of Prosper and Marie Lagaye. Maria Tombeux, a pregnant mother of two young children, left the cellar where she had been hiding with her husband and neighbors and tried to walk with their children in their arms to the local hospital. Tank gunners opened fire on the group, killing Tombeux's husband and possibly one of her neighbors, and wounding her in both legs.[45]

As the battle group's advance slowed and then halted west of Stavelot and as it began to disintegrate, pockets of soldiers lashed out at civilians. "All of the people around here are terrorists," an unidentified battle group soldier told Ernest Natalis, a schoolteacher in Stoumont.[46] Battle group men told civilians hiding in the nearby St. Edouard sanatorium that they were forced to shoot civilians in Stavelot because they had been firing on the battle group, though Belgian historians have found no evidence of armed civilian resistance.[47] The hamlet of Wanne was the scene of a particularly gruesome series of murders. Claiming that the village's inhabitants were feeding Americans tactical intelligence, battle group soldiers abused and executed men and women, seemingly at random. In the chateau of Petit-Spay near Trois Ponts, where war orphans were being cared for, SS men dragged a bedridden chaplain outside and shot him. When battle group men left the chateau in the hands of German Army Volksgrenadiers (reserves of often older soldiers mobilized following the army's massive manpower losses in Russia and Normandy), these men rationed bread and water to feed the inhabitants for the next ten days.[48]

His attempts to break through Stoumont having failed, Peiper fell back to La Gleize on December 21 to await reinforcements or a chance to retreat. American artillery subjected the town to intense bombardment, destroying much of it, while terrified civilians hid in cellars or braved the firestorm above and attempted to flee to surrounding hamlets. Peiper's men nonetheless managed to defend the roads into the town, and by the evening of December 23, the fighting had subsided. His request to retreat from La Gleize having been approved, Peiper led the surviving remnant of his battle group on foot toward Wanne, abandoning vehicles, his own wounded, and over one hundred American prisoners.

Peiper's escape from La Gleize may have been facilitated by Major Hal McCown, a battalion commander in the U.S. 119th Infantry captured near Stoumont on December 21. McCown claimed he and Peiper (who could speak near-fluent English) conversed for hours and that he, McCown, had been impressed by Peiper's conduct and that of his men. Two battle group officers, Erich Rumpf and Rolf Reiser, found the cordiality of the exchange comical. "I stood together with some other officers around the Major," Rumpf told

American interrogators, "and we had to keep from laughing as we knew that the American prisoners of war were shot." Reiser admitted much the same: "I have to admit that the manner in which this Major was treated . . . touched me comically as [Peiper and Poetschke] took care of him and troubled themselves, and talked to him as friends, while orders existed to have other American prisoners shot."[49] Peiper arranged for the American officer to accompany the battle group as it retreated with the hope of later exchanging him for a handful of German medics Peiper had left behind. McCown left La Gleize with Peiper's men, but managed to escape to American lines.

McCown was later to testify for the defense at the trial. The chief defense counsel presented the decorated officer as a star witness whose firsthand account of Peiper's supposed benevolence would, he hoped, undermine the prosecution's sweeping claims of a conspiracy to commit an unbroken series of war crimes.[50] Yet it may have been McCown's willingness to talk rather than Peiper's adherence to the Geneva Convention that saved the American officer's life in La Gleize. Lieutenant Russell Heginbotham, a 30th Infantry Division platoon leader captured in Stoumont and less willing to talk to Peiper, was told he and two other officers were being confined in a house in the middle of La Gleize on Peiper's orders "so we would all be killed by our own artillery." When American forces intensified the shelling of the village, Heginbotham and one other officer were wounded and the third was killed.[51]

Early in the morning of December 24, what remained of Battle Group Peiper, now nearly surrounded by American forces, slipped out of the town by foot, arriving in Wanne a day later. Of the three thousand men in the battle group, Peiper estimated that perhaps eight hundred survived the attempt to reach the Meuse. All Personal Standard forces were finally withdrawn from Belgium on January 12. Despite the failure to achieve his principal objective, Peiper was awarded the Swords to the Knight's Cross on January 11, 1945, the recommendation noting that his leadership "displayed decisive recklessness and cold-bloodedness." Among the long list of successes cited by Wilhelm Mohnke was the "annihilation" of a supply column of American soldiers at Baugnez.[52]

The fate of Battle Group Peiper in Autumn Mist reflected in miniature that of Hitler's entire Ardennes gamble. Half a million German troops had charged into a quiet sector of the front and taken the enemy by near-total surprise. American forces recovered quickly and contained the German advance to a "bulge" in southern Belgium, the tip of which nearly reached the Meuse River town of Dinant, roughly eighty miles west of the German border but far short of Antwerp. On January 7, Hitler ordered German forces to withdraw from the Ardennes, though sporadic fighting continued until the end of the month. Around one hundred thousand German soldiers had been killed, wounded, or captured. The manpower and material losses for the Wehrmacht, Waffen SS, and Luftwaffe were irreplaceable, making Autumn Mist the last major German offensive operation of the war.

The Waffen SS waged terror war in the Ardennes as it had done in other theaters over the course of the entire war. Peiper and other young Waffen SS field division officers were not mindless fanatics, but neither were they ordinary soldiers up in a desperate effort to stave off an inevitable and calamitous defeat. They were expected, of course, to demonstrate unwavering loyalty to Adolf Hitler and to each other. The motto of the SS was, after all, "My Honor Is Loyalty." Himmler, moreover, had implemented the "mission command" system of administration, which for the SS meant that trusted subordinates were expected to act on their allegedly superior "racial" instincts and take bold initiatives that their consciences assured them were in line with Hitler's wishes.[53] Peiper's disdain of authority that did not emanate from higher echelons of the SS—he bragged of his "insubordination" to Himmler's mistress—or comport with his instincts for quick offensive thrusts regardless of risk or strategic considerations was not simply a matter of arrogance or incompetence.[54] Rather, he believed that the "boldness" of an individual battalion commander would compensate for inadequate material support and the inability (or unwillingness) to relate tactical maneuvers to a larger strategic objective.

The combination of loyalty and the responsibility to act on one's instincts permeated Personal Standard battalion command structures. Erich Rumpf, the commander of a battle group engineer company in the Ardennes, explained the dynamic to an American interrogator in early 1946: "Not only [were] the orders he gave for the commitment in the west . . . decisive, but the knowledge of every member of his troop that the commander generally recommends this ruthless way of fighting and that he appreciates especially those who conduct warfare in this sense and made them an example to the others as men of courageous and daring decisions."[55] Peiper's "ruthless way of fighting" proved extremely costly to his own men. That the Personal Standard was almost completely destroyed four times by the conclusion of the Ardennes offensive was not solely the result of its facing overwhelming odds.[56]

Peiper's charge to the Meuse was also typical as a Waffen SS field division operation in that the killing of prisoners and civilians was not an incidental or accidental feature of its operations. Attempts—first made during the trial at Dachau—to explain or justify the Baugnez massacre as the result of heat of battle conditions are unconvincing. At the crossroads, very little heat was generated in the brief exchange of fire between the battle group and the lightly armed Americans. The prisoners were then held for over an hour before the attempt to execute them began. Under orders to advance rapidly and ruthlessly, battle group soldiers executed an unexpectedly large and unwanted group of American prisoners. This massacre was similar to those committed previously by Peiper and the men under his command: premeditated, brutal, and undertaken in the spirit of "that excellent weapon, the dread and terrible reputation which preceded us."

Yet Peiper's men did not execute all American prisoners wherever they were captured, nor did they kill every Belgian they encountered. Shifting circumstances provides part of the explanation as to why some were killed and others not. The largest number of prisoners who were not executed—those captured in Honsfeld and Büllingen—were spared in the very first hours of Peiper's advance into Belgium, when there was a secure rear to which they could be marched, and even then some were abused and shot. A few were needed to refuel or drive support vehicles. One week later in La Gleize, the battle group's forward momentum finally exhausted, "spreading fear and terror" served no military purpose. As the core of the battle group around his command prepared to retreat from that town, Peiper kept some American prisoners alive to deploy them as hostages or human shields. In and around Stavelot, poorly trained and undisciplined recruits—their aggressive impulses intensified by alcohol or doses of a methamphetamine-based drug distributed widely to German soldiers—lashed out at civilians as the battle group's military situation deteriorated.[57]

These distinctions, while not lost entirely on some observers during and after the trial, are primarily those of a historian and not a contemporary. Certainly, they would have been of little interest to the American public in the middle of January 1945 as American soldiers discovered the frozen corpses of some eighty of their comrades in a field near Malmedy.

TWO

Now It Comes Home to Us

Creating the "Malmedy Massacre"

In June 1945, Leon Jaworski, a young lawyer serving in the U.S. War Department's legal division, the Judge Advocate General's Corps, wrote to a superior officer that "of all the atrocities committed against American personnel the Malmedy incident is the most vicious and brutal. . . . Its atrocious nature has been widely publicized and it is expected by the public and military authorities alike that the perpetrators be brought to justice."[1] Jaworski would soon prosecute several of the U.S. Army's early war crimes cases and, much later, serve as a special prosecutor in the Watergate investigation. One month after VE Day he was advocating making the "Malmedy incident" the highest-priority investigation for a new division within the War Department created to prosecute what became known in the Anglo-American context as "traditional" war crimes cases. That is, alleged violations of the Geneva and Hague Conventions regarding the treatment of prisoners of war and civilians.

Jaworski's confidence that this case would be pursued with particular determination was not misplaced. A directive signed by Supreme Allied Commander Dwight Eisenhower on October 29, 1945, ordered that the investigation of the "Malmedy Massacre of American Prisoners of War" be given the "highest priority by all commanders concerned."[2] The case was given such high priority in large part because of the creation of the "Malmedy massacre" story. Constructed by survivors, army officials, and American reporters in the immediate aftermath of the encounter at Baugnez, the story described in vivid detail an unprecedented and possibly premeditated war crime perpetrated by the SS against some one hundred American prisoners of war.

This is not to suggest that the massacre itself was a fabrication concocted by vengeful army officers and headline seeking reporters. Rather, the dramatic characterization of the incident and the way the story was disseminated to the American public produced powerful responses from the frozen fields of the Ardennes to the highest circles of power in Washington. The rhetorical ammunition it provided then influenced the investigation demanded by Jaworski and other War Department officials, the ensuing trial, and the post-trial controversy. An explanation of the story's creation and its significance begins with a look at the unusual circumstances of the massacre's aftermath.

Survivors

Most unusual was the fact that fifty American soldiers survived the encounter at Baugnez. First Lieutenant Virgil Lary's ordeal was typical. Like most members of Battery B of the 285th Field Artillery Observation Battalion en route to St. Vith that day, Lary surrendered after coming under fire from the lead elements of Battle Group Peiper just south of the crossroads. And like many of the prisoners assembled in a field alongside the roadway, he dropped to the ground when the soldiers who had been guarding them opened fire. For nearly two hours Lary played dead, waiting until it was nearly dark before crawling out of the field alone. Though shot through the ankle and in considerable pain, he almost reached Malmedy by foot before convincing a nervous Belgian family in the hamlet of Floriheid to drive him the rest of the way.[3]

Most of the other survivors crawled out of the field in groups of two to four. They stumbled across various outposts and roadblocks or were picked up by American soldiers scouting the area. Crucially, a handful would provide the first eyewitness accounts of the incident to American officers and reporters in Malmedy and in nearby Spa, where First U.S. Army's headquarters was based. Six, including Lary, would testify as prosecution witnesses at the trial of the alleged perpetrators sixteen months later.

The fact that so many of Peiper's intended victims spoke to reporters within hours of the massacre distinguished its aftermath from similar incidents. Previous massacres perpetrated by the Personal Standard and other Waffen SS field divisions either left few survivors or the military situation made it impossible for those who did survive to record detailed accounts soon after the event. Only two soldiers, for instance, survived the massacre of nearly one hundred British prisoners by elements of the Death's Head Division in the French village of Le Paradis in May 1940. In an incident similar to the Baugnez massacre, soldiers of the Hitler Youth Division executed thirty-five Canadian prisoners of war on June 8, 1944, near the Norman town of Fontenay-le-Pesnel. Five survivors managed to escape but were recaptured almost immediately. Only one survivor of the massacre of over six hundred inhabitants of Oradour-sur-Glane by the Das Reich Division in June 1944 was available to give testimony at the trial of the alleged perpetrators nine years later.[4]

Another survivor's account prompted First Army commander General Courtney Hodges to record one of the earliest versions of the Malmedy massacre story in his war diary on the night of December 17. Private Homer Ford, a military policeman (MP), reported that approximately two hundred men were taken prisoner at a crossroads and "herded together into a side field and an SS officer fired two shots from his pistol and immediately there came the crackle of machine-gun fire and the whole group was mowed down in cold blood." Hodges indulged in hyperbole in claiming that the wounded MP's account "measures up to and matches anything thus far published of Boche brutality and atrocity."[5] Such hyperbole would become a fixture of press reporting on the incident over the next two months and of the popular memory of the massacre long after.

By the night of December 17 Hodges considered the situation in his sector to be "serious if not yet critical." The first German artillery barrages that hit Malmedy the previous day were, he initially believed, merely attempts to disrupt the U.S. V Corps' advance on German-controlled Urft and Roer River dams. The intensification of artillery and aerial attacks throughout the day and night of the 16th changed his mind. As if to erase any lingering doubt, a German plane strafed the street in front of his house in Spa. By the evening of the 17th, Hodges's intelligence estimate warned that the counteroffensive's lead elements might actually capture Meuse River bridgeheads. His conclusion that "the Boche was staking his life on this drive" was only reinforced by Ford's incredible story. As other eyewitness accounts consistent with that of the badly shaken MP's were collected, Hodges decided to give them "immediate publicity." He ordered the story disseminated among U.S. forces in the Ardennes and his intelligence officers informed Supreme Headquarters Allied Expeditionary Force (SHAEF) of the incident.

By that point in the war, SHAEF's public relations division had become an enormous operation that tracked and censored thousands of reporters' stories, photographs, and many hours of film footage. Hodges and Eisenhower ensured that news of the mass execution near Malmedy bypassed this bureaucracy and reached American forces in the Ardennes and the American public without delay. The immediate effect on American soldiers was predictable. A desire for revenge and the fear of being captured incited GIs to fight with particular tenacity. "It made fightin' fools out of [my] guys for a while," Lieutenant Philip Cole, Jr. wrote his father at the end of January. Associated Press reporter Tom Yarbrough wrote on December 19 that First Army troops were "fired . . . with a new measure of hate as they face the Nazi counter-offensive." A United Press report the same day noted "news of the massacre has spread up and down first army lines and has increased the urgency with which the Yanks desire to finish off the attacking Nazis."[6]

Coinciding as it did with the uncertainty and disorder of the surprise German counterattack's first days, reports of the massacre also provoked retaliatory executions of captured German soldiers, above all Waffen SS men and paratroopers. "Immediately after the Malmedy massacre became known to us," the German-born American interrogator William Boehme admitted in 1949, "you could hardly expect any prisoners to be taken for awhile from any of the SS units."[7] Prior to an attack on German positions, the headquarters of the 328th Infantry ordered "no SS troops or paratroopers will be taken prisoners but will be shot on sight."[8] An entry in a Ninth Army war diary reported that "American troops are refusing to take any more SS prisoners, and it may well spread to include all German soldiers."[9]

Forrest Pogue, at that time a master sergeant in the V Corps serving as an army combat historian, was one of the GIs who learned about the Baugnez massacre via this lightning-quick publicity campaign. Though aware that U.S. soldiers had also executed German prisoners in the region, Pogue grasped that the distinctive modus operandi of the Waffen SS—terror war—would unleash a particularly deadly spiral of retaliation. "A massacre like the one at Malmedy," he wrote in his diary on December 20, "is brutal only because it is larger and calculated to provoke terror."[10] The massacre had indeed provoked terror, but of brief duration and without the results that had fired the imaginations of Hitler, Himmler, and Peiper. The commitment to maintaining a bad reputation was backfiring.

Yet it was not only news of the massacre that threatened to replicate conditions on the Eastern Front in a small slice of Belgium. Rumors—true, though exaggerated—were spreading that English-speaking German soldiers wearing U.S. Army uniforms had infiltrated American lines. When captured, some reported that their objective was to rendezvous at a Paris café and then assassinate Dwight Eisenhower. The operation, if not the plot to kill the supreme allied commander, was real. Codenamed "Greif" and led by SS Colonel Otto Skorzeny, SS men driving captured American jeeps and a few tanks targeted a handful of Meuse River bridges in advance of the larger German attack force and otherwise sowed confusion behind Allied lines. Nervous GIs manning checkpoints took to quizzing other nervous GIs, at one point detaining General Omar Bradley until he could identify the capital of Illinois and arresting British general Bernard Montgomery when he refused to submit to similar questioning. An unknown number of American and British soldiers were shot accidentally—native German-speaking GIs were particularly vulnerable—and hundreds of Germans were killed after being captured wearing pieces of American uniforms. Most of them were not part of Skorzeny's operation.[11]

The exact number of German soldiers executed summarily by Anglo-American forces in Belgium is unknown. What is clear is that the "war by rules," as Gerald Linderman called it, that had largely obtained between Allied and German forces in North Africa, Italy, and France had frayed badly by the fall of 1944 and broken down completely in the immediate aftermath of the Baugnez massacre. While this breakdown was temporary—the surge of retaliatory violence in the Ardennes subsided as the German counterattack stalled and then failed—the potential for similar eruptions simmered just below the surface as Anglo-American forces pushed into Germany. Captured members of the SS remained the most likely targets of on the spot killings, most notably when American soldiers liberated the Dachau concentration camp in April. There they executed some SS camp guards and allowed others to be killed by inmates.[12] That very day, a few miles northeast of Dachau in the tiny town of Webling, members of the U.S. 222nd Infantry Regiment executed forty-one Waffen SS prisoners in retaliation for the killing of one of their men by sniper fire.[13]

The Massacre in the Press

For the American public, including political and military officials, it was two waves of press reporting in December 1944 and January 1945 that defined the "Malmedy incident" in a way that would remain intact in American popular memory for decades after the war. A day before First Army headquarters issued a statement about the execution of "more than 100" American prisoners by "Nazi [SS] and Panzer men" south of Malmedy, reporters had already transformed raw survivor accounts into a story of Nazi barbarity that appeared on the front pages of hundreds of American newspapers on December 18 and 19. The headlines conveyed the shock and outrage expressed by Courtney Hodges and GIs throughout the region: "Brutal Germans Mow Down American Prisoners with Machine Gun, Pistol Fire" and "German Tank Force Pours Fire into 150 Unarmed Americans."[14]

The Associated Press reporter Hal Boyle was the first American journalist to file a story about the incident. He had encountered wounded survivors in Malmedy on December 17 and captured the immediate impact of the incident in a story published across the county the following day: "Weeping with rage, a handful of doughboy survivors described today how a German tank force ruthlessly poured machine gun fire into a group of about 150 Americans who had been disarmed and herded into a field in the opening hours of the present Nazi counteroffensive."[15] Boyle and other reporters' first dispatches emphasized German brutality, especially in their descriptions of how many of the men wounded in the initial volley of fire were then shot, stabbed, and beaten to death. William Summers, a 285th Field Artillery Observation Battalion sergeant, told Boyle, "We had to lie there and listen to German non-coms kill with pistols every one of our wounded men who groaned or tried to move."[16] In the versions of Boyle's report published in *Stars and Stripes* and the *Washington Post* the same day, the editors included the portion of Summers's statement indicating the desire for immediate retaliation: "Damn them. Give me my rifle and put me in with the infantry. I want to go back and kill every one of them."[17]

The first reports in the American press emphasized the unprecedented nature of the Baugnez massacre. "Despite their other crimes," *Time* magazine's editors noted, "the Germans had generally observed the rules of war in their treatment of captured U.S. and British fighting men. But last week even that record was blotched by the coldblooded murder of scores of U.S. soldiers."[18] Some reporters in Belgium grasped for comparisons, if only to highlight the massacre's supposedly unprecedented nature. Lee Carson, the First Army correspondent for the International News Service, described the incident as "a mass slaying that made Custer's famed last stand pale in bloody comparison." Only a few made references to the Pacific theater or the Eastern Front or to a similar series of executions carried out by the Hitler Youth Division of the Waffen SS against Canadian and British prisoners near Caen the previous July. "We've heard—repeatedly—of similar German atrocities on the Russian front," one commentator wrote in the Las Cruces, New Mexico, *Sun-News* on December 21, "but many Americans refused to believe. Now it comes home to us, with grim reality."[19]

A dearth of reliable information on other shootings, either of American prisoners or Belgian civilians, also cast the Baugnez incident in even sharper relief. While Lee Carson could file a detailed story on what happened at Baugnez, for instance, he could add only that a "supply and medical convoy" near St. Vith was ambushed, the Germans "carr[ying] out their bloody attack just as did the Nazi panzer men on the Malmedy highway."[20] Over the next several weeks, however, accounts of massacres multiplied as reporters were shown intelligence obtained from captured German soldiers or after they witnessed firsthand the carnage wrought by Peiper's men or other SS units in towns like Stavelot or Parfondruy.[21]

As these stories proliferated another element of the "Malmedy incident" narrative took shape: that German forces in the Ardennes had been ordered to execute prisoners and civilians. In late December and through January, American interrogators in Belgium collected numerous accounts from captured German soldiers of massacres they had committed or witnessed, with some prisoners admitting they had been ordered or encouraged to kill their captives. Summarizing interrogation reports and photographic evidence, the U.S. Army's Communications Zone Headquarters in Paris concluded at the end of January that "the policy of SS troops as well as Volksgrenadier troops under SS Command, is not to take any prisoners, but to destroy them."[22] The army had already provided some of this intelligence to reporters. A January 17 *Stars and Stripes* report, for instance, cited U.S. Army sources that "Belgian women and children were stabbed, shot and burned by German SS storm troopers at Parfondruy last week in an organized massacre which was an integral part of the Nazi master plan." Army investigators concluded that Peiper's men fighting in and around Stavelot were "acting under orders" to kill civilians, speculating that after killing at least sixty-three, they "had neither leisure nor ammunition" to continue their murderous rampages as American resistance intensified west of Stavelot.[23]

Murder in the Snow

By mid-January the Malmedy massacre story had taken definite shape and by the end of the month newspapers were using the term "Malmedy massacre" on a regular basis.[24] On January 26, *Yank*, a weekly wartime newsmagazine published by the army, and the Washington edition of *Stars and Stripes* ran the first narrative account of the "massacre at Malmedy" to draw on survivor accounts and statements by German prisoners. *Yank* correspondent Ed Cunningham wrote that a German tank column surprised a unit of an American Field Artillery Observation Battalion heading to St. Vith from Malmedy and that a brief exchange of fire took place before the lightly armed Americans surrendered. The Germans stripped the prisoners of their valuables and herded them into a field. An officer in a "command car" "stood up, took deliberate aim with a pistol at an American medical officer in the front rank of the prisoners and fired." Machine gun fire from the tanks along the road followed, killing some but not all of the prisoners, who had been standing motionless in the field "with their hands raised over their heads."

Cunningham opened his story with a bit of gruesome speculation. The victims' frozen corpses "may still be where they fell." He was right. At the moment his report appeared in print, American forces recovered the bodies of the victims. The result was a second wave of stories on the massacre even more graphic than the first. On January 14, a Graves Registration Company team, along with army cameramen and a medical officer, arrived and began uncovering the bodies, well preserved in the deep snow. Photographs of the site and the autopsies made it clear that a massacre of unarmed American soldiers had taken place. Close examination indicated that more than half of the victims were likely killed at close range by coups de grace.[25]

Hal Boyle's reports on the recovery were published the most widely. The circumstances of the Graves Registration Company's work enhanced the drama of his and other reporters' dispatches. A final burst of German artillery

AN AMERICAN SOLDIER LOOKS NUMBLY AT BODIES OF AMERICAN PRISONERS WHO WERE SHOT BY THE GERMANS. SOME OF DEAD LIE IN ROWS WHERE THE GERMANS LINED THEM UP

MURDER IN THE SNOW

Americans find a field of horror where Germans shot U.S. prisoners

On the second day of the breakthrough the Germans added a detail to the frightful total of their guilt.

At a road junction near Malmédy, German tanks overpowered a little column of American trucks. The Germans herded some 159 Americans into a field by the road. A German officer spoke to a tankman, who shot at the prisoners with a pistol. Another German then set up a Schmeisser machine pistol in an armored car, massacred the Americans at point-blank range.

The men who were still alive lay among the dead for an hour. Some of them moaned and the Germans shot them in the head. Finally many of the Germans went away. Then the survivors, most of them wounded, got up and ran to a woods. Fifteen of them, weeping with rage, got back to tell what happened.

When the Americans took back the road junction in January they looked to see what the Germans had done. Brushing away the snow, they found 115 bodies.

HUDDLED TOGETHER IN THE SNOW, MANY OF THE MEN ARE FROZEN IN THE SAME POSITIONS IN WHICH THEY DIED. SOME OF THEM STILL HAVE THEIR HANDS ABOVE THEIR HEADS

"Murder in the Snow," *Life*, February 5, 1945 *(Life)*.

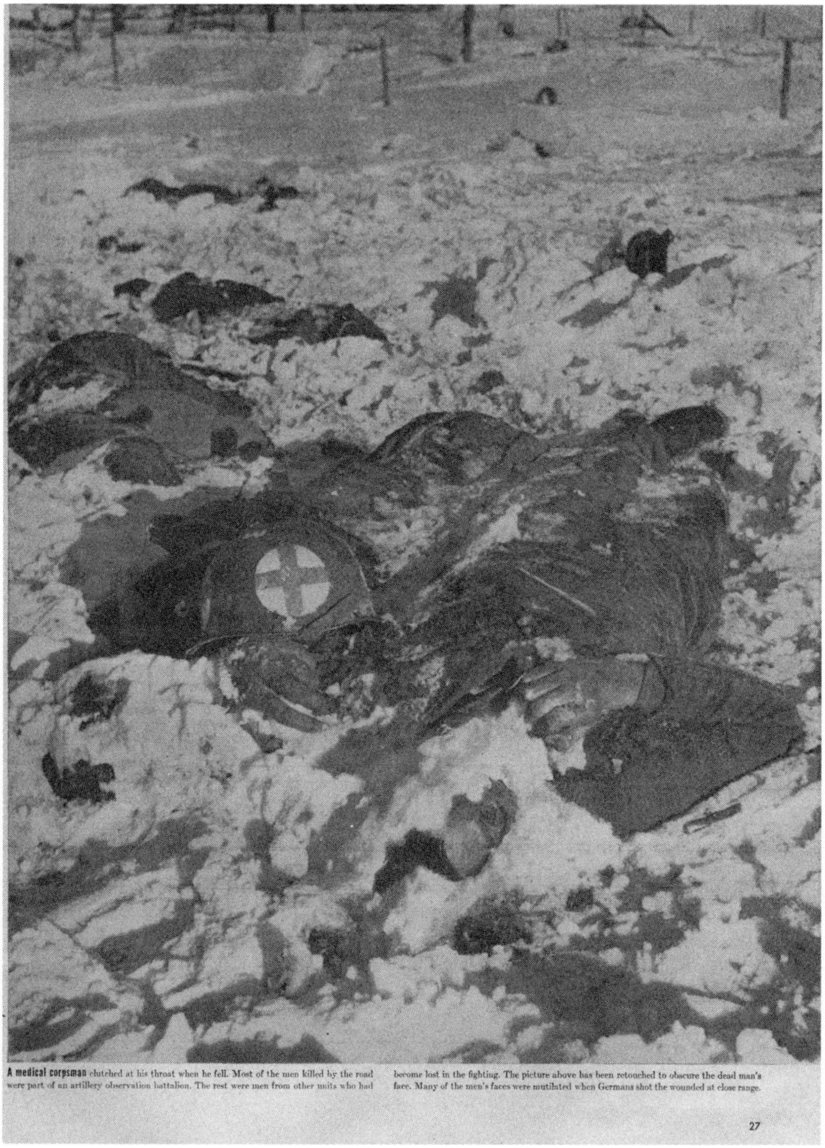

A medical corpsman clutched at his throat when he fell. Most of the men killed by the road were part of an artillery observation battalion. The rest were men from other units who had become lost in the fighting. The picture above has been retouched to obscure the dead man's face. Many of the men's faces were mutilated when Germans shot the wounded at close range.
27

The body of Corporal Ralph Indelicato as it appeared in *Life*'s "Murder in the Snow." The magazine retouched the photograph to conceal part of the victim's face *(Life)*.

fire delayed the recovery of the bodies. And in a scene that may have been contrived for the benefit of the cameras, a group of German prisoners was marched, hands in the air, past the field as the team did its work. "American and German Treatment of Prisoners Contrasted" read the caption over the photograph of the German captives being led to a prisoner of war camp in Malmedy and published on the front page of the January 14 edition of the *New York Times*. As he had done in the first reports of the massacre, Boyle emphasized feelings of anger and vengefulness among GIs at the scene. "'The way to do with them is the way they did with us,'" he quoted Private William Babcock as the young rifleman watched the enemy prisoners "march[ed] back to the safety, good food, and warmth available behind the front."[26]

Another GI at the recovery site told Boyle that images of the morbid scene could provide the right kind of "'propaganda'" for the American public. "Maybe if the folks back home could see a few things like this," the sergeant told Boyle, "they wouldn't be so sure the war was nearly over." *Life*, the most popular American news magazine of the time, ran just such a story three weeks later. Titled "Murder in the Snow," it consisted of few words—only 166 describing the incident in much the same way as Boyle had in December—but included three large photographs of the dead before their bodies were removed by the Graves Registration Company. The photographs were among the most graphic provided to the American public in wartime. The most striking was of Corporal Ralph Indelicato, one of seven medics killed in the field, his bare hands revealing the preserved state of the bodies and his helmet bearing the medic's red cross next to his body. His face is partly visible—the image had to be retouched to obscure Indelicato's identity—though the portion of the photograph exposing his missing right eye was unaltered.[27]

Assessing the impact of this reporting on American public opinion is difficult. Certainly, Americans were unaccustomed to news of wartime atrocities involving GI prisoners of war in North Africa and Europe, in part because such incidents were relatively rare and in part because the War Department's Office of War Information (OWI) controlled the flow of information to the press and public. Published photographs of American casualties were almost nonexistent. OWI censorship rules aimed at shaping the war's image to suit a shifting array of domestic and military purposes. *Life*'s editors could display the grisly images from Baugnez because by early 1945 OWI officials perceived the need to manipulate public opinion, as the Allies had not won the war in Europe as quickly as expected following the liberation of France the previous summer. And not only had German forces repulsed a British-led assault on Rhine River bridges in September, the Wehrmacht and SS launched a surprise counterattack in Belgium three months later. The discovery of the preserved state of the Baugnez victims' bodies thus offered American officials an opportunity to counter a possible "peace bloc" or flagging anti-German sentiment among civilians and soldiers.[28]

It is possible, however, to overstate the impact of the Malmedy massacre story and related images on American public opinion. Polls taken from the fall of 1944 to early 1945 revealed ambiguous views of the soon-to-be-vanquished enemy. On the one hand, opinions had hardened after D-Day and support for harsh occupation policies and war crimes trials increased. On the other, most Americans still viewed the Germans as a basically good, if politically incompetent, people who were suffering under a dictatorship most of them did not support. These conflicted attitudes extended into the postwar years with considerable significance for the political fallout of the Malmedy massacre trial.[29]

In addition, both those who wished to punish the perpetrators and those who demanded clemency would make self-serving references to a deafening "public outcry" over Malmedy. Advocates of a prompt and severe judicial reckoning, such as Leon Jaworski, argued that the public and the nation's political and military leadership had demanded no less. Conversely, defenders of the accused and some of the accused themselves would claim they had been prosecuted unjustly because the American public had become enraged by reports of the massacre and incapable of administering justice with any degree of impartiality. The Malmedy massacre story as formulated by the press by early 1945 would become a metaphorical lodestar for those seeking punishment and those seeking amnesty.

The narrative had other reverberations beyond the battlefields of the Ardennes and the front pages of American newspapers. The first reports of the massacre became, albeit briefly, a matter of wartime diplomacy in the form of a formal protest lodged on December 29 against the German government by U.S. Secretary of State Edward Stettinius. Responding to survivor reports, Stettinius charged that German forces had killed "about 130" American prisoners in "gross violation of the Geneva Prisoners of War Convention and the generally accepted international rules of warfare."[30] Such protests, submitted by the aggrieved party via their respective legations in neutral Switzerland, were not purely symbolic. They were part of a broad effort—not always successful—undertaken from the battlefield to the desks of diplomats to contain escalating spirals of retaliation in the theaters of operation and in prisoner of war camps. German, British, and American officials were well aware of the "mutual hostage factor" and the need to prevent or at least limit the maltreatment of prisoners of war. In the case of the Baugnez shootings, of course, the U.S. Army had resorted to instant publicity and retaliation had followed just as instantly. Stettinius's protest was therefore mostly symbolic.[31]

It remains unclear how extensively, if at all, the Wehrmacht, Waffen SS, or German Foreign Ministry looked into the incident in response to the American protest. During his trial at Nuremberg, Alfred Jodl, the former chief of the operations staff of the Armed Forces High Command, claimed that on December 22 Hitler had demanded to know who was responsible for the massacre being reported in American newspapers and that he (Jodl) had "on my own initiative" ordered an investigation.[32] At the Dachau trial, Sepp Dietrich also claimed to have ordered a formal investigation, as did Peiper, allegedly on Wilhelm Mohnke's orders.[33] Regardless of whether such inquiries took place, Field Marshal Gerd von Rundstedt's headquarters reported to the Foreign Ministry that "the accusations constitute nothing but foul enemy agitation." Using more diplomatic language, the Foreign Ministry informed the Swiss Legation in early March that German Army investigators had concluded that the accusations were false.[34]

Press reports and reprisals by American forces provoked a rather different response by German military propaganda radio broadcasts directed at American troops in mid-February. The broadcasts revealed not only awareness of the massacre but admitted, indirectly, that German forces had been responsible. One such broadcast justified the killings: "If you have a numerically superior opponent fighting a smaller one and the smaller one knows his very existence is at stake, he will, to make up for his inferiority, have to resort to means that appear hard and brutal. That is a right that his urge for self-preservation accords him."[35]

Despite the fact that it came from a source no American soldier in Belgium would take seriously, it was not entirely preposterous for German military propagandists to hope such reasoning might have some effect on the enemy by calling attention to what underpinned the rough sense of "fair play" between combatants that had prevailed throughout much of the war in the North Africa, Italy, and France. That is, that the men responsible were soldiers reacting as any might in similarly desperate circumstances. This explanation for the Baugnez massacre foreshadowed a pillar of the defense's case in the trial and in the amnesty lobby's subsequent efforts to free the convicted perpetrators. It would also become foundational to the attempt by Waffen SS veterans and their apologists to present themselves to German and non-German publics as nothing more than ordinary soldiers.

Finally, American soldiers and civilians were not the only ones reading accounts of the massacre published in *Stars and Stripes, Yank,* and *Life.* Rolf Reiser, a second lieutenant in the Personal Standard's First Panzer Regiment during the Ardennes offensive, told American interrogators that he and other officers being held in a prisoner of war enclosure in Austria had read Ed Cunningham's *Yank* story. The effect was to alert battle group veterans, many of who were interned together in makeshift camps in that country and Bavaria, that the Americans had labeled one of numerous atrocities perpetrated by the Personal Standard as the "Malmedy massacre" and identified Battle Group Peiper as the responsible unit.[36] As we will see, the effect was to encourage battle group veterans to coordinate their stories in the expectation that they would face trial, a development that complicated the war crimes investigation that was about to begin.

The Channel of Organized Justice

As late as the fall of 1944, Allied leaders had not agreed on the fate of war criminals. The issue was first raised in early 1942 when representatives of governments-in-exile rejected "acts of vengeance" in lieu of "punishment . . . through the channel of organized justice." Nearly two years later a United Nations War Crimes Commission was established, but it could do little more than gather evidence. During a conference held in Moscow in October and November 1943, the American, British, and Soviet foreign ministers declared their determination to send accused German war criminals to the countries in which crimes had been committed but withheld for themselves the authority to pursue those whose "offenses have no particular location."

Beyond this rather important distinction, however, their declaration lacked specifics, and at that point in the war planning trials anywhere was not a high priority.[37]

Agreement among most Allied leaders and governments-in-exile that trials were preferable to "acts of vengeance" sat uneasily alongside powerful urges for just such acts. The wording of the Moscow Declaration contained the threat of summary executions by stating that many Germans would be "judged on the spot by the peoples whom they have outraged." Such language reflected Winston Churchill's hostility to the idea of holding trials of Nazi Party leaders and German military officers. All British officials of Churchill's generation recalled the farcical affairs held in post–World War I Germany. And while they were amenable to the prospect of trials held in different European nations for "lesser" criminals, they also advocated summary executions for leading Nazis on the grounds that their actions had placed them outside the boundaries of law.[38]

Churchill's counterparts, however, favored trials for major war criminals. An ailing and distracted Franklin Roosevelt, who had briefly given tacit support to a British summary execution scheme, changed his mind and backed the idea of an international tribunal. His successor, Harry Truman, was an even stronger supporter of high-level trials, as was Charles de Gaulle. Moreover, Joseph Stalin had taken what a chagrined Churchill referred to as an "ultrarespectable line" on dealing with major war criminals by backing plans for an international tribunal. Creating such a court could not be put off for long. In the early months of 1945, Allied armies were pushing into Germany and everyone understood that the war in Europe would soon be over.

It would be within the U.S. War Department that the legal framework for the court that would try the highest-level cases—the International Military Tribunal (IMT)—was formulated. The idea of an international court was not a new one. Nor was the concept of such a court prosecuting prewar crimes committed against specific groups of people. What was novel was a proposal first put forward in September 1944 by a War Department lawyer named Murray Bernays to charge Nazi Party organizations with "conspiracy to commit murder, terrorism, and the destruction of peaceful populations in violations of the Laws of War." An individual could thus be found guilty on the basis of membership in a criminal organization, with the extent of his or her knowledge of or participation in its crimes determining the severity of punishment. Bernays had in mind above all the SS, the organization he and many other Allied government officials held most responsible for the Nazi regime's worst crimes.[39]

The most important convert to Bernays's scheme was Secretary of War Henry Stimson. As a former federal prosecutor in Theodore Roosevelt's administration, he had successfully prosecuted antitrust cases on criminal conspiracy charges. Stimson understood immediately that Bernays's proposal would facilitate the prosecution of crimes authorized by a state and committed by hundreds of thousands of individuals. Franklin Roosevelt seemed to favor the idea, but left it to Stimson to convince other officials in the War, Navy, State, Treasury, and Justice Departments. For over a month, however, the criminal organization and conspiracy idea came up against strong resistance in the War and Justice Departments, with opponents favoring a much narrower interpretation of war crimes and skeptical about the need for an international tribunal.

The Malmedy massacre story tipped the debate in favor of those including criminal organization and conspiracy categories in a future international tribunal. Timing was one factor: news of the incident broke just as opposition to Bernays's proposal had gathered significant momentum. It was the story's content that provided the critical leverage to supporters of the conspiracy charge. The fact that the massacre had been perpetrated by a branch of the SS, the principal Nazi Party "criminal organization" in the eyes of American officials, was decisive, as was the widely held belief that the responsible Waffen SS battle group had been "acting under orders," as Attorney General Francis Biddle recalled assuming in early 1945.

Biddle was among those officials who had opposed a conspiracy category in the weeks leading up to the German counterattack in the Ardennes. The Malmedy massacre story changed his mind. At the very least, the narrative made it difficult for those opposing Bernays's proposal to prevail in intra- and intercabinet debates, particularly as it applied to a court in which everyone expected members of the SS to be among the principal defendants. Events in the war's last months were charging the atmosphere in high-level Washington policy circles with a current of "utter hatred" for that organization.[40] Two weeks after the recovery of the victims' bodies at the Baugnez crossroads, the Red Army liberated Auschwitz and Allied armies would soon overrun the vast network of concentration camps in Germany.

It was in this atmosphere that Stimson and proponents of the criminal organization and conspiracy categories prevailed, allowing them to present the idea as American policy during negotiations with other Allied governments over the international tribunal's charter. By the late summer of 1945, American officials had succeeded in persuading their British, Soviet, and French counterparts to include both categories in the IMT's charter. The Malmedy case, however, would not be among those prosecuted by the famous court that convened in Nuremberg's Palace of Justice from November 1945 to October 1946. Rather, it would become one—albeit the best known—of hundreds handled by U.S. Army courts in occupied Germany.

Stimson again played the critical role in shaping this lesser-known dimension of postwar judicial reckoning with Nazi crimes. He was aware that American occupation forces would have thousands of war crimes cases to handle in the U.S. zone alone. Despite this daunting prospect and his sense that "a great many people think that the question of the guilt of some of these people is already decided," he was determined that trials would be held.[41] Right before the debates that produced the "Nuremberg ideas" took place, Stimson ordered the Judge Advocate General to create a special division charged with "collect[ing] evidence of cruelties, atrocities, and acts of oppression against members of the United States armed forces or other Americans . . . and arranging for the apprehension and prompt trial of persons against whom a prima facie case is made out."[42] In late December 1944, the Judge Advocate in the European Theater formed the War Crimes Group to coordinate investigations by War Crimes Branches deployed at the level of army groups. Authority to conduct trials was transferred to the commander in chief of U.S. forces in Europe the following July.[43]

As military courts created to prosecute violations of the laws of war had not been used extensively by the American military since the Civil War, Stimson had no recent models from which to base a new post-hostilities program. Given the high number of expected cases and the expected short duration of the occupation, he demanded a structure "cut down to its bare bones." He expected expeditious but fair proceedings, and as long as the courts were "absolutely free of the restrictions of courts-martial" the Judge Advocate General's Corps could constitute them as it saw fit. One innovation that would distinguish the army's courts from earlier incarnations was Judge

Advocate General Myron Cramer's decision to adopt Bernays's criminal organization and conspiracy scheme.[44]

While Stimson's priority was justice for "members of the United States armed forces or other Americans," the Joint Chiefs of Staff directed the American occupation zone commander to undertake investigations of crimes against civilians and "other atrocities and offenses, including atrocities and persecutions on racial, religious or political grounds, committed since 30 January 1933."[45] If this expansive mandate guaranteed a huge caseload, the language and notoriety of the Malmedy massacre story made the encounter at Baugnez the highest priority case for the new War Crimes Group. As relayed in hundreds of American newspapers in December and January, the story laid bare the Nazi regime's base criminality for the American public, its political leaders, and the War Department. The new division thus had an opportunity to prosecute a case that could compete in terms of public visibility—at least in the United States—with that of the planned international tribunal at Nuremberg.

THREE

Like a Division Reunion

Launching the Investigation

On July 22, 1945, the second day of the annual holiday celebrating Belgium's creation in 1831, the American ambassador, Charles Sawyer, presided over the dedication of a thirty-six-foot-tall wooden cross at the site of the Malmedy massacre. Present were the country's foreign minister, Paul Henri Spaak, a contingent of Belgian military officers and troops, and most of Malmedy's six thousand inhabitants. On hand to bless the memorial was the Bishop of Liege and his entourage of priests and altar boys. In honor of the victims' memories, local schoolchildren sang "The Star-Spangled Banner" to the accompaniment of an American artillery salute. Absent were survivors of the massacre until a U.S. Army truck carrying nine GIs appeared at the crossroads during the ceremony. In a bizarre coincidence, all nine happened to be survivors of the encounter with Battle Group Peiper the previous December. Taking their first furlough in three years, they were passing through Malmedy en route to the French Riviera. "I remember this place," one of them told a *New York Herald Tribune* reporter. "I'll certainly have something to tell the boys when we get back to the outfit."[1]

Deploying the language of the Malmedy massacre story that had become so well known in the United States since January, Sawyer described it as "one of the most senseless and brutal mass murders of Germany's horrid history." He was well aware that his comments were being made at a transitional moment in the war's aftermath. The first sharp gusts of the Cold War could be felt cutting through the still hot atmosphere of anger at Germany for the devastation it had wrought across Europe. Though spared the massive destruction inflicted upon the Soviet Union or Poland, the liberation of Belgium in the fall of 1944 had been amply destructive, and the months following liberation were extraordinarily difficult for most Belgians. Heading into the winter of 1944, the country was fraying at the seams. Fuel and food shortages were widespread and labor unrest was increasing. Mounting public anger at the new Belgian government's leniency toward collaborators along with the growing strength of a communist-led resistance group portended a breakdown of public order. While American and British troops did a great deal to ameliorate material hardships, their presence meant more disruptions and competition for scarce resources and, not least, robbery and rape. Then came the German counteroffensive, which turned the southeastern corner of the country into a battle zone in which thousands of civilians were trapped in the ferocious fighting between determined German attackers and their equally determined American opponents.[2]

Against this backdrop, Sawyer's remarks had a dual purpose. One was to direct attention away from the problems with the American occupation and the divisions within Belgian society by emphasizing Germany's responsibility for the war. At a time when Belgians and Luxembourgers continued to suffer from the damage wrought by the Germans, he told his audience, "We are told we cannot let the Germans starve and that we must maintain Germany's economy." "My hope," he added, "is that we will remember and not forget the atrocities of the Germans; that we will remember and not forget the great contribution of our allies and the sacrifices made by them and by us to win the victory." For Sawyer, a veteran of World War I, Allied unity won both wars but disunity after 1918 failed to maintain the peace. Now it was imperative to prevent history from repeating itself.

Justice Paying Tribute to Memory

Voices like Sawyer's were dominant among American officials in the summer of 1945. That summer marked the beginning of what Jeffrey Herf called the "Nuremberg interregnum"—the years between the end of the war and the hardening division of Cold War Europe. It was in this period, lasting through 1947, that the most extensive judicial reckoning with the perpetrators of war crimes in Europe and Asia took place. Across Europe, justice paid tribute to memory. Suspected German war criminals were tried in recently liberated nations. Thousands of former collaborators were purged from their posts and many faced trial. A similar purge in occupied Germany—known as "denazification"—was in full swing, above all in the American zone. The four occupying nations were conducting trials in their respective zones—the U.S. Army held its first trial in June—and the IMT was preparing to convene in Nuremberg in November.

For American officials, the IMT and Army courts were to serve multiple purposes. They were to bring to justice the perpetrators of war crimes and crimes against humanity. The IMT, its architects hoped, would set new precedents in international law and deter future wars of conquest. The courts would be held to high legal standards, with the prosecutors aiming to demonstrate to the publics of Germany and Japan that crimes on an unprecedented scale had been committed in their names. And this time, there would be no doubt as to which states bore responsibility for starting the war.

For critics, who were by no means limited to the accused and their defenders, vengeance and hypocrisy were driving forces behind the IMT and other tribunals. In their view, the trials took place at a time when anger at vanquished and now helpless former enemies compromised the victors' ability to take a more dispassionate and farsighted approach to assigning guilt. Critics questioned the legal legitimacy of the IMT and decried the imposition of ex post facto law. Many also found the presence of Soviet representatives on the tribunal an outrage against the ideals of liberal democratic jurisprudence and, not least, memory. After all, it was the Nazi-Soviet alliance that had given Hitler a free hand to invade Poland and then much of Western Europe. Even defenders of the trials would admit that Allied forces had also violated some of the laws their governments were preparing to prosecute others for committing. While all postwar trials were subjected to variations of this double-edged critique, in no other case was the charge of hypocritical vengefulness masquerading as justice made so aggressively and persistently than in the Malmedy massacre case.

Though Army courts had plenty of German and American critics, the focus of the controversy was the pretrial investigation. Before, during, and long after the trial, many of the convicted men and their supporters claimed that the investigation was not only a sham—rushed and unprofessional with the outcome predetermined by a vindictive U.S. Army and an angry American public—but that vengeance-seeking "un-American" interrogators had deployed an array of psychologically and physically abusive methods to obtain false confessions. This claim dominated the transatlantic debate over the Malmedy trial in the late 1940s and early 1950s and has informed accounts of the entire affair to the present day. Given the intensity of the attack on the Army's handling of the Malmedy case, a close look at how the investigation was conducted is necessary. Who were the interrogators? What was the nature of the evidence they collected and how did they obtain it?

The Strangest Place in the United States

By the beginning of 1945 the War Department had created a basic infrastructure for investigating war crimes and prosecuting the perpetrators—at least on paper. Setting up a functioning war crimes unit in Europe, however, proved to be very difficult in the months leading up to VE Day. The biggest problem was a shortage of qualified personnel. In June the head of the War Crimes Group's Investigation Section assigned the Malmedy case to Dwight Fanton, a Connecticut attorney. Fanton was less than two years out of Yale Law School and working in a private firm when he entered the service in 1942. Once commissioned as an officer he served as an air force quartermaster before being assigned to the War Crimes Group. The other lead investigator, Raphael Shumacker, was a more seasoned lawyer, though like Fanton had no experience pursuing suspected war criminals. Neither spoke the German language.[3]

Despite their lack of experience, Fanton and Shumacker had been given responsibility for the Army's highest profile case, which they would pursue with tireless determination. Fanton also had an invaluable asset in the person of Lieutenant William Perl. Born in 1906 in Prague, Perl studied law and psychology in Vienna. From 1930 to 1938 he worked in a large firm in that city and gained extensive experience dealing with criminal cases. He had also become a militant Zionist. Beginning in 1937 he organized an operation to transport European Jews to Palestine in defiance of both the Germans and the British. SS Lieutenant Adolf Eichmann, who was overseeing the forced emigration of Jews in postannexation Austria, had refused Perl permission to continue the transports. At the same time, the British government was trying to restrict Jewish immigration to the territory. Perl and his agents were undeterred. Between 1938 and 1944 they utilized an array of ingenious bureaucratic deceptions and freighters of dubious seaworthiness to bring, by Perl's estimate, some forty thousand Austrian and Eastern European Jews to Palestine.[4]

In 1940 Perl was arrested by the British in Greece but managed to escape his captors after faking a suicide attempt. He reached the United States in September after months of transitory stays in Portugal, England, and South Africa. Like some twenty thousand other Jewish refugees from Nazi Germany, he served in the U.S. Army during and after the war. With their native fluency in German, knowledge of the country, and—not least—hatred of the Nazi regime, they were an invaluable resource for wartime intelligence and psychological warfare operations.

When the United States entered the war in December 1941, the War Department had virtually no infrastructure devoted to training interrogators. A former Maryland National Guard camp was quickly converted into the principal instructional facility for interrogators and psychological warfare operatives. Known formally as the Military Intelligence Training Center (MITC) but informally as Camp Ritchie, the Army began producing combat intelligence specialists there in June 1942. Most were trained to gather tactical intelligence in small "Interrogator Prisoner of War" (IPW) teams that would operate at or close to the front lines. A smaller number would collect strategic intelligence, usually from captured higher-ranking officers imprisoned in the United States, England, or France. By the war's end, Camp Ritchie had produced nearly twenty thousand such specialists, including 2,641 interrogators, most of them Jewish refugees pulled out of basic training to become "Ritchie Boys."[5]

The MITC was like no other military camp. It was, as the writer and Ritchie Boy Walter Hasenclever remembered it, the strangest place in the United States.[6] Ritchie earned a reputation as kind of throwback to a nineteenth-century European aristocratic officers' club. The columnist Drew Pearson referred to it as a "country club for boys."[7] There was some justification to the charge, if only a superficial one. The Washington lawyer Kingman Brewster made his nearby hunting preserve available for recreational forays by off-duty Ritchie Boys and a cook in the officer's mess hall had been a chef at the Waldorf Astoria hotel in New York.[8] A poem recalled by Ritchie Boys long after the war points to the self-perception of its trainees as forming a special sector of the Army and the joy they took in flouting standard military discipline:

> Was you ever in Camp Ritchie?
> The very schönste [beautiful] Camp of all!
> Where the sun comes up with Donner [thunder],
> and recorded bugle call.
> Where the Privates are professors
> And the Corporals write books
> And all of them scare Captains
> With their supercilious looks![9]

Some of the privates were indeed professors, or at least had obtained far more formal education than the average American GI, and among the trainees were a French baron, a Bourbon prince, and a White Russian count. In addition to Hasenclever, the writers Klaus Mann, Stefan Heym, and Hanus Burger were among the many intellectuals, journalists, screenwriters, actors, psychiatrists, and musicians that passed through Ritchie's training courses.[10]

The image of a country club for boys was belied by the rigorous course of instruction for interrogators. Instructors were often German-born and of high quality. William Perl became one of them. Already thirty-seven years old when he was inducted into the Army in February 1943, he was transferred to Ritchie after fumbling through less than a month of basic training in Virginia. His talents were put to considerably better use in the MITC, where he took the standard eight-week course for combat intelligence specialists before becoming an instructor.[11] The course centered on mastering the German order of battle—the structure and insignia of German military, including SS divisions and regiments, the names of commanding officers, and other pertinent details. Trainees also had to possess an understanding of German Army small-unit tactics, how squads conducted patrols, and the features of German weaponry from pistols to artillery pieces. This knowledge allowed interrogators to avoid wasting time gathering such basic information from prisoners. A well-informed interrogator could catch a prisoner off guard or at least convince him that the interrogator knew more than he actually did about the disposition and capabilities of enemy forces.[12]

Familiarity with the organization of enemy forces was one prerequisite for effective interrogation. Knowing how to question individual prisoners was the other. Though interrogators at theater- and U.S.-based strategic interrogation centers could deploy informants and electronic eavesdropping devices, most interrogations involved face-to-face encounters with everyone from terrified teenaged recruits to the German military's most experienced NCOs and its highest-ranking officers. As trainees completed the courses at Ritchie versed in the provisions of the Geneva Convention—an introduction to which formed the first part of an interrogators' formal training—they had to learn how to convince a prisoner to proffer information willingly. German-speaking Ritchie Boys learned and then developed in the field a method that relied on a combination of verbal persuasion—"ways of influencing people and making friends (the Dale Carnegie approach applied to [prisoners of war])," as an official camp history put it—and myriad forms of psychological pressure and ruses like good cop / bad cop routines and empty threats.

The Ritchie Boys proved to be highly effective in the field. The collection of tactical intelligence was crucial to the effective fighting capacities of Allied armies from the army group level down to individual regiments, and the most consistently reliable source of actionable intelligence came from German prisoners of war. U.S. Army intelligence officers surveyed immediately after the war concluded that IPW teams collected one-third of combat intelligence in the European theater and that the quality of this intelligence was the highest provided by all branches of military intelligence. Survey respondents also estimated that perhaps 33–50 percent of all information received at the corps level was produced from prisoner interrogations and most divisions surveyed concluded that prisoners provided a steady stream of valuable information from D-Day to VE Day, with one division noting that prisoners provided 90 percent of information obtained by its regiments and battalions. Intelligence officers from the First, Third, Ninth and Fifteenth Armies similarly reported that the interrogations of prisoners proved to be "by far the most important single source of intelligence."[13]

After VE Day, the men and women of "Generation Exodus," as Walter Laqueur called them, formed a deep talent pool for war crimes investigations and would play prominent roles as interrogators and translators in every important case.[14] It was not only Perl's background, then, that made him indispensable to Fanton's team. By the end of the war he had become an experienced interrogator in the European theater. He had been transferred from Ritchie to England in 1944, where he questioned German prisoners about conditions in Germany for the Army's Psychological Warfare Branch. By September he was conducting interrogations in France. Shortly after VE Day, Perl joined the War Crimes Group, which was "badly handicapped," he was told, "by its lack of German-speaking personnel."[15]

The American Doughboy's Number One Criminal

By May 1945, Allied forces had captured or accepted the surrender of millions of German soldiers. Nearly all were convalescing in hospitals or being held in camps—often no more than poorly guarded "Prisoner of War Temporary Enclosures"—in Britain, the United States, North Africa, and Germany. Fanton issued wanted notices for members of the First SS Panzer Division and was particularly interested in locating Joachim Peiper. At that point, American military intelligence sources, probably influenced by assertions of Waffen SS prisoners attempting to cover for Peiper, speculated that he had been killed in the fighting around Vienna in May.[16]

Peiper had in fact been captured by American forces in Bavaria two weeks after VE Day. He spent several months being shuttled between various camps, undetected by his captors as the presumed principal perpetrator of the Malmedy massacre.[17] On August 19, the Associated Press's Wes Gallagher reported that a CIC team had identified Peiper in a prisoner camp outside Nuremberg. Gallagher labeled Peiper "the American doughboy's number one criminal" and described him as "arrogant," "six foot two inches" (Peiper was in fact shorter), and a "tough, cold military strategist who impressed battle-hardened men of the [U.S.] First Division as being one of the most dangerous men they have ever met."[18] Edmund King, a CIC officer among the first to question Peiper, dismissed him as a pompous "typical SS officer" and a compulsive liar who could not be trusted.[19] An interviewer for an Army historical project, Major Kenneth Hechler, also found his subject to be "a very arrogant, typical SS man, thoroughly imbued with the Nazi philosophy," though added he was "not as tall as published reports indicate." Hechler noted that Peiper spoke excellent English and took pleasure in correcting the interpreter.[20]

Other opinions about Peiper among American intelligence and War Crimes Group officials in Germany at that moment were not as uniformly hostile as Gallagher's characterization suggested. Like Hechler, Dwight Fanton found Peiper cooperative and informative regarding details of his battle group's operations in the Ardennes when he interviewed him in late August. Peiper also spent six weeks working closely with Paul Guth, a German Jewish U.S. Army investigator (and Ritchie Boy) who was looking into the administrative structure of Himmler's SS, but not into war crimes committed by the Personal Standard.[21]

Colonel Burton Ellis, head of the War Crimes Branch's Investigation Section and the future prosecutor in the Malmedy trial, also spoke with Peiper in September. Like many other Americans at the time and since, Ellis was fascinated by the young German officer. His initial impressions echoed those of Peiper's former prisoner in La Gleize, Hal McCown. "Definitely not the sadist type," Ellis wrote to his wife, Dee, on September 30, "but a bold, courageous soldier." The language in the press reports following Peiper's capture infuriated him: "It offends my sense of fair play until I can hardly stand it. . . . Why the hell can't we be honest about it[?] If we want revenge let us say so [and] [n]ot pretend to be such goddamned moralists."[22] A month later the deputy theater judge advocate, Colonel Claude Mickelwait, having read McCown's assessment of Peiper's conduct in La Gleize, concluded "it is very doubtful that he is guilty of any war crimes," an opinion shared at that moment by Burton Ellis.[23]

There is irony in the fact that the U.S. Army provided Peiper with the first opportunity to articulate the myth of an apolitical, ordinary soldier. Both Peiper and Hechler were aware of the Malmedy massacre story, and the American officer speculated that Peiper must have feared for his "future disposition." But when it was clear that Hechler would avoid references to war crimes, Peiper seized the chance to distance himself and the Waffen SS from its record of terror war by portraying his battle group as having fought an honorable duel with American forces in the Ardennes. He speculated that he might have reached the Meuse in a single day had it not been for terrible road conditions, fuel shortages, the failure to capture a crucial bridge in Trois Ponts, and poor planning on the part of generals, whom Peiper thought would have been more useful directing traffic at congested intersections. As for the encounter at Baugnez, Peiper stated only that "our tank point fired at an American convoy proceeding along the road from Malmédy to Ligneuville. . . . Eleven to fifteen of their trucks were destroyed, and we moved through their convoy with little difficulty." Peiper admitted to committing no crimes, adding that General Wilhlem Mohnke ordered him to investigate reports of an alleged massacre of American soldiers at the Baugnez crossroads.[24]

Peiper would have many more such opportunities to restate this self-serving myth. Indeed, he remained willing to talk to American officers and historians right up to his murder in 1976. He must have found their attention flattering. More importantly, he used it to shape his image as an ordinary soldier rather than a lifelong loyal servant of the SS, a member of Heinrich Himmler's inner circle, and a military commander responsible for war crimes in Russia, Italy, and Belgium.

Fashioning this myth in the summer of 1945, however, required more than a handful of American officers willing to give him the benefit of the doubt or unwilling to ask questions about civilians and prisoners of war. Aware of his newly conferred bad reputation as the "American doughboy's number one criminal," Peiper likely assumed he would soon be prosecuted. He needed to communicate with those of his men willing to back up his sanitized version of events, and his ability to do so diminished immediately after his capture and public identification as the prime suspect in the Malmedy case. As Fanton's investigation intensified in the fall and hundreds of Personal Standard prisoners were transferred to a single enclosure outside Stuttgart, Peiper alone was kept isolated from his former comrades.

The Atmosphere Was Like That of a Division Reunion

Peiper, of course, was only one of hundreds of possible suspects being sought by Fanton's team. Survivor accounts and interrogations by Ritchie Boys of German soldiers captured during the Ardennes counteroffensive led First Army officials to identify elements of the Personal Standard's First SS Panzer Division as the likely perpetrators of the Malmedy massacre. In early February 1945, a SHAEF Standing Court of Inquiry convened to determine whether a prima facie case could be established on which to base indictments.[25] It concluded "a heinous crime had been committed" near Malmedy and speculated that the killing of prisoners of war was probably "accepted policy" for German forces in the Ardennes. Establishing the identities of the perpetrators, however, was another matter. The court could not indict a

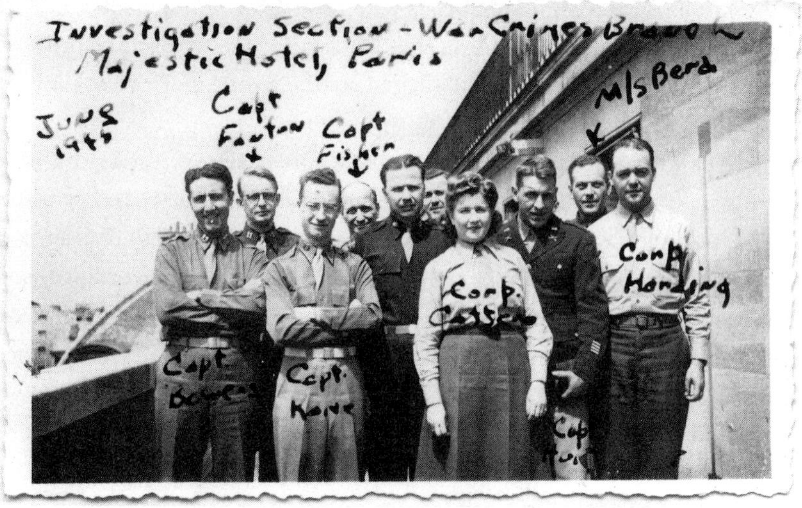

U.S. War Crimes Branch Investigations Section, Paris, June 1945. Dwight Fanton stands second from left, Burton Ellis fifth from left (Special Collections and Archives, University of Idaho Library, University of Idaho).

single individual. It could only identify battle group Peiper's constituent units and list the names of forty-two officers and NCOs, Peiper included, known to have served in them.[26]

Locating surviving First SS Panzer Division men among the millions of German prisoners held by the Allies proved easier than one might have expected. Wanted notices having produced no results, Fanton and his investigators spent several months traveling to various prisoner of war camps and hospitals seeking battle group veterans. SS men were often confined together in the camps, thus making identifying members of the First much easier. However, the conditions of group confinement compromised the security of the investigation from the beginning. Some battle group veterans had read about the Malmedy massacre in *Yank, Stars and Stripes,* and *Life* and had also learned of Peiper's capture. Any inquiries into the battle group's record in the Ardennes confirmed to Fanton's targets that the Americans were investigating war crimes.

In this early stage of the investigation Fanton found that many prisoners—including those in the unit present at the Baugnez crossroads on December 17—were willing to talk to him and other interrogators, albeit in ways that omitted self-incriminating statements. Clearly, some coordination of stories had already taken place. The result was a mixture of abundant details about the battle group's attempt to reach the Meuse alongside evasiveness when it came to questions about the fates of captured GIs at specific locations, above all Baugnez. Peiper and other higher-ranking officers were similarly cagey when asked about the existence of orders to execute prisoners. Benoni Junker, a First SS Panzer Regiment first lieutenant and company commander, told a U.S. Army investigator in January 1945 that he only learned of American prisoners being executed when he was shown an American magazine article shortly after his capture. He claimed illness prevented him from attending the preoffensive briefing in which the disposition of enemy prisoners was discussed and asserted that his men would never commit the kind of atrocities described in the American press. Nor, he added, would Peiper order or tolerate such a thing.[27] A few months later, Sepp Dietrich pretended to be incredulous when asked by Burton Ellis about the fate of enemy prisoners:

> *Q:* Did you ever hear of any of your commanding officers making any statements [to kill prisoners of war]?
>
> *A:* No, never. I would have kicked them around.
>
> . . .
>
> *Q:* General, how do account for the fact that so many of the officers in command under you gave orders to shoot American prisoners?
>
> *A:* . . . I cannot understand it. Are they crazy or what is the matter with them?[28]

Major Josef Diefenthal, in whose armored personnel carrier Peiper rode just before American prisoners were executed at the crossroads, told Fanton in mid-November: "We did not have any orders or instructions concerning prisoners of war. There is no instruction necessary. It is a Geneva Convention regulation."[29]

The investigation could make no progress in these conditions. Complicating matters was a lack of documentary evidence. Malmedy would be the only high-visibility war crimes case in which the prosecution lacked a significant documentary basis for preparing its case. By contrast, the prosecution at the main Nuremberg trial amassed a small mountain of files and reports—some three thousand tons of it. Prosecutors in the twelve Nuremberg "successor trials" also had the benefit of large quantities of damning documents. The prosecutors in the U.S. Army's concentration camp trials were similarly blessed with an abundance of official records, photographs, and eyewitness accounts.[30]

Thus Fanton's investigation could make headway if surviving battle group men could be gathered in one secure location and questioned intensively. At the end of October, the commanding general of the Third U.S. Army issued orders to all personnel involved in screening German prisoners to separate members of three SS divisions within their respective enclosures: the Personal Standard, Viking, and Prinz Eugen. The target, of course, was the Personal Standard, but by including the other divisions the investigators hoped to cloak their intentions. From the Personal Standard, those belonging to companies of regiments known to have been operating in the vicinity of Malmedy were to be separated again. They were to be "interrogated thoroughly" but "absolutely no mention of 'Ardennes' or the period covering that offensive should be made until individual interrogation reveals that subject participated therein."[31]

These steps were taken in preparation for the evacuation of about one thousand Personal Standard men to a single enclosure in the town of Zuffenhausen, near Stuttgart. The theater provost marshal had assured Burton Ellis that the suspects could be held there in separate confinement, by which Ellis believed he meant separated from each other. Instead, SS prisoners were being confined together in a single complex of barracks. The investigators then observed the inevitable take place. "The atmosphere," Raphael Shumacker recalled, "was that of a division reunion."[32] Many of those being screened in Zuffenhausen, aware that they were suspected of having committed war crimes, were given another opportunity to coordinate stories and intimidate comrades who might be inclined to divulge the truth. Ellis was apoplectic when he learned of the mistake. "These stupid asses have thrown those who have been questioned in with those who have not been," he raged in a letter to Dee. "Now they can frame their story and what a job it will be to ever crack them."[33]

That prisoners were coordinating stories in Zuffenhausen became apparent when Fanton noticed certain explanations being repeated to his investigators: numerous mysterious "vehicular breakdowns" that prevented soldiers from reaching the crossroads in time to have been involved in any executions, or claims to have been either at the column's head or its rear and thus nowhere near the crossroads at the time of the shooting. Investigators also learned that Peiper, despite being isolated from the other prisoners in Zuffenhausen, had managed to convey an order not to discuss the incident in any detail and to blame the dead Werner Poetschke for issuing the orders to shoot the prisoners at the crossroads.[34]

Some prisoners were being intimidated by other Waffen SS veterans in the enclosure. Perl had learned early in the investigation that more than residual loyalty to the SS or group solidarity was responsible for the prisoners' silences and evasions. Otto Wichmann, a sergeant in the First SS Panzer Regiment's Headquarters Company, told him in January 1946 that "the word was circulated that Colonel Peiper was [in Zuffenhausen] and that he had the following words passed on: that we should say that Poetschke gave the order to shoot the Americans before [Ligneuville], for Poetschke was dead anyhow." It was clear to Wichmann that anyone defying Peiper's "order" would face retribution.[35] "I openly admit that I am afraid of being persecuted and murdered by one of Peiper's followers if I say anything against [him]," Wichmann recounted in one of his sworn statements: "My fear of being executed by one of the followers of Peiper as a traitor is probably incomprehensible to the Americans, but I am certain that the same fear holds many of my comrades back from telling the truth." In the Zuffenhausen cell he shared with about ten other prisoners, Wichmann added, "it was generally said that he who makes a statement against his superior, is certain to be punished for that one day by Peiper and to disappear."[36]

Fanton's team managed to make the best of a bad situation. They screened about one thousand former Personal Standard members, eliminating half that number as suspects. They avoided specific questioning about war crimes, particularly the Malmedy massacre, focusing instead on compiling complete rosters of men belonging to the battle group's various battalions, companies, and regiments and reconstructing in remarkable detail the route of march toward the Meuse River. They also collected a large amount of ancillary information about the battle group's culture in the process—gossip, nicknames, personal grudges between officers, a sense of which officers were particularly disliked by the men under their command, and some information on individuals who may have committed crimes.

Their work was facilitated by the fact that a united front among former Personal Standard men did not form in Zuffenhausen. By late November, one of Fanton's investigators, Morris Elowitz, had noticed that small, exclusive groups were forming and not speaking with one another. It also seemed as though younger prisoners were more willing to talk than older veterans.[37] The interrogators would attempt to exploit these divisions during the investigation's final phase.

Despite the willingness of the prisoners to talk to their captors, however, it was clear to Fanton by December that the investigation was heading for a dead end. Given the lack of documentary evidence, he understood that the suspects would have to "convict themselves," as one of his investigators put it, meaning that they would have to confess to crimes they had committed or accuse others of committing crimes. The suspected perpetrators would have to be broken down as a group and as individuals, and this would not be possible in Zuffenhausen.

FOUR

The Psychological Approach

American Interrogators

Beginning in December 1945, members of the First SS Panzer Division being held in Zuffenhausen and other internment camps were conveyed in small groups to the undamaged town of Schwäbisch Hall, located roughly forty miles northeast of Stuttgart. American officials had commandeered part of a civilian prison large enough to hold several hundred suspects, and it was here that the investigation's final stage took place between December 1945 and April 1946. Six American interrogators questioned around seven hundred prisoners and obtained the sworn statements that established the prosecution's case. They sought to disrupt whatever group solidarity remained from the war and confinement in Allied prison camps and to break through the individual suspects' lies and omissions to obtain voluntary confessions admissible as evidence before a military court. The investigators relied on what they would later refer to as the "psychological approach."

To regulate the prisoners' secure transfer, confinement and questioning, Dwight Fanton had drawn up a series of standard operating procedures (SOPs). He ordered that men from the same company not travel together or share cells, and tried to keep as many suspects as possible—especially officers and other high priority suspects—in single cells before they were interrogated.[1] Preventing prisoners from communicating with each other or with Germans working in the prison's facilities was another essential security measure. These precautions were taken primarily to protect prisoners' safety and increase the interrogators' effectiveness. If the prisoners' identities were not kept from one another they would remain vulnerable to threats, intimidation, or reprisals. Guards would accompany them to the barber and prisoners were not to have contact with any German medical personnel. When this was unavoidable, American personnel had to be present. Other than the investigators and certain prison staff, no one was to speak to a prisoner without Fanton's permission. Prisoners were hooded as they were moved about the prison, a basic security provision that later became a point of considerable controversy regarding the conditions of their confinement.

These precautions did not create a completely secure environment. Prisoners found ways to communicate with each other. They tapped out coded messages on the pipes of the prison's heating system and tried to pass written notes between floors.[2] At one point William Perl learned that some were using their mess kits to convey messages, a practice that he let continue briefly in order to monitor what was being said. There were at least two escape attempts. Shortly before the trial, two prisoners who had implicated Joachim Peiper in multiple crimes attempted to escape. Some suspects were clearly trying to evade both the perceived wrath of the Americans and that of Peiper and his loyalists.

Fanton also drew up an SOP for interrogating prisoners. The Theater Judge Advocate had already issued guidelines for War Crimes Branch interrogators, intending to provide them with "latitude of judgment and an elasticity of investigative procedure." The objective was to obtain a voluntary, highly detailed confession. To the greatest extent possible, the confession should be based on the suspect's direct, personal knowledge of the incident in question. Statements based on hearsay, while admissible as evidence in a military court, were to be avoided.[3] Prisoners also had to be made to feel secure in the presence of their interrogators. "To get the prisoner to 'open up,'" the guidelines stressed, "there is no substitute for gaining his confidence and having quiet, unostentatious talks with him." Coercion in the form of threats and abuse had to be avoided. Multiple interviews were recommended, the expectation being that the first encounter would not produce any information of value. Further, the number of people present in the room had to be kept to a minimum, lest the prisoner conclude that some kind of "trial" was taking place. When a confession was obtained, finally, it had to be written down by the prisoner in his own handwriting. "The average German prisoner," Judge Advocate officials asserted, "has been found to possess an extreme weakness for wanting to write."[4]

The unique circumstances of the Malmedy investigation to date led Fanton to augment these guidelines. The interrogators aimed to produce in the subjects, as Fanton described it, "resignation and hopelessness." First, a suspect had to be made to believe that any plan to block the investigation by relying on stories coordinated at Zuffenhausen had failed. Then he had to be convinced that the interrogators knew everything and that lying or not answering their questions was pointless. Raphael Shumacker summarized the interrogators' approach to a suspect in Schwäbisch Hall:

> We always began with the assertion that we knew all about the man being questioned, all about his unit and its men, and the part that each man played in the events of December 17 and the week that followed. We would then ask questions about inconsequential's, the answers to which we knew from the mass of information obtained from the usually non-combatant personnel. Almost invariably we received false answers. Whereupon we would proceed to tell the man being questioned the whole history of his unit, the names of his comrades, their "jobs," their vehicle numbers, their positions in the march column, even where they had stopped along the route to urinate. The man being questioned apparently thought, as we had hoped he would, that we knew the whole story, and he proceeded to tell us what we didn't then know—whether he shot prisoners, who else shot them, and on whose orders and under what circumstances the shootings took place. In short, if guilty he confessed and then "ratted" on everybody else involved with him.[5]

To increase the pressure by giving credence to the assertion that "we know all," the interrogators might also confront a subject with his former comrades who had already confessed to committing or witnessing a crime.

The point of the psychological approach was to draw information—which may or may not have included an admission of guilt—from a suspect voluntarily. "We know all" did not mean simply telling the suspect "we know you are guilty." A great deal of preparation was thus required for the approach to work. In addition to lengthy information-gathering sessions with prisoners, interrogators examined each prisoner's personal possessions, noting in particular any articles of American manufacture. They also studied prisoner pay books and a personality card compiled by the investigators, noting both the unit to which he belonged and the identities of his cellmates. Fanton also ordered that a detailed record of all interrogations and cell assignments and reassignments be maintained.[6]

While "threats, duress in any form, physical violence, or promises of immunity or mitigation of punishment" were to be "scrupulously avoided," interrogators were free to deploy "any ruse or deception." The most common form of deception was a simple bluff in which the interrogator claimed to possess more information than he actually did. "Stool pigeons" were deployed on a few occasions, but Perl and Morris Elowitz did not find them particularly useful, as they did not trust the informers. Breaking down loyalty was another tactic, directed mainly at NCOs and enlisted men whom the interrogators suspected hated some of the officers. Fanton assumed—not without some basis in fact—that Waffen SS officers had brutalized their own men regularly. To amplify what resentments may have existed, the interrogators would show an enlisted man a former superior officer's cell made up to appear well-appointed with books and comfortable furnishings.

Of all the forms of psychological pressure exerted by Perl and the other interrogators, the most controversial was a ruse Perl referred to as the "quick process" or "quick procedure" *(Schnellprozess)* used on perhaps a dozen prisoners. Critics later labeled this technique a "mock trial," a term also used occasionally by some of the interrogators. In the "quick process," a few individuals who had refused to make statements or divulge information were led to a cell used in regular interrogations in which two candles and a crucifix had been placed atop a cloth-covered table.[7] Two or three prison staff members pretending to be officers sat behind the table. One German-speaking interrogator questioned the prisoner and the other took his side. The prisoner was told to take an oath, but was told only that this was the "quick process." Another suspect was brought in to "confront" the subject. If the target lied or was reluctant to provide information, he would be dismissed abruptly. Perhaps believing that he had been tried and would now be executed, he would often ask for a second chance. If he was still unwilling to confess or provide information, he might be approached by an interrogator who would suggest that perhaps the prisoner could have one more chance at a "quick process." If he remained recalcitrant, he was returned to the rotation of regular interrogations.

Perl adopted the ruse from a pretrial examination procedure found in some continental European legal systems. In certain criminal cases, a judge hears evidence from interested parties and this evidence may later be presented to trial judges. Perl assumed that a version of this procedure would not be completely alien to the men being subjected to it.[8] There were in fact two versions of the "quick process," the first resembling a hearing, which Perl recalled as being successful only twice on reluctant witnesses and not principal suspects who later became defendants. The second version was "more dramatized." Taken together, Perl estimated that at most three were successful, with the first iteration of the "quick process" being the more successful of the two. The witnesses who confessed were not used at the trial, but the information they provided led Perl to other witnesses whose stories proved more useful. Perl and Shumacker never denied that the ruse was designed to give the prisoner the impression that he was finally being tried. They assumed that German soldiers were "accustomed to summary hearings, if any at all" and that "the very stupid might believe and conclude, without being so told, that this was a trial."[9]

Departing from the Theater Judge Advocate's guidelines, Fanton recommended that once a confession was obtained, the prisoner himself was to write out his own statement and the interrogator would then dictate it to a stenographer. As some prisoners were better able to express themselves than others, their statements were "dictated or supervised" by the interrogator, though the final statement had to be sworn to by the suspect. Fanton's concern was to head off potential defense objections to the statements' validity by ensuring they were as detailed as possible. "In dictating or supervising the preparation of the statement," Fanton ordered in his SOP, "all possible defenses should be anticipated and answered. . . . For instance, it should be made clear that the soldiers who were killed were Americans, not merely because the prisoner making the statement says they were Americans, but because they wore American uniforms, spoke English and were armed with American weapons, or because an examination of their personal effects disclosed that they were Americans."[10]

As the prosecution would learn at the trial, defending the legitimacy of this elaborate procedure was difficult. Most sworn statements did contain abundant details—such as place names, the caliber of firearms, the configuration of towns, buildings, and even individual rooms—some of which had been supplied by the interrogators based on the knowledge of the battle group and the terrain amassed in the course of the investigation. Also, the statements shared certain similarities in composition and phrasing, a fact that would lead defense lawyers, and later amnesty advocates, to claim that they were simply concocted by the interrogators. This was precisely the accusation leveled at the prosecution by defense attorneys in the Mauthausen trial, the case that immediately preceded Malmedy at Dachau.[11]

There were other assumptions about prisoners in general and members of the SS in particular that underpinned the interrogators' strategy and methods. One was that an individual guilty of committing or abetting a crime wants to unburden himself. It was therefore necessary for the investigators to encourage him to confess and make it easy for him to do so. That the suspects were, as members of the Waffen SS, "thoroughly indoctrinated," and the officers more so than the NCOs and enlisted men, was another. This idea determined the strategy of focusing first on enlisted men and moving up the chain of command. The investigators considered the relative youth of most of the suspects as incidental to the commission of war crimes. "Only the utmost ingenuity on the part of the investigators get confessions . . . from the hard boiled, dangerous and courageous, too, S.S. troops," Burton Ellis wrote his wife, Dee, on March 5. "These SS are only babies 18, 19, 20 years old but they have nerves of steel and are the toughest babies in the whole armies of the world."[12]

Perl also believed that former Waffen SS soldiers would be particularly susceptible to appeals to their honor. The SS's motto, as Perl was aware, was "My Honor Is Loyalty." He asserted to prisoners that their adherence to a code that defined "honor" in terms of loyalty to, and self-sacrifice for, Hitler's vision of Germanic racial superiority and conquest should not have simply evaporated after Germany's defeat. It was therefore beneath the dignity of a former member of the SS to behave like a "little chicken thief"—as Perl put it to his subjects repeatedly—who had been caught red-handed and now refused to admit responsibility.[13] Here Perl was indulging in a bit of manipulative flattery, as he was suggesting to his subjects that they should remain proud that they had fought in the "SS spirit" expected of them by Hitler, Himmler, and their superior officers.

In a few cases Perl resorted to a ruse that played on another aspect of this code of honor. He blamed a prisoner he suspected of committing a serious crime merely of stealing from a dead American soldier, a transgression he did not really believe the prisoner had committed. Perl assumed, rather, that an "honorable" SS man would consider pilfering boots, wedding bands, or some other trophy from the body of a dead enemy was a worse offense—at least in principle—than executing him after he had surrendered, an act that Perl believed most SS soldiers considered within the proper bounds of warfare. An appeal to the honor-loyalty dyad could backfire, however, as the interrogators were urging individuals to betray their comrades, hardly an honorable or loyal act. As we will see, the fact that so many suspects did just this likely encouraged some of them to claim that they had been physically abused by Perl and the other interrogators.

The interrogators also believed that the prisoners made assumptions about *them*. One was that the investigators were stupid. Another was that they would be abused while imprisoned or during interrogations. Some also assumed they would be executed immediately following their confessions, a belief that may have induced one suspect to commit suicide in his cell on the night of March 6–7. Arvid Freimuth, a driver in one the battle group's armored personnel carriers, had just confessed to shooting Belgians and American prisoners, including using disarmed GIs as target practice in La Gleize. He had been taken to a cell to write out his confession, nearly completing it before hanging himself—Freimuth's statement ends in mid-sentence—just after describing his participation in the "sharpshooting" of American prisoners. Raphael Shumacker thought it was likely that Freimuth believed he'd be hanged after writing the confession. Indeed, the investigators were struck by the frequency in which prisoners assumed that once they had confessed they would be executed without a trial.[14]

The First Shot at the Americans

The first weeks of work in Schwäbisch Hall were devoted not to interrogating prisoners but to completing rosters of each unit that might have been involved in the battle group's various crimes, above all the Malmedy massacre, and to gathering more background information to use in interrogating the principal suspects.[15] Collecting this information was facilitated when Fanton's team informed prisoners before they were interrogated that they were now suspects in a war crimes investigation. Fanton noticed that this tactic had the effect of "flushing out" those who were most likely innocent of any crimes, as they usually rushed to tell their stories. The tactic worked to the interrogators' advantage in that it not only reduced the number of interrogations that had to be conducted but also provided the investigators with even more information about the various units and personalities. Another benefit was that a few such prisoners volunteered to work as informants.

On the assumption that the highest-ranking and presumably most thoroughly indoctrinated battle group veterans would be the hardest to "break" and that numerous enlisted men disliked some of their officers, Fanton and Perl aimed first at the lower ranks. An important exception was Friedrich Christ, a first lieutenant and commander of the Second SS Panzer Company. Christ, Perl discovered early in the investigation, was "hated by his own men for his cruelty toward them." Moreover, preliminary screening of enlisted men in Christ's company indicated that he had conveyed an order to his men to "fight a ruthless fight and . . . spread terror among the American troops" and take no prisoners.[16] Perl decided to interrogate him at this early stage, bluffing a man he considered "less intelligent" than other commanders with details about his own unit—mentioning gossip and nicknames—and using the names of subordinates Perl knew disliked Christ intensely. Thanks to Fanton's security measures, Christ was unaware that Perl did not even have these men in custody.[17]

On December 17, Christ signed a statement admitting that he attended a meeting of company commanders on December 15 in which Werner Poetschke demanded that "we should behave toward the enemy in such a way that we create amongst them panic and terror and through our behavior should precede our troops so that the enemy should be frightened ever to meet them" and that "no prisoners should be taken." He also confessed to repeating the order to his company. Christ claimed that while he could not recall whether Peiper was present during Poetschke's speech, he was "under the impression that Peiper knew about the order to take no prisoners of war." For Perl, his success with Christ demonstrated how "security, [the] psychological approach and the use of permissible ruses interlocked in eliciting the truth."[18]

Over the following weeks, the interrogators uncovered more details about the preoffensive conferences involving Poetschke, Peiper, and other commanders and the orders they conveyed to their regiments, battalions, and companies. They were to disregard rules that had governed engagements in the West and fight "in the old spirit" of the SS, meaning as the Waffen SS had fought in the Soviet Union. Allied "terror bombings" of German cities were to be avenged and the spearhead would "spread fear and terror" among American soldiers and Belgian civilians. Some officers ordered that no prisoners were to be taken at all, while others ordered that they be shot only if unspecified "conditions" necessitated it.

Among NCOs and enlisted men, the main effect of these preoffensive briefings and exhortations seems to have been that they would not need a direct order to shoot a prisoner or a civilian. A member of Christ's company who recalled his commander's speech on the afternoon of December 15, for instance, concluded that "as far as the officers were concerned, I could shoot every prisoner of war, not only without fear of being punished, but would be rewarded for my actions." Similar statements reinforced what the investigators already assumed about the battle group—that it launched its spearhead assault prepared to kill prisoners and civilians out of perceived necessity and to "spread fear and terror."[19]

Determining who was responsible for the Malmedy massacre—who ordered the execution and the identity of the shooters—remained the highest priority. By early January, Perl and the other interrogators had obtained the confessions of several Baugnez executioners, including from those who had walked into the field and killed the wounded. On January 5, Georg Fleps, a private in the Seventh Company's Third Platoon, claimed to have been the first man to have shot into the field where the American prisoners had been assembled, thus initiating the deadly fusillade that killed or wounded over half of them. He admitted an unidentified officer ordered his tank commander, Hans Siptrott, to shoot the prisoners and that Siptrott, seeing that Fleps was holding a pistol, "gave me the order to shoot. I then fired a shot at one of the Americans. . . . As far as I know, this shot of mine was the first one shot at the Americans." Two days later, Siptrott confirmed giving Fleps the order, though would not name the officer who had ordered him to begin shooting. Both men cited their company commander Oskar Klingelhoefer's repeated preoffensive admonitions to his men to not take prisoners, though others present at the crossroads implicated Max Beutner, a sergeant in the Second Platoon of the Third Panzer Engineer Company who was killed in action three days later. Beutner's orders, further investigation suggested, had most likely come from Werner Poetschke.[20]

The interrogation of Siegfried Jäckel in mid-February 1946 offers a window into how the interrogators' questioned individual suspects and what suspects told them about the Baugnez executions. Jäckel, eighteen years old in December 1944, had been drafted into the Waffen SS in 1943. He was a private in the Second Platoon of the Third Panzer Pioneer Company. Fanton, Perl, and Shumacker had been developing the case against members of this company. They had five of its members in custody who were known to be present at the crossroads before the shooting, including Jäckel. On February 15, he was interrogated by Shumacker and Perl. A crucial segment of the interrogation is worth quoting at length, as it reflects how interrogators obtained and deployed background information and, not least, the tedious and time-consuming nature of the psychological approach. The transcript also illustrates a point made by Dwight Fanton during the controversy over the investigation: that most subjects, when questioned in this manner, talked freely:

Jäckel: When we came in front of the field, Beutner's SPW was parked on the left side of the road in front of the field. Beutner halted our SPW and spoke to Witkofsky. At this time Beutner was not in his SPW. He told Witkovsky that they were going to shoot the prisoners and to move on down the road out of the way so that they would not be in the line of fire.

Q: How far down the road did you go, Jäckel?

Jäckel: We stopped a little more than halfway down the field, on the right hand side of the road with nothing between our SPW, the ditch, and the pasture.

Q: What SPW was in front of you?

Jäckel: Lozensky's SPW was directly in front of us.

Q: How much distance was there between the front end of your SPW and Lozensky's SPW?

Jäckel: 8 to 10 meters, something over the length of an SPW distance between us.

Q: When you stopped, what was behind you, if anything?

Jäckel: There was no vehicle behind us. Beutner's vehicle was on the left side of the road but to the extreme left, and we passed it by passing by its right side.

Q: After Beutner spoke with Witkofsky and you parked in the position you have described, were these American prisoners still standing in the field?

Jäckel: After we stopped at the place I have previously described, all of the prisoners in the field were still standing.

Q: How long after you stopped did you remain standing there with all the soldiers standing in the field before the first shot was fired?

Jäckel: Three to five minutes before the first shots were fired.

Q: What happened in those three to five minutes?

Jäckel: During the three to five minutes we made our machine guns ready.

Q: Who is "we?"

Jäckel: Toedter and Stueckel. We removed the cover. This was after Beutner shouted from his vehicle "we will start firing!"

Q: Then what happened?

Jäckel: Hofmann and Neve left our vehicle. Hofmann aimed with his machine pistol and aimed toward the field and Neve took his fast firing rifle and made it ready to shoot. I did not leave the vehicle because I was loading the ammunition into the machine gun while Toedter and Stueckel were pointing the gun towards the field. Witkofsky too left the vehicle and took a machine pistol and he aimed at the field too.

Q: Where did Witkofsky, Hofmann, and Neve go with respect to your vehicle? Where on the road? You say they left the vehicle.

Jäckel: They stood at the right front corner of our SPW so that they should not be in the line of fire of our own machine gun.

Q: Up to this time nobody had fired a shot. Is that right?

Jäckel: Up to this time nobody had fired a shot.

. . .

Q: Jäckel, you have given us a picture of everybody getting ready with rifles, machine guns, machine pistols and so forth and aiming them at the field. Then what happened after you got all set and everybody placed themselves and so forth?

Jäckel: Then Beutner gave the command to shoot or fire. He said "shoot!"

Q: Who shot first after the command was given?

Jäckel: Goldschmidt's vehicle starting shooting with machine pistols and then everybody started.

Q: After you had made these preparations, Jäckel, and everybody was all set, apparently you were waiting for your order from this platoon leader, Beutner. If you were waiting for the order from Beutner, you were certainly looking towards him so that when he gave the order, certainly you must have seen who in his vehicle shot with his machine pistol?

Jäckel: Yes, I saw who shot from his vehicle.

Q: Who did shoot and with what?

Jäckel: Goldschmidt with his machine pistol; Beutner and Dieckmann with their machine pistols, Hanke with a rifle, Schlingman with a rifle, Max Hammerer with either a rifle or a pistol.

Q: What about Dibbert?

Jäckel: I saw Dibbert shooting with a rifle.

Q: Did you see all those men shoot before you fired?

Jäckel: My machine gun was pointed at the prisoners in the field and I was standing on the left side of the gun so as I guided the ammunition belt into the gun I could do this and was looking right at Beutner's vehicle at the same time. Of course, I could look at the field at the same time.

Q: Did you see, during this first shooting, any of the men in the vehicles in front of you shoot?

Jäckel: Yes. Standing in my position, you look in all directions, especially when you are firing behind you, as I did.

Q: Did you see the firing from Bode's SPW?

Jäckel: Yes.

Q: What about firing, if any, from his [tank]?

Jäckel: The [tank] was shooting with the machine gun.

Q: What men or officers did you see around this [tank] during the time these preparations were being made?

Jäckel: There was the commanding officer of the 9th Pioneer Company.

Q: What does he look like?

Jäckel: He is about the same size as I, but he was blonde and slim.

Q: How tall are you?

Jäckel: I am 1.72 [meters].

Q: You mean that this officer was about your height?

Jäckel: Yes, maybe one-half inch taller or shorter, but he was slimmer.

Q: How long had you known the commanding officer of the 9th Pioneer Company before this occasion?

Jäckel: I did not know him before.

Q: Had you ever seen him before?

Jäckel: I never saw him before. I know now and I knew a short time afterwards that he was the commanding officer of the 9th Pioneer Company because in La Gleize the company medic of the 9th Pioneer Company, a [sergeant], told me of this officer when I saw him there again. "This is our company commander." He did not mention the name.

Q: You would certainly know him again if you saw him?

Jäckel: Yes.

(1st Lieutenant Rumpf was shown to Jäckel and [Jäckel] identified him without any difficulty)

. . .

Q: How many rounds did you fire with your machine gun?

Jäckel: A belt of approximately 75 shots. Ordinarily the belt contains 50 rounds but we had made them longer so that there were about 75.

Q: How many rounds did the rear gun in Bode's SPW fire?

Jäckel: I cannot say.

Q: Do you know how many rounds the rear gun on your vehicle fired?

Jäckel: I believe about 50 or 60, approximately the same . . .

Q: Do you know that they didn't use up one belt and load another—the other gun?

Jäckel: I don't know. They shot in bursts of about 10 shots.

Q: How many did you fire?

Jäckel: Approximately 10 bursts.

Q: Who pulled the trigger, you or Stuecker?
Jäckel: Toedter.
Q: What did the prisoners do when the firing started?
Jäckel: They hit the ground.
Q: Are you sure of that?
Jäckel: As far as I remember, all of them hit the ground.
Q: This machine gun on the tank, was that a machine gun mounted up through the turret or was that the machine gun that was parallel to the cannon that was fired?
Jäckel: I believe it was below the turret. I cannot remember. It looks like an "eye" and can be turned. I believe it is below the turret.

. . .

Q: How long did you stay in your SPW firing the machine gun?
Jäckel: A short time—2 or 4 minutes.
Q: Did anyone give you the order to cease fire or not?
Jäckel: No one said anything. I didn't hear anything.
Q: Tell your story as to what you did and what everybody else did from there—the truth.
Jäckel: First I threw all the brass out of the car. Then we drove ahead approximately 50 meters beyond the end of the field. I stopped my vehicle behind an American truck—maybe 10 or 15 meters behind it.
Q: When you moved your SPW down behind the American truck, which of your men were in the vehicle when it was moved?
Jäckel: Toedter, Stueckel, Ende, Hofmann, and I.
Q: After you stopped your vehicle, then what did your men do?
Jäckel: We first left the vehicle, then we went to the field.
Q: Who went to the field from your vehicle?
Jäckel: Toedter, Stueckel, Ende, and I. I don't know whether Hofmann went with me.
Q: Before you went down and parked behind the American truck and while you were firing the machine gun, who else did you see shoot with their pistols, machine pistols, rifles and so forth, from your vehicle?
Jäckel: Hofmann, Hergeth, Neve, Storch and Witkofsky. I saw them shooting between the bursts.

Q: They shot with the weapons that you previously said you saw them aiming with, is that right?

Jäckel: Yes.

Q: Now, when you came up the road, where did you go, what did you do, and so forth. You, Stueckel, Toedter, Ende, and Neve?

Jäckel: First we stood for a few seconds in front of the field in a ditch and looked into the field to see who was still moving. Then we picked out those who were still moving and went towards them in order to shoot them and then we shot them.

Q: You told me the other day that you shot how many?

Jäckel: 4 or 5.

Q: Where did you shoot them, in the head or in the heart?

Jäckel: Into the heart.

Q: How many shots into each one?

Jäckel: Only 1 shot in each.

Q: What makes you so sure that you only shot 4 or 5 shots with your—you were shooting with a machine pistol or a pistol?

Jäckel: Pistol.

Q: What makes you so sure you only shot 4 or 5 rounds?

Jäckel: Because I didn't have more bullets in my pistol.

Q: How many rounds does your pistol hold?

Jäckel: 8 or 9.

Q: You had shot the other 4 or 5 rounds at Honsfeld or Büllingen?

Jäckel: I shot in Satzvey before the offensive started.

Q: You went into an offensive with a half loaded pistol?

Jäckel: I shot in Satzvey. Then I didn't reload again.

Q: What weapons did the man who went into the field use?

Jäckel: Toedter, Stueckel, and Ende shot with pistols.

Q: How many men each did they shoot?

Jäckel: I do not know how many but each of them fired several times, that is, Toedter, Stueckel, and Ende, shot with machine pistols.

Q: And Neve, what did he shoot with?

Jäckel: Neve shot with a fast-firing rifle.

Q: How many shots did he fire?

Jäckel: I don't know.

Q: What about Storch? Was he in the field?

Jäckel: Yes.

Q: What did he shoot?

Jäckel: With his rifle.

Q: Did you see him shoot with his rifle?

Jäckel: I did not see Storch shooting but he had his rifle and he was in the field and everyone in the field was shooting.

Q: What about Boltz?

Jäckel: He was in the field.

Q: What did you take from those soldiers. I don't care what you took, but I want the truth.

Jäckel: I took a few cigarettes, a pair of gloves, and a lighter.

Q: What kind of lighter?

Jäckel: A round and tall lighter.[21]

On March 1, Jäckel signed an eleven-page statement in which he described his participation in the offensive. Though he admitted "the truth of the matter is that I saw and heard about so many American prisoners of war who had been shot or were being shot during this offensive that I cannot remember the details of every case," he provided the Americans with a extraordinarily detailed account of his role in the battle group's operations, which began with the capture of Honsfeld and ended with the retreat on foot out of La Gleize twelve days later. A foot injury prevented him from attending the preoffensive briefing on December 12, but he named four comrades who told him their platoon leader, a first lieutenant, had told them "substantially the following": "We will make a counter-offensive which should develop into something very big. We will have three smoke-laying battalions, a battalion of Germans dressed as Americans will make the first thrust and put the enemy on the run. No prisoners of war will be taken. You will remember the cities which were subjected to terror attacks day after day. . . . We shall strike the enemy wherever we meet him. Whoever shows himself to be a coward will be shot."

Jäckel confirmed what he had admitted to Shumacker and Perl two weeks earlier about his role in the Malmedy massacre and admitted to having shot at American prisoners outside two towns overrun by the battle group before it reached Baugnez. In the case of these incidents he did not claim that he had been ordered to shoot by a superior officer. He also identified by name numerous members of his and other units whom he saw shoot prisoners or learned at the time that they had done so.[22]

As with most other suspects, the case against him was not based solely on his own confession. Just as Jäckel had provided the interrogators with the names of comrades who had executed prisoners (and, as the portion of his February 15 interrogation reveals, information not related directly to his participation in war crimes), he had been identified by others as a participant. Taken together, their statements—which did not contradict each other—provided one of the most detailed accounts of the Malmedy massacre from the perspective of the perpetrators.[23]

The U.S. Army court at Dachau would convict Jäckel and sentence him to death. The deputy theater judge advocate for war crimes later recommended a reduction in his sentence to twenty years on the grounds of his age and the mitigating factor of superior orders. Like most of his fellow defendants in the trial, Jäckel would then repudiate his pretrial confession, this time swearing that he had not divulged voluntarily any of the information contained in his eleven-page affidavit.

Like Trying the Whole German Army

A little over one month into the investigation, Burton Ellis replaced Dwight Fanton as the chief investigator in the case and was given the job of prosecutor in the upcoming trial. Ellis, then the chief of the War Crimes Group Investigation Section, had taken an increasingly keen interest in the Malmedy case and came to covet the high-profile job of prosecutor.[24] William Denson, the American prosecutor who had been racking up an unbroken record of convictions in the army's concentration camp trials, was the obvious choice, but he was committed at that time to those cases. Ellis convinced the deputy theater judge advocate for war crimes, Lieutenant Colonel Clio Straight, to give him the Malmedy case. Though the forty-three-year-old Ellis, a former tax attorney, had relatively little experience as a prosecutor and trial lawyer, he had served as an assistant staff judge advocate in the China-Burma-India theater before being tapped to serve in the new War Crimes Group headquarters in France. By the fall of 1945, he was overseeing all investigative teams operating in the Low Countries, France, Germany, and Austria.[25]

Like the other investigators, Ellis was focused initially on the Malmedy massacre, assuming the case would be about this infamous incident and thus involve a relatively small number of defendants. He believed the investigators had broken the case and expected a three-week trial would take place in late March, presumably with a victorious outcome for the prosecution and a high-visibility win for both the War Crimes Group and, not least, for the army's prosecutor.[26]

He was disabused very quickly that his job would be a simple one. As the investigation progressed, the extent of the battle group's crimes became clearer and the number of defendants exploded. "If we don't get to trying it soon," he wrote Dee on March 3, "it will be like trying the whole German army." While the Malmedy massacre would remain the central crime pursued by the investigators, a much more extensive record of war crimes emerged in the following weeks. "I am following their line of march and trying to get all the perpetrators of war crimes," he wrote Dee nine days later: "They killed actually hundreds of American P.W.'s and many civilians. They used p.w.'s for target practice at La Gleize, tanks shot down women and babies at Stavelot, etc. etc. I can prove all this and I have over 40 of the perpetrators. It will be the bloodiest campaign ever put before the public's eye."[27] If the number of prisoners to be named as defendants increased almost daily, so did the list of suspects who had not been located. Some, of course, were dead, and others likely escaped or managed to conceal their identities. The fact that the investigators did not try every battle group member implicated in a war crime has fueled the charge that the investigation was a sloppy and rushed affair. The truth is more prosaic: Ellis simply could not find them among the millions of German prisoners held in camps in Europe and the United States.

Like Fanton, Ellis did not limit the investigation to the interrogation rooms in Schwäbisch Hall. In February Fanton dispatched Lieutenant Robert Byrne to Belgium to locate eyewitnesses. Using maps drawn by some of the prisoners, Byrne found the buried personal effects of an American prisoner shot in Petit Thiers on Peiper's orders. Of greater significance to the prosecution's case, he identified around thirty Belgians who had witnessed some of the battle group's crimes. The investigators also tracked down six American survivors of the Baugnez shootings to testify at the trial. In early April,

Ellis and all six men traveled to Belgium and retraced the battle group's route of march.[28]

Before his departure from the case, Fanton summarized the investigation's progress for Ellis. By February 19, Fanton's team had obtained multiple admissions of a "no mercy" order being handed down to four panzer companies, including the one present at the Baugnez crossroads at the time of the shootings. The first thing to be proved in the case, then, would be the existence of orders throughout Peiper's command to execute prisoners of war and murder civilians. In addition to admissions that verbal orders to kill prisoners had been given right before the counteroffensive was launched, the investigators at that point had amassed details about shootings in Honsfeld, Büllingen, and Baugnez.

Fanton's desire to implicate Peiper directly in the upcoming trial's central crime must have been enormous. The interrogators, however, were coming up against resistance to identifying him as having given the order to shoot the prisoners at the crossroads. It is entirely possible, of course, that those claiming firsthand knowledge of Poetschke's actions that afternoon were telling the truth and that as the second-most senior officer present he gave the order to execute the captured GIs. Yet Fanton could not ignore the suggestions of a coordinated effort among prisoners to deflect the blame from Peiper. A sergeant in the First SS Panzer Regiment's Headquarters Company, Otto Wichmann, had told Perl that he was being pressured to blame the dead Poetschke for issuing the order. Fanton also had evidence that Paul Zwigart—a Personal Standard sergeant with long experience serving under Peiper in Russia and Belgium—had told several fellow prisoners in the fall of 1945 that Peiper was responsible for giving the order to shoot, but Zwigart did not admit this in his sworn statement.

In the end, Peiper signed three statements in March. He claimed to have been informed of the counteroffensive at a late date and, once he received his orders, concluded the preparations were "highly defective" and the entire operation to be a "desperate undertaking." In a staging area command post in Blankenheim on December 14, he admitted that he had received written orders from Sepp Dietrich, "that prisoners of war must be shot where the local conditions of combat should so require it." Dietrich, according to Peiper, was only passing along an order he had received from Hitler in Bad

Nauheim two days earlier. When Peiper assembled the battle group's commanders for a briefing later that day, he claimed not to have said anything about shooting prisoners of war in certain circumstances "because those present were all experienced officers to whom this was obvious."[29]

Peiper's only other substantive statement, sworn to on March 26, admitted that after conferring with Poetschke and two other officers about their increasingly desperate situation in La Gleize, he decided that the American prisoners they were then holding would have to be shot if the battle group received no reinforcements. He also claimed to have heard that some prisoners were "disobedient." Two NCOs, Hans Hennecke and Rolf Reiser, both asserted that he ordered the execution of some American prisoners in La Gleize.[30] More serious was evidence that in Stoumont on December 19 he had ordered a First SS Panzer regiment sergeant, Hans Hillig, to shoot an American prisoner who had refused to provide Peiper with information he wanted. "In spite of my greatest efforts," Peiper declared to Perl, "I could not remember such an execution," but once he had been "confronted" by Hillig and another eyewitness, he finally admitted: "I am remembering that I caused an American prisoner of war to be shot there, but to my own mind I do not recollect any details."[31]

Peiper deployed similar evasive language to describe his decision to have an American prisoner executed in Petit Thiers in early January. Otto Wichmann had admitted that he had brought an exhausted American soldier, clearly suffering from hunger, exposure, and frostbite, to Peiper and the regimental surgeon, Kurt Sickel. After questioning him with no success, Peiper asked for Sickel's recommendation, which was to administer a "mercy shot": "'Alright! Take the poor devil away!' I then had not given further orders but had left the rest up to [Sickel]. It was clear to me that the prisoner would be shot! . . . Dr. Sickel and I acted obviously out of pity."[32] Wichmann shot the prisoner.

Fanton's team had only begun to obtain admissions of other crimes along the battle group's route when Ellis took over the investigation. Over the following weeks, the interrogators collected sworn statements tying numerous individuals to the murder of American prisoners and civilians all along the battle group's route of march from Honsfeld to La Gleize. The interrogators' strategy produced dramatic, though not always conclusive, results. After over four months of investigation, the focal point of the Malmedy case—the

Baugnez shooting—could be described in detail from the perpetrators' perspectives rather than solely that of the survivors. Beyond Baugnez—in Honsfeld, Büllingen, Ligneuville, Stavelot, Stoumont, Wanne, La Gleize, and Petit Thiers—Ellis had statements confessing to or implicating several dozen battle group officers and enlisted men in the murder of possibly hundreds of prisoners of war and civilians. The many admissions that battle group officers, NCOs, and enlisted men had either received or given orders to "spread fear and terror" and kill prisoners of war and civilians would allow the prosecution to make the case for a conspiracy linking Adolf Hitler to the crimes of his "personal" Waffen SS division.

On April 11 in Schwäbisch Hall, Ellis served seventy-two former officers, NCOs, and enlisted men of Battle Group Peiper with formal charges. Two more defendants were served on April 22. They were accused of violating the laws and usages of war as enumerated in the Geneva Convention Relative to the Treatment of Prisoners of War and The Hague Convention (IV) Respecting the Laws and Customs of War on Land. In the wording of the charges, the defendants did "willfully, deliberately and wrongfully permit, encourage, aid, abet and participate in the killing, shooting, ill-treatment, abuse and torture of members of the Armed Forces of the United States of America, then at war with the then German Reich, who were then and there surrendered and unarmed prisoners of war in the custody of the then German Reich, the exact names and numbers of such persons being unknown but aggregating several hundred, and of unarmed Allied civilian nationals, the exact names and numbers of such persons being unknown." They were accused of committing these crimes in or around twelve Belgian towns and villages between December 16, 1944, and January 13, 1945, and were to be tried by a General Military Court in Dachau in early May.[33] The defendants were transferred to Dachau between April 16 and 18, where they were again confined to separate cells.

Despite the confessions, the identification of American and Belgian eyewitnesses, and the fact that the prosecution was drawing on well-established international law and would present its case to a court that would make its own determination of the value of hearsay evidence, convictions were not assured. With the exception of the Baugnez crossroads, photographic and forensic evidence was lacking, particularly in La Gleize, where prosecutors would claim that more American prisoners were killed than at Baugnez.

Reliable eyewitnesses could testify to only some of the alleged crimes confessed to by former battle group soldiers and a skilled defense attorney might cast considerable doubt on the accuracy of their memories.

Moreover, despite the detail contained in most sworn statements, some contained language that avoided an unambiguous admission of guilt or in some cases did not identify other culpable individuals by name. A few statements provided contradictory accounts of various incidents, including the Baugnez shootings. Nearly all suggested the existence of mitigating circumstances. While pointing to preoffensive briefings in which company commanders spoke of "revenge" for Allied "terror bombings" and admonished their men to "spread fear and terror" and take no prisoners would likely work to the prosecution's advantage, it offered some defendants the possibility that the court would consider such orders as mitigating factors.

The highest-ranking Personal Standard officers in American custody were evasive to varying degrees on orders to kill prisoners and spread fear and terror. In his preoffensive briefing to his officers, Peiper claimed he said nothing about shooting prisoners of war because he believed experienced officers would need no instructions on the matter, an ambiguous statement that could be interpreted multiple ways. As for Dietrich's order regarding prisoners, Peiper insisted that "the order to use brutality was given by Sepp Dietrich out of his own initiative but that he only acted along the lines which the Fuehrer expressly laid down." Dietrich himself admitted that he had ordered the spearhead to spread a "wave of terror and fright and that no humane inhibitions should be shown" but denied giving any specific orders to shoot prisoners: "Whoever claims anything of the sort is speaking the untruth!"[34]

Brigadier General Fritz Kraemer, the Sixth Panzer Army's chief of staff, wrote that during an interrogation he admitted to knowing of orders to take no prisoners of war but insisted in his written sworn statement that the meaning of that order was merely that follow-up units would have to be responsible for handling any captured American soldiers. The former commanding general of the First SS Panzer Corps, Lieutenant General Hermann Priess, who, like Dietrich, was present at Hitler's December 12 briefing, stated that Hitler never explained what he meant by "terror." Priess believed that he meant avenging Allied bombing raids on Germany. Regardless, he interpreted Hitler's words as "propaganda." He concluded that there would be no deviation from the "fighting methods on the western front" and assumed his commanders shared this understanding. Priess claimed to remember no references to a wave of fear and terror in the Sixth Army's orders, though conceded such language might have been used.[35]

The posttrial attacks on the investigation and the efforts by the interrogators to explain and defend their methods have placed into the background the most important dimension of the investigation: most suspects admitted freely to varying degrees of responsibility for the battle group's multiple war crimes between Honsfeld, La Gleize, and Petit Thiers. They had spent many hours over four months being questioned by mostly German-speaking interrogators who seemed to know a great deal about the battle group. When engaged in this manner, they talked. The tricks and ruses that became so central to the ensuing controversy formed a relatively small part of the hundreds of interrogations, most of which did not involve trickery but were aimed at acquiring a minutely detailed account of the battle group's personnel and operations over a four-week period.[36]

The problems the ambiguities and evasions contained in these statements might present to the prosecution aside, Ellis knew that the defense would attack the validity of all of the sworn statements by attempting to discredit the investigators' methods. The extent to which this effort reached went far beyond what he, Fanton, Perl, and the other investigators imagined as they pieced together their case in Schwäbisch Hall.

FIVE

Nazi Method Boys

The First Torture Allegations

Burton Ellis's confidence that he would reveal the "bloodiest campaign ever put before the public's eye" at the upcoming trial was not shared by his counterpart, chief defense counsel Colonel Willis Everett.[1] The forty-six-year-old Everett, an Atlanta general practice attorney in civilian life, had applied to the U.S. Army's Reserve Officer Corps immediately after World War I, and in 1932 sought a transfer to the Military Intelligence Reserve. He remained in the Atlanta-based Fourth Corps Area and led the Fourth Service Command's intelligence division during the war, an assignment that combined investigating foreign and domestic subversion, very little of which was ever uncovered. After completing a fourteen-week European studies course at the Post Hostilities School at Columbia University in January 1945, he was sent to France in late March and then on to Frankfurt, where he was ordered to report to the Theater Judge Advocate's headquarters in nearby Wiesbaden.[2]

Like many occupation officers, Everett was shocked at the extent of the physical destruction in and around Frankfurt and found himself sympathetic to the daily hardships endured by civilians he considered victims of a criminal regime. Conversely, he was appalled by what he perceived as the wastefulness and disorganization of American occupation. The sight of American soldiers—many of them married—consorting openly with German women and contributing to a thriving black market offended his deeply conservative moral and religious sensibilities.

At the Judge Advocate's office in Wiesbaden he may have been led to believe he would be assigned as a court "law member"—military courts required at least one member to have a background in the law—or a prosecutor in an important war crimes case. On April 8, he was driven to Schwäbisch Hall and was shocked to learn that he had been appointed chief defense counsel in the Malmedy case, with the trial scheduled to open in little over a month. Though he considered himself unqualified for the task—he had no courtroom experience—and disliked the idea of representing men he believed to be murderers, he was nonetheless determined to do his best to defend them.

They Were All Lying

Everett's efforts to this end got off to a bad start. For one thing, the War Crimes Branch had done little to prepare any of the necessary facilities for him and his staff at Dachau. Simply getting up and running took the better part of a week. He met Ellis in Schwäbisch Hall on April 11 and disliked him immediately (he wrote to his family that "he has no chin and wears a moustache"). Ellis was dilatory in handing over copies of the sworn statements to the defense team, finally doing so after the Third Army's Judge Advocate threatened to delay the trial by six months. One bright spot for Everett was the fact that his team of six American attorneys included Herbert J. Strong, who had defended accused German war criminals in several Dachau cases and was a Jewish refugee from the Nazis whose fluency in German was an important asset. As the army permitted the defendants to retain German lawyers, Everett dispatched Strong to Munich to recruit them.[3]

Everett also found the defendants to be uncooperative and suspicious. He had first encountered them in Schwäbisch Hall when Ellis served them with charges. Now that they had been transferred to Dachau, he and his team expected to be able to work with them in crafting their defense. One of Everett's lawyers, Lieutenant Colonel John Dwinell, recalled that the defendants at first thought they were yet more interrogators, this time impersonating defense attorneys. To break through the wall of suspicion, Everett asked Joachim Peiper to speak to his former subordinates and urge them to trust the men responsible for their defense in court.[4]

It was in these circumstances that the first accusations of abuse at the hands of American interrogators were brought to Everett's attention. On

April 23, he and his staff began interviewing prisoners and heard accounts of mock trials, threats, dictated statements, and physical abuse. Peiper had already submitted to Everett the names of prisoners who claimed they had been beaten and threatened with hanging. He also told Everett that he had been told that Arvid Freimuth had been beaten before hanging himself in his cell in early March.

Everett was unsure of what he should do. He seemed convinced from the start that the interrogators, to whom he referred privately as Ellis's "Nazi method boys," had resorted to abuse and unacceptable forms of trickery in the form of "mock trials." Given that the defendants had remained in separate confinement in Dachau, he doubted they could have "coordinated" their stories in advance, though he later admitted to a U.S. Senate investigator "there was an absolute pattern of the same type of force or threat being used on one defendant as another." Herbert Strong, however, found enough variation in the claims to convince him that they were not coordinated. In any case, Everett was concerned about the implications of going public with the allegations. "I am afraid the case will smell really bad and if the newspapers pick up this stuff you will really see the headlines," he wrote his family on April 23, adding that he had no desire to "[inform] the American public about the atrocities the Americans perpetrated."[5]

Everett and his staff prepared a questionnaire and demanded each defendant complete it. The questionnaire informed defendants that the information it requested was "necessary to enable your counsel to initiate his preparation of your defense" and that it was in his best interests to be "accurate." Thirteen of the forty-three questions dealt with the prisoners' treatment: Had he received any instructions regarding the Geneva Conventions and the treatment of prisoners of war? How was he treated when he was captured, where was he interned, and was he ever denied food or privileges or placed in solitary confinement? Eight questions related directly to interrogations and sworn statements.[6]

Was the questionnaire a deliberate attempt to encourage prisoners to fabricate stories of abuse? Ellis and his investigators certainly saw it that way after one of Everett's secretaries provided them with a blank copy. Questions such as "Did you at any time make a statement or confession not voluntarily?" provided an opening to the defendants to invent or exaggerate. More likely, however, the defense was trying to determine whether the abuse accusations made during the initial interviews with the prisoners were truthful and widespread and how they might be used to cast doubt on the prosecution's case.

Despite his fears of embarrassing the army with negative publicity, Everett got his concerns relayed to Colonel Claude Mickelwait, the head of the War Crimes Group in Wiesbaden, who immediately dispatched an officer to Dachau to investigate the matter. It would be the first of many formal inquiries into the abuse allegations. Everett provided the investigator, Colonel Edward J. Carpenter, with a sample of completed questionnaires emphasizing mock trials and Carpenter spoke with some of the defendants. Everett's selection suggests that he remained skeptical about the truthfulness of the claims and concerned about the implications should they be publicized.

Nonetheless, a few told Carpenter that they had been treated roughly by some of the guards and four said they had been hit. No one claimed to have been forced to confess, and in his testimony before the Senate subcommittee in 1949, Carpenter stated that "none of the accused in their statements claimed that they had been brutally treated or beaten up in an effort to obtain statements." Further, he could not get anyone to identify an abusive interrogator by name, except for William Perl, and only then when Carpenter used his name first. He also noticed that the defendants he interviewed were suspiciously vague about details and simply repeated what they had written in their questionnaires. "I just could not get anything out of them," he testified, when he asked them about anything "not contained in the statement."[7] Carpenter enlisted the help of Paul Guth, the Austrian-born chief interrogator in the Mauthausen concentration camp trial then taking place in Dachau. Some of the abuse claims had, as Guth remembered it, "melted to nothing when they were probed." Moreover, despite the fact that their main complaint was the use of mock trials, he could not coax out of them convincing accounts of this procedure. As for Perl, some prisoners described him as "loud" and "relentless," but not violent.[8]

On April 28, Carpenter reported on his inquiry to Mickelwait and the deputy theater judge advocate for war crimes, Lieutenant Colonel Clio Straight, in Wiesbaden in the presence of both Everett and Ellis. Mickelwait concluded that the court would determine the statements' validity, though ordered Ellis to withdraw any confessions found to be signed under duress. When Ellis returned to Dachau the following day his staff assured him the accusations were baseless. The meeting, however, only deepened the difficulty of Everett's position. Everett's good-faith effort to have the matter investigated by a War Crimes Group officer failed to produce the results he desired—a delay in the trial's opening date or perhaps the dismissal of certain charges. Confirming to his opponent his strategy of casting doubt on the veracity of the sworn statements was particularly distressing. It was, he recalled three years later, "probably the hardest decision I had been called upon to make throughout my entire Army career."[9]

The four defendants who told Carpenter they had been abused were Gustav Sprenger, Friedel Bode, Siegfried Jäckel, and Gustav Neve. Sprenger, a Third Panzer Pioneer Company private and SPW driver who had fought with the Personal Standard in Russia, had been perhaps the most cooperative of all suspects. The longest of his three sworn statements totaled sixteen typed pages in which he both confessed to committing multiple crimes and implicated many others, including Peiper. In Schwäbisch Hall he provided the investigators with six unusually detailed maps showing both the route of march and the sites of various crimes. Sprenger's memory seems to have been so precise that Ellis cursed himself for not bringing him along when he retraced the route in April. Indeed, Ellis considered his willing cooperation so important to the entire investigation that he recommended clemency shortly after Sprenger's conviction and death sentence.[10]

Gustav Neve was another Third Company SPW driver. He confessed to participating in the execution of prisoners at Baugnez and confirmed Sprenger's admissions of executing multiple American prisoners in other locations. Siegfried Jäckel, the Third Company rifleman who admitted freely to participating in the initial shooting at Baugnez after hearing Max Beutner give the order and then walking into the field to kill survivors, had named numerous others who had shot prisoners along the route of march. Finally, Friedel Bode, a Third Company sergeant also under Beutner's immediate command, was the only one of the four to have not confessed to committing any crimes, confirming only the names of the men in his SPW and to have been "present when German soldiers, among them numerous members of my platoon shot at these American prisoners of war" at Baugnez. Jäckel and others, however, identified him as one of the soldiers who administered coups de grace in the Baugnez field.

Not only were these four men implicated in the upcoming trial's main crime, but three of them had provided the Americans with a great deal of information. Between them, they implicated many of their comrades and several officers in serious crimes. They had, in short, enormous incentive to extract themselves from their confessions. Despite the fact that they were confined separately in Dachau, they may have found some way to communicate with each other. Whatever their motives or ability to communicate, Everett was soon forced to concede that they were lying. "We had four young kids (18 & 19 yrs.) back for reinterrogation as it looked very suspicious that they were all lying," he wrote his family on April 30. "We were able to break one and then all admitted that they were not telling the truth in some details." Though he later denied doing so, he conveyed this information to Ellis.[11]

Could Everett trust any of the claims made on the questionnaires? He asked Paul Guth to address the defendants together and impress upon them the importance of being completely honest with their lawyers. Everett also turned once again to Peiper, who made, he thought, a "fine appeal" to the defendants on May 1. Peiper, however, also confided in Guth that his men were lying about being abused. Guth had gotten to know Peiper when he interrogated him shortly after his capture in Bavaria in May 1945. The acquaintance had been more than passing. Guth was seeking information on Heinrich Himmler's staff and not only questioned Peiper but put him to work in his office for six weeks. The relationship appears to have been a cordial one—Guth delivered letters from Peiper to his wife, Sigurd. A year later in Dachau, Peiper told Guth that he was disgusted with his men's behavior. Hoping to save themselves, they had betrayed him and each other and were desperate to find a way out of their confessions "now that they were all in the same boat."[12]

Peiper admitted the same to Colonel Charles Perry in early 1947. Perry, a Theater Judge Advocate lawyer, had been dispatched to Landsberg prison, near Munich (where the men convicted in the Malmedy trial were serving their sentences or awaiting execution), to investigate another case. Perry asked him whether he had in fact ever been "struck or threatened with bodily harm" in Schwäbisch Hall. Peiper was, Perry reported, "emphatic in expressing a negative answer." He went on to state that some of the men formerly under his command had told him about beatings and threats at Dachau right before and during the trial. Perry offered that Everett's plea to Peiper to "keep the best interests of his men ever present in his mind" and to "encourage [them] to confide in him" might have been a deliberate ploy by the defense to elicit stories about abuse. Peiper responded, perhaps obsequiously, that "no American officer would resort to such unsportsmanlike conduct." Rather, he repeated the explanation he had given to Guth: that he was "disgusted" by his men's behavior and believed that they were trying to redeem themselves in his eyes.[13]

Peiper's account was confirmed at the same time by another convicted perpetrator, Benoni Junker. Junker, who also spoke fluent English, had been the commanding officer of the Sixth Panzer Company and was sentenced to death for issuing preoffensive orders to shoot prisoners and civilians. He told Perry that he had never been abused, threatened, or humiliated, only "intensely interrogated" at Schwäbisch Hall. "Frequently," Perry reported, Junker believed "his answers to direct questions were distorted and colored to suit the ideas of his interrogators in an effort to solicit further information, but that such methods were not unusual and were probably a great deal milder than the methods which would have been used by German interrogators had the situation been reversed." Like Peiper, Junker also suspected his former comrades had invented abuse stories to extricate themselves from the confessions they believed—or had been led to believe—would work to their advantage. Junker speculated that this coordinated attempt to "discredit the prosecution" in fact originated with the defense.[14]

Small Matters Easily Exaggerated

Testifying before the Senate Armed Services subcommittee in 1949, Paul Guth offered an explanation as to why some defendants claimed to have been abused by American interrogators. "What had been a rude gesture at first became a threatening move, became physical contact, and finally became mistreatment."[15] His assessment is supported by other sources. In early February 1947, one of the former investigators, Harry Thon, interrogated Willy Schäfer in Landsberg prison. Schäfer, a Third Panzer Pioneer Company sergeant sentenced to death for ordering and participating in the execution of American prisoners in Stoumont and La Gleize, offered similar insight into how some of the defendants might have concocted stories of torture at the hands of Thon and Perl:

Thon: I can only say, Schäfer, that I did not force anyone to any testimony. I didn't find it necessary. . . .

Schäfer: Small things do happen. I'd like to call your attention to a thing which is probably being elaborated on. That is the case of [Friedel] Bode. I, myself, was a witness and had an understanding for it, but eventually one will try to present it in a different fashion. As Bode was called in after my deposition, First Lieutenant Perl asked: You were at the crossroads at such and such a time? He denied it. First Lieutenant Perl said: I know it better than you do. Bode said in a rather snotty tone: Were you at the crossroads at all? First Lieutenant Perl got mad and got hold of him and pushed him forcefully against the wall. These are things that can be explained.

Thon: Was I present?

Schäfer: You were present. Hofmann, Sprenger, and Jäckel were present. These are small matters which, however, are easily exaggerated. These are matters which as they stand do not carry any weight.[16]

Another account of prisoner inventions or exaggerations was provided by one of the defense counsels, Granger Sutton, in his testimony before the Senate subcommittee two years later. Sutton, who was assigned to prepare the defense of twelve of the accused, all of them privates, had helped Everett write up the questionnaire. When asked about their contents by a subcommittee staff lawyer, Sutton testified that "those questionnaires did not develop by any means what was developed later." He recalled "four or five" complained at the time of mistreatments: "One, I believe, said he was kicked, and two or three said they were hit by either [of the interrogators]—one or two said they were hit by Polish guards." When the defendants were shown photographs of the interrogators, according to Sutton, they singled out Morris Elowitz, Thon, and Perl, claiming that one or more of these men had "just pushed them around, hit them or kicked them."[17]

There may have been yet another factor encouraging both prisoners and their lawyers to concoct stories of abuse. In his subcommittee testimony, Guth also noted that in the final week of the Mauthausen concentration camp trial in early May some of the accused had tried to extricate themselves from their sworn statements by accusing him of tricking, insulting, and threatening them. One even claimed that Guth was so "friendly" that the defendant fell into a "hypnotic state" and signed a false confession. None of it worked. On May 13, the month-long trial concluded with the conviction of all sixty-one defendants. All but three received death sentences.[18]

In reflecting on his role in the Mauthausen and Malmedy trials, Guth concluded that the Malmedy defendants knew that in other cases defendants had not been able to get out from under their confessions. Indeed, Guth pointed out that some of the men charged in the Malmedy case had sat in on sessions of the Mauthausen trial and may have seen firsthand how attempts to retract confessions had failed. Guth also knew that they followed reporting on the concentration camp trials in German newspapers, which were "at a premium on the black markets in the camps." In Guth's estimation, some of the Malmedy defendants must have concluded that if claims of ruses would not be enough to cast doubt on the contents of their sworn statements, perhaps accusations that interrogators—particularly those who, like Guth, were Jewish refugees from Nazi Germany—beat confessions out of suspects would be "strong enough to take away from the force of their confessions."[19]

The very first accusations of abuse originated with a small number of prisoners. Though Everett seemed inclined to believe the worst of Ellis's "Nazi method boys," he worried about embarrassing the army if he made the charges public and they turned out to be false, a concern that must have been intensified when it became clear that at least four of the defendants claiming duress were lying. Nonetheless, Everett's team of American and German lawyers would attempt to convince the judges that the sworn statements were obtained by duress and trickery. The defense had little more to go on. Everett had not been successful in delaying the opening of the trial or having some defendants excused because they had claimed to have been coerced or tricked into signing false confessions. As Ellis handed over the sworn statements in late April, it must have become even more apparent how damaging they would be should the court accept them as "evidence of probative value."

SIX

A Monstrous Slaughter Machine

The Prosecution's Case

Recalling his role as chief prosecutor in the Malmedy trial, Burton Ellis boasted to a U.S. Army interviewer in 1988 that he "had the case prepared. I knew what I was going to do every damn minute." He had sworn statements from the accused, six American survivors of the Baugnez massacre, and Belgian civilian eyewitnesses from other locations. He had dozens of former German soldiers willing to give corroborating testimony, though he considered some "shaky as hell," as they, too, were prisoners who would be vulnerable to intimidation by the defendants. He also knew that the defense would attempt to discredit the investigator's methods. In court he would be supported by the men with whom he had been working for months. Raphael Shumacker, Barney Crawford, and Morris Elowitz were assigned as assistant trial judge advocates, along with Robert Byrne, the investigator who had collected evidence and eyewitness accounts of the battle group's crimes in various Belgian towns. William Perl was assigned as special assistant to the prosecution. Ellis expected to "breeze through" his case, he wrote his wife, Dee, ten days before the trial opened.[1]

The United States participated in three categories of war crimes trials in Europe. From November 1945 to October 1946, the IMT at Nuremberg, its judges representing the United States, the Soviet Union, Great Britain, and France, tried the surviving highest-level leaders of the Nazi Party and German armed forces. The second, the Nuremberg Military Tribunals, also known as the subsequent Nuremberg trials, were conducted solely by the United States in 1947 and 1948. These trials involved the German Army High Command, perpetrators of medical crimes, various German government ministries, several industrial concerns, and Einsatzgruppen leaders.[2] The U.S. Army would conduct the third category of trials, those involving "traditional" war crimes and "mass atrocities committed in the U.S. area of control or in concentration camps overrun by American troops."[3]

The Malmedy trial, designated *United States of America v. Valentin Bersin, et al.*, was one of hundreds held by army courts from 1945 through 1947. These courts presided over three categories of cases. In the "fliers cases," 640 "Axis nationals" (nearly all Germans) were tried in 311 cases for the murder of over 1,200 American airmen whose planes had been shot down over Germany. Eight "mass atrocity" cases involved the personnel of six concentration camps (Dachau, Mauthausen, Buchenwald, Flossenbürg, Nordhausen, and Muehldorf); the perpetrators of the Malmedy massacre and other crimes committed during the Ardennes offensive; and the personnel of the Hadamar hospital in west-central Germany, where over ten thousand Germans and Allied nationals were murdered. Finally, army courts tried 170 "subsequent" concentration camp cases involving personnel at subcamps and those not tried in the six major camp trials.[4]

The fact that the army's courts did not adhere to the procedures of American civil courts left them vulnerable, then as later, to charges that they were "un-American." The use of such courts, critics contended, was detrimental to one of the main objectives of war crimes trials: the demonstration of liberal democratic jurisprudence to the German people. The military court as a venue to try violations of the laws and usages of war, however, was anything but alien to the American legal tradition. The opposite was the case—the military commission was distinctly American. Its use dated back to the revolutionary period, though it would be during the Mexican-American War that an American army general, Winfield Scott, created the first recognizably modern military commission to try—rather than summarily execute—Mexican irregulars who had attacked American soldiers. They were also convened during and immediately after the Civil War and again in the U.S.-Philippine War.[5]

Moreover, what became the body of twentieth-century international law aimed at regulating the treatment of prisoners of war and civilian populations in wartime, and thereby justifying the prosecution of those who violated these regulations, was developed in the United States during the Civil War. Its principal architect was Francis J. Lieber, a Prussian-born professor of law and Waterloo veteran who had two sons serving in the Union Army and one in the Confederate. Lieber wrote a code of conduct for the Union Army that became a landmark in the history of the laws of war. Adopted widely in Europe, the code formed the basis for the 1899 Hague Convention with Respect to the Laws and Customs of War on Land, the first multilateral agreement that codified the rules of warfare in international law. While Lieber's code allowed for a commander "in great straits" to "direct his troops to give no quarter . . . when his own salvation makes it impossible to cumber himself with prisoners," the provisions of the Hague Convention made no such allowance.[6] Another major international convention, held in Geneva thirty years later, refined and expanded upon the Hague provisions dealing with the treatment of prisoners of war. Ratified by the United States, Britain, Germany, and Italy (though not the Soviet Union and Japan), its articles provided much of the legal justification for post—World War II Allied war crimes prosecutions.

Neither this body of law nor the wartime agreements between Allied nations, however, determined the makeup, rules, and procedures of military courts. These were determined in part by precedent and in part by circumstantial factors. One of the latter was that the war was over. While Allied governments had made their intention to hold war criminals accountable clear to the Nazi regime in hopes of deterring atrocities, the U.S. War Department would not allow any trials to take place before the end of hostilities for fear of inciting reprisals against Allied prisoners by their German captors.[7] After VE Day, however, trials would serve multiple purposes. They would bring at least some perpetrators to justice and reveal to the German people the magnitude of the crimes committed by the Nazi regime. The IMT would demonstrate the application of international law in what the occupiers hoped would be perceived by the German public and its future political leaders as a fair trial. The precedent set by the IMT would, its creators hoped, serve to deter future wars of conquest.

Another factor was that the earliest trials in Germany and Asia established the precedents that had the most immediate impact on subsequent trials, including Malmedy. In the trial of Bergen-Belsen concentration camp personnel conducted by a British military court in the fall of 1945, the prosecution pursued—successfully—a conspiracy and criminal enterprise strategy. The Hadamar trial, held in October 1945, was the first "mass atrocity" case conducted by the Americans and established the jurisdiction of military courts and the charge of "common intent" to commit murder. Prosecutors in the Hadamar case also deployed the conspiracy strategy that would be adopted by American prosecutors in the concentration camp cases and also by Ellis in the Malmedy trial. That commanders could be held accountable for the actions of their subordinates, even in the absence of orders, was established in the aftermath of the trial of General Tomoyuki Yamashita by an American military court in November 1945. The court held Yamashita, an Imperial Japanese military governor of the Philippines, responsible for massacres of Filipino civilians carried out by forces under his command in early 1945.[8]

Finally, the number of cases to be tried shaped the courts' procedures and makeup. With the large number of traditional war crimes committed against American airmen and soldiers and the expanded scope of crimes prosecutable by army courts, the Joint Chiefs of Staff insisted that these courts rely on "simple and expeditious procedures designed to accomplish substantial justice."[9] Hence, military courts would not follow "the rules of procedure and evidence applicable in British and American municipal criminal proceedings." Particularly important in this context was that hearsay evidence was admissible, a feature of continental European legal traditions, including those of Germany, but not the Anglo-Saxon. Judges were also granted wide latitude in determining what evidence was of probative value. And while all verdicts were subject to multiple reviews by the Theater Judge Advocate and, finally, the commander of U.S. occupation forces, there was no independent court of appeal.

As for the courts, they were common law military courts appointed by the commanding generals of the Third or Seventh U.S. Armies.[10] Defendants were presumed innocent and the burden of proof rested on the prosecution. A panel of at least five senior officers would serve as judges, with one serving as the court's president and another as the "law court member." Only the latter, who advised the court on legal matters, had to have formal training in the law. There was no jury. The Theater Judge Advocate appointed both the prosecution and defense counsel attorneys, though defendants could also choose their own attorneys. Following the presentations of the prosecution and defense cases, in that order, the judges would deliberate and announce their findings. In the case of convictions, the court would hear additional prosecution and defense statements. All death sentences required a two-thirds vote by the judges. The proceedings, findings, and sentences could not be invalidated by errors or on technicalities.[11]

The determination to hold expeditious trials and the rules regarding evidence may have seemed to favor the prosecution. The accused, however, had the right to read the indictment before the trial and be present during the trial itself. He or she could give evidence in self-defense, examine all witnesses giving opposing testimony, introduce material witnesses or have them summoned, and choose his or her own lawyer. The trials were open to the press and the public. And while doing so did not lend itself to expediency, the proceedings were translated simultaneously into German. At least a few German defense lawyers in the early "fliers" cases, the American prosecutor Leon Jaworski recalled, were impressed with the basic fairness of the proceedings. Herbert Strong, the German-born lawyer who served as an army-appointed defense counsel in multiple fliers cases and was on Willis Everett's team in the Malmedy trial also remembered these trials as having been conducted fairly. "The courts leaned over backward to give the accused a fair trial," he testified to the U.S. Senate subcommittee investigating the Malmedy case. "The courtroom was filled with Germans most of the time, who during and after the trial, repeatedly expressed to me their admiration for the scrupulously fair way in which it was conducted. . . . I also had the same impression of absolute fairness in the conduct of the Mauthausen and Flossenbürg concentration camp trials."[12]

Opening Skirmishes

From the start of the investigation at Schwäbisch Hall, Dwight Fanton and Burton Ellis had built a conspiracy case. Ellis knew that the prosecution in other high-profile cases, notably Mauthausen, had pursued this strategy successfully. The evidence amassed by the investigators suggested the existence of a conspiracy to commit murder. A conspiracy charge, moreover, would give Ellis's case a kind of narrative coherency that might otherwise be lost in the complexity of prosecuting seventy-four defendants accused of committing hundreds of crimes in eleven obscure Belgian towns over the course of nearly a month.

War crimes trials, the historian John Dower observed, were part law, part politics, and part theater, and Ellis was hardly immune to the prospect that his case would be a big publicity draw.[13] The trial would take place at a time when voices advocating judicial reckoning with the surviving leaders of Nazi Germany, war criminals, and collaborators commanded more authority than those urging leniency for the sake of rapid economic recovery. The Malmedy massacre trial would be unique among the army's Dachau cases, as it involved the widely publicized mass execution of American prisoners of war. That Ellis's conspiracy case included evidence that orders to spread terror by murdering Americans prisoners and Belgian civilians originated with Adolf Hitler and were then carried out by Hitler's "own" Waffen SS division only added to the trial's publicity-attracting potential. Since the War

Members of the prosecution in the Dachau courtroom. From right to left: Burton Ellis, Raphael Shumacker, Harry Thon, William Perl, Morris Elowitz, Robert Byrne, Joseph Kirschbaum, and unidentified (Special Collections Research Center, Estelle and Melvin Gelman Library, George Washington University).

Department had decided to film the trial, the presence of lights would not only make the courtroom uncomfortable—they almost "baked" us, Everett remarked privately—but provided Ellis with even more incentive to dramatize his case.[14]

The timing of the trial's opening also encouraged dramatization. Ellis knew that the IMT would continue to attract the bulk of media and public attention. He was also concerned about the impact of the just-completed Mauthausen case might have on his own. Toward the end of April, he learned that five of the judges in that trial would serve in the Malmedy case and became determined to change the court's composition. "I'm afraid they will not be impressed by the killing of a few hundred Americans after having listened to the fiendish murders of thousands for the past six weeks," he wrote Dee on April 23.[15] As it turned out, only two judges from the Mauthausen case sat on the bench in the Malmedy trial, but one of them was Colonel Abraham Rosenfeld, the law court member whose opinions would have the strongest influence over the rest of the judges.

Everett and the other defense lawyers would pursue a three-pronged strategy. First, they would challenge the court on its jurisdiction and the admissibility of the sworn statements as evidence. Second, in the likely event that their motions to dismiss would be denied, the defense would attempt to discredit the confessions. Defense witnesses would testify that there had been no conspiracy and that the defendants were not guilty of the crimes with which they were charged. Like the prosecution, the defense would offer its own simplified version of Battle Group Peiper's record in the Ardennes. Namely, that its commander had been ordered to spearhead a desperate counteroffensive operation and any crimes committed by the men under his command were the result of heat of battle conditions. The underlying assumption was that the men sitting before the judges, most of them young, had been ordinary soldiers and not instruments of the murderous conspiracy claimed by the prosecution.

The third involved pressuring some defendants and prosecution witnesses to retract portions of their sworn statements or change their testimonies. Defense lawyers tried to get Hans Hillig and Otto Wichmann, both of whom had signed sworn statements accusing Peiper of giving them direct orders to shoot American prisoners, to renounce their statements. A year after the trial's completion, Wichmann told an American investigator that the defense had pressured him and other former NCOs to "take responsibility upon themselves and not to blame . . . their superior officers."[16] As defendants and prosecution and defense witnesses were confined together in the Dachau enclosure, prosecution witnesses were easy targets for intimidation by their former comrades. Ellis was aware of the problem, and at one point tried to separate some of the witnesses. But the security measures taken at Schwäbisch Hall to prevent the coordination of stories among prisoners could not be replicated in Dachau.

That precedents set in previous trials would determine the course of *United States of America v. Valentin Bersin, et al.* became clear on the trial's opening day, which was taken up with defense motions challenging the court's jurisdiction. Assistant defense counselor Wilbert Wahler introduced two motions to have charges dropped against the twenty-one defendants accused of committing crimes against Belgian civilians, arguing that the proper site for prosecuting such crimes would be Belgium.[17] The prosecution responded that it would indeed be appropriate to try the case in Belgium, were this a common law court. But this was a case involving violations of international law and "all civilized belligerents have an interest in the punishment of offenses against the laws of war." Further, the United States had custody of the accused and had received the cooperation of the Belgian government. Rosenfeld rejected the motions, stating "the United States has as much interest in punishing offenses against nationals of its Allies as it does in the punishing of offenses against its own nationals." In any case, the Hadamar trial, in which seven doctors, nurses, and staff members had been tried for committing crimes against "Allied nationals," had set the relevant precedent.[18]

Undeterred, one of the German defense lawyers immediately challenged the court's jurisdiction on the grounds that since the accused were being tried for allegedly violating international laws, they should be tried by an as-yet-undetermined international court and "not between the victorious State and individuals of the defeated one." Again the prosecution referred to recent precedents, noting that in the Yamashita case the U.S. Supreme Court had ruled that military courts could try such cases and, as the Hadamar and other recent cases demonstrated, the United States has an interest in trying such cases and that American military courts had jurisdiction. Pointing to similar defense motions in the Dachau and Mauthausen cases, Rosenfeld denied this motion and another claiming that the accused should only be tried by the same courts that would try members of the U.S. armed forces (i.e., courts-martial).[19]

Defense counsel Benjamin Narvid introduced a motion for severance—that is, to conduct two trials, one for those who gave orders (or "aided and abetted in the giving of such orders") and the other for those accused of "actual participation." The reasoning was that since there was, according to the defense, no "common design" it would not be possible to determine degrees of responsibility if all seventy-four defendants were tried together. If they were, they would have to defend themselves against both the prosecution and each other. The prosecution's response, delivered by Shumacker, produced one of the more vivid characterizations of its strategy. They were being charged, Shumacker pointed out, as "joint perpetrators." If it was true that there had been a conspiracy or "common design" to kill prisoners and civilians, then "each accused became a cog-wheel in a monstrous slaughter machine. Now each such cog-wheel or group of such cog-wheels comes into court and demands a severance as a matter of right because their teeth mesh less smoothly when they drip with blood than when oiled with the prospects of victory."[20] Narvid retorted that the case was really about "a series of isolated, unrelated incidents," a heat of battle situation and not one involving any conspiracy. Concentration camp cases provided no applicable precedent because they involved "brutality and killings during a long period of time under normal conditions."[21]

In denying this motion, Rosenfeld again referred to the Dachau and Mauthausen cases, in which forty and sixty-one defendants were tried, respectively. Moreover, military courts were created to conduct trials quickly and efficiently "in the name of military security," an odd choice of words given that the security of the occupation one year after VE Day was not in question. The final defense motion asked the court to be more specific in charges against twenty-three defendants. Again referring to the Yamashita decision and the Mauthausen case, Rosenfeld ruled that charges in war crimes cases would not need to be "stated with the precision of a common law indictment."[22] The charges and particulars were then read to the defendants. All pleaded not guilty the following day.

A Wave of Fright and Terror

Ellis's opening statement introduced the prosecution's conspiracy case and described the pretrial investigation. Battle Group Peiper's objective in the Ardennes, Ellis asserted, was not simply the capture of Meuse River bridges. Peiper and his men also sought revenge: "We expect to show that for this offensive there existed a general policy to spread terror and panic, to avenge the so-called terror bombings, and to break all resistance by murdering prisoners of war and unarmed civilians." Ellis referred to the Bad Nauheim meeting during which Hitler ordered that a "wave of fright and terror should precede the Army." The Sixth Panzer Army under Sepp Dietrich's command "passed on the tenor of Hitler's speech in an order to its subordinate commands in words and substance," including the order that "prisoners of war must be shot when the local conditions of combat should so require it." This order was then passed down through corps, division, and regimental levels. Near the Blankenheim staging area on December 15–16 and in "varying degrees of boldness and callousness," the orders were given to companies, platoons, and tank groups. The message was clear—battle group soldiers "could disregard the rules of the Geneva Convention with impunity" and that the lawless forms of warfare that characterized German operations on the Eastern Front were now to be transferred to the west.[23]

Ellis then traced the battle group's route of march from Blankenheim to the border at Losheim, then into Belgium, with the furthest advance being a railroad station near Stoumont, with the subsequent retreat to La Gleize. Throughout the offensive, Ellis claimed, members of the battle group killed prisoners of war and civilians with "zeal and enthusiasm" and gave a summary of crimes and casualties amounting to the killing of 538 to 749 Americans and over 90 Belgians in dozens of incidents in towns and villages along the group's route of advance and retreat. The final crime was the murder on January 13 of a single American prisoner—already suffering terribly from frostbite and exposure—in Petit Thiers on Peiper's direct orders.[24]

Ellis also attempted to preempt what he knew would be the defense's main strategy by describing in detail the investigation's two phases. He recounted how the ability of prisoners to communicate with each other at Zuffenhausen had produced "the stock answer to all questions," namely, that the deceased First Battalion commander Werner Poetschke was blamed "for all their misdeeds." The security problem was resolved in Schwäbisch Hall, where Ellis described how prisoners were placed in individual cells and transferred within the prison while hooded. Perhaps fearing the youthful faces of many of the defendants—twenty-eight were between seventeen and twenty years old at the time of the Ardennes counteroffensive—might sway the court, Ellis concluded with what would become the most notorious passage of his opening statement: "Despite the youth of these suspects, it took months of continuous interrogation in which all the legitimate tricks, ruses and stratagems known to the investigators were employed. Among other artifices used were stool-pigeons, witnesses who were not bona fide and ceremonies." These methods were necessary, Ellis insisted, as the suspects were all members of the SS and knew that if captured they were bound by a "conspiracy of silence" not to reveal anything about the killing of prisoners and civilians.[25]

Everett asked the court for a chance to respond, and the court president allowed it over Ellis's strenuous objections. In a brief and eloquent statement, Everett asked the judges to be dispassionate and "rise above any spirit of victor or vanquished." As the court was part of the "American jurisprudence system" and as such was obliged to "guarantee the immutable rights of the individual under our Constitution to these defendants by throwing around each the cloak of 'America's fair trial.'" A fair trial would also serve to demonstrate democratic practices to the German people. Hoping to separate the Malmedy case from the concentration camp cases in the judges' minds, and certainly sensitive to the fact that the accused had belonged not to the Wehrmacht but to the Waffen SS, Everett rejected the prosecution's conspiracy or "common design" charge and asserted that "this is entirely a heat of battle case."[26]

It was a deft rhetorical strategy, given that the judges were line officers with combat experience sitting in judgment not of sadistic camp guards or murderous doctors, but young soldiers. Everett's statement also foreshadowed what would become a principal American and German criticism of the trials: that they were supposed to be providing an example of "American jurisprudence" and as such were not compatible with the procedures of military commissions.

The first four days of the prosecution's case focused on the defendants' statements regarding orders to "spread terror" by killing prisoners and civilians. As the accused were not taking the stand at that point, their statements were read and prosecution witnesses were examined and cross-examined. Sepp Dietrich's statement was, fittingly, the first to be read. Dietrich had attended the Bad Nauheim conference and recalled Hitler's order that the spearhead fight with brutality and without humane inhibitions. His statement was followed by Fritz Kraemer's and Hermann Priess's, the Sixth Panzer Army's chief of staff and the commanding general of the First SS Panzer Corps, respectively. Priess, who also attended the Bad Nauheim meeting with Hitler, had claimed in his sworn statement that Hitler had never explained what he meant by "terror" and that he, Priess, assumed that there would be no "irregularity in fighting methods." Kraemer, whose job it was to draft orders for the Sixth Panzer Army for Dietrich's approval, insisted that he had written that spearhead units were to leave prisoners to follow up infantry so as to avoid delays. Peiper's March 21 statement, in which he claimed that Dietrich had ordered prisoners of war to be shot "where the local conditions of combat should so require it," was also read into the record. The others were read to the court over the following two weeks, accompanied by testimony from former Waffen SS soldiers not charged by the court.[27]

The prosecution's strategy of laying bare its investigative methods was not novel. The American prosecutor William Denson pioneered the tactic in the concentration camp cases preceding the Malmedy trial. So it was appropriate that Ellis's first witness was William Perl. In the direct and cross-examinations of Perl and other investigators, the "legitimate tricks, ruses and stratagems" such as confronting suspects with their former comrades, "mock trials," the use of informants, and attempts to convince prisoners that the interrogators already knew everything were explained, attacked by the defense, and defended in a process that would be repeated many times over the following weeks.[28] The interrogators also described how statements were taken and defended the measures necessary to maintaining the investigation's security, such as hooding prisoners and confining them in single cells while they were being interrogated.

In the first of Perl's forty-seven appearances on the stand, Ellis questioned him about his interrogations of Dietrich. Perl denied using any duress, including threats or promises. Regarding the taking of Dietrich's statements, he explained: "Dietrich was first interrogated as to the subject this statement covers. During this interrogation he made oral statements. When the information was obtained he was asked to write it down. I told him that I would

William Perl on the witness stand before being cross-examined by one of the German defense counsels. Note the lights for the filming of the trial (Special Collections Research Center, Estelle and Melvin Gelman Library, George Washington University).

dictate the statement because we had the experience that statements written by the defendants themselves become outstandingly long. I stressed, however, that it is his statement and that if I say or dictate something with which he does not agree, he should object right away. Then I started dictating the statement and [regarding] many of the sentences I had discussions with him whether one or the other quotation should not be put in." Ellis then pressed him on other details of Dietrich's treatment in Schwäbisch Hall:

Ellis: With respect to Dietrich, were any special security measures employed during his interrogation?

Perl: Yes.

Ellis: What were they?

Perl: He was brought into the interrogation room blindfolded and was brought back to his own cell blindfolded again.

. . .

Ellis: Do you know of any mistreatment by the Polish guards of Dietrich?

Perl: Yes.

Ellis: How did this come to your knowledge?

Perl: Dietrich once mentioned to me that when being brought into the interrogation room he was kicked by someone he could not identify into his behind. At the same time he told me that he would not like me to do anything about it and I shouldn't even tell Colonel Ellis about it because it was not worthwhile.[29]

In another typical exchange, Benjamin Narvid sparred with Perl over what constituted "pressure" in obtaining crucial admissions of responsibility for the Baugnez crossroads shootings:

Narvid: Lieutenant Perl, you will agree undoubtedly that the [Personal Standard Adolf Hitler] was composed of rather tough troops?

. . .

Perl: Yes.

Narvid: Surely Lieutenant Perl you did not obtain the statements from both [Hans] Siptrott and [Roman] Clotten without some considerable pressure?

Perl: What do you understand of "pressure?"

Narvid: You stated that the statements were made voluntarily. I will ask you what you mean by voluntarily?

Perl: No pressure was used.

Narvid: If you do not know what I mean by the word "pressure."

Perl: I know what I mean by "under pressure."

Narvid: On the basis of your understanding of the word "pressure," will you please answer this question: did you obtain the statements from Siptrott and Clotten without any pressure whatsoever?

Perl: No pressure was used as far as what I mean by "under pressure." Maybe you mean something else, and I mean something else of "under pressure."

. . .

Narvid: Do you recall if at any time during the interrogation the words "execution" or "hanging" were used?

Perl: They certainly were not used. Now I know that I understand something very differently of "under pressure." I want to say that when I spoke of "pressure" I meant due to the previous confession of [Georg] Fleps.[30]

Fleps had signed a statement on January 5 confessing to being the first or among the first to fire on prisoners at Baugnez on Hans Siptrott's orders. Two days later, Siptrott confirmed that he had ordered Fleps to start shooting. Perl had "pressured" Siptrott by informing him that Fleps had identified him as having ordered him to fire on the prisoners and that he, Fleps, had admitted to doing so. Pressure of the kind alluded to by the defense and "tricks," however, were a sideshow. As Ellis, Perl, and the other interrogators would stress repeatedly during and after the trial, the most effective approach to a suspect was to present him over many hours with "an avalanche of facts and information we had about him and his unit and what they had done," as Raphael Shumacker put it during one his numerous appearances on the stand.[31] The results of this approach produced the detailed confessions presented to the court.

The first American survivors of the Baugnez shooting began testifying on May 21, followed by fifteen Belgian witnesses from seven towns a week later. Their testimonies injected the proceedings—which had turned into a repetitive, tedious routine of reading sworn statements, corroborating witness testimony, and cross-examining interrogators—with surge of drama. Clearly with an eye to the reporters present and whirring courtroom cameras, the only American officer to have survived the Baugnez encounter, Lieutenant Virgil Lary, identified Georg Fleps as the first German soldier to have fired into the group of American prisoners on December 17. Lary's testimony was followed by those of five other survivors of the Baugnez shooting. Belgian eyewitnesses testified to the brutality of battle group soldiers in Ligneuville, Stavelot, Wanne, and other towns.[32]

A week later the prosecution read from portions of the first U.S. Army report on the Baugnez massacre, emphasizing the more gruesome aspects of the autopsies conducted in Malmedy in mid-January 1945. Regarding

Virgil Lary, the only American officer to have survived the Malmedy massacre, being sworn in as a prosecution witness, May 21, 1946 (NARA).

Corporal Ralph Indelicato, the altered photograph of whose body had been published in *Life* magazine, the medical examiner concluded: "Both eyes are gone. Examination reveals bilateral enucleation with a sharp instrument. The skin edges show definite knife marks. . . . Presence of blood in the region of the sockets and the ragged appearance of the skin substantiates the opinion that it was performed while the soldier was still alive and it was done by an inexperienced person."[33]

Ten days into the trial, Ellis was in high spirits. He seemed to be "breezing through" his case as he had expected. Everett, conversely, was despondent. The members of his large team of American and German lawyers were at odds with each other. They seemed reluctant in the first week to cross-examine German eyewitnesses assertively, though were doing so by early June. They also refrained from aggressive cross-examining of American and Belgian survivors. While he could not have expected the judges to rule favorably on the various motions proposed on the trial's opening day, Everett was convinced that the court was implacably hostile. He was also convinced that Ellis was "trying the case in the press and movies." His suspicion was reinforced with the news, published in the *Stars and Stripes,* that Ellis had been elected district attorney in Mariposa County, California. While the truth was that he had no intention of assuming that position, the timing of the story could only have reinforced Everett's suspicions and would later be used to discredit Ellis as an unscrupulous showboater preening for voters.[34]

Indeed, American newspaper and newsreel coverage was entirely sympathetic to the prosecution, and reporters would not stay to cover the defense's presentation of its case. Newspapers around the country published stories focusing on the most dramatic moments of the prosecution's case, with headlines like "Bulge Nazis Used GI Prisoners for Target Practice," "Malmedy Nazi Admits He Shot Yank Who Aided Hurt German," and "Laughing Germans Slew Captives, 'Bulge' Massacre Survivors Say."[35] The narrator of a Movietone newsreel feature described "the trial at the infamous Dachau concentration camp, where it's testified that the murder of prisoners, directed by Hitler, was ordered by the Nazi plug-ugly Sepp Dietrich" as the camera panned across the faces of the defendants. The feature ended at the moment in which Virgil Lary pointed his finger, pistol-like, at Georg Fleps, an image reproduced on the front page of the *Washington Post* on May 23.[36]

SEVEN

Entirely a Heat of Battle Case

The Defense

With the prosecution resting on June 7, Willis Everett requested five days of recess. To his surprise and to Burton Ellis's annoyance, the court granted the defense ten to finalize its case. Everett's mood was also buoyed by the imminent arrival of Colonel Hal McCown as a defense witness. McCown, it will be recalled, was captured outside La Gleize and held in that besieged town during the last days of desperate fighting before Joachim Peiper's retreat on December 23 and 24. Shortly after his escape he had been quoted in an Associated Press report that Peiper and his men adhered scrupulously to international law in La Gleize. He then wrote an official account of his treatment as a prisoner, insisting that Peiper's conduct had been proper and that he, McCown, was unaware of mass executions of American prisoners in that town. At Dachau during the recess, McCown told Everett that he thought American newspaper reports on the trial had been full of "lies," quelling Everett's suspicion that McCown had received instructions from the Theater Judge Advocate's office in Wiesbaden not to embarrass the prosecution.[1]

The defense opened its case with two unsuccessful motions to dismiss the charges on the grounds that the confessions had been obtained by tricks and duress and that without corroborating evidence the court could not consider their contents as evidence of probative value. Lieutenant Colonel John Dwinell then delivered a brief opening statement, arguing that there was no "preconceived murderous plan." The defendants had belonged to a spearhead "fighting desperately under the worst battle conditions" and that it would not have been possible for a spearhead operating in such conditions to secure prisoners of war. Once its advance was halted, the prisoners were treated correctly. As for the Baugnez crossroads shooting, Dwinell promised the defense would demonstrate that the prisoners assembled in the roadside field had attempted to flee, thus negating their status as prisoners, and were fired upon by their captors. When the court took these factors into consideration, manslaughter would be the "maximum" conviction. As for the "confessions," they had been obtained by "duress and promises" and the court had an obligation to consider the defendants' "extreme youth and susceptibility to such tactics."[2]

McCown testified on June 20. Everett hoped that the appearance of the handsome, decorated combat veteran of five campaigns in the European theater would serve as a compelling counterpoint to the testimonies of Virgil Lary and other survivors and puncture Ellis's conspiracy case. He would

Burton Ellis and Willis Everett confer with Judge Josiah Dalbey and law member Abraham Rosenfeld (NARA).

argue that if the battle group was the "monstrous slaughter machine" claimed by the prosecution, why hadn't it executed over one hundred American prisoners in La Gleize, including, presumably, McCown himself? And if that many GIs had been shot in that town, where were their remains?[3]

McCown and Everett overplayed their hand. McCown's claim, confirmed by Peiper the following day, that he held several lengthy and seemingly friendly conversations with the battle group's commander struck the judges as inappropriate. Possibly more problematic for the defense was McCown's rather forthright admission that he fed tactical information to Peiper that aided the combat group's escape from La Gleize. And while Everett may have welcomed an airing of his witness's assertion that American soldiers had also murdered hundreds of German prisoners of war, the Dachau courtroom was hardly an auspicious place to voice such opinions. Then, under cross-examination, McCown had to admit that he had not in fact seen the entire town—including the location where the prosecution claimed a large number of American prisoners had been executed—and therefore could not be certain that no one had been killed there.[4]

Everett believed the court had silenced McCown and treated him disrespectfully, and his disappointment brought his prejudices to the surface. His correspondence with his family during the trial reveal a paranoid, conspiratorial anti-Semitism that would underpin his posttrial efforts to have the verdicts overturned or the case retried. He was particularly hostile toward the "Jew law member" Abraham Rosenfeld, who had "gloated through the Mauthausen trial." When the court president asked McCown to direct his answers to the court, Everett, confusing Rosenfeld with court president Josiah Dalbey, wrote privately that the "Jew law member" shouted at McCown in "a louder voice than I would yell at a nigger." He even referred to his codefense counsel, Herbert Strong, as a "nosey-talking-arguing Jew." It was also significant that in addition to the "gloating" and high-handed Jewish law court member who seemed dead set on convicting the defendants, the lead interrogator was a Jewish refugee from Nazi Germany. At the end of the trial, he fumed to his wife about the "over-production" of Jews in military government, war crimes trials, and the United Nations Relief and Rehabilitation Administration, and feared for the long-term consequences of what he termed the "Jewish occupation."[5]

Unbeknownst to Everett, a real fiasco for the defense was barely averted a few days later when Ellis received a copy of an American intelligence report regarding the content of McCown's conversations with Peiper in La Gleize. A month after his capture in Bavaria, Peiper told a CIC officer that McCown had facilitated his escape from La Gleize by providing him with specific information about the disposition of American forces, information that proved accurate. Further, McCown told Peiper that he regretted the American alliance with the Soviet Union against Germany and Japan, and believed that what the United States was really doing in Europe was "pull[ing] British chestnuts out of the fire, as the British preferred to let their Allies do their fighting for them." Since McCown did not expect to return to American lines, he offered to join Peiper in fighting the Russians. In return, Peiper could "[come] to America after the war and help him hang the Jews."[6] Regardless of the accuracy of Peiper's statement, the presentation of this report in court would have done even more damage to McCown's credibility as a defense witness.

I Was No Genghis Khan

On June 21, Peiper took the stand as a defense witness. He was the third defendant to testify, having been preceded by Fritz Kraemer and Hermann Priess. Their testimonies had gone well for the defense, as both continued to deny the existence of a "terror order." Putting Peiper on the stand, however, was riskier. He had led the combat group and admitted to ordering the execution of prisoners. His subordinates had also accused him of giving general orders to shoot prisoners and of ordering several executions personally.[7]

Dwinell first asked him about his interrogation in Zuffenhausen. Peiper claimed he had been held in solitary confinement for five weeks in a pitch-black cellar without the opportunity for exercise and only one opportunity to bathe. William Perl questioned him there and Peiper claimed to have taken notes in his apparently not-quite-so-pitch-black cell after the interrogation, notes so detailed that he could now recount the interrogation "almost word for word." According to Peiper, Perl told him that among the battle group's victims were the sons of an unnamed American senator and a "business man" who incited the public to demand Peiper's execution. "You must not overlook the influence of the press or that the President would not be able to save you," Perl allegedly warned Peiper, "because the will of the people has quite a different power in [the United States] than in Germany." Following this almost comically simple ruse, Perl then tried to appeal to Peiper's sense of duty as an officer and also to his vanity. He was popular among most of his men and while he had been, in Perl's words, "an extraordinary soldier," the SS was about to be declared a criminal organization by the IMT and his life was now "completely ruined." Peiper then declared that he would take responsibility for his men's crimes if it would exonerate them.[8]

The interrogators increased the pressure at Schwäbisch Hall. Since Peiper's superiors had been evasive on the question of a no prisoners order, Peiper was now the highest-ranking holdout who could confirm its existence. Yet he now asserted that it was only in Schwäbisch Hall that he was informed about a general order to shoot prisoners of war "in cases of military necessity" and that his battle group was to fight without "humane inhibitions." He recalled that he was "confronted" by four officers, including his former adjutant Hans Gruhle, all of whom insisted that Peiper had transmitted or given orders not to take prisoners of war and to spread "a wave of fright and terror."[9]

Peiper then conceded that he allowed Perl to dictate his statement of March 21, in which he admitted to having received orders from Sepp Dietrich, Hermann Priess, and Wilhelm Mohnke that prisoners of war were to be executed "where the local conditions of combat should so require it." But this "admission," Peiper now claimed, was based on the information provided to the Americans by his adjutant. Further, Peiper recalled that Perl seemed to be "in a big hurry" but assured him that he would have the opportunity to review his statement. "I was stupid enough," Peiper admitted, "to sign it without having read through it."[10]

When the confrontations with his former subordinates continued, Peiper realized that the "comradeship which had been made very firm through blood in the front lines" had been broken by "trickery" in Schwäbisch Hall. Despite believing his men had been tricked, he claimed that he was "disgusted" by their behavior and that he would sign anything Perl wrote. In his testimony he did not claim to have been abused by any interrogator, only struck in the face and "several times in my sexual parts" while hooded the day before he left Schwäbisch Hall for Dachau by what he presumed was a "Polish guard."[11]

Despite his professed disgust at his subordinates' behavior in Schwäbisch Hall, Peiper also insisted that he tried to protect them. In a statement signed

From left to right: John Dwinell, Willis Everett, and Joachim Peiper (NARA).

on March 26, in which he admitted to ordering Josef Diefenthal to shoot a few American prisoners in La Gleize to set an example among the large number being held in that besieged town, he now claimed on the stand that he did so only to protect Diefenthal. He took responsibility for ordering a wounded American prisoner shot in Petit Thiers for the same reason.[12]

Peiper was then asked to give his own account of the offensive. What followed was a more detailed version of the one provided to U.S. Army interviewers the previous summer. He claimed that on December 14, Mohnke ordered him to lead a "rapid break through" and that "every man was to commit himself relentlessly and that we should ignore all threats to our flanks fundamentally." Peiper interpreted "fighting fanatically" in the Ardennes to mean nothing more than the total, selfless commitment of his own forces to reaching the Meuse.[13] Regarding prisoners of war, he now recalled reading orders that "it was not the job of the armored spearhead to worry about prisoners of war." It would be left to infantry units following the spearhead to secure any prisoners. As for civilians, he expected to encounter resistance and that any armed civilians would be treated as partisans.

Near the Baugnez crossroads, Peiper told the court he had heard the brief exchange of gunfire between the surprised American forces and the lead elements of his battle group and, angered at the delay and "at having these beautiful [American] trucks, which we needed so badly, all shot up," immediately issued cease-fire orders.[14] As he continued south toward Ligneuville, he recalled seeing "40 to 60" American prisoners on or just off the main road. He described a chaotic situation at odds with the description of unambiguous surrender presented by American survivors: "Some of the American soldiers played dead; some of them slowly crept toward the woods; some of them suddenly jumped up and ran toward the forest and some of them came towards the road. Grenadiers which were in the half tracks driving behind me fired on those which carried rifles and were running toward the forest." He did not "at that moment" consider them to be prisoners of war. As Peiper knew that more than "40 to 60" bodies had been recovered at Baugnez, he added that since the spearhead's lead elements had fired on the American convoy with twenty-five machine guns and five cannons, this "concentrated fire . . . must necessarily have caused a lot of casualties."[15]

After passing through Ligneuville, again without having seen any prisoners shot, Peiper recounted entering Stavelot on the morning of December 18. Here "many civilians" fired on the advancing column, though Peiper kept driving toward Trois Ponts. He recalled learning that Belgian civilians severely maltreated some of his wounded men, but that they managed to get their wounded out despite the arrival of American reinforcements. His advance at Trois Ponts blocked, he decided to detour through La Gleize. As he remembered seeing no American soldiers in the villages in and around the town, the multiple sworn statements claiming that his men had executed dozens of prisoners in this area must have been false.[16]

He denied having anything more to do with prisoners, as he remained set on advancing through Stoumont and resuming the drive toward the Meuse. When he could not break through there he returned to La Gleize. Almost completely surrounded, he ordered all his troops to withdraw to that town. It was there that he tended personally to the welfare of both wounded German and American soldiers, thus confirming McCown's assessment of his behavior as proper: "I told [McCown] that I was no 'Genghis Khan.'" Peiper also confirmed that the two had lengthy conversations and that he—

Peiper—was "very glad to find out that front-line soldiers always spoke the same language."[17]

Ellis's cross-examination began the following morning. He pressed Peiper on inconsistencies in the multiple statements he made to American investigators since his initial confinement and on whether he believed in the "sanctity" of an oath. Was it not suspiciously convenient, Ellis argued, that Peiper would confirm the truth of self-exculpatory statements while denying those that were not? It was a ham-fisted approach on Ellis's part as it gave Peiper a chance to repeat the claim that he had been tricked and not given the opportunity to correct his own statements. Besides, it could hardly be surprising that multiple statements taken over the course of a year might contain some inconsistencies, a common-sense observation that the prosecution itself had made in regard to the defendants' sworn statements.

Peiper admitted that at various moments he may have recalled some events with more clarity than others. In any case, he had learned many things during the course of his interrogations. He restated that he had been given an extremely difficult assignment and remained determined to reach the Meuse. "The only important matter . . . was to break through fanatically at maximum speed and that anything which in the course of our break-through would remain lying in the ditches, be it prisoners of war or material or tools of war, that they would later be picked up by the infantry following us."[18]

Ellis also believed that he could demonstrate that high-ranking Waffen SS officers must have known what Hitler really meant by "spreading fear and terror." The prosecution had been waiting to pounce on these officers' professed ignorance with information it had obtained only recently on the significance to Heinrich Himmler of Michael Prawdin's writings about Genghis Khan. A week after the trial opened, Perl had interrogated Gottlob Berger about Himmler's fascination with Prawdin's books. Perl could not have found a more authoritative living source on this matter than Berger, who had served as Himmler's chief recruitment officer and had done more than any other individual to create the structure of the Waffen SS. Himmler, Berger told Perl, impressed upon him the importance of spreading "fright and panic" as he believed Genghis Khan had done. Himmler's fascination with this "theory" of combat, he added, "was commonly known among the higher SS officers" and that in 1943 Himmler ordered him to distribute twenty thousand copies of one of Prawdin's books to Waffen SS personnel. Only a paper shortage made the distribution of more copies impossible.[19]

In his cross-examination of Priess on June 19, Morris Elowitz asked him if he had ever heard of Prawdin's writings. Priess admitted that he had been given a copy of a book by Prawdin as a Christmas gift, but when pressed about whether thousands of copies had been the distributed among Waffen SS officers and enlisted men, Priess professed ignorance. In response to defense objections that an obscure book about Genghis Khan had nothing to do with Priess's background as a Waffen SS officer, Elowitz replied that the prosecution would demonstrate that Himmler intended the Waffen SS to emulate Genghis Khan's methods of terror war as described by Prawdin. When pressed further, Priess admitted that the gift of Prawdin's book came from Himmler's office, but then denied that Himmler had any real authority over the Waffen SS. He was, Priess insisted, "in charge of personnel and philosophical matters" and nothing more. Undaunted, Elowitz began quoting from Prawdin's book, citing a passage in which Prawdin had admonished Europe to "become familiar with what Mongolian warfare meant. The first attack . . . had to carry terror and panic into the remotest part of the country. . . . Nothing was to remain of the cities but what might be of use to the Mongols. . . . Escapees who had escaped the massacre carried the picture of the terror." When asked whether he recalled that particular passage, Priess denied ever having read the book, and Elowitz let it go at that.[20]

Priess's lawyer was incensed. He dismissed the book as nothing more than a "presentation of Russian history." Since his client stated he never read the book all references to it should be struck from the record. Elowitz maintained that the prosecution would soon show that the book was in fact distributed widely to Waffen SS officers such as Priess. As Priess had dismissed any alleged references made by Hitler or Dietrich to spreading terror as mere "propaganda," Elowitz was suggesting that the charge was more substantial: spreading terror was an operational order.

Peiper was in an even better position than Priess to know about Himmler's enthusiasm for Prawdin's books. When questioned on the matter, he denied ever having told Perl that "it was a sort of hobby of Himmler's to inculcate to the SS the idea of fighting like Genghis Khan." Perhaps sensing the court's limited patience for arguments over the influence of a seemingly obscure Russian writer on the head of the SS, Ellis did not press Peiper on the issue. A day later, however, Peiper explained that like other officer candidates he was assigned to write a paper on law in the Mongolian empire and that Prawdin's books were made available as one of several sources. The idea that the Waffen SS sought to fight in the spirit of marauding Mongols was laughable "propaganda." "When I first talked to Major McCown," Peiper said on the stand, "I said, laughingly, 'You are really suffering from a stroke of bad luck by falling into the hands of us bloodhounds here.' Upon that [McCown] himself laughed and said, 'That is propaganda. I know very well that these are the best troops in the world, for any other troops in your position would have surrendered a long time ago.' And in that connection we came to talk about propaganda in general and the reputation of the SS which was created in such a manner."[21]

Given his proclivity during the war to boast of waging the kind of warfare that would have made "old Genghis Khan proud," the prosecution's questions about Prawdin, Genghis Kahn, and Himmler must have been unsettling to Peiper. Like Priess, however, he managed to frustrate the prosecution's attempt to link the book to the conduct of terror war in the Ardennes. The prosecution had grasped that Prawdin's interpretation of Genghis Khan was indeed meaningful to Himmler and that the admonition to spread terror was more than "propaganda" dismissed so casually by Priess and Peiper. The problem was that Perl discovered the significance of Prawdin's books too late to have made much effective use of it. The place to have questioned the highest-ranking suspects on the matter was Schwäbisch Hall and not the Dachau courtroom.

Peiper's lengthy account of his record was directed at multiple audiences. One was the judges, though he likely assumed that his fate was sealed and that he would be hanged. To them, he presented himself as an ordinary soldier and conscientious officer determined to reach his objective despite near impossible odds. Another audience was the gallery of codefendants. He, and by extension those under his command, had done everything in their power to achieve their objective. While he never claimed that his men failed him on the battlefield—other than causing some delays—their behavior in captivity "disgusted" him as it had broken a bond "made very firm through blood in the front lines." Yet despite the betrayals, he understood why some of them signed statements he believed to be false and allowed that he, too, had been tricked, if not abused physically, by the interrogators. Despite the trickery and the betrayal by his own men, he remained committed to them by confessing to crimes he did not commit in order to spare their lives.

Peiper was also speaking to posterity, to the judgment of history and future generations of Americans and Germans. His testimony was not the first—nor would it be the last—instance in which he would describe his record in Russia and Belgium. He had already been interviewed by American officials about the Ardennes counteroffensive, interviews that gave him the opportunity to influence how its history would be written. In the Dachau courtroom, he used what he expected would be his final public platform to justify his own record and to glorify the military exploits of the elite of Nazi Germany's armed forces. In a private letter to Willis Everett dated July 4, he indicated that he had forgiven his men's lapses and understood why some had invented stories of being abused by their interrogators. What counted now was their legacy, and that legacy lay in the memory of a heroic, if doomed, effort in the forests of the Ardennes rather than in the interrogation rooms of Schwäbisch Hall or the Dachau courtroom. "They are not evil and no criminals," Peiper wrote. "They are the product of total war. . . . The only thing they knew was [how] to handle weapons for the Dream of the Reich. They were young people with a hot heart and the desire to win or to die."[22]

Given his descriptions of the Ardennes counteroffensive as an operation in which his battle group did not violate the rules of war nor break with the standards of fighting in the West, it may seem odd that Peiper did not deny his close connection to Heinrich Himmler and the SS. Shortly after his capture, he had cooperated with the American counterintelligence officer Paul Guth in his investigation of Himmler's staff and was forthcoming about his experiences on the stand, to the point of admitting freely—and to the distress of his defense counsel—that he had witnessed the gassing of death camp inmates. While he may have endeavored to portray himself as an ordinary soldier, he would not define that identity as one independent of the organization he had served since he was eighteen. For Peiper, the fight for the "Dream of Reich" was the fight of the SS, including the Waffen SS.

"Peiper's Order"

Only a week into its case Everett's team believed the defense should rest. Everett, however, wanted to push on. Though he believed Peiper had done well in his duel with Ellis, the fact that seventy-four men of varying ranks, nearly all of whom had signed statements admitting degrees of responsibility while incriminating others, made it highly undesirable for multiple defendants to testify. Following Peiper's testimony, however, others insisted on taking the stand, and Everett assented.

Certainly, they hoped to extricate themselves from their confessions. But Peiper's performance was the more important catalyst. He had presented himself as a self-sacrificing leader on and off the battlefield, and the defendants who demanded to testify in their own defense wanted to justify themselves in Peiper's and their comrades' eyes. The risk, of course, was that they would further incriminate each other. And how would they account for their own confessions? Most likely with the encouragement and guidance of their German lawyers, six of the seven defendants who testified claimed that they signed false statements because they had been tricked, threatened, and abused. Friedrich Christ, a First Panzer Regiment company commander and one of the first defendants to confess to having received and transmitted Werner Poetschke's orders to spread "panic and terror" and shoot prisoners of war, now parroted Peiper's claim to have ordered his men to not waste time dealing with prisoners and to allow follow-up infantry to secure them. On the stand, Christ claimed that he ordered his men to "treat prisoners of war the same way as they would expect to be treated in case they were to fall into enemy hands."[23]

As for his sworn statement, Christ accused his interrogators in Schwäbisch Hall of subjecting him to verbal abuse and threatening him with hanging. One told him that his mother would be denied ration cards and would starve as a result, and that if he refused to cooperate he would be shot "while trying to escape." When the unnamed interrogators insisted to him that Poetschke and Peiper had issued orders for prisoners to be executed and confronted him with former comrades, he became confused and disoriented: "I got into such a spiritually forced situation and I was so depressed that I didn't know any more what was to be true and what was a lie. I became completely confused about this order and said that this order meant that the prisoners of war should be shot and that we had to spread fright and terror and this was then dictated to me immediately."[24]

Sergeant Hans Hennecke followed Christ. In his sworn statement, Hennecke had not only claimed that the order to shoot prisoners was "always called 'Peiper's order' " and that this was "well known in the 1st Panzer Division," but that Peiper had ordered him to convey a command to assemble a detail to execute some American prisoners. Hennecke had also passed along "Peiper's order" to his own crews. Now on the stand, he insisted he never gave any speeches about such orders to anyone. In Schwäbisch Hall, Elowitz had confronted him with former comrades who accused him of giving a take no prisoners order. So Hennecke confessed and his statement was dictated to him. He wrote it down because "I was not conscious of . . . how much damage I could do with any such untruth." Now he admitted to being "ashamed . . . that I denounced my regimental commander." On the stand, he retracted his confession and confirmed Peiper's testimony about being ordered to fight "without any regard for ourselves or our machines."[25]

The first Third Battalion officer to confess to receiving and transmitting orders to kill prisoners, Lieutenant Heinz Tomhardt, took the stand on June 26. He repeated Christ's claim that he had ordered his men to treat prisoners humanely and to leave them to the "infantry that follows." Like Christ and Hennecke, he echoed Peiper's testimony by claiming to have ordered the men under his command to drive forward relentlessly "without regard to machine and man." He signed a false confession because he had been in "solitary confinement" for three months and had been beaten while hooded. He also claimed that the former comrades who confronted him showed signs of physical abuse and that the inside of the hood used to conceal his identity was "full of blood." Perl threatened him with hanging if he did not confess to passing along the order to shoot prisoners. He was then placed in what he referred to as the "death cell" for six days and deprived of sleep. During the night, he heard "cries of agony" and the sounds of prisoners being beaten from neighboring cells: "a voice cried out constantly: '. . . Do you want to lie to us? Do you want to tell us the truth: yes or no?' "[26]

Another company commander to take the stand, Franz Sievers, had confessed to having heard Peiper's boast regarding the "commitments of a bad reputation" and to have passed along Poetschke's terror speech to his platoon leaders. In the courtroom, Sievers claimed he never received such orders. The "real" orders were to drive forward relentlessly and that prisoners were to be handled by follow-up infantry. Like Tomhardt, he referred to three months of solitary confinement and testified that he was beaten while hooded and subjected to verbal abuse during his first interrogation at Schwäbisch Hall. He recounted a good cop / bad cop routine played by Perl and Harry Thon, in which the latter, among other things, offered to provide him with enough rope to hang himself. He was also confronted by several comrades. Perl then attempted to reason calmly with him, telling him that once he confessed, the conditions of his confinement would improve and that he would only get six to eight months. They didn't want him or even Peiper, Perl allegedly insisted, but Sepp Dietrich. "I was moved by that and made my first statement, which was immediately torn up by Lt. Perl because he was not satisfied with the contents. Then I wrote another statement, which was dictated to me also." When he still claimed he could not recall any order to shoot prisoners, he was taken to the "death cell." Exhausted by this charade, he wrote a third and final statement. Despite this, beatings, threats, and hours of forced standing allegedly followed.[27]

Sergeant Anton Motzheim's claims were the most extreme. His sworn statement contained an accusation that Peiper ordered two American prisoners shot. When he refused to confess in Schwäbisch Hall to shooting a prisoner, an interrogator—possibly Thon—beat him several times and then threatened to torture him to death. Then Perl and Thon beat him for a half hour. Perl "kicked me four times in my sexual parts and Mr. Thon kicked [my leg]." Threatened the next day by Thon with hanging unless he admitted to having shot a prisoner in Stoumont, he wrote out a confession as dictated by Elowitz.[28]

The last defendant to testify, Private First Class Marcel Boltz, claimed that Thon assured him he would only serve three months "at most" if he admitted to shooting prisoners, as the interrogators already knew that he had orders to shoot and that he did so. And, like Sievers, he was assured that the interrogators were interested only in Dietrich. After being confronted with a former comrade, he confessed to having shot at prisoners at Baugnez. Raphael Shumacker allegedly dictated his statement.[29]

By this point, Everett had realized his error and was anxious to rest his case. Though the defendants who took the stand had tried to avoid implicating codefendants, doing so was unavoidable. Their reversals could hardly have been credible to the judges and likely damaged the defense's efforts to cast doubt on the veracity of the confessions. The testimonies were too consistent to be believable, as nearly all of them repeated what Peiper had said in his testimony about prisoners, and the accounts of physical abuses strained credulity. At one point the testimony spiraled into the realm of farce when Sievers, who stood six feet in height, accused the much smaller William Perl of beating him brutally. Nonetheless, Ellis recalled the interrogators one last time to deny any abusive methods.[30]

In light of the controversy that would erupt in 1948 over accusations that Perl and other interrogators subjected nearly all of the defendants to systematic torture, it may seem strange that neither Ellis nor Everett sought testimony or records from Schwäbisch Hall administrators and, especially, from the medical personnel responsible for treating the prisoners. Indeed, it is unclear whether either lawyer even considered going this far during the trial. Without the benefit of hindsight, however, the reasons are clear enough. Ellis most likely thought it unnecessary while Everett was not just pressed for time to prepare his case but knew the defendants were lying about being abused. As he must have understood at the time and as would become clear, the testimony of guards, wardens, and physicians, would have done grievous harm to his case.

The defense rested on July 6. Forty-two defendants, nearly all of them the youngest members of Battle Group Peiper, submitted pleas for mitigation, with references to superior orders and duty to the nation being the most common. Only three admitted to committing the crimes of which they were accused, and not one made any reference to coerced confessions.[31]

The trial's final days were taken up with each side's lengthy closing arguments. Shumacker summarized the prosecution's case: the officers and enlisted men of Battle Group Peiper had been ordered to spread "terror" in their drive for the Meuse and did so willingly, and it was incumbent upon the judges to render the appropriate verdicts so that "the people of the world will know what the instigators and perpetrators of unrestrained Genghis Khan warfare can expect when they are brought before the bar of justice." He again defended the methods of the interrogators, adding that if the sworn statements were entirely invented, why then did some defendants confess to certain crimes but not others? As for defense witnesses, their testimonies could not be credible. Not only were nearly all of them prisoners of war and former members of the Waffen SS, but Peiper himself had stated in his courtroom testimony that it was at Dachau before and during the trial that their comradeship had been "reborn again."[32]

Members of the defense team restated their attempt to demonstrate the opposite. There had been no conspiracy or "common design" to commit war crimes. The "monstrous slaughter machine" was pure fiction. "One cannot help having the impression that it is all a construction, an artificial edifice, that one stone was shaped to fit in with the other," German defense counsel Otto Leiling argued. Rather than a conspiracy, there was simply war and its attendant confusion and chaos. In places like Stoumont, the fighting was intense and it could very well be the case that American and civilian casualties were the result of combat. As for the Malmedy massacre—the trial's centerpiece—a confused situation resulted in the deaths of perhaps a few prisoners but also those who had attempted to escape or resume fighting after having surrendered. Casualties of war, yes, but not victims of a war crime. The fact that Peiper's men did not murder every captured American in La Gleize should alone be sufficient to discredit the prosecution's claim of a conspiracy to murder prisoners.[33]

Everett spoke last for the defense. He repeated the argument that war produces not only casualties, but a "spiral of inhumanities" and that the "primitive impulses of vengeance and retaliation among victimized peoples are often called forth in the heat of battle or as the culmination of a war-weary last struggle against an overwhelming enemy." Most of his brief statement, however, dealt with the interrogators' alleged methods, offering a preview of the posttrial controversy that he would be instrumental in unleashing. He informed the judges that the accused had been unwilling at first to cooperate with the lawyers charged with defending them, as they had been in "solitary confinement" and subjected to "what the Prosecution has called '. . . months of continuous interrogation in which all of the legitimate tricks, ruses and stratagems known to investigators were employed.' "[34]

Yet Everett went beyond quoting Ellis's opening statement about "legitimate tricks" and hinted at the supposed hidden truth of the Malmedy massacre investigation: "a complete picture of these tricks, ruses and beatings would have been shown" had he not prevented more defendants from taking the stand. Everett claimed, preposterously, that the defendants remained too fearful of the men who had tormented them to continue testifying, and he could not in good conscience force them to do so. Here Everett offered a glimpse of the conspiratorial mind-set that would emerge with such reckless force over the next three years.[35]

Accorded a Soldier's Death

The judges delivered the guilty verdicts on July 11 and announced the sentences five days later. Forty-three defendants, including Peiper, received death sentences, 22 were sentenced to life terms, and 8 to terms ranging from 10 to 20 years.[36] Those receiving death sentences were to be executed by hanging. On July 11, Peiper asked Everett to request that those receiving death sentences be permitted to face a firing squad and die "as soldiers." Court president Dalbey concurred, noting in his recommendation to the commanding general of European forces that "the impression which these defendants made upon the court was extremely favorable and . . . that these men are soldiers and should be accorded a soldier's death."[37] The request was denied.

We do not have a record of the judges' deliberations. No doubt the weight of the sworn statements, combined with the explanations of the how they were obtained, and eyewitness testimony were the deciding factors. Like the members of any court, the judges could not have been immune to other in-

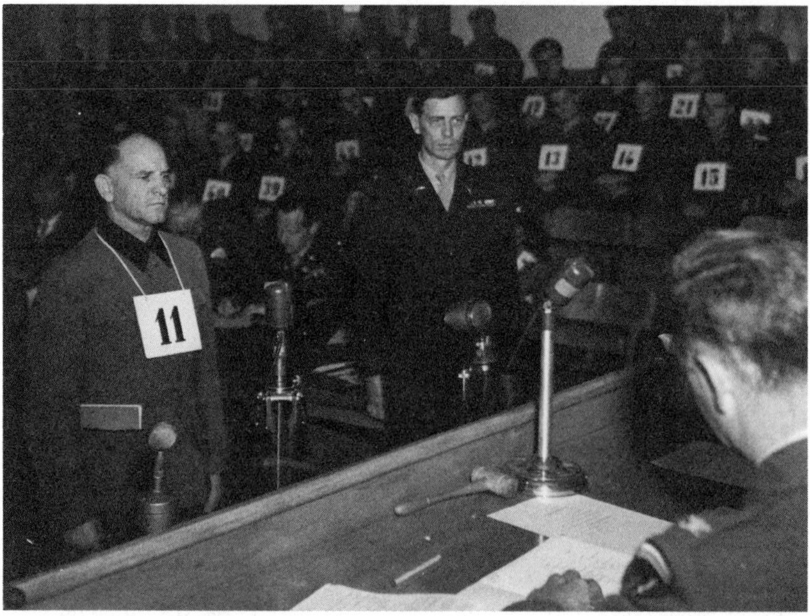

Sepp Dietrich receiving a life sentence from the court, July 16, 1946 (NARA).

fluences. For the U.S. Army and the wider American public, the Malmedy massacre had become a symbol of heroic sacrifice and Nazi criminality. Though overshadowed by Nuremberg, the Malmedy case was the army's highest-visibility trial. The accused were members of the Waffen SS, and that organization's notorious reputation was well known to the judges, all of them line officers sitting in judgment of other soldiers.

The proceedings were not flawless. Most of the judges had little or no training in the law. Aware that *United States v. Valentin Bersin, et al.* would be the army's prize war crimes trial and hoping to compete for public attention with the Nuremberg tribunal, the prosecution overdramatized its case. Evidence that a war crime had been committed near Malmedy was incontrovertible but less so in other locations along battle group Peiper's route of march. And just because the accused were not tortured does not mean that every word of their confessions was accurate or truthful. Certain interrogation methods—including elements of the "psychological approach"—may produce false confessions, and eyewitness testimony is notoriously unreliable.[38] The rules regarding what constituted admissible evidence, however, worked in the prosecution's favor.

Yet the trial was not the totalitarian monstrosity portrayed by the amnesty lobby and then by historians. Everett and the other defense lawyers had done an admirable job defending their clients. They had challenged, if unsuccessfully, the court's jurisdiction and called into question the existence of a "monstrous slaughter machine" operating on Hitler's direct orders. While heat of battle conditions may indeed have played a role in some of the encounters between Battle Group Peiper, American soldiers, and Belgian civilians, the defense overreached in trying to explain every encounter in such terms, above all the Malmedy massacre. Permitting defendants to testify, other than the cagey Peiper, was another error, and Hal McCown's testimony was of dubious value.

Most of the amnesty lobby's arguments and accusations were introduced in the defense's case. In July 1946, however, no one outside the overheated Dachau courtroom was listening. German press coverage was muted and focused on the Nuremberg trial. The handful of American reporters covering the Malmedy trial stayed for the prosecution's case then vanished, returning only to report on the verdicts and sentencing. The one-sided and sensationalist American press coverage of one portion of the trial made no mention of the investigators' methods. The proceedings had, of course, been public. But press reports were the wider public's sole source of information, and reporters had conveyed only a story of an SS murder rampage and justice served.

While the lack of any skeptical or sympathetic reporting infuriated Everett during the trial, it may have ultimately redounded to the benefit of the amnesty lobby. The American public and its political leadership had no idea that the matter of interrogation methods had come up repeatedly throughout the trial. When Everett and then other American and German critics of the trials later raised the issue in the press, albeit from their point of view, it hit an unprepared public. Everett and others were thus able to position themselves as "crusaders" for truth and justice, men and women who appeared to have broken a public and official "silence" about the matter.

As we will see, the strategy was successful. Having spent two months in court explaining their methods, Ellis, Perl, and the other interrogators had every reason to believe the matter of interrogations had been settled. Ellis in particular was dumbfounded that the trial record proved useless in squelching the controversy. He and the other investigators would watch in dismay as lurid stories of broken teeth, mangled fingers, crushed testicles, solitary confinement, "death cells," blood-soaked hoods, and mock trials exploded across the headlines of American and German newspapers and magazines. The alleged abuses and the trial they corrupted would ignite an already smoldering transatlantic controversy over war crimes trials.

EIGHT

Other Battlefields

Willis Everett and the Amnesty Campaign

The men convicted in *United States v. Valentin Bersin, et al.* were transported from Dachau to Landsberg prison, roughly forty miles west of Munich, to await execution or to serve out their sentences. Like Dachau, Landsberg was freighted with symbolic significance. In the minds of Germans and informed Americans it was associated with Adolf Hitler's emergence from obscurity and the rise of the Nazi Party to national prominence. Hitler had served nearly a year in the facility in 1924 following his conviction for treason in the aftermath of the failed Beer Hall Putsch. Confined in relatively comfortable conditions, he spent his time reading, dictating what would become *Mein Kampf,* and thinking about the party's future. After 1933, the prison's real and symbolic significance would be reinforced to a young generation of German boys whose Hitler Youth detachments would pay reverential visits to the Führer's cell.

For those with more than a passing knowledge of the Weimar Republic's fate, Landsberg represented the relative leniency with which the republic's conservative nationalist judiciary treated the perpetrators of politically motivated crimes and would-be putschists like Hitler. "Leniency," however, was not the word Germans would associate with Landsberg after World War II. They would have considered "vengeance" and "injustice" more appropriate descriptors. As it had done with Dachau, the U.S. Army transformed the fortress-like prison into an important site of judicial reckoning with the regime's crimes against civilians and American military personnel. Beginning in December 1945, the army began using the undamaged prison to incarcerate Germans convicted in the Dachau and subsequent Nuremberg trials.[1] Reflecting the significance of the population housed within its walls, the army designated the facility "War Criminal Prison No. 1." Executions, nearly all by hanging, were carried out in the prison's courtyard with the condemned men identified by the inmates and German newspapers as "red jackets" after their distinctive prison uniform.

In 1947 and 1948, a campaign aimed at discrediting the army's war crimes trials and securing the release of convicted war criminals took shape in the United States and occupied Germany. For American and German critics, "Dachau" connoted sham courts where American interrogators deployed methods similar to those of the camp's previous overseers and judges disregarded traditions of Anglo-American law in the service of victor's justice. With the conclusion of the Dachau and subsequent Nuremberg trials, the critics' focus shifted to saving the "red jackets" in Landsberg who had not yet been executed. The Malmedy investigation and trial occupied a central position in this campaign, which was initiated in the United States by Willis Everett.

Mad as a Hornet

The trial left Everett exhausted and very angry. He had little desire to remain in the army and by the fall of 1946 his application for discharge had been approved. In January he departed Germany "mad as a hornet," as an unnamed American officer in Dachau put it to an Associated Press reporter.[2] Everett would not forget the Malmedy case, however, and made his displeasure at its outcome known to anyone who would listen, including Theater Judge Advocate Claude Mickelwait, who advised him to let the matter go. Instead, Everett intended to see the verdicts of what he considered "one of the most farcical trials imaginable" overturned and the case retried.[3] He began by spending his final months in Germany working with former defense counsel John Dwinell on a petition that he hoped would sway the review of the case.

Everett and Dwinell based the long document on a highly selective reading of the trial record. Though he claimed the army denied him a copy, Everett had in fact taken one in violation of regulations. With the entire record at his disposal he could present a detailed but also one-sided and distorted version of the trial. Battle Group Peiper's crimes, he argued, amounted to nothing more than "technical and incidental transgressions of international conventions without preplanning" and were no worse than multiple war crimes committed by American forces. Moreover, the trial was an exercise in victor's justice "totally lacking in standards of American justice." The defendants had been convicted under "totalitarian law," by which he meant that they had been convicted on the basis of their own confessions and those of their codefendants and prosecution witnesses.[4]

Everett went on to charge that the court had failed to dispense "just and measured retribution" because it was blinded by wartime passions and by a "hatred created by a race persecution now supposedly ended." Hence he accused the judges of denying every defense motion he believed to be grounded firmly in precedent, Anglo-American legal traditions, and the provisions of the Geneva Convention. Further, the court was eager to appease the American public, which Everett believed—with considerable justification—had been fed an account of the proceedings entirely sympathetic to the prosecution by a sensation-seeking press.

Regarding interrogation methods, Everett cited Ellis's forthright admission during the trial that "all manner of tricks and ruses" were used on the prisoners to secure sworn statements and asserted that nearly all the evidence presented by the prosecution was produced by "illegal and fraudulently procured confessions." By ripping the investigators' repeated and detailed explanations of their methods out of their contexts, Everett presented them as shameless braggarts boasting of their conquests while enjoying the protection of the court's law member, Abraham Rosenfeld.

As to why more than just seven defendants did not retract their statements during the trial, he repeated his claim that the presence of the interrogators in the courtroom had cowed them into silence: "after ten long months of duress, beatings, interrogations, and mistreatments by the prosecution at Schwäbisch Hall they plainly had developed a fear psychosis with respect to interrogations by members of the prosecution's staff." To make matters worse, he added, the court (again meaning Rosenfeld) aided the prosecution by preventing more defendants from revealing the "beatings and mistreatment by members of the prosecution staff." Everett leveled these accusations without any evidence to back them up. Rosenfeld had certainly not "prevented" defendants from repudiating their confessions. And if any "fear psychosis" in fact existed among them, it was more likely brought about by fears of retaliation by Joachim Peiper and those loyal to him than the presence of American interrogators in the courtroom. Though only a few defendants claimed on the stand that Perl and other interrogators forced them to sign false statements, Everett now asserted that "beatings and mistreatment" lasting over nearly a year were pervasive.

What was driving Everett? In one of his many follow-up letters to War Crimes Branch officials he insisted that he had no desire to pursue his appeal but that "an obligation greater than you may realize exists within me . . . to defend justice and moral rights." He would also state repeatedly that he honored this obligation at great personal expense. "Please remain assured that I have been faithful to my duty to advocate for each of the accused," he wrote Fritz Kraemer in September 1948. "I have given up more than one thousand dollars of my own assets in order to see that justice prevails. I have expended more than two thousand hours of work for this case and am still not finished."[5]

Yet more than self-sacrificing principle was at stake. He held the entire occupation to be corrupt and misguided. His sympathies lay not with the victims of Nazi Germany but with Germans—including former Nazis—victimized, in his mind, by ignominious defeat and a vengeance-fueled occupation. Such feelings were intensified by his self-identification as a Georgian and a "rebel," a man of the American South acutely sensitive to the injustices and humiliation inflicted by an occupying power on a proud and defeated nation.[6] The fate of men like Kraemer, Peiper and other Waffen SS veterans, men whose apparent stoicism in the face of long prison terms or impending execution, moved him deeply. Certainly, he was susceptible to their obsequious and self-serving flattery, especially when it came from Peiper and his wife, Sigurd.

Everett also believed the army had treated him shabbily. He had been given an assignment for which he did not have the requisite experience or enough time, in his view, to prepare his case. Though he and the other defense lawyers had nonetheless mounted a vigorous defense, they lost the case, and badly. Facing the prospect of returning to his struggling Atlanta law firm and professional obscurity, he viewed a challenge to the outcome of the Malmedy trial as an opportunity for personal and professional redemption.

Not least, there was the possibility of considerable financial gain, as he believed he had a story worth a great deal of money to the press.

Everett's assertion that the Malmedy trial court was motivated by a "hatred created by a race persecution now supposedly ended" revealed, in thinly veiled form, the conspiratorial anti-Semitism that underpinned his view of a corrupt American occupation. He held that the real reason "Anglo-American standards of justice" were disregarded, reasonable defense motions rejected, and defendants coerced into signing false confessions was because the Office of Military Government, United States (OMGUS), including the Theater Judge Advocate's office and War Crimes Group branches, had been subverted by vengeance-seeking Jews. During and immediately after the trial, Everett had raged in letters to his family about Jews in the Dachau courtroom and within OMGUS more generally. He was more circumspect in his petition and correspondence with U.S. officials and sympathetic Germans, resorting to euphemisms and oblique references that nonetheless revealed his belief in conspiratorial, vengeful Jewish "power" stretching from Washington to occupied Germany.[7]

These views were hardly unusual among American and British officials, including occupation personnel. For those who shared Everett's outlook, Rosenfeld and William Perl were but two of many "Morgenthau boys." The reference was to former U.S. Treasury Secretary Henry Morgenthau and his widely publicized "plan" to pastoralize and divide postwar Germany. Morgenthau conceived the scheme, which entailed stripping Germany of its industrial infrastructure, in the late summer of 1944 after learning of State Department proposals to support the rebuilding of the German economy. President Franklin Roosevelt initially backed Morgenthau's idea, though he backed off in the face of strong opposition from his Secretaries of State and War. Roosevelt distanced himself further after the plan was leaked to the press. Joseph Goebbels, the Nazi regime's propaganda minister, immediately publicized the story in Germany as proof that Jews were behind a conspiracy to destroy the country. A deeply alarmed Army Chief of Staff General George C. Marshall told Morgenthau that Goebbels's propaganda was working, as the Germans were now fighting even harder against Allied forces, an assessment shared by Allen Dulles, the chief American intelligence officer in wartime Europe.[8]

The "Morgenthau plan" took on a new life after VE Day. Those American officials favoring Germany's rapid economic reconstruction would link his name to any occupation policies they considered unduly harsh, including war crimes trials. As they saw it, while Morgenthau had resigned following Roosevelt's death in April 1945, the supposedly vengeful intent of his plan had informed the Joint Chiefs of Staff's initial occupation directive, which ordered American forces in Germany to "take no steps looking toward the economic rehabilitation of Germany [or] designed to maintain or strengthen the German economy."[9] Though Morgenthau's opponents, notably Assistant Secretary of War John J. McCloy, managed to ensure that loopholes in the directive would give occupation officials enough leeway to manage the U.S. zone effectively and humanely, for Americans and Germans the name "Morgenthau" had become associated indelibly with vengeful victor's justice.

The terms "Morgenthau clique" and "Morgenthau boys" also became unmistakable references to Jews serving in OMGUS's offices, the IMT, and the CIC. In the eyes of American and German critics of the occupation and war crimes trials, this "clique" not only continued to hold sway in Washington, but also on the ground in Germany. For these critics, "Morgenthau boys" serving in the sprawling occupation apparatus were the "clique's" agents of vengeance working to undermine the noble efforts of the American military governor, General Lucius Clay.

Willis Everett, then, was typical of the many Americans and Germans who would deploy these and other euphemisms in their official correspondence and public statements. References to Morgenthau were particularly useful, as it allowed them to avoid crassly anti-Semitic language while making it clear that "vengeful Jews" were responsible for what they believed were unjust war crimes trials and potentially disastrous occupation policies.[10] German-speaking Jews who had fled Nazi Germany in the 1930s were particularly suspicious, given their backgrounds and the fact that they were "recent Americans."

What was the reality? Thousands of German Jews—now American citizens—wearing U.S. Army uniforms did hold important positions throughout OMGUS, and the success of the American occupation owes much to their efforts. Many had transitioned from wartime intelligence gathering to the work of overseeing the first years of Germany's reconstruction.

They staffed the bureaucracies of the military government's Civil and Legal Affairs Divisions and were particularly important to the functioning of the Information Control Division, the responsibility of which was to monitor and license the postwar German press. Their work as CIC agents was particularly important. Across the American occupation zone during the period of the denazification purges, they examined the pasts of Germans seeking to regain their former positions. German-born CIC agents were also an essential resource for tracking down war crimes suspects and others who fell into SHAEF's automatic arrest categories, and for investigating war crimes cases. And as recently declassified American intelligence records have revealed, they monitored the unrepentant postwar German right, thus making a long-underestimated contribution to the creation of a stable liberal democratic political system in Western Germany.[11]

To a degree unique among American occupation officials, they understood the depth of the Nazi regime's reach throughout German society and, conversely, the defensiveness and willful ignorance among Germans after VE Day. Though most had lost family members in the Holocaust and had themselves been betrayed by former friends and neighbors before being made refugees, German Jewish occupation personnel did not see themselves as agents of vengeance, but as agents of Germany's reconstruction, something most believed could only be accomplished by a thorough purge, trials of suspected war criminals, and a concerted program of reeducation.[12]

By the fall of 1946, American occupation policies had officially shifted to emphasize Germany's rapid economic rehabilitation. But war crimes trials continued, and it would be during and after the trials that fear and resentment of "vengeful Jews" among judges, prosecutors, lower-level staff, and American and German defense attorneys became particularly acute. In the Nuremberg trials, American and British officials had limited the prominence given to Jewish suffering by prosecutors. A similar unwritten rule may have been operative in some U.S. Army courts at Dachau. As Tomaz Jardim pointed out in his study of the Mauthausen camp case, American and German defense lawyers treated Jewish prosecution witnesses with extreme hostility and contempt, arguing to the judges that the witnesses' backgrounds had compromised their capacity to be truthful on the stand.[13] As war crimes trials remained broadly punitive from 1945 and into 1948, American, British, and German defense counsels and trial opponents identified the source of their continued courtroom defeats: the Jewish prosecutors, interrogators, and personnel.

An analysis of the trials written for Pope Pius XII by the American lawyer Warren Magee offers insight into the conspiratorial anti-Semitism animating this fear of Jewish revenge. Magee had served as a defense counsel in the subsequent Nuremberg trial involving Reich ministers, state secretaries, and high-ranking Nazi Party officials accused of war crimes and crimes against humanity. The chief prosecutor in that trial was Robert Kempner, a German-born lawyer of Jewish descent who had fled Germany in 1935 and emigrated to the United States a few years later. "A Mosaic justice stalks the halls of the Palace of Justice at Nuremberg," Magee wrote to the pope:

> We all know Jews suffered much under Hitler. We also know that Christian tenets of "humility, and charity which, together with the Church, have their source in the Heart of Christ" have no real place in the hearts of many Jews. "An eye for an eye and a tooth for a tooth" is the driving force behind the prosecutions at Nuremberg. While it grieves me to say this, the prosecution staff, its lawyers, research analysts, interpreters, clerks, etc. is largely Jewish. Many are Germans who fled their country and only recently took out American citizenship. Jewish influence was even apparent at the first trial, labeled the IMT. Atrocities against Jews are always stressed above all else. . . . With persecuted Jews in the background directing the proceedings, the trials cannot be maintained in an objectivity aloof from vindictiveness, personal grievances, and racial desires for revenge. . . . Basic principles have been disregarded by "new" Americans, many of whom have imbedded in their very beings European racial hatreds and prejudices.[14]

Magee, of course, had Kempner chiefly in mind. But for him, Everett, and other American and German anti-Semites intent on discrediting all Allied war crimes trials and reversing the growing number of guilty verdicts, the real problem was not a single prosecutor or interrogator, but a conspiracy to exact vengeance. The challenge for Everett and others, then, would be to reveal the conspiracy to military and political officials and the wider public.

Where There Is Smoke

Everett sent copies of his petition to War Crimes Group officials and several U.S. congressmen. However, a written critique was only the beginning of his campaign. Throughout 1947 and 1948, he pressed American officials for a retrial. He wrote Claude Mickelwait at the end of February 1947, insisting that "errors committed during the trial, and certain acts and procedures followed prior to the trial, invalidate the entire procedure." If the Theater Judge Advocate's review of the case did not correct these "errors" then he wanted to be given time before the death sentences were carried out to submit a petition for a writ of habeas corpus to the U.S. Supreme Court. A favorable ruling from the Court would remove the case from the army's control.[15]

Real leverage, Everett hoped, would come from a threat to wield the "sword of public opinion." An enlisted man posted to Dachau leaked the existence of his petition to the press, and in late January and early February 1947, the *New York Times, Stars and Stripes,* the *New York Herald Tribune,* and dozens of other American papers ran reports fixating on the abuse allegations and suggesting that the army was attempting to suppress evidence of a corrupted trial. On January 24, Edwin Hartrich of the *Herald Tribune* reported that the U.S. Army Public Relations Office in Frankfurt had imposed "official secrecy" on Everett's allegations until the American military governor approved or disapproved the Theater Judge Advocate's review of the case. As an example of the alleged abuses, Hartrich wrote that during the trial Joachim Peiper had accused American soldiers of beating him "to force a conviction [*sic*] from him." Peiper made no such claim, though he understood why his subordinates concocted such stories. Hartrich also repeated Everett's contention that American soldiers were guilty of similar war crimes and suggested that the integrity of the trial program and the occupation was at stake, as "German civilians are free in their private expressions that American soldiers and airmen also committed atrocities which should make them eligible for war crimes trials, too."[16]

A week later, another story by Hartrich provided more details from Everett's petition, now "flushed" from United States Forces European Theater (USFET) headquarters in Frankfurt. Though Hartrich quoted an USFET statement noting that the memorandum "'did not disclose any material matters of fact or evidence which were not brought out . . . at the trial,'" he repeated Everett's unsupported assertion that "80 to 90 percent of the evidence . . . consisted of these illegal and fraudulently obtained confessions." Making another reference to Peiper, he cited the former battle group commander's assertion that William Perl told him that "the people were enraged and demanded [his] head" because the sons of two unnamed "prominent Americans" were among his many victims. While conceding that the petition did not offer "an air-tight case of alleged third-degree prosecution tactics," Hartrich's two reports suggested that the army was trying to hide an ugly episode of revenge, hypocrisy, and malfeasance from the public.[17]

The sympathetic reporting suggested the potential of negative publicity to embarrass and perhaps influence the army. Everett's letters to Judge Advocate and occupation officials subsequently contained repeated threats to go to the press with what he knew, allegedly, about what happened at Schwäbisch Hall and Dachau. "Newspapers and editors have been and still are hounding me for the inside story," he wrote the acting chief of the War Crimes Branch in June: "I have kept my faith and issued no statement due to my desire not to expose certain facts until definite word has been received as to the findings."[18] Having received no official communication since the summer, Everett wrote Clay in January 1948. He repeated his claim that reporters and "several strong political friends and representatives in Washington" had been requesting the "inside facts" about the Malmedy case but that he had still not responded. The price for his silence was a retrial, with this attempt to pressure Clay being "a final personal appeal to correct those irregularities of trial [*sic*] as I am still determined to appeal this matter to our Supreme Court and any other battlefields I can honorably approach."[19]

To convince Clay that his was not a one-man crusade, Everett pointed to a strongly worded editorial in *Life* magazine criticizing American policies in occupied Germany and enclosed a copy of a speech given by Representative John E. Rankin of Mississippi to the House of Representatives on November 24. Referring to forthcoming indictments in the High Command case at Nuremberg, Rankin asked, rhetorically, "Suppose that Lee had won the Battle of Gettysburg and brought that unfortunate conflict to a close in our favor and we had proceeded to hunt down Abraham Lincoln and Andrew Johnson, U.S. Grant, General Meade, and all the great leaders on the northern side and then gone into the business world and destroyed the people who fought on your side or supported your cause, how would you have felt over it?" In addition to reflecting Everett's self-identification as a Southern "rebel," Rankin's conception of Jewish vengefulness mirrored his own: "[A] racial minority, 2 1/2 years after the war closed, are in Nuremberg not only hanging German soldiers but trying to hang German businessmen, in the name of the United States."[20] This was the second time Rankin had made reference to vengeful Jews. The previous summer he had praised President Truman for rejecting the "Morgenthau plan" and demanded that the United States "treat the people of Germany . . . with human decency and . . . not permit racial minorities to vent their sadistic vengeance upon them and charge it up to the United States."[21]

By early 1948 other American officials involved with war crimes trials were expressing critical views in public, and Everett hoped the publicity would provide him with even more leverage. In late February, the Chicago *Daily Tribune* published a report of an interview with Charles F. Wennerstrum, an Iowa State Supreme Court justice who had presided over the "Hostages Case" or "Southeast Case," one of the subsequent Nuremberg trials involving high-ranking German Army officers accused of ordering the massacre of civilians in the Balkans. Wennerstrum blasted the IMT and the subsequent Nuremberg trials using the same arguments Everett was using to critique the Malmedy case. They were exercises in victor's justice and nothing more, Wennerstrum told reporter Hal Foust, and succeeded only in conveying to the Germans that they had been beaten by "tough conquerors." Tough and corrupt, as he also accused the chief counsel in the subsequent Nuremberg trials, General Telford Taylor, of scheming to restrict the defense's access to documentary evidence.

Wennerstrum also seized on the use of "self-incriminating statements made by the defendants while prisoners for more than 2 1/2 years and repeated interrogation without presence of counsel," a practice he labeled "abhorrent to the American sense of justice," despite the fact that the American justice system offered no such protections to citizens at that time. Like Everett, Rankin, and Magee, he believed vengeful Jews to be behind the trials. "The entire atmosphere here is unwholesome," he told Foust. "Linguists were needed. The Americans are notably poor linguists. Lawyers, clerks, interpreters, and researchers were employed who became Americans only in recent years, whose backgrounds were imbedded in Europe's hatreds and prejudices."[22]

Wennerstrum's public critique further energized Everett. He contacted the judge and sought his advice. Wennerstrum seems to have kept Everett at a distance, though praised his efforts in an international forum on war crimes trials held in September, in which he reported that Everett's petition "charged the prosecution staff with acts of fraud and coercion quite comparable to the conduct of Hitler's Gestapo." And while it might be difficult to prove the truth of his charges, "it is an old adage that where there is smoke there will undoubtedly be some fire."[23] Everett also endeavored to get the *Daily Tribune* to send a reporter to Atlanta. In mid-March, he wrote to the chief of the War Crimes Branch to suggest that Wennerstrum had only encountered the "'gentlemanly' aspect of some of OUR American prosecution teams." So Everett took the opportunity to be more forthright about what happened before the Malmedy trial and the party responsible, in the process implying that he, too, could embarrass the army: "It is quite reasonable to assume that you have not been appraised of all the underhanded methods used by OUR American prosecution team while they spent about eighteen months investigating this case, because the unwritten record has never been exposed. The beatings, threats, promises and duress used by many of these 'German Refugee' Americans who were members of OUR American Investigation Team are reprehensible." He added that in the Malmedy trial his "newly organized and generally unqualified" team had just nine days to prepare their case and that Burton Ellis was hungry for publicity to boost his election campaign for the District Attorney's office in his home county in California, both untrue statements.[24]

Everett's threats to expose the "unwritten record" was, by his own admission, a bluff. "I have made it so hot for the Army, from within, that they are afraid to carry out the execution of the 43 death penalties," he bragged to Wennerstrum in early March: "Consistently I have told [Clay] that I was going to the U.S. Supreme Court and the papers if they do not send the case back for retrial. Frankly I know of no way to get to the Supreme Court but have done a lot of 'bluffing' along this line to force them to send the case back for retrial."[25] As Clay's final decision approached, Everett's bluff would be called were he unable to produce a writ petition or expose the real story of the Malmedy trial to the legions of reporters he claimed were "hounding" him.

The problem for Everett, of course, was that he did not possess credible evidence of "unexposed" prisoner abuse. So he resorted to fishing about for what he had been hinting for over a year to be withholding from the public. In March 1948, he wrote Sally and Irving Hayett, two court reporters with whom he had become friendly during the trial. He made clear that his "price for keeping my mouth shut" was a retrial but in the same letter pleaded with Sally Hayett for "some details of what went on in Schwäbisch Hall." She was the wrong person to ask for damaging information, however, as she considered Everett's accusations of prisoner abuse baseless and, like former Schwäbisch Hall medical and security personnel, would defend Ellis and his investigators against attacks in the American press.[26] As during the trial, Everett did not seek out the prison personnel who would have been in a better position than two court reporters to substantiate claims of rampant prisoner abuse.

Yet his bluffing had some effect. Everett's demands prompted a brief debate among Theater Judge Advocate and War Crimes Group officials over the appropriate response. A retrial was out of the question. War Crimes Group attorneys reviewed the Supreme Court's denial of a writ of habeas corpus submitted on behalf of the Japanese Imperial Army general Tomoyuki Yamashita and concluded that a positive decision by the court on Everett's expected petition was highly unlikely. Yamashita, however, had been granted a stay of execution until the court made its ruling. As Judge Advocate officials were sensitive to the negative publicity of early 1947, Mickelwait recommended a similar approach to Everett's request. In late March, Clay's chief of staff informed Everett that he expected the formal review of the case to be completed the following month but that Everett would be given enough time—sixty days following Clay's final decision—to submit his petition before any executions were carried out. Over the following months Judge Advocate officials assured Everett that all "reasonable" requests for extensions would be given sympathetic consideration.[27]

A Saturnalia of Persecution

Unbeknownst to Everett, Judge Advocate officials' concerns about negative publicity had another source. In August the deputy theater judge advocate for war crimes, Lieutenant Colonel Clio Straight, received reports of myriad logistical problems, procedural irregularities, and prisoner abuse within the War Crimes Enclosure at Dachau. Around the same time, a group of detainees complaining of poor conditions in their bunker, capricious behavior by Polish guards, and inadequate legal representation staged a four-day hunger strike.[28] A bundle of written complaints, including a statement by prisoners representing the hunger strikers, was intercepted by American staff and revealed considerable discontent, though not an explosive situation. Two prisoners claimed they had not been given reasons for their arrests. Another accused the court of sentencing a defendant to twenty years in prison based on a faulty translation of a sworn statement. According to another, three prisoners signed false statements out of fear of retribution by an interrogator. Other statements claimed interrogators beat prisoners—one prisoner allegedly committed suicide because of "severe interrogations"—or threatened to turn them over to the Russians. A German defense attorney was alleged to have accused Jewish prosecution witnesses of perjury.[29]

Though unable to determine who assembled the statements or the identity of the recipient, it was clear to War Crimes Group officials in Dachau that the intention was to smuggle them outside the enclosure. If their contents were taken at face value, Straight concluded, then "atrocious things are going on at Dachau." While he was willing to believe that "improper conduct" had occurred on occasion, he suspected that the statements contained "grave exaggerations" and that there was a "quiet hand" in- or outside the enclosure encouraging prisoners to claim they were being abused. Straight also suspected that members of the "indigenous side" of the War Crimes Group operation—that is, German civilians and prisoners who were working for the U.S. Army in administrative capacities—and even some American personnel were involved in manufacturing or collecting the complaints. The CIC, he believed, needed to investigate both.[30]

The Judge Advocate at Clay's headquarters dispatched an inspector to Dachau. While the veracity of a few statements could not be determined, the inspector confirmed Straight's suspicions of "grave exaggerations" and outright falsifications. The claim of a faulty translation resulting in a twenty-year prison sentence turned out to be baseless. The prisoner who claimed that fellow detainees told him they had signed sworn statements because they feared retribution by interrogators admitted that he did not know the men making the complaint. Two prisoners named in different complaints were never interned at Dachau. Others told the inspector they had never been coerced into signing false confessions or harmed by interrogators or threatened with imprisonment in Russia.[31]

One of the accusations of physical abuse was directed at Joseph Kirschbaum, an Austrian-Jewish refugee who had assisted with the Malmedy investigation as an interpreter and had remained with the War Crimes Group at Dachau after the trial. A prisoner, Otto Eichler, accused Kirschbaum of beating him. The inspector, Major Paul Foster, reviewed the camp's medical records, which identified finger marks and a small blood clot on part of Eichler's chin and noted the patient's complaints of pains in his throat. Kirschbaum, however, denied the incident. Foster wrestled with the complexity of the situation. Clearly, Eichler had received an injury. But Foster had already determined that many similar accusations were being concocted and circulated within the camp, leading him to conclude that "the evidence concerning [Eichler's] purported mistreatment is equally as compatible with a planned attempt to discredit Kirschbaum as it is with the contention that [Kirschbaum] abused Eichler."[32]

Foster's investigation also revealed that Kirschbaum was despised by the prisoners for his role in running the procedure at which potential prosecution witnesses were asked to identify suspects in concentration camp cases. Prisoners and their advocates would later deride the procedure as "stage shows" or "fashion shows," claiming that they were held for the amusement of investigators and prosecution witnesses and resulted in innocent men being charged with serious offenses. It was a gross mischaracterization of how prosecutors in the army's Dachau cases identified witnesses, which was in fact a complicated and lengthy process involving interviews of hundreds of people by prosecutors and investigators.[33]

Burton Ellis, then deputy chief of operations at Dachau, had considered relieving Kirschbaum of his duties, but remained confident in his subordinate's integrity, having worked with him closely on the Malmedy case. Even Everett, who would later caricature Kirschbaum as one of the "Morgenthau boys" and among the "evil forces who either perpetuated or aided in the original Malmedy trial," had held him in high enough regard to have recommended him a month after that trial for future employment as an investigator. Ellis also understood the risks in removing Kirschbaum: if prisoners believed their complaints had resulted in his reassignment they would only intensify their efforts to discredit his successor. Similarly, Straight and Foster recognized the danger of making inquiries among the prisoners and their defense counsels. Doing so was necessary to determine the validity of the statements, but the two feared that once it became known around the camp that army officials were investigating prisoner complaints, "it is only logical to assume that in desperation more such assertions will now be forthcoming from other detainees."[34]

In early September, the new theater judge advocate, Colonel James Harbaugh, met with Straight in Munich to discuss the problems being reported in Dachau. The war crimes operation in the camp seemed to be fraying at the seams. Shortages of qualified personnel had been the "cardinal impediment," Straight recalled, to the War Crimes Group's operations.[35] Supervision of guards and investigators had been lax. Even before the Munich meeting Straight had ordered the removal of two guards and sought to secure more interpreters and court reporters. Oversight of witness identification needed to be strengthened and Straight ordered Ellis to track the involvement of witnesses in the various trials more carefully. Regardless, Clay's chief of staff dispatched another officer to conduct a surprise inspection of conditions in Dachau. He too found no evidence that prisoners had been abused and, like Straight, suspected that someone outside Dachau was attempting to discredit the army's trial program.

Harbaugh concluded that the army had to complete its trials by the end of the year, with cases against those accused of committing crimes against American soldiers given priority over those involving concentration camp personnel. At work here was less the effects of a "Cold War climate," as is often assumed, but the prospects of a public relations fiasco in the United States and Germany should the army be unable to contain the stories of abuse in Dachau. Clearly, some prisoners, encouraged and aided by indigenous and possibly American personnel, were attempting to discredit the trials by fabricating or exaggerating incidents of maltreatments and procedural lapses. The fact that most of the accusations had been refuted following multiple internal investigations would do little to dissuade the press from publishing sensational stories. The publicity generated by Willis Everett's first salvo and his repeated threats to take his campaign to "other battlefields" were threatening signs.

NINE

The Sword of Public Opinion

The Torture Stories in the United States

The Theater Judge Advocate's review of the Malmedy trial proceeded slowly and fitfully. The army's trials were reviewed for legal sufficiency by the Deputy Judge Advocate for War Crimes, who possessed the authority to disapprove verdicts or commute sentences in cases not involving the death penalty. Death sentences were subject to approval or disapproval by the commander in chief of the U.S. European Command (EUCOM). Contrary to Willis Everett's prediction of a perfunctory review, Theater Judge Advocate officials devoted considerable attention to the case, in part due to the Malmedy massacre's notoriety but also because of the publicity generated by Everett's petition. A close look at the multiple reviews of the case is necessary to understand how the amnesty campaign developed in the United States.

The first review took over a year to complete. A month after the trial, Straight gave the job to Maximilian Koessler, a prolix Austrian-born lawyer. Koessler labored away until he was relieved in January 1947 and the task given to William Denson, the prosecutor with an unbroken record of convictions in the concentration camp trials. Despite Denson's experience and seeming boundless capacities, he, too, could not finish the job. The final version submitted to the Deputy Theater Judge Advocate that October stuck to the trial record closely. The reviewer, Major Richard Reynolds, was charged with determining whether or not the trial was conducted in accordance with the army's procedures for military courts. On the matter of interrogation methods, Reynolds confirmed that confessions obtained by tricks and ruses were admissible as evidence in military courts, as they were in American and British municipal courts. As for instances in which defendants claimed their interrogators' methods went beyond tricks and ruses, Reynolds described the complaints and the rebuttals, concluding that the "evidence is conflicting as to the methods used in the pretrial interrogations of the accused" and that it had been up to the court to determine whether the accused's statements were voluntary.[1]

Reynolds recommended that thirty-eight of the original verdicts and sentences be approved. Of those, twenty-five were death sentences. One conviction was recommended for disapproval on the grounds of insufficient evidence. He believed the verdicts in thirty-four others, among them those of the battle group's youngest and lowest-ranking members, should be confirmed but the sentences reduced. Reynolds and Clio Straight, who concurred in the recommendations, were convinced that while these men had been aware of the illegality of their actions, they had been conscripted into the Waffen SS at a very young age and late in the war.[2] They had been "brought up in the shade," as Straight testified before the Senate subcommittee two years later, and "taught doctrines that are quite far-reaching for our imagination to grasp." He thought they could be saved, in a political sense, and that this possibility merited clemency.[3] Straight also knew that while no war crimes tribunal accepted superior orders as a viable defense, all recognized that a degree of compulsion could accompany a superior officer's orders to commit an illegal act and could be considered a mitigating circumstance in sentencing and, by extension, in posttrial reviews.[4]

Complicating matters was the existence of an advisory body—the War Crimes Board of Review—created by EUCOM's Judge Advocate in August 1947. As the division was in the problematic position of reviewing the cases it had prosecuted, it seemed appropriate to appoint an advisory board of military and civilian lawyers unconnected with the trials to serve as a check on the formal review and, not least, to facilitate the onerous job of certifying the ongoing trials for legal sufficiency. Since the board's members were unfamiliar with the Malmedy case, Theater Judge Advocate James Harbaugh appointed former defense counsel John Dwinell as a technical adviser. None of the former investigators or members of the prosecution were consulted.

Dwinell's influence on this second reviewing body's recommendations was decisive. He was its sole guide to the massive record and represented the defense's position daily for the three months it took to prepare the report.[5] It was, not surprisingly, highly critical of Reynolds's review. The report claimed that Abraham Rosenfeld was determined to limit the defense's ability to examine witnesses on the stand and accused Reynolds of misstating defense testimony in his review of the case. The board was particularly critical of the use of "mock trials" and accused interrogators of dictating written confessions.[6]

While it recommended confirming twelve death sentences, the board also urged the Judge Advocate and U.S. military governor General Lucius Clay to reduce most other sentences and disapprove the guilty verdicts of twenty-nine individuals. The principal reason in twenty-one of these was that the prosecution had relied solely on the confessions of the accused and coaccused to demonstrate that a crime had been committed. It had failed, in other words, to produce a corpus delicti, and the "confessions" in any case were not credible because of the methods used to obtain and record them. In the case of Sepp Dietrich, a star defendant in the trial, the board argued that the prosecution had offered no proof that he had issued orders to execute prisoners of war and civilians. The board, however, ignored the fact that while Dietrich denied giving such orders, he had confessed to "order[ing] that our troops . . . be preceded by a wave of terror and fright and that no humane inhibitions should be shown." The board did not accuse interrogators of torturing the defendants, and mentioned accusations of serious physical abuse in only one case.

The task of reconciling the recommendations of these two very different documents fell to Harbaugh. He pointed out that in war crimes trials, judges could accept confessions alone as evidence that a crime had been committed. He also rejected the advisory board's contention that none of the confessions were worth believing because the interrogators had tricked some of the defendants. As for "dictated confessions," he noted that none of the twenty-one individuals testified in court that his confession was false. Harbaugh was, however, convinced by the board's arguments that the evidence was insufficient to sustain the convictions of ten of the twenty-nine defendants. In two cases—including one of the accused who did take the stand to testify that his interrogators beat him—Harbaugh conceded that the possibility of extreme duress, along with no other corroborating evidence, was enough to warrant disapproval. His recommendations to Clay had, clearly, been influenced by the board's critique, as he had acknowledged that more than the mitigating circumstances of youth and superior orders warranted the disapproval of some verdicts and the reduction of most sentences.[7]

The final decision was Clay's. The burden of confirming death sentences was, he recalled, the most onerous of his years as military governor. He held to tough standards of evidence, telling his chief of staff in March that "a life sentence can be corrected, a death sentence cannot. If there is the slightest doubt, a death sentence should never be administered."[8] He concurred in all but one of Harbaugh's recommendations: 19 verdicts and sentences were upheld, including 12 death sentences (among them Joachim Peiper's), while 26 death sentences were commuted. Clay approved the reduction of 32 other sentences and ordered the disapproval of 13. Like Harbaugh, then, he had been convinced that nearly all guilty verdicts were justified but that most of the sentences were excessive. He agreed that interrogators had used some questionable methods but that Waffen SS veterans, along with their lawyers and sympathetic clergymen, were engaged in a campaign to discredit the trial by inventing instances of torture.

Clay's decision called Everett's bluff. The long petition had no direct effect on the review of the trial, verdicts, and sentences. Nor had Dwinnel's input on the War Crimes Board of Review's report produced the desired result. Moreover, as Everett was unable to do more than threaten to go to the press with the inside story of Schwäbisch Hall, he never made it "hot" enough for the army to invalidate the convictions and retry the case. The problem, of course, was that Everett had taken a maximalist position by insisting that the entire enterprise was a farce and only a retrial was acceptable. There was no possibility he could accept the modification of some sentences and not others.

Undeterred, Everett submitted his writ petition to the U.S. Supreme Court in May 1948. He repeated the legal arguments against the trial laid out in his petition to the Theater Judge Advocate and amplified his previous accusations of prisoner abuse. Everett not only charged that all the verdicts in the Malmedy case were "utterly void" because the accused had been abused by army investigators but that "many" defendants and defense witnesses "were given severe and frequent beatings and other corporal punishments," such as being denied food and having their blankets taken from their cells in winter. His description also suggested that every suspect was subjected to a "mock trial," a claim refuted during the trial. The investigators in Schwäbisch Hall, he added, hooded their suspects then beat them before subjecting them to mock trials in a "completely dark cell."[9]

Another assertion was that an unspecified number were held in a special "death cell" for "days and weeks." A particularly graphic detail was the claim that prisoners would be shown "bullet holes in the wall where gruesome human flesh and hair would be imbedded from one of their 'latest executions.'" The prosecution's "endless tricks, ruses [and] so-called stratagems" were bolstered by promises of immunity or light sentences in exchange for confessions implicating their comrades. In another distortion of the trial record, Everett claimed that an unspecified number of prosecution witnesses were abused by investigators and that a few took the stand to deny their previous testimonies, claiming that they, too, had been "the victims of force, duress, beatings and other forms of torture." All of these methods "were laughingly or jokingly admitted" by the prosecution team during the trial.

The Court denied Everett's request. The vote was close—4 to 4—with Chief Justice Robert H. Jackson having recused himself because of his role in the IMT. The decision had effectively exhausted Everett's legal appeals. He subsequently turned his attention to preparing an appeal to the International Court of Justice in The Hague.[10] Exerting political pressure on the army, however, might salvage his campaign. Everett convinced Congressman James Davis, a personal acquaintance who represented Everett's Atlanta district, to intercede on behalf of his cause with Secretary of Defense James Forrestal and Judge Advocate General Corps officials. Davis in turn convinced Georgia Senator Walter George to urge Secretary of the Army Kenneth Royall to reconsider the case.

Royall was in difficult position. He was opposed to continuing war crimes trials and believed that many occupation policies in the U.S. zone were impeding Germany's recovery.[11] The Supreme Court's decision on Everett's petition had been picked up by the press and on May 21, the Chicago *Daily Tribune,* a reliable critic of war crimes trials, published a strongly worded critique of the army's conduct and demanded that the prosecutors in the Malmedy case be court-martialed.[12] In addition to the interest of two congressmen who had taken Everett's side, Royall had received pleas for clemency from some of the convicted men's family members. But he would also receive letters from Virgil Lary, the only officer to have survived the Baugnez massacre, and from some of the victims' families, all of whom expressed dismay that the death sentences had not been carried out nearly two years after the trial's conclusion.

As there was no legal basis or precedent for a retrial, which would in any case be a public relations disaster for the army, Royall chose a prudent, if convoluted, course of action. In January Clay had halted executions in Landsberg to allow the Supreme Court to determine whether it would hear arguments in the Malmedy and other cases. After the Court rejected Everett's petition request, the twelve men whose death sentences Clay had upheld in March were scheduled for execution. However, Clay had informed Royall, mistakenly, that a total of 550 convicted war criminals were awaiting executions. The correct figure was 150. Royall seized the opportunity provided by Clay's inflated figures and press reports on the Court's decision to order a halt the impending executions of the twelve convicted men.[13] He instructed Clay to have Everett's accusations investigated and then appointed his own commission to review the entire trial program. Though Congressman Davis had insisted that Everett and Dwinell be appointed to such a commission, Royall wisely chose to select three men with no direct connection to the case.[14]

No General or Systematic Use of Improper Methods

These two new bodies worked through the summer of 1948 and reached surprisingly similar conclusions. The first, called the Administration of Justice Review Board (AJRB) and directed by Clay on Royall's orders to investigate Everett's charges, was comprised of Harbaugh, John Raymond, a military government legal adviser, and a civilian adviser, the political scientist Carl Friedrich. They reviewed Everett's two petitions and the previous reviews of the case, interviewed one of the Malmedy trial defense counsels, Benjamin Narvid, and assessed a batch of petitions submitted by a German lawyer representing the convicted men that accused William Perl and other interrogators of outright torture. Unlike the first advisory board assigned to review the case, however, the AJRB's members considered statements and testimony from Burton Ellis and two of the former investigators along with a statement provided by Lieutenant Colonel Charles Perry, an investigator who had spoken with several of the convicted men in the fall of 1946, Peiper among them, who told Perry that they had never been maltreated by their interrogators.

The AJRB's first of two reports, submitted to Clay in August, found no credible evidence to support any of Everett's most serious charges. It concluded that the defense had adequate time and support to prepare its case. Though the court "might have been more considerate of the position of the defense," the board did not find that it had been hindered in presenting its case. As to the investigators' methods, the board suggested that Everett had at the very least distorted the circumstances of the investigation in Schwäbisch Hall. Hoods, for instance, were used on prisoners, but as a security measure. "Solitary confinement" in reality referred to single-occupant cells, the use of which was intended to prevent prisoners from intimidating each other and coordinating testimony. Further, the difficulties encountered in breaking the case justified the interrogators' use of tricks and ruses, including the limited use of mock trials. As to the most extreme claims of physical violence, the board concluded that "there was no systematic use of physical violence but that undoubtedly on occasions the interrogator would use some physical force on a recalcitrant individual such as pushing him up against the wall, slapping him, grabbing hold of him, and similar tactics." The report added that such incidents "were not general but were due to the heat of the particular moment." Moreover, the AJRB's members found it "difficult to understand" why the defendants did not take the stand to repudiate false confessions. Harbaugh, Raymond, and Friedrich had, in short, provided a corrective to the distortions of both Everett's petitions and the first advisory board's critique of the investigation and trial.[15]

The other three-man commission appointed by Royall reached the same conclusion. Its members were Charles Lawrence, a Judge Advocate General Corps lawyer, and two state court judges, Gordon Simpson of the Texas State Supreme Court and Edward Leroy Van Roden, a Pennsylvania county judge. Both Simpson and Van Roden were familiar with military law. The three spent six weeks in Germany reviewing sixty-five cases, including the Malmedy trial. As the Simpson Commission, as it became known, estimated the volume of all trial records weighed 12 1/2 tons, they limited their review to the cases involving 139 confirmed but unexecuted death sentences. Even then its members had to rely not on the actual investigation and trial records but on the various official reviews, petitions, and interviews with American officials and Germans representing the interests of the convicted.[16]

In the Malmedy case, the judges interviewed John Dwinell and, later, Willis Everett. They also spoke with German lawyers and clergymen who, as we will see, were instrumental in manufacturing, collecting, and disseminating stories of torture in Schwäbisch Hall and Dachau. Though Simpson had access to the AJRB's intial report, his commission did not interview or seek testimony from a single person with firsthand knowledge of the Malmedy investigation and prosecution.[17]

Crucially, a coincidence linked Willis Everett to the commission. He and Edward Van Roden were acquainted—they had shared quarters briefly in Frankfurt in 1946. When Everett learned that Van Roden had been appointed to the commission, he sent the judge materials he had collected about the case, warned him that Clio Straight and Abraham Rosenfeld could not be trusted, and suggested he consult with sympathetic German lawyers and clergymen. The two then corresponded throughout the commission's investigation in Germany, thus making Everett, as his biographer revealed, a "shadow member."[18] Van Roden, however, was not a puppet. He shared Everett's disdain for war crimes trials and his sympathy for men he believed had done their duty as soldiers but then suffered victor's justice at the hands of German-Jewish interrogators.[19]

Despite this connection and the lack of testimony from Ellis or any of the interrogators, the commission's report handed Everett yet another disappointment. The judges accepted his central contention that Battle Group Peiper's crimes were committed in heat of battle conditions, adding that it was "extremely doubtful that an American court-martial would fix any punishment more severe than life imprisonment if it were trying members of the American Army who committed like offenses." Moreover, they added that "the propriety of many of the methods [mainly mock trials] employed to secure statements from the accused is highly questionable" and "cannot be condoned." The army's trials, however, were "essentially fair," and "there was no general or systematic use of improper methods to secure prosecution evidence."[20]

The commission concluded that while the evidence warranted the guilty verdicts, "any injustice done the accused against whom death sentences have been approved will be adequately removed by commutation of the sentences of imprisonment to life." Most of the death sentences reviewed by the commission should not be carried out except for those of twenty-nine individuals, among them the twelve convicted Malmedy trial defendants whose death sentences Clay had confirmed. The final report rejected the claims of two prominent German clergymen who had petitioned the commission with rafts of documents alleging pervasive torture and insisting on the creation of an appellate court. The judges recommended instead that EUCOM institute a permanent clemency board, an idea that had also found favor with Clay.[21]

Despite its moderate conclusions, the army did not make the details of the Simpson Commission's report public for another four months. Just as the commission was concluding its work in Germany, the army revealed that Clay had reduced the life sentence of Ilse Koch, the wife of the Buchenwald concentration camp's commandant, to four years on the grounds that the evidence against her was insufficient to justify the life sentence.[22] Furious press commentary followed. Lurid accusations—most of them untrue—of Koch's brutality, sexual depravity, and her alleged use of tattooed human skin to decorate lampshades had been publicized widely during the army's Buchenwald trial in 1947. By the fall of 1948, when, as Clay put it years later, the "Iron Curtain had become much thicker," Soviet occupation officials and German communists used the story to highlight alleged American leniency toward convicted war criminals.[23] The public furor led to a three-month Senate subcommittee investigation, which concluded that Koch's crimes were indeed very serious and that the sentence reduction was unjustified. It did not, however, challenge the verdict or demand that Clay reverse his decision. The problem, the subcommittee's final report concluded, was not the army's trials but a malfunctioning review process.

American press commentary was far less forgiving. John O'Donnell, the popular Washington-based columnist for the New York *Daily News,* referred to "these so-called trials in Germany" as "a sadistic farce by any standards of justice." The army's mismanagement had failed to present to the German public "an example of impartial, even-handed American justice and fair play."[24] More moderate in tone but also highly critical was Leon Poullada, a Judge Advocate General Corps lawyer who had served as a prosecutor and defense counsel in several army trials. In a long letter published in the

Washington Evening Star on October 2, 1948, Poullada attempted to place the Ilse Koch scandal in the broader context of the army's trials at Dachau. He believed that most of the defendants in the army's war crimes trials were in fact guilty. The problem with the Koch case and many others, however, was not with what he considered a "careful, dispassionate, and unhurried process of review," but with the pretrial investigations and trials themselves.[25]

Poullada's editorial was the most extensive attempt to date in the American press to summarize the main points of American and German critiques of the army's war crimes trials. Like Everett, Charles Wennerstrom, and others, he identified Jewish interrogators as part of the problem. It was bad enough that the dismal surroundings of Dachau were reminiscent of a "third-rate police court," where "ubiquitous dark-uniformed Polish guards slightly reminiscent in appearance of Gestapo men" policed the camp and army prosecutors rushed to convict thousands of suspected war criminals. Further poisoning the atmosphere were the "emotional strains of combat" under which the first trials were conducted, which he believed accounted for the relatively high number of convictions and harsher sentences than would be handed down at later trials. And while Poullada considered members of the army's courts to be "honest, competent men" given a difficult assignment, most had no background in the law. Justice was further compromised by the wide latitude they were given in considering evidence, above all hearsay.

Adding to this, he claimed some investigators were hardly impartial, as many were "former refugees from Germany who had escaped Hitler's persecutions, migrated to the United States, obtained American citizenship and returned with our armies as 'avenging angels.'" He recalled witnessing on one occasion the identification of suspects in the Buchenwald case in which an unnamed "avenging angel" (possibly Joseph Kirschbaum) allowed former Buchenwald inmates to verbally abuse suspects during what the prisoners referred to as a "fashion show." To make matters worse, Poullada pointed out that many prosecution witnesses were not Jews or victims of political or religious persecution, but criminals—"murderers, embezzlers, homosexuals, rapists, etc."—who would have been "lifers" in American prisons. Nowhere were all these problems more apparent than in the Malmedy case. In that investigation, Jewish "avenging angels" had deployed mock trials to secure confessions. Here, Poullada perpetuated Everett's insinuation that mock trials had been the rule in the Malmedy investigation rather than the exception.

With the army's war crimes trials under close scrutiny in the United States and Germany, then, Royall delayed the release of the Simpson Commission's full report until January 1949.

A Walloping Fine Job

In the interim, he allowed executions at Landsberg to resume. This authorization, along with a desire for self-promotion, prompted Van Roden to start speaking to the press, Rotary Clubs, and other organizations about the Malmedy case.[26] His public comments departed radically from the commission's conclusions. In early October, he provided a statement to the United Press from his home in Media, Pennsylvania, describing how solitary confinement and mock trials were used to secure confessions, with hoods—"some of them bloody"—placed over suspects' heads to heighten a suspect's anxiety and fear. Van Roden also noted "evidence of brutality in that a dentist employed by the Government had to work overtime fixing up teeth knocked out and jaws that were broken." The commission's findings, he added, substantiated the charges leveled by Willis Everett's petitions.[27]

Van Roden ratcheted up the drama over the following months. In a speech to a group of federal court attorneys on December 8, he claimed interrogators had admitted that they placed suspects in "solitary confinement" for four-month stretches, dictated confessions, and resorted to "rubber hosing" and "kicking and beating with fists and brass knuckles." He then claimed to have seen one of the blood-soaked hoods and referred again to German dentists who had treated prisoners who had teeth—"in some cases every tooth in their heads"—knocked out. He kept the charge of allegedly ubiquitous mock trials in circulation, only now adding the account of a suspect who "had his hands clamped on a table with match sticks placed under his fingernails and each one lighted and allowed to burn until it went down to his fingers. All of his fingers became infected from the burns and the trial was delayed until he was able to go into court."[28]

The judge's comments drew the attention of a Philadelphia-based Quaker organization called the National Council for Prevention of War (NCPW). Pacifist and isolationist, with ties to liberal peace activists and right-wing isolationists, the NCPW had opposed American entry into World War II and then became a determined opponent of what it considered to be the occupation's punitive orientation. It became most active in opposing all war crimes trials, basing its objections on the insistence that there was no substantial difference between crimes committed by the Germans and those it believed had been committed by Allied forces. The NCPW pushed its agenda mainly through a constant stream of press releases and attempts to influence members of Congress. It also became a conduit for German amnesty advocates who were attempting to influence public opinion in the United States.

In the Malmedy case, James Finucane, the NCPW's second in command, found his most important cause. Citing Van Roden's recent speeches in the Philadelphia area, Finucane released a statement to the press and members of Congress on December 18 demanding that all executions in Landsberg be halted until a "full judicial review" could be carried out. Further, for having "abused the powers of victory and prostitut[ing] justice to vengeance," the interrogators in the Malmedy case should be "exposed in a public process" and charged with suborning perjury. This demand was based on Van Roden's descriptions of pervasive mock trials and torture in Schwäbisch Hall. Quoting at length from the judge's speech to a Rotary Club meeting four days earlier, the statement cited, among other alleged actions, "knocking out teeth and breaking jaws" and "torture with burning splinters." In the 139 cases investigated by the Simpson Commission, Van Roden had claimed "all but two of the Germans . . . had been kicked in the testicles beyond repair. This was Standard Operating Procedure with our American investigators."[29]

Finucane had not cleared the first version of the NCPW's statement with Van Roden, who immediately protested, albeit in private, about embellishments and the details of certain claims. By insisting that a reference to a Schwäbisch Hall dentist as the source of his statements about broken teeth and jaws be omitted, Van Roden was admitting that he did not have conclusive evidence of torture in the prison. Finucane complied, and the NCPW's revised statement quoted Van Roden as having relied on Everett's Supreme Court petition and an unspecified "stream of testimony" taken in Munich. The judge's equivocations, however, did not deter Finucane and the NCPW's chief, Frederick J. Libby, from pressing members of Congress to investigate the Malmedy trial on the grounds that every word of Van Roden's speeches was true. The judge's credentials were, after all, most impressive. Not only had he served as an officer with the Judge Advocate General Corps, he had been twice decorated after going ashore at Utah Beach on D-Day. His two sons had flown sixty-seven missions over Germany and Italy. One had been shot down and held for a year in a German prisoner of war camp where he was, Van Roden asserted, "fairly well treated." Van Roden had also vouched for Everett's integrity, describing him as "a very able lawyer, a conscientious and sincere gentleman" and "not a fanatic."[30]

Other American newspapers and magazines picked up the story immediately. In its January 5 issue, the *Christian Century* reported on the NCPW's December 18 press release, calling it "one of the most horrible documents we have read in years." Citing Van Roden's December 14 Rotary Club speech as the NCPW's principal source, the article reported that American interrogators had used "such torture, both physical and mental, to extort 'confessions,' as even the Nazi sadists never surpassed."[31]

In early January, Morris Rubin, the editor of the liberal monthly the *Progressive* wrote Finucane, praising the NCPW's statement as a "walloping fine job." Would it be possible, Rubin asked, to prepare an article for the magazine under Van Roden's byline? A day later, Finucane had secured the judge's agreement and ghostwrote the article.[32] "American Atrocities in Germany" appeared in the February edition of the *Progressive* under Van Roden's name. Based largely on his recent speeches, the article repeated the catalog of medieval horrors inflicted by American interrogators upon suspected German war criminals. "I am convinced the German populace had no idea what diabolical crimes that arch-fiend, Himmler, was committing in the concentration camps," it read, adding that "[ordinary Germans] fought the war as loyal citizens with a fatherland to support, and a fatherland to defend."[33] Further, it claimed William Perl admitted during the trial to resorting to "violence" to secure confessions, an admission Perl never made.

Van Roden's statements and the *Progressive* article offered what must have struck many readers as the inside story of the whole ugly affair. Newspaper stories following the army's release of the Simpson Commission's full report on January 7, 1949, hinted darkly at the prevalence of mock trials and unspecified "questionable methods." While major newspapers and wire services noted that the commission had found the guilty verdicts justified, they omitted reporting its other major finding: that there was no use of systematic physical force.[34] Upon receiving a copy of the *Progressive* article, however, Van Roden began to distance himself—again in private—from the NCPW.[35] When questioned by the leadership of the National Catholic Welfare Conference about his claims that the interrogators had misused the sacrament of confession during mock trials, Van Roden admitted that he did not have a "single scrap of evidence" nor could he recall when or where he had heard the stories or the name of anyone who might corroborate it.[36]

In terms of the "sword of public opinion," however, the damage had been done. Over the following months, the press treated Van Roden and Everett rather than the commission's final report as authoritative sources on the pretrial investigation, despite the fact that Everett had not been speaking publicly about the case. Both men's accounts were accepted as truth by an uncritical press seeking sensational headlines or stories that confirmed its publishers' animosity toward the occupation and war crimes trials. Van Roden's startling claims attracted far more press attention than Gordon Simpson's public repudiation of his former commission colleague. "Americans have nothing to be ashamed of," he told the Associated Press, as they had "bent over backwards to give fair trials to Nazis who had never given fair trials to many they sentenced to death." Van Roden's "inordinate" statements—which Simpson found all the more inexplicable because Van Roden had signed the commission's final report—"[are] doing us a disservice."[37]

The *Chicago Daily Tribune* remained particularly determined to discredit the Malmedy and other army trials. Beginning in mid-February, the paper published a four-part series by reporter Larry Rue focusing on abuse. It would be the lengthiest, most detailed summary of the pretrial investigation written wholly from the perspective of its most determined critics published in the American press. Rue cited Everett and Van Roden but also identified by name, for the first time in a major American newspaper, German sources of the torture accusations. Rue had corresponded with Georg Froeschmann, a German lawyer who, as we will see, was one of the most important German figures collecting and disseminating the particularly gruesome accusations. Froeschmann provided Rue with some of the most sensational material that would have substantiated Van Roden's claims. He identified two Germans by name, a dentist named Eduard Knorr and a prisoner who worked as a medical orderly, Dietrich Schnell. Both swore to have treated prisoners who had suffered serious injuries at the hands of Perl, Kirschbaum, Morris Elowitz, and Harry Thon, and Rue quoted extensively from their affidavits. The final installment of the series focused on Peiper, who had by that time had further exaggerated the claims made in his first posttrial affidavits. Readers of the *Tribune* learned, for instance, that Perl had threatened Peiper's family and told him he would be deported to Russia. Nowhere in the series did Rue indicate that he had tried to confirm the accuracy of any of these assertions.[38]

Van Roden's speeches also inspired the Anglo-American conservative writer Freda Utley to devote nearly an entire chapter of a book titled *The High Cost of Vengeance: How Our German Policy Is Leading Us to Bankruptcy and War* to what she labeled "our crimes against humanity." A former member of the British Communist Party, Utley had transformed herself into an outspoken and widely published anticommunist journalist and commentator. *The High Cost of Vengeance,* written after a visit to Germany in 1948 and published by the conservative Henry Regnery Press right as the U.S. Senate hearings on the Malmedy case were taking place, was a three-hundred-page, unsparing attack on American occupation policies. Utley's main point was—unsurprisingly—that harsh occupation policies would drive Germans into the arms of the communists. Her chapter on war crimes trials repeated Van Roden's charges and quoted at length from affidavits written by some of the men convicted in the Malmedy trial containing descriptions of horrendous abuse by American interrogators. Utley made repeated and stark comparisons between the Allies and the Nazis, seeing very little difference in the actions of the Americans, British, Soviets, and Nazis. Typical is the warning following her description of a catalog of tortures allegedly inflicted on young Germans by American interrogators: "The names . . . Kirschbaum, Metzger, Enders . . . like those of Lieutenant Perl and Mr. Harry Thon, will be remembered in Germany as long, and with as much loathing, as the names of Himmler, Bormann and other Nazi bullies and criminals are remembered in America."[39]

Publications with less editorial hostility were no less irresponsible. The January 17, 1949, issue of *Time* magazine ran a story on the abuse allegations. The case against the accused perpetrators seemed "open and shut," until Willis Everett "discovered facts which turned the case into one of the ugliest in the history of war crimes trials." Everett reported to the army and the U.S. Supreme Court a catalog of abuses "which read like a record of Nazi atrocities." Everett, the article concluded, was no longer representing the convicted German soldiers, "most of whom he believed guilty." Rather, he was taking a stand on principles, namely that his clients deserved, and did not receive, a fair trial.

INTERNATIONAL

THE NATIONS

No Footsie-Wootsie

For a month Berlin had been deceptively quiet, as though the antagonists, while not relaxing their holds, had paused for breath. Last week the silence was broken by a brass-lunged blast from Colonel Frank L. Howley, hard-bitten commander of the city's U.S. sector. On New Year's Day, two or three U.S. officials telephoned their Russian opposite numbers to wish them a prosperous New Year. When he heard of this incident last week, Howley's quick-triggered temper exploded:

"Prosperous New Year—like hell! Instructions in the Russian army manual are not to mix with us except when essential to fulfill their missions. These days we aren't trying to help the Russians fulfill their missions." Howley promptly ordered all fraternizing with Russians in Berlin to stop, forthwith. Cried he: "None of my men are going to play footsie-wootsie with the Russians!"

WAR CRIMES

Clemency

The Malmédy massacre of captured U.S. soldiers, during the Battle of the Bulge in December 1944, was one of the most vicious atrocities committed by Germans in combat during the war. By the testimony of one survivor (who escaped by feigning death after he was shot in the foot), some 160 U.S. soldiers were lined up in a snow-covered field, eight deep and 20 abreast, and raked by machine-gun fire for three minutes.

The survivor heard the "agonized screams" of wounded and dying comrades, and single pistol shots—*coups de grâce* administered by Germans who walked among the fallen victims after the machine-gunning stopped.

After war's end, the Germans responsible for the massacre fell into Allied hands. Among them were two *SS* bigwigs, General Josef ("Sepp") Dietrich, commander of the 6th Armored Division, and Colonel Joachim Peiper of the 1st Armored Regiment (known as "Peiper's Task Force"). But most were youngsters whom Dietrich and Peiper had commanded. In 1946, in Dachau, 73 Germans were brought to trial for the Malmédy massacre. All were found guilty and 43 sentenced to death. It seemed an open-&-shut case. But the Germans' defense counsel (appointed by the U.S.), an Atlanta lawyer named Willis Meade Everett Jr., had discovered facts which turned the case into one of the ugliest in the history of the war crimes trials.

Candles on the Table. Everett submitted an incredible report (first to the U.S. Supreme Court, then to the U.S. Army), which read like a record of Nazi atrocities. He charged that, to extort confessions, U.S. prosecution teams "had kept the German defendants in dark, solitary confinement at near starvation rations up to six months; had applied various forms of torture, including the driving of burning matches under the prisoners' fingernails; had administered beatings which resulted in broken jaws and arms and permanently injured testicles."

He also charged that false confessions were obtained in mock trials, at which "the . . . plaintiff would see before him a long table . . . with candles burning at both ends . . . and a crucifix in the center . . . [The Germans] were informed or led to believe that they were being tried by Americans for violations of international law. At the other end of the table would be the prosecutor, who would read the charges, yell and scream at these 18- and 20-year-old plaintiffs and attempt to force confessions from them . . ."

Blot on the Record. Everett was no longer defending the Germans, most of whom he believed guilty; he was defending justice. For two years, at his own expense, Everett pleaded his case. Finally, last July 29, an Army commission under Justice Gordon Simpson of the Texas Supreme Court was set up to review the records.* The commission corroborated Everett concerning the mock trials and did not dispute or deny the rest. General Lucius D. Clay had already commuted the death sentences of 31 of the 43 condemned Germans. In Washington last week the Simpson commission recommended clemency (commutation to life imprisonment) for the remaining twelve.

This action, however, could not remove the blot on the record of U.S. military justice. It would remain as a terrible warning that, at times, the judges can be conquered by the forces of evil they are supposed to try.

* Three weeks ago a congressional committee, set up to review the case of Ilse ("Bitch of Buchenwald") Koch, whose life sentence had been reduced to four years, concluded that the U.S. prosecution had bungled. Ilse could have been given a life term for any one of several proved crimes; instead, she was tried and convicted on the shaky charge of participating in the management of Buchenwald. "Our soldiers," said the committee, "are not lawyers." Ilse will be free next September, but a German court will then almost certainly try her for crimes against German nationals.

U.S. Army Signal Corps

MALMÉDY MASSACRE

Acme

LAWYER EVERETT

Judges are sometimes conquered by the evil they judge.

TIME, JANUARY 17, 1949 19

"Blot on the Record," *Time*, January 17, 1949 *(Time)*.

In March 1949 Willis Everett suffered a massive heart attack and ceased playing an active role in the campaign to free the men convicted in the Malmedy trial. For nearly three years he had sought, without success, a retrial. His persistence had, however, pressured the army to pay particularly close attention to the case. Contrary to Everett's claims and those of later critics of the Dachau courts, the army had not attempted a cover-up of the pretrial investigation.[40] Rather, the opposite was the case. Between 1946 and 1948 it conducted four official reviews of the case, all of which concluded that while most guilty verdicts were justified, sentence reductions were warranted in most cases. Along with the sentence reductions and the release of thirteen convicted men, the multiple reviews had resulted in the delay of Joachim Peiper's and eleven other men's executions.

Not one review found any credible evidence that the defendants had been coerced into signing their confessions. While Everett may have been nonetheless convinced that the "Nazi method boys" in Schwäbisch Hall had in fact resorted to Nazi methods, to his credit he refrained from making accusations to the press he could not substantiate. It was a stroke of good fortune, then, that an obscure Pennsylvania county judge and a pacifist organization vehemently opposed to all war crimes trials were able to draw close—if careless and sensationalist—press attention to alleged prisoner abuse. By early 1949, American newspapers and news magazines had seized upon unverified accusations of systematic and brutal torture. Comparisons of American interrogators with "Gestapo men" abounded, accompanied by thinly veiled references to vengeful Jews ("recent Americans") who had turned the tables on their former tormentors.

Despite his lack of success in convincing the army to retry the case, then, Everett must have been pleased with the flood of reports that seemed to expose an "un-American" and corrupt program of war crimes trials. *Time* magazine's portrayal of his efforts was particularly flattering. The article was accompanied by two photographs: one of the Baugnez crossroads field littered with the frozen corpses of American soldiers and one of Everett holding a large bound volume titled "Malmedy Case." The handsome lawyer bore a passing resemblance to Henry Fonda or Jimmy Stewart, the actors Everett may have envisioned portraying him in a war crimes trial version of *12 Angry Men* or *Mr. Smith Goes to Washington.*[41]

Unlike Everett, of course, Van Roden was not reluctant to proclaim that suspects had their teeth knocked out, jaws broken, testicles crushed, and fingers burned by American interrogators. Where did Van Roden get this information? In these years, he and Everett were not the only sources of pressure on American officials. German lawyers, prominent clergymen, Waffen SS veterans, and wealthy sympathizers had been mobilizing to discredit the Malmedy and other trials. As we will see in Chapter 10, the members of this network of amnesty advocates were most responsible for manufacturing and disseminating such stories in Germany and, ultimately, the United States.

TEN

The Daring Fists of Lieutenant Perl

Tales of Torture in Schwäbisch Hall

In a three-page statement written in the summer of 1947, a thirty-one-year-old former Waffen SS sergeant calling himself Otto Eble described a nightmarish ordeal at the hands of unnamed American interrogators in Schwäbisch Hall. Eble claimed that after being arrested by American MPs in October 1945 he was transferred to the prison on the grounds that he had belonged to Joachim Peiper's regiment and had been in the vicinity of Malmedy at the time of the massacre. While in Schwäbisch Hall he was underfed and subjected to eight continuous days of intensive interrogation. After insisting repeatedly that he had not belonged to Peiper's regiment, Eble accused his interrogators of tying his hands to a table, driving sharpened matchsticks under "all" of his fingernails, lighting them, and allowing the flames to burn his fingertips. When he still refused to give the interrogators the answers they wanted, he was tied to a table and stabbed repeatedly in the arm. Although he was given bandages for the knife wounds, his injured fingers went untreated. His ordeal ended after he was subjected to a mock execution by hanging. Eble closed his affidavit by noting that the "same mistreatments were accorded many comrades of the Personal Standard." He heard them shouting, as did "people passing by in the street" who had "stopped to listen."[1]

Eble's was one of many similar statements conveyed to the Simpson Commission in the fall of 1948 by Eugen Leer, a German lawyer who had defended some of the accused at the Malmedy trial. By December of that year, Edward Van Roden was repeating the most gruesome details of Eble's story to the press and in his public talks. When one of John O'Donnell's "Capitol Stuff" columns in the New York *Daily News* repeated the charges and named Eble, the army's Judge Advocate General asked Lucius Clay to investigate.[2] Several months of inquiries revealed that "Otto Eble" was in fact Friedrich Eble, a Waffen SS sergeant who had escaped repeatedly from three different civilian internment enclosures. He had falsified his identity multiple times and had never been imprisoned in Schwäbisch Hall. The principal interrogators had no memory of him.[3] Investigators also learned that on four different occasions between 1937 and 1943 he was sentenced to terms of penal servitude ranging from ten months to three years for theft, embezzlement, and fraud.[4]

If Eble's criminal record and dizzying array of postwar escapes and name changes were not enough to make American officials question his reliability, there was his boast that he had served as an officer in the Swiss Army who deserted to Germany carrying classified documents before becoming involved in a secret operation to ferret out alleged plans by General Friedrich Paulus to surrender to Soviet forces at Stalingrad. "Any story given by [Eble]," one War Crimes Group investigator concluded with considerable understatement, "is open to serious doubt."[5] Three American physicians who later examined Eble to determine whether he had in fact suffered the injuries described in his affidavit concluded he was "a psychopathic personality and a pathological liar."[6] As to where he might have heard stories of prisoner abuse at Schwäbisch Hall, the same War Crimes Group investigator noted that Eble had admitted to meeting several escapees from the Dachau enclosure and suspected he might have picked up tales of torture from them.[7]

As he was never charged with any crimes, Eble was released from American custody in August 1948. A German denazification tribunal in the French occupation zone, where Eble resided, categorized him as a "chief delinquent" and forbade him from voting or holding a civil service job for four years. He was living quietly near Freiburg when he was called to testify before the Senate subcommittee when it convened in Germany in September 1949. Although Eble had already admitted to changing his identity multiple times after the war, he stuck to his account of his ordeal in Schwäbisch Hall, adding that unnamed German "camp leaders" had asked him to write his statement.

He also finally identified his abusers by name: William Perl and Joseph Kirschbaum.[8]

Clay realized what was going on long before American senators arrived in Germany. By early 1948, most of the men convicted in the Malmedy trial had signed affidavits repudiating their pretrial statements. They now asserted that American interrogators had tortured them in Schwäbisch Hall and forced them to confess to crimes they did not commit. Clay, for one, was not fooled. He was convinced that the convicted men and other Waffen SS veterans had concocted the stories of beatings, burning matchsticks, and other abuses that had been sent to him in large batches as petitions. "I think it only fair to say," an exasperated Clay wrote to the Judge Advocate General in response to O'Donnell's column, "that statements of German SS personnel, uncorroborated by other evidence, particularly when they were suspects, must be taken with a large grain of salt as [the] SS was notoriously famous for [its] ability to manufacture lies out of all reason."[9] While Clay conceded that American interrogators had used some questionable methods, stories like Eble's were simply not believable.

The torture accusations became the basis for a campaign in Germany by a network of SS veterans and their lawyers, clergymen, and wealthy sympathizers to discredit the Malmedy and other trials and free the convicted men of Battle Group Peiper from Landsberg. The network's basic argument was simple: charges of war crimes were baseless and Allied courts had exacted what the prestigious *Frankfurter Allgemeine Zeitung (Frankfurt General Newspaper)* would refer to in 1954 as "revenge justice." The network's organization was somewhat more complicated.

In June 1958, after the last prisoners in Landsberg, Wittlich, and Werl had been released, former Luftwaffe general Hans Korte described the origins of this network ten years earlier and boasted of its long-term success to readers of the right-wing newspaper *Deutsche Soldaten Zeitung (German Soldiers' Paper)*. The network, Korte wrote, was coordinated by lawyers representing the convicted men and otherwise advocating for a general amnesty. To evade censorship or possible disruption by occupation authorities, its efforts were dispersed among a number of groups with innocuous-sounding names like "The Committee for Christian Aid to War Prisoners" and "The Committee for Justice and Trade." The lawyers would work closely with Catholic and Protestant church leaders, who, along with proliferating veterans groups, would play particularly important roles as amnesty advocates. A special bank account was created to receive contributions and a flood of pamphlets, circulars, press releases, and editorials were issued to solicit donations and influence public opinion, especially through the respectable press. The network also supplied packages to prisoners and provided material support for their families. Korte was an active participant and became a vocal critic of the Malmedy case in the pages of both the *Deutsche Soldaten Zeitung* and more mainstream newspapers.[10]

Korte's celebratory account of this network's campaign to "reel in the stars and stripes from atop Landsberg" portrayed it not as an act of subversion but as a grassroots effort by those Germans who rejected an Allied accusation of "collective guilt" for "alleged" war crimes. Korte was less charitable toward the Americans who had contributed to undermining the trials. Willis Everett, for one, went unmentioned. Korte conceded, however, that the Simpson Commission, "despite strong opposition from the Morgenthau clique," had attempted to rectify the worst errors of the Malmedy trial. Nor did he acknowledge the many West German government officials who had, as we will see, adopted the network's position and benefited from its publicity work. For Korte it was the ceaseless work of many Germans—some well known, others desiring anonymity—in keeping the plight of the convicted men alive for the public that brought to a close what he termed "the most unpleasant and saddest chapter of the postwar period." By doing so they had redeemed the honor of the German people.

Fortunately for the network, the drawn-out American review process and the emerging public controversy over the Malmedy trial had provided the necessary window of opportunity to act. Armed with sheaves of affidavits like Eble's, German lawyers attempted to persuade the apparently wavering Americans to overturn the Malmedy court's verdicts. While they were not successful in the short run, the public endorsement of the torture stories by the leaders of Germany's Catholic and Protestant churches—sources most Germans considered credible beyond reproach—fueled public opposition to war crimes trials and brought intense pressure on American officials to release the convicted men. In the process, the reputation of U.S. Army courts would be damaged severely by what frustrated War Crimes Group officials considered nothing more than a smear campaign.

Why did the convicted men accuse American interrogators of torturing them, and how were these stories conveyed beyond the walls of Landsberg prison? The answer to the first question lies in the circumstances in which former members of the SS found themselves in the first postwar years.

Claiming Distance from Himmler

Through 1947, the bad reputation sought by Peiper and other Waffen SS officers during the war had become a fatal liability. Allied governments had long been aware that the SS was responsible for countless crimes across Europe. For their publics, the liberation of the camps in the war's final year connected the SS indelibly to the horrors of Dachau, Auschwitz, and other camps. Massacres of hundreds of civilians in Italy and France, along with the executions of Canadian and American soldiers in the months following D-Day, revealed to the populations of those countries what Polish and Soviet citizens had known since the war's beginning: that the Waffen SS was a particularly murderous element of the German military. As British and American armies entered Germany, all members of the SS were subject to automatic arrest and it could have surprised no one that the IMT declared the entire SS to be a criminal organization.[11]

The scope and brutality of SS crimes were laid bare in the twelve subsequent Nuremberg trials. Three of these centered on the SS, most notably the trial of former Einsatzgruppen leaders and officials of the Race and Settlement Main Office. The chief defendants in the third, the Economics and Administrative Main Office trial (or "Pohl Case"), were high-ranking Waffen SS officers (all but one of the others were officers in the General SS). Even in one of the putatively non-SS trials, the "Doctors' Trial," ten of the twenty-three defendants were SS officers, and seven of the ten served in the Waffen SS. Their sentences were harsh relative to other defendants in the subsequent trials.

SS members also figured prominently in trials held in the four occupation zones, with the U.S. Army being the most aggressive prosecutor. In the army's trials at Dachau, a majority of the 1,672 defendants belonged to the SS, most of them serving as concentration camp personnel. Waffen SS members were prominent in that category as well. In the Mauthausen trial, for instance, fifty-five of sixty-one defendants had belonged to the Waffen SS.

This fact only reinforced the prosecution's assertion in the main Nuremberg trial that it was "impossible to single out any one portion of the SS which was not involved in these criminal activities."[12]

The Malmedy massacre case was the highest-profile trial held by any Allied nation to involve the Waffen SS exclusively.[13] Unlike trials of Waffen SS personnel held around this time by other Allied states, more than a handful of high-ranking officers were in the dock. Most defendants were middle-ranking officers, NCOs, and enlisted men. The prosecution portrayed all of them as gears in "a monstrous slaughter machine" acting on Hitler's orders to wage terror war in the Ardennes. This conception of a major Waffen SS field division also comported with the way Allied prosecutors in Nuremberg had characterized the SS: as a "highly disciplined organization composed of the elite of National Socialism."[14]

Prosecutors were not the only ones to describe the Waffen SS as part of a larger, fundamentally criminal organization. During the war, the Wehrmacht and the Waffen SS had fought side by side, with both forces becoming deeply complicit in crimes against combatants and civilians. After the war, however, surviving Wehrmacht officers distanced themselves from their former comrades in arms. Indeed, this attempt to draw a clear line between the two forces began before VE Day, as surreptitiously taped conversations among Wehrmacht officers captured by the British and Americans have revealed.[15] During the Nuremberg and other trials, Wehrmacht officers portrayed themselves as dutiful soldiers who had led a conventional fighting force and directed blame for war crimes to the Waffen SS or other armed SS units.[16]

Waffen SS veterans responded by characterizing their organization as a purely military entity. They insisted the various field divisions were comprised of ordinary soldiers who had fought for their nation honorably and within the bounds of international law. And just as former Wehrmacht officers attempted to distance themselves from the Waffen SS, veterans of the latter insisted that their wartime operations had nothing to do with those of the General SS—by which they meant the SS of Heinrich Himmler, the concentration camps, and the extermination of European Jews. One of the earliest members of the Personal Standard, Lieutenant Colonel Robert Brill, articulated what would become the standard justification among Waffen SS veterans and their sympathizers in his testimony for the defense at Nuremberg in August 1946: "We were always trained in honor, discipline, and decency. For five years we fought in faithful duty for our fatherland, and now we sit behind barbed wire and everywhere we are called murderers and criminals. . . . We have nothing to do with, and have known nothing of the abominable atrocities of Himmler who betrayed and deceived us, too, by preferring death to responsibility."[17] The highest-ranking Waffen SS officer to testify for the defense, General Paul Hausser, insisted that his men were well versed in "the Hague rules of Land Warfare" and, like Brill and other Waffen SS veterans, downplayed the connection to Himmler and claimed to know nothing of the murder of civilians in Russia and France by Waffen SS field divisions.[18]

The defense at the Malmedy trail made the same argument two months before Brill's and Hausser's testimonies. Like their counterparts in Nuremberg, the highest-ranking officers to take the stand denied that Himmler had any significant connection to the Waffen SS and derided the prosecution's attempt to connect his fascination with Genghis Khan to their operations on the battlefield. Though during his testimony Joachim Peiper discussed his role as one of Himmler's adjutants, it would not be long before he distanced himself from the SS chief, at least in public. In April 1947, he told an American war crimes investigator that he had nothing to do with the deportations of non-Jewish and Jewish Poles in 1940 and 1941, as involvement in any such actions would have "despoiled" him "as a soldier." All he did for Himmler, he now insisted, was maintain his appointment calendar, adding for good measure that the two never discussed anything other than "purely military matters."[19]

This effort to redefine the reputation of the Waffen SS by its veterans and sympathizers would go on for decades and, in the longer term, achieve considerable success. In the immediate postwar years the appeal fell on deaf ears. The conception of the entire SS as a "homogenous and all-powerful elite," as Jan Erik Schulte put it, was entrenched among prosecutors at Nuremberg, and former Wehrmacht officers were in eager agreement.[20] At the most important trial of Waffen SS soldiers—the Malmedy trial—the defense could not convince the judges that the defendants had been ordinary soldiers and that their actions in the Battle of the Bulge were not part of a conspiracy to wage terror war.

The Landsbergers' Favorite Sport

Through 1947, then, the situation facing the convicted men in Landsberg appeared grim. The outcome of the army's reviews of the Malmedy case only seemed to make matters worse. None of the death sentences could be carried out until the formal review of the trial had been completed, and this process took over a year. When the review was finally completed in late 1947, Clay confirmed nearly all of the verdicts and upheld twelve of the forty-three original death sentences. Willis Everett was only just starting to urge American officials to reopen the case and his criticisms had not yet generated enough publicity—or the threat of it—to convince Secretary of the Army Kenneth Royall to order a halt to the executions.

With the encouragement and assistance of their lawyers, a few trusted comrades outside Landsberg, and sympathetic prison clergy, most of the convicted men prepared new statements repudiating those made in Schwäbisch Hall. These depicted the prison as a complex of torture chambers. Accusations ranged from kicking, being slammed or "pressed" against walls, shoving, broken teeth, being thrown down stairs, unspecified "beatings," slapping, beatings with clubs, being kicked or "beaten" in the genitals, or being subjected to mock trials and threatened with immediate hanging. Nearly all of the affidavits also described atrocious conditions of imprisonment: weeks of solitary confinement and denial of blankets, baths, and medical treatment. Seven claimed to have been forced to drink from the toilets in their cells. Perl was named as an abuser in 30 of the statements, Kirschbaum in 11, and Harry Thon in 26.[21]

Paul Zwigart's statement was typical. Zwigart, a sergeant and personnel carrier driver, had been convicted of executing an American prisoner near the village of Cheneux and sentenced to death. Like most defendants, he never took the stand to deny his confession. Unlike most, he admitted his guilt in his plea for mitigation. He began to challenge his pretrial statements and the posttrial statements he made in October 1947, in which he insisted that his commanding officer had ordered him to shoot the prisoner and that he did so out of fear of being punished for disobeying the order.[22]

Four months later he had recanted all admissions of guilt. Zwigart now asserted that he was kept in solitary confinement for over a month without adequate food or clothing before being forced to sign a false confession. Physical abuse, which began upon his arrival when he was beaten by guards, only became extreme when he was interrogated by Perl and Thon. When he was taken out of his cell for questioning, he now claimed, "the guard threw a [hood] over my head. Outside of the questioning cell someone pulled me, my face towards the wall, to the wall and pulled up my hands. In this position I was repeatedly kicked for about 20 minutes. When my head was vehemently pulled against the wall for the second time, I collapsed. Then someone led me into the cell, where Lieutenant Perl took off my [hood] with one blow. . . . Perl told me briefly that I was standing before a Schnellgericht ["quick process" or "mock trial"]. Then I had to describe the course of the offensive. But as soon as I had started to speak Lieutenant Perl [hit] me in the face and at the same time Mr. Thon kicked me in the genitals." Zwigart then recounted being subjected to a mock trial, and when his responses did not come fast enough, Perl again struck him in the face while Thon kicked him "in the genitals." Zwigart's silences or denials of responsibility were met with yet more beatings and, finally, a mock execution by hanging. Perl then ordered him to write out a dictated confession, punching him whenever he refused to write out an "untruth."[23]

The reversal in Benoni Junker's statements was particularly striking. Junker, a first lieutenant and First Panzer Regiment company commander sentenced to death for ordering his company's tank commanders to execute prisoners of war, told an American investigator in 1947 that the abuse allegations were completely false and had originated with the defense attorneys. Junker found a rumor circulating among the prisoners—that certain interrogation cells in Schwäbisch Hall were pockmarked with bullet holes dripping with human flesh and blood—so ludicrous that he composed a limerick about it and asked that it be passed along to Burton Ellis.[24] Evidently, however, his former comrades—and perhaps Leer—had convinced him to revise his assessment of Schwäbisch Hall. In January 1948, he prepared a statement describing beatings while hooded, presumably administered by Perl. According to this revised version of events Junker had confessed not "based on the daring fists of Lieutenant Perl" but because he was confronted by "false witnesses" and deceived by a few "well-placed lies" and "intimate appeals to my duties as an officer." As with other affidavits, Junker swore to having heard the cries of his tormented comrades echoing around the halls of the prison.[25]

Even Peiper, who had been reluctant to accuse any American official of such brutalities, also reversed his earlier denials of ever having been abused. During the trial he testified only that he had been struck on one occasion by what he presumed were "Polish guards." In his February 1948 statement he claimed to have been robbed of his personal possessions—including his battle decorations, which he learned were being worn by Thon as he interrogated Peiper's men—and held in solitary confinement for four months. He was "softened up" before his own interrogation by being placed in an unheated cell for six days and subjected to verbal threats by three unnamed armed U.S. officers. When he was led to the interrogation room his head was covered in a hood "caked with blood on the inside."

Peiper's statement differed from most of the others in that he did not accuse Perl of striking him, though like other prisoners claimed, "I frequently heard the cries of pain of my comrades coming from the interrogation cells as well as the clattering noises of beatings and name-calling." Perl's demeanor with Peiper, however, was calm and businesslike: "He knew how to get to my softest spot and to put me under psychic pressure by appealing to the ethics of an officer and [to] Prussian tradition," Peiper wrote. Perl told him that he thought Peiper had been "an exceptional soldier" who had nothing to do with the Malmedy massacre. He had, however, the misfortune of having been "hanged" by American public opinion and the press.

To compound these indignities, he claimed the interrogators showed him "numerous falsified statements" from former subordinates. In the end, Peiper signed what he now insisted were totally bogus confessions prepared by Perl because "the unfortunate end of the war, the psychic state of emergency and not least my disgust at the supposed attitude and faithless betrayal of my comrades created in me a feeling of apathy-like-fatalistic lethargy."[26]

As we have seen, a few accounts of abuse had come to Everett's attention before the trial, but they had been investigated and discredited. Several more were presented late in the trial, though without positive effect on the judges. Now freed from the constraints of the courtroom and facing long prison sentences or executions, the convicted men had nothing to lose by writing such lurid fictions. The seeming desperation of their situation through 1947, however, does not by itself explain why they wrote them.

For one thing, an unwavering belief in their own innocence and victimization was pervasive among the men and women convicted by war crimes tribunals and imprisoned in Landsberg.[27] Werner Hess, a Lutheran pastor serving a six-month sentence for participating in the beating of a captured American pilot, described the prison's atmosphere to another pastor as being pervaded by a "psychosis of blamelessness." Tension, nationalism, and "prison-induced psychotic exaggeration" ruled in Landsberg, Hess warned his confrere, and above all among the SS men. From them one could expect to hear the "most gruesome stories" about what happened at the trials. Hess advised listening to them "with the patience of a lamb." Within a few weeks, he believed it would become clear who was telling the truth and who was not.[28]

For an individual convicted in the Malmedy trial, however, repudiating a confession by swearing that it had been coerced by men seeking revenge on their defeated enemy would do more than demonstrate his innocence: it would absolve him of blame for his betrayals. American interrogators had made a mockery of the SS motto "My Honor Is Loyalty." In Schwäbisch Hall, and again in the sweltering Dachau courtroom, the accused had turned on each other. This fact, along with the fear of reprisals by their comrades, provided a powerful incentive for some defendants to exaggerate or invent claims of extreme duress applied to secure confessions. By participating in a collective effort in Landsberg, then, individuals could join a community of persecution, suffering, and redemption.

Conditions within Landsberg proved highly conducive to such an effort. "An observer," one American intelligence officer who had been investigating smuggling and other subversive activities noted, "would be under the impression that the Germany of 1933–1945 is being preserved."[29] Prisoners, who had many opportunities to associate with each other freely on a daily basis, had formed into distinct groups, one of them being comprised of former SS officers with Dietrich and Peiper as the figures commanding the most authority. Whatever personal animosities and disputes divided the members of the battle group, they could now be united on two related matters: the belief in the possibility of amnesty and a determination to never again reveal the truth about war crimes.[30] To write their own affidavits and those for other prisoners, the convicted men worked together in the prison's lecture hall, the process becoming what they referred to as "the Landsbergers' favorite sport."[31]

Eugen Leer was responsible for formatting the statements as legal documents and presenting them to Clay and then to the Simpson Commission.

He had served as Peiper's lawyer during the Malmedy trial and continued to represent many of the men convicted in that and other Dachau cases. In 1947 he began collecting statements from men he called "witnesses." That is, Waffen SS veterans not then in prison and eager to provide "new evidence" regarding imprisoned comrades. In his testimony before American senators in 1949, Leer insisted that the defense had been unable to locate these witnesses during the trial and that afterwards he had not sought them out. Rather, they had contacted him and inundated his office with statements proclaiming the convicted men's innocence.[32]

Leer was in fact working closely with several Waffen SS veterans who tracked down former comrades and coordinated their statements with the lawyer. Dietrich entrusted this task to Dietrich Ziemssen and Rolf Reiser. The former, a Personal Standard lieutenant colonel and defense witness in the Malmedy trial, would become one of the most active Waffen SS veterans in the amnesty campaign in 1949 and into the 1950s. Reiser, a second lieutenant in the First SS Panzer Regiment of Battle Group Peiper, had his sentence reduced by Clay and was released from Landsberg in early 1948. He began assisting Leer immediately, contacting other Waffen SS veterans, coordinating their statements, and also bringing the materials to the attention of high-level Protestant and Catholic church officials. The Munich address of another comrade from Peiper's regiment, Rudolf Woch, became a collecting point for correspondence with veterans in Germany. Woch also opened a bank account for donations to support Leer's work.[33] Over the next few years, veterans would be admonished to support their imprisoned comrades, as doing so was a matter of eradicating "the remains of a long-discredited revenge-justice."[34]

Intimidation of uncommitted comrades was also an important factor in producing such a large number of statements alleging very similar types of maltreatment and identifying repeatedly three interrogators by name as the abusers. In and outside Landsberg, Waffen SS veterans pressured their fellow veterans into renouncing their confessions. In mid-September 1947, Gerald Coates, a War Crimes Group investigator, took sworn statements from two men convicted in the Malmedy trial, Hans Hillig and Otto Wichmann, with the latter certifying that he had told the truth to interrogators in Schwäbisch Hall but had been pressured by defense lawyers to change his statement to avoid implicating superior officers. When Coates returned the following day to take another statement, Wichmann "gave me the very clear impression that he must have talked overnight with some of his comrades who must have changed him completely." Wichmann had in fact already told Coates that he feared that he would be "given a tough time" for his original statement.[35]

A few among the committed core of Waffen SS veterans outside Landsberg were willing to go further than this. In April 1948, CIC agents discovered a plot by some of Peiper's former subordinates to free him from Landsberg by force. The conspirators knew that Clay, unconvinced by Peiper's renunciations of his pretrial statements, had just confirmed his conviction and death sentence. They were apparently unaware, however, that Clay had stayed Peiper's execution pending the Supreme Court's decision on Everett's writ petition. They therefore conspired to break Peiper out of the prison. As Peiper had many supporters in Baden-Württemberg and Bavaria, the agents were unable to identify the individuals involved in the plot and decided to take no action other than tightening security at Landsberg and other war crimes enclosures.[36]

Also important were the sympathies and assistance of prison clergy, who aided the convicted men in transmitting documents to their church superiors. August Eckardt, the pastor warned by Werner Hess to beware of fictitious stories of torture, became active in smuggling out unapproved materials for the prisoners. Eckardt was a former member of the Stormtroopers and a Wehrmacht officer. He was convinced that the men in Landsberg were not war criminals, though admitted privately the torture stories were totally unbelievable. Yet he believed the prisoners, tortured or not, had been victimized in the trials. In March 1949, American officials uncovered Eckardt's smuggling operation and the commandant had him removed.[37]

More influential was Father Karl Morgenschweis, the Catholic prison priest. Morgenschweis had served in this post since 1932 and was esteemed highly by American officials. Their trust was misplaced, however, as Morgenschweis was even more determined than Eckardt to smuggle written materials out of the prison. He did so as part of what he later referred to as a "rescue action" aimed less at saving the souls of convicted murderers than helping them appeal their sentences. Unlike the Protestant pastors, who "unwisely" left materials prisoners had given them in their offices only to be discovered by the Americans, Morgenschweis simply took the documents home with him. In a speech in Munich in 1966, he boasted of his role in launching the amnesty campaign in Germany: "When [the prisoners] were brought here in 1947, they declared to me: 'we are not guilty. We were mistreated. They extorted the confessions from us.' . . . I collected everything they gave to me and in October 1947 and brought it to [Cardinal Josef Frings]. . . . He said to me 'I cannot do much with this material. You'd better go to his Excellency [Bishop Johannes] Neuhäusler.' When I went to Neuhäusler, he said the same to me: 'It seems right that you brought this, there are indeed Senators from America with whom I can discuss it and bring to them. At that was the beginning of it, because then the rescue action had been brought together with the American Colonel Everett, who led the defense in Dachau." Like Eckardt, Morgenschweis believed the convicted men in the Malmedy and other cases to be guiltless victims of Jewish "avenging angels." For Morgenschweis, they were responsible for what he considered the "real crimes" at Dachau.[38]

The Best, Most Immediate Witnesses

In the spring and summer of 1948, Leer submitted batches of affidavits as petitions to the War Crimes Group. In the first, sent while Clay was reviewing his Judge Advocate's recommendations on the Malmedy trial sentences, Leer requested the case be reopened. Should that not be possible, the sentences—above all the forty-three death sentences—had to be commuted. He based the request on what he considered "new evidence" from fifty-one affidavits, nearly all signed by Waffen SS veterans of Battle Group Peiper who had not been charged in the Malmedy case. Leer considered these men (and the many more who had yet to submit statements) "the best, most immediate witnesses for all phases of this offensive and consequently for all the assertions of the accused." Their credibility was enhanced, he believed, because they had all been cleared as war crimes suspects.[39]

The affidavits provided alibis for the convicted men, and thirty-two contained statements seeking to exonerate Peiper. His conduct, and that of other officers, was defended by assertions that they gave no orders to shoot prisoners and civilians in advance of the counteroffensive. On the contrary, NCOs and enlisted men had received clear instructions on the relevant provisions of international law. When prisoners were taken during the offensive they were invariably treated decently and "sent to the rear." As for the convicted triggermen, these new "witnesses" insisted that the accused were never at the places where crimes were supposed to have been committed. Indeed, most of the petitioners claimed that they—and by extension the accused—had never heard anything about any prisoners being executed. To these statements Leer added the argument that the conditions of combat in the Ardennes had led soldiers on both sides to fight with a savagery unconstrained by the formal rules of war.[40] For good measure he cited a long essay published in the *Atlantic Monthly* in February 1946 by Edgar L. Jones, a British Army veteran of the North African campaign and a wartime correspondent for the magazine who denounced war crimes trials on the grounds that the victors had also "fought a dishonorable war" and were thus in no position to pass judgment on the vanquished.[41]

The fact that nearly all the convicted men had either confessed to committing serious crimes or accused others of doing so had to be addressed, so Leer cited interrogation methods as another reason the case needed to be reopened. Like Everett, he asserted that *all* of the defendants had been subjected to "physical and psychological duress." Beginning in April, he submitted fifty affidavits from the convicted men that described repeated violent encounters with interrogators, interpreters, and guards.

Among them were two of what would become the most widely publicized statements concerning conditions in Schwäbisch Hall. One was from "Otto Eble." The other was from a German dentist, Eduard Knorr, who treated some Schwäbisch Hall prisoners and was identified by name in the *Chicago Daily Tribune*'s series on the torture allegations published in February 1949. Knorr wrote that "about 15 or 20 men had to be treated because of mouth and jaw injuries. Almost all of them showed distinct marks of blows. When I asked one young man how he was, he answered: 'How can I be, if almost every day, at any rate in every interrogation, I am beaten in such a manner.'" In a particularly dramatic flourish that would be repeated in the American and German presses, Knorr added that residents of the town of Schwäbisch Hall "heard the cries of pain and that great excitement and indignation arose amongst the population."[42]

Leer was not the only German lawyer submitting such petitions to American officials. Parallel to his efforts were those of Georg Froeschmann, a Nuremberg-based attorney. Froeschmann, a former Nazi Party member and unrepentant National Socialist, represented accused war criminals in the subsequent Nuremberg trials, notably Viktor Brack, the mastermind behind the Nazi regime's program of murdering the mentally and physically handicapped, and Gottlob Berger, the chief recruitment officer of the SS. His less well-known clients included hundreds of convicted war criminals imprisoned in Landsberg, notably former SS members.[43]

As we have seen, prisoners being held in the Dachau war crimes enclosure had attempted to smuggle written accusations of abuse at the hands of the mostly Jewish investigators—especially Joseph Kirschbaum—out of the camp. After intercepting some of these statements in the summer of 1947, American officials investigated conditions in Dachau and concluded that while the claims were largely baseless there were some disciplinary problems with respect to guards and that Kirschbaum in particular had become the object of intense hatred for his role in identifying prosecution witnesses. The more serious problem was the possibility that some prisoners were engaged in an organized attempt to discredit the army's trials and that there was likely a "guiding hand" outside the prison soliciting the statements for this purpose.

It is possible that Georg Froeschmann initiated some of this activity. He was certainly well informed about it. By early 1948, Froeschmann had in fact become the "guiding hand" in amassing statements from many of those convicted in the Dachau trials. In what was known as the "Froeschmann action," he and a handful of Waffen SS veterans then imprisoned in Landsberg collected statements—mostly from other prisoners—alleging witness tampering and abusive pretrial investigative methods by American interrogators in several Dachau trials. A few prisoners involved in the "action" who became disillusioned after it became apparent that Froeschmann was interested only in aiding Waffen SS veterans, told American officials that "former big-shot Nazis who had money are trying to discredit the Americans and are willing to pay for it," and that false statements were being made.[44]

While Leer was focused on the Malmedy case, Froeschmann targeted all the Dachau trials. In a series of letters, petitions, and cables sent to Clay and Judge Advocate officials in Germany in the summer and fall of 1948, Froeschmann insisted that dozens of sworn statements demonstrated that investigative misconduct, procedural irregularities, and severe limits placed on defense lawyers were pervasive at Dachau. Indeed, he suggested that another version of a "guiding hand" was at work, as "the similar, recurring observations, with which those affected in various camp cases made independently of one another, gives the impression that what was involved was a systematic depriving of the rights of the accused through the methods applied by prosecution officials."[45]

Froeschmann's statements described an intensifying ordeal of abuses that began when suspects arrived at Dachau. Unnamed American officers and "soldiers of the CIC" first stole their rings, watches, cigarette cases, and whatever money they had on them. Prisoners were then subjected to various forms of humiliation and abuse, including denial of medical care, periods of solitary confinement, and bans on letter writing, the cumulative effect of which was to "make these people gradually psychically and physically softened up." These measures had the desired effect. The suspects soon made incriminating statements the prosecution would later use against them in court. Froeschmann contended that since their ordeals had rendered the accused "spiritually and physically tormented," with undernourishment weakening their powers of recall, they were unable to be of any assistance to their own lawyers at trial.

Froeschmann singled out Kirschbaum and two other Jewish émigré officers as the prosecution officials responsible for the worst abuses. He accused these men of turning one of the barracks in Dachau into a macabre theater of abuse by paying (or perhaps coercing) former concentration camp inmates to "identify" suspects in a series of "stage shows" in which terrified and bewildered suspects were paraded before a howling mob of "witnesses" who would identify them as the perpetrators of crimes in the camps. Froeschmann did not question that the witnesses had been prisoners in the Dachau and other camps, but insisted that the investigators had selected common criminals and former kapos (prisoners who helped the Germans control the prisoner populations) and turned them into "professional witnesses." The alleged pattern of abuse documented in his clients' sworn statements, Froeschmann concluded, could only leave one with the impression that the prosecution was seeking the largest possible number of convictions "in order to effectively prove the allegation, already widespread before and after the war's end, of the vast extent of the atrocities in the concentration camps."[46]

In his longest petition to Clay, Froeschmann noted that criticism of war crimes trials was intensifying in the United States. The American judge Charles Wennerstrum's dustup with Telford Taylor over the former's characterization of the subsequent Nuremberg trials as simple victor's justice had taken place a few months earlier. In late July, Froeschmann reminded

Clay—as if it were necessary—that Secretary of the Army Royall had just ordered an independent review of the army's trials by the Simpson Commission. Less than two months after Froeschmann sent his first long petition, a U.S. Senate subcommittee opened hearings on Clay's decision to commute Ilse Koch's life sentence. By early October 1948, American newspaper commentators were referring to the army's trials as "a sadistic farce by any standards of justice." It was then that the American lawyer Leon Poullada explained to readers of the Washington *Evening Star* that Jewish "avenging angels" were corrupting the army's trials.[47] At the beginning of 1949 the controversy over the Malmedy case was intensifying to the point where Froeschmann began to worry that Americans might think the methods of Kirschbaum and other German-born Jews had been limited to that case.[48]

What Froeschmann wanted was for the Americans to overturn the death sentences and approve a "neutral investigation" of all army trials. By "neutral" he meant a review by "qualified American jurists" completely unconnected to the Dachau prosecution staff and taking into account the "guidance of German magistrates." After examining Froeschmann's materials, however, EUCOM's Judge Advocate concluded that they offered nothing that warranted halting executions, let alone a retrial of hundreds of cases. American officials had investigated alleged abuses at the Dachau war crimes enclosure a year earlier and had conducted multiple reviews of the Malmedy and other Dachau cases. As Froeschmann had twice met with the Simpson Commission, the Judge Advocate recommended that his request for a meeting with Clay be denied.[49]

Throughout the summer and early fall of 1948 War Crimes Group lawyers and the Judge Advocate's War Crimes Board of Review examined the petitions and concluded that they were without legal merit. In their views, Leer had added nothing new in terms of the law or fact that had not been dealt with at the trials or in the posttrial reviews.[50] The "new evidence" gathered by Leer, moreover, strained credulity to the breaking point. It would have been difficult for an American observer, let alone a Judge Advocate lawyer, to take seriously the claim that the former Waffen SS comrades of the convicted men were "the best, most immediate witnesses for all phases of this offensive and consequently for all the assertions of the accused." Even more incredible were the accusations of torture. They were of a suspiciously uniform nature, with some of the descriptions—"if you do not write we shall crack your testicles just as in concentration camps," "it is a pity to waste bullets on you. We only have strong pieces of rope which we tie onto a tree. Then you can take one more deep breath and up you go"—reading like a hack screenwriter's attempt at dramatizing interrogation.[51]

Leer and Froeschmann, like Everett, would not accept the official American contention that the trials had been reviewed adequately. Also like Everett, they had taken a maximalist position on the army's trials. For them, nothing less than new reviews involving German jurists and retrials of all cases would be acceptable. The fact that Clay had already reduced many sentences—including most of those in the Malmedy case—meant nothing. That Royall had ordered a halt to executions and dispatched the Simpson Commission to Germany had seemed promising: the commission's members had no connection to army prosecutors and they did not speak to a single person with firsthand knowledge of the pretrial investigation. Indeed, most of the individuals they interviewed—including Leer and Froeschmann—were hostile to the army's trials. Yet in the end, the commission's final report found the torture accusations unbelievable and Clay ordered the execution of Landsberg prisoners under death sentences to be resumed.

Despite this setback, the two lawyers' efforts had a powerful effect on the emerging Malmedy controversy in the United States. The affidavits provided the most important sources for the spate of newspaper and magazine stories appearing in early 1949. Like other German critics of the Malmedy and other trials, Leer reached out to Americans he believed to be in sympathy with his clients' situation, or at least those who were critical of war crimes trials. His affidavits were cited by Larry Rue, the *Chicago Daily Tribune* reporter responsible for the four-part expose of supposed prisoner abuse in February. Another target was Everett. Leer sent him his petition, though it could not be translated in time to be included with the writ petition to the Supreme Court. Most important, however, were both Edward Van Roden's willingness to relay the grotesque details of the torture stories to audiences in the United States and the gullibility of the American press in publishing them without considering that they may have been utter nonsense.

In Germany, what was to be more effective than formal petitions was a version of Everett's "sword of public opinion." In this case, the sword would be wielded by two of Germany's most influential Catholic and Protestant church officials.

ELEVEN

Avenging Angels

German Clergy and the Massacre

"From my experience," the German Protestant bishop Theophil Wurm wrote the director of the U.S. Office of Military Government Württemberg-Baden in May 1948, "petitions do not always manage to reach the crucial departments; they are in the habit of reacting only when the public is brought into play."[1] This missive from one of Germany's most influential clergymen captures the strategy pursued at the time by American and German opponents of war crimes trials: if American officials could not be convinced to retry cases or overturn unjust sentences, then public pressure might force them to do so. The seventy-nine-year-old Wurm, who had served as Württemberg's bishop since 1933, became one of the most aggressive practitioners of this approach. In 1948 he and his counterpart in the Catholic Church, Archbishop Johannes Neuhäusler, used their considerable authority to discredit the Malmedy and other war crimes trials in occupied Germany.

In the first postwar years, lower-level clergy provided invaluable assistance to former Nazi Party members and convicted war criminals. They aided wanted war criminals in hiding their identities and escaping Europe. During the height of the denazification purges in 1945 and 1946, they wrote countless testimonials in support of Germans facing the loss of their positions, including for those who were guilty of serious crimes. As we have seen, they transmitted the Landsberg prisoners' torture affidavits to German lawyers and to their superiors. But only the leadership of both churches had the visibility and authority to challenge American and British occupation officials directly and to appeal to influential sympathizers abroad.[2]

It would be the accusations of prisoner abuse that intensified preexisting opposition to denazification and war crimes trials. Not content with pleading with skeptical officials like Lucius D. Clay, Wurm and Neuhäusler turned to more sympathetic Americans and then the German press to publicize what they considered irrefutable evidence that the verdicts in the Malmedy and other cases were illegitimate. For Wurm in particular, the trials were nothing more than base acts of vengeance. While both men were convinced that Jewish "avenging angels" were responsible for the abuses, they could not use such language in public. They could, however, present the accusations as graphic proof that the Allied war effort, which many Germans believed to be a war of revenge against them, was continuing "clad in sham forms of law," as Wurm would put it after receiving copies of the torture affidavits.[3]

The emerging controversy in the United States over the Malmedy case was a godsend for amnesty advocates like Wurm and Neuhäusler. By pointing to Secretary of the Army Kenneth Royall's hesitation to see the death sentences carried out and the growing number of American press reports on the torture allegations, some of which identified the backgrounds of the interrogators, German critics were able to "giv[e] 'authenticity'" to their claims of corrupt pretrial investigations, as William Perl would shrewdly observe.[4] By the end of 1948, American War Crimes Group and intelligence officials were admitting—privately—that the campaign against the Malmedy and other Dachau trials was having the intended effect on German public opinion. It would be for good reason, then, that the former Luftwaffe general Hans Korte would credit Wurm and Neuhäusler in the pages of the *Deutsche Soldaten Zeitung* with playing a crucial role in the campaign to free the men convicted in the Malmedy case.[5]

Bowing before Baal

Germany's Christian churches occupied a position of unique authority and influence in the early postwar years. This authority had several sources. One was the fact that that they were the only institutions to have remained intact in the wake of Germany's defeat and occupation. They were in a position to provide spiritual and material aid to millions of traumatized and uprooted Germans, including soldiers and Nazi functionaries being held in Allied prisoner of war camps. Another emerged from the efforts of both churches to forge an exculpatory self-image as victims of a criminal and fundamentally anti-Christian dictatorship. In statements issued from the highest levels of their hierarchies, Catholic and Protestant clergy declared that the churches had resisted the regime and suffered the consequences, thereby granting themselves enormous moral authority in the war's bleak aftermath. Going even further, they claimed that despite intensifying persecution, the vast majority of Christians had never willingly worshipped the false gods of Adolf Hitler, the Nazi Party, and National Socialist ideology.

There was a degree of truth behind this explanation of the churches' fate in Nazi Germany. But support for the regime, or at least quiet compliance, had been the rule in both churches and among the vast majority of Christians. Most church leaders, priests, and pastors never resisted the regime in any active, meaningful way. Both churches' records on the persecution of the Jews and the Holocaust are especially dismal. Theological, political, and even racial anti-Semitic sentiments were common currency among most Catholic or Protestant clergy, and very few spoke out against the regime's anti-Jewish policies or acted on behalf of Jews. Prominent Protestants who denounced the persecution of *all* Jews (and not just those who had converted), like Dietrich Bonhoeffer or less prominent clergy or lay Christians who took enormous risks protecting individual Jews, were exceptionally rare.[6]

Immediately after the war, the churches were not entirely uncritical of their own records, nor were they unwilling to admit the failings of the lay public. As German Catholic bishops convening in Fulda in August 1945 declared, "We profoundly deplore the fact that many Germans, even within our own ranks, allowed themselves to be deceived by the false teachings of National Socialism, [and] remained indifferent to the crimes against human freedom and dignity, many by their attitude lent support to the crimes, many became criminals themselves." A similar statement from the Council of the Protestant Church in Germany came two months later. In the Stuttgart Declaration of Guilt, the leaders of Germany's Protestants wrote "we not only know that we are with our people in a large community of suffering, but also in a solidarity of guilt. With great pain we say: By us infinite wrong was brought over many peoples and countries." While the signatories, writing "in the name of the whole Church," added that "we" struggled against

National Socialism, "we [nonetheless] accuse ourselves for not standing to our beliefs more courageously."[7]

Yet these statements were hedged, qualified, and controversial within both churches' establishments and among the laity. The bulk of the Catholic bishops' statement praised the great majority of Catholics for having "never bowed before Baal." Since it could not be denied that many Catholics had joined the Nazi Party, the bishops argued that most had done so "with the good intention of preventing evil" or out of ignorance or because they had been coerced. Left out of the statement's final version were passages critical of the church and references to anti-Semitism and the Holocaust. These omissions provoked a critical reaction among some conscience-stricken lay Catholics and a few lower-level clergymen. The bishops had not really taken responsibility for the failures of the church, according to Eugen Kogon, the most prominent of the lay critics and a survivor of seven years' internment in Buchenwald. Nor had most Germans acknowledged the "bitter truth" that Germans knew of the regime's crimes and did next to nothing.[8]

The Protestant Church's Stuttgart Declaration was also controversial from within and outside the church. The declaration was the result of a demand by non-German members of the Ecumenical Council of Churches that the German Protestant establishment issue a formal statement of contrition and responsibility. Eleven of the church's most prominent leaders signed it. With the notable exception of Martin Niemoeller, who spent eight years in concentration camps, all the other signatories were not the active resisters to National Socialism they claimed to be. Despite its forthright assertion that the Protestant Church joins with the laity in a "community of guilt" for inflicting "infinite wrong . . . over many peoples and countries," the statement's wording was opaque. Specifics about victims and perpetrators were absent. Rather, any meaningful distinction between the two was erased by the claim that *all* Germans in 1945 belonged to a "community of suffering." What was needed now, the signatories insisted, was the unification of Germany's fractured Protestant churches and "a new beginning," a spiritual renewal that would "cleanse" the church "of the influences alien to faith."[9]

In what might be seen as a preliminary salvo in the church's fight against denazification and war crimes trials, the Stuttgart Declaration concluded with a plea that a renewed Protestant Church would also seek to "control the spirit of violence and revenge, which wants to become powerful again."

While very few Germans would object to blunting the vengeful urges of the victors, many found the phrase "by us infinite wrong was brought over many peoples and countries" highly objectionable. For these critics, the signatories had ignored the suffering of Germans from the hungry years of World War I to the expulsion of millions of ethnic Germans from Eastern Europe. Where the statement's reference to "solidarity of guilt" did find support was among Germans imprisoned in Allied camps, who welcomed a sharing of responsibility rather than having all of the blame for the war and the Nazis' crimes heaped on them. A pastor ministering to prisoners in the Moosburg internment camp near Munich recalled this telling response to the declaration among his flock, the majority of which was comprised of ex–Nazi Party functionaries and members of the SS: "At least they [the signatories] did not arrogantly distance themselves from everything."[10]

A Mistake but Not a Crime

From the end of the war through the early 1950s, Catholic and Protestant church leaders made opposition to denazification and war crimes trials their most important political causes. In principle there was no disagreement with Allied officials that German society had to be purged of Nazism's influences and that those who had committed crimes should be punished. The difference was that church officials had defined themselves, their institutions, and the lay population as blameless victims of a godless regime. In their collective view, there was little to expiate. Statements expressing regret that the churches had not taken a stronger stand against the regime and acknowledging that terrible crimes had been committed had already been issued. Moreover, individual Christians were obligated to confess their sins and seek atonement for any injustices they may have committed. On a collision course with this position was the American determination to implement a sweeping program of denazification and prosecute those who had committed war crimes and crimes against humanity.

Denazification was intended to remove all traces of Nazi influence from German society. This involved everything from taking down street signs bearing Hitler's name to purging individuals from positions of responsibility in public life, including businesses large and small, and possibly punishing them with fines or prison sentences. While the governments of all four

Allied nations agreed denazification should take place, each was responsible for carrying it out in its respective occupation zone. The Americans cast the widest net. Before the war ended, SHAEF had identified automatic arrest categories for Nazi Party functionaries, including all members of the SS, and tens of thousands were arrested in the American zone alone in the summer and early fall of 1945. At the same time, all adult Germans were required to fill out a lengthy questionnaire about their backgrounds. This was mainly in order to reveal whether an individual had been among the 8 million members of the Nazi Party or the 4 million belonging to one or more of its affiliated organizations. The standard for judging whether a person was to be removed from public office or "positions of importance in quasi-public and private enterprises" was whether he or she had been a "nominal" participant, an "active supporter of Nazism or militarism," or "hostile to Allied purposes."[11]

Defenders of denazification pointed out at the time that it accomplished the "clearing away work for a new, democratic German society," as an American official with extensive experience with the program in Bavaria put it. But the policy proved to be so burdensome and unpopular that it was effectively abandoned by 1948.[12] For the occupiers, there was the problem of carrying out the purges while dealing with the destruction and dislocation of the war's immediate aftermath. "You can imagine our difficulties," the first head of the regional military government in Württemberg-Baden wrote to a friend four months after VE Day, "if you can place yourself in the position of trying to reorganize the state of Indiana—throwing out of office everybody that had a pleasant word to say for [former governor] Paul McNutt. No, I am wrong; you cannot imagine the situation because you would have to throw in destroyed cities, no coal or gas, and a food ration about one-half that the people have been accustomed to."[13]

Because the parameters of the purge were so expansive, Germans saw a charge of collective guilt being leveled at them. This was despite the fact that the decision to remove an individual from his job was to be based on the extent to which he had demonstrated more than "nominal" commitment to the Nazi Party. But what did that even mean? How could it be determined in so many cases with fairness and accuracy? And few failed to notice that ex-Nazis still found ways to assume their former positions. "The whole blessed caboodle of the Nazis' heyday, that we thought destroyed," one infuriated

German lawyer wrote in an editorial for a Mannheim newspaper, "has reappeared at this provincial witches' Sabbath, disguised as good, honest democratic fellows. . . . They sneak into office and help each other to position and honors, and the renazification of Germany is being achieved by brazen bureaucratic tactics."[14]

Clergy at all levels denounced denazification repeatedly to American officials and in the press, and then actively impeded its implementation. They pointed out—with some justification—that it punished an individual not for what he or she had done, but for simply belonging to the party or one of its organizations. Joining the party may have been a political mistake, they insisted, but it should not be regarded as a crime.[15] "How can those who joined for idealistic reasons now be called guilty?" Bishop Wurm asked in an interview with the *New York Times*. He and other clergy also feared that the purges were allowing leftists and possibly even communists to take positions once held by Nazi Party members.[16] At the most basic level, however, the purges challenged the clergy's assertion that most Germans had been anti-Nazis.

As denazification affected millions of their congregants, clergy responded to the endless pleas for help that flooded their offices by providing affidavits testifying to the good Christian character of the accused. Such affidavits became known as *Persilscheine*, after a popular brand of detergent. The irony, of course, was that clergymen issuing *Persilscheine* were now guilty of what they had been denouncing the Americans for doing: certifying the innocence of an individual with little or no knowledge of whether that person had been more than a "nominal" Nazi. In early 1948, almost two years after the Americans had turned over most of the responsibility for handling cases to local German denazification boards, Martin Niemoeller went so far as to insist that Protestants stop assisting the prosecution and forbade clergy in Hesse-Nassau from "justify[ing] this scandal any longer by doing any work in connection with denazification."[17]

Pressure to Revisit the Cases

As the Americans limited and then ended denazification, the churches' opposition to war crimes trials intensified. The most influential voices in both churches took the position that very few were responsible for committing war crimes or crimes against humanity, a position that contradicted the first postwar statements admitting that "many Germans . . . became criminals" or "by us infinite wrong was brought over many peoples." Similarly, while the August 1945 bishops' statement had affirmed that those guilty of crimes should be held accountable in courts of law, Catholic church leaders soon began denouncing war crimes tribunals, including the IMT, which most Germans supported at the time. Both Catholic and Protestant bishops objected to the tribunal on the grounds that Germany was not the only nation guilty of starting the war—a clear reference to the 1939 Nazi-Soviet nonaggression pact—or of committing war crimes, and the related accusation that the tribunal was merely a vehicle to dispense victor's justice.[18]

The leadership of both churches became much more outspoken after the subsequent Nuremberg trials got under way in 1947. For one thing, this court prosecuted individuals from Germany's pre-Nazi military, political, and economic elite. Of the twelve trials, four involved high-ranking officers of the Wehrmacht or Luftwaffe; three prosecuted directors of the IG Farben, Flick, and Krupp conglomerates; and one focused on officials in government ministries. In the eyes of the clergy, most of these men were never committed National Socialists, let alone guilty of criminal acts. Church leaders ignored the abundant incriminating evidence that in most cases suggested otherwise. That the trials were coming under increasing critical scrutiny in the United States and Great Britain only bolstered their confidence and encouraged them to continue pressuring American and British officials to end the trials and release those convicted.

The U.S. Army's trials, and especially the Malmedy case, became the other target of intense opposition by the churches. Here their attacks were directed primarily at the pretrial investigations. On the Catholic side, the cause of the men convicted in the army's cases was taken up by Archbishop Johannes Neuhäusler. Neuhäusler's anti-Nazi credentials were impressive. In 1932 Cardinal Michael Faulhaber, then archbishop of Munich and Freising, brought Neuhäusler to the Munich Cathedral chapter, where he served as a political adviser. One of his responsibilities was to collect evidence of violations of the Concordat signed in 1933 between the regime and the Catholic Church. In early 1941, he was arrested after refusing to obey a regime order to prevent one of Faulhaber's pastoral letters from being read in public. It is also possible that the Gestapo had traced to Neuhäusler's office the source of materials for the book *The Persecution of the Churches in the Third Reich*, which

Archbishop Johannes Neuhäusler (Archiv des Erzbistums München und Freising).

had been translated by the Vatican into English and published in London in 1940. Neuhäusler would spend the remainder of the war in Sachsenhausen and Dachau.

In February 1947 the pope appointed Neuhäusler archbishop of Munich and Freising, making him the most influential German Catholic Church official in the American occupation zone. Neuhäusler had already become an important purveyor of the church's postwar narrative of victimization and resistance. His profile as a victim of the Nazis was raised by his testimony at the army's trial of Dachau concentration camp personnel. In a two-volume book published in Germany in March 1946, Neuhäusler documented the church's resistance to the Nazis. His prominence and wartime experience as a camp inmate ensured that the hefty volumes would become landmark works in the Catholic Church's efforts to refute charges of complicity with the Nazis. It would not be until the 1960s that it was revealed that he had distorted and falsified some of the material to present the church's record in a more positive light.[19]

Catholic and Protestant clergy in Landsberg were Neuhäusler's most important source of prisoner complaints about the Dachau trials, and it was largely at their prompting that he took up the matter with American officials. In September 1947, Neuhäusler, along with members of the new Bavarian state government and representatives of the Protestant Church, met with a delegation of five American congressmen. When asked for his opinion of the Nuremberg trials, Neuhäusler replied that they had been justified in the cases of the highest-level Nazi officials. The trials at Dachau, however, were another matter. At that point, Neuhäusler was concerned with the selection of prosecution witnesses, which prison clergy had assured him were giving false testimony in exchange for money, housing, and food.[20]

In March 1948, Neuhäusler wrote the same five congressmen about the Malmedy case, this time focusing on the torture accusations. Since his meeting with them the previous September, Karl Morgenschweis had assured the archbishop that "many of [convicted men] are absolutely to be believed when they protest again and again, not to have committed the crimes of which they are accused, saying that their 'confessions' were brought about by terrible ill treatments and threats." On top of Morgenschweis's smuggled documents, Neuhäusler had received copies of Eugen Leer's petition and the prisoners' affidavits. The latter reinforced his belief that the pretrial procedures in the other Dachau cases were totally corrupt. "It is appalling to learn what the different defendants had to suffer during the inquest," Neuhäusler wrote the congressmen, "how—besides legal tricks—by ill treatment of every kind, starving, exposure to cold, faked 'confessions' of others, threats, promises in the case of a confession, fictitious shrivings by examining magistrates disguised as clergymen, coercive dictates and so on, these 'statements' were brought about."[21]

While Neuhäusler told the congressmen that he had no desire to see the crimes of National Socialists "left unexpiated"—he reminded them that he had spent over four years in a concentration camp—he could not bear to see innocent men executed. Aware that Willis Everett's efforts to expose the interrogators' methods and nullify the verdicts had been unsuccessful, the archbishop beseeched the congressmen to demand a halt to further executions and begin a new investigation "without threats and torture-like coercive measures."

Neuhäusler did not know that Clay had commuted all but 12 of the death sentences to life terms, reduced 29 other sentences, overturned 13 convictions, and halted executions. One of the congressmen, Francis Case, while also unaware of Clay's decision, was highly sympathetic to Neuhäusler's plea. "It just so happens," Case wrote in his reply to the archbishop, "that some weeks ago an American lawyer told me of his own feeling that the sacred principles of evidence and justice were violated in the Malmedy process" and that "the United States has everything to gain and nothing to lose in assuring competent authority that the convictions and sentences awarded are merited." Case delivered Neuhäusler's letter and the supporting documents to Kenneth Royall just as the army was facing the likelihood of greater political and public scrutiny over the Malmedy case. Case asked that they be given "the most expeditious consideration possible," adding that Neuhäusler was a victim of the Nazis who then "impressed [the congressional delegation] with his general sincerity and honesty."[22]

As criticism of the Malmedy and other army trials became more persistent in the United States, Neuhäusler and his legal advisers continued to pressure American officials to revisit the cases. While he assured Case and the other congressmen that he had withheld supposedly incriminating materials from the public, the Christian News Service, a Munich-based German Catholic and Protestant agency licensed by the Americans, publicized the archbishop's appeal. The agency reported that in March 1948 Neuhäusler had received hundreds of pages of documents about the Malmedy trial, most notably "several dozen sworn statements from the convicted concerning severe mistreatment and deceptions through which confessions had been extracted." Noting that he had transmitted the material and his demand for stays in executions pending a new inquiry to Clay and U.S. congressmen, the wording of the press release implied that it was Neuhäusler's intervention that resulted in the sentence reductions Clay had ordered several months earlier.[23]

Leer sent Neuhäusler more petitions on behalf of Landsberg prisoners and by the summer the archbishop's demand for new reviews of the trials became more specific. "Where there is such a great probability that witnesses gave wrong evidence, avowals were forced, witnesses for the defendants and exonerating material could not be produced quickly enough and so on," Neuhäusler wrote Clay's chief political adviser Robert Murphy in July, "only a revision-trial together with a new inquiry . . . can redress the balance and give consolation."[24] By "revision-trial" Neuhäusler did not mean the creation of a court of appeals. What he wanted was entirely new trials. In August the Catholic Church's bishops backed Neuhäusler's demand.[25]

Neuhäusler received more prisoner statements that summer from Georg Froeschmann and Rudolf Aschenauer. Like Froeschmann, Aschenauer was a former Nazi Party member and lawyer who would play an increasingly important role in discrediting the Malmedy trial in Germany. In a new petition delivered to Lucius D. Clay in late August, Neuhäusler cited the quantity of sworn statements he had received—this time from men convicted in the "fliers" and concentration camp trials—as the reason he could no longer "remain silent," though at this point he claimed he was still unwilling to make the material public. Rather, he wanted to convince American officials of the need for new trials, for "even if only fragments of the statements made by the condemned men proved true, I think it would be a claim of justice as well as the honor of the American [jurisprudence] to try everything in order to find out the truth." His petition included accusations that interrogators, notably Joseph Kirschbaum and Josef Metzger, tricked and coerced suspects, that defense witnesses were threatened or bought off, and that dozens of prosecution witnesses had perjured themselves in court.[26]

Neuhäusler's reticence to release this material to the press is understandable. The petitioners had been convicted of very serious crimes in the camps. Among the material submitted to the Americans was a ten-page letter from Karl Mayer, a former kapo in the Flossenbürg concentration camp. At Mayer's trial before an army court, multiple witnesses accused him of beating prisoners, participating in executions, and stealing personal possessions. The court sentenced him to life imprisonment. Mayer now insisted that it was "communists" in the camp who dominated the prisoners at the behest of the SS. "In their very ranks," he wrote, "there were mostly criminal elements and today the communist party has to be considered as the pool for all 'professional criminals.' From their ranks were taken the professional witnesses for the prosecution in the KZ [concentration camp] trials." Mayer believed these "communists" were successful because they were aided by "the great many German emigrants occupied at the American court of inquiry at Dachau who often themselves because of their communist intrigues were persecuted by the Hitler regime and therefore went abroad." Mayer also accused the CIC, which counted many German Jewish émigrés among its ranks, of paying witnesses to testify against him and other defendants,

"90 percent" of whom were "professional criminals and communists, professional bullies, notorious loafers, homosexual people, [and] therefore the dregs of the KZ inmates."

That German clergy and the lay population would believe accusations that concentration camp inmates were unreliable witnesses because they were nothing more than criminals should not be surprising. The Nazi regime had told the public repeatedly that the camps were used to hold not only political subversives but "asocial" elements—a broad category encompassing criminals, the homeless, the "workshy," homosexuals, and sometimes Roma and Sinti peoples.[27] While Neuhäusler may have been skeptical about some of the petitioners' accusations, his receptivity to their complaints reflected his agreement with the basic position taken by the convicted men: that most inmates of the concentration camps were not truly victims of Nazi persecution. Neuhäusler, of course, could not state this publicly after 1945, let alone endorse Mayer's linkage of communists and Jews. He could argue that merely the existence of statements such as Mayer's should justify a retrial or at least an independent clemency board.

Neuhäusler's criticisms were by then familiar to War Crimes Branch officials, but the archbishop's stature in Germany and his connections to prominent Americans made yet another review of the materials necessary. The frustration of the officer given this responsibility, Major Joseph Haefele, is palpable in his response to the chief of EUCOM's War Crimes Branch. Haefele pointed out that all of the cases in Neuhäusler's petitions had been reviewed, some of them multiple times by different reviewing bodies. Every review concluded that the accused had received fair trials and the evidence presented had justified the verdicts and sentences. As for Neuhäusler's charge that prosecution witnesses had given false testimony, Haefele noted that "the cry of 'perjury' has long been a favorite with the accused in War Crimes cases, particularly in petitions submitted subsequent to trial" and that none of the accused had been convicted solely on the testimony of the alleged perjurers identified by the archbishop.[28]

Haefele was also unimpressed by complaints about the behavior of interrogators in identifying suspects. Neuhäusler's understanding of how prosecutors had obtained witnesses was based entirely on the assertions of the convicted. When War Crimes Group officials first became aware in 1947 that convicted concentration camp personnel were claiming that the mostly

German Jewish interrogators had presided over "stage shows," they investigated and concluded that such accounts were gross exaggerations and distortions of how the process of identifying suspects actually worked. Haefele was well aware of this of this "old familiar song," as he put it in response to the archbishop's attempt to revive the "stage show" charge. Those unfamiliar with the "peculiarly American institution" of the police lineup, he wrote, seemed to believe that their convictions were predetermined during the process of eyewitness identification. For Haefele, this was "such a far cry from the truth that it needs no answer."[29]

Clay's advisers were no doubt relieved to pass Neuhäusler's petitions along to Judge Gordon Simpson, who was at that time preparing his report on the sentences in the army's cases. Neuhäusler and other trial critics were heartened by the opportunity to present their petitions to a body of American officials unconnected to the trials and appointed by the secretary of the army. Neuhäusler, Froeschmann, and Aschenauer all met with Simpson and members of his commission. But neither it nor the AJRB's initial report on Everett's writ petition found convincing evidence of the abuses reported by Neuhäusler or the convicted men's lawyers.

Clay's decision to resume executions at Landsberg incited Neuhäusler to turn to the press. In late October, the *Muenchner Allgemeine (Munich General)* newspaper published a statement in which the archbishop informed readers that he had resisted making public comments about the trials out of a desire to avoid creating a "sensation." But now Neuhäusler deemed it necessary to publicize his criticisms in hope of pressuring the Americans to hold retrials. The same newspaper also published verbatim a copy of the archbishop's August petition to American officials. Though he remained unwilling to make the convicted men's statements public, the message was clear enough to anyone reading his letter: the second-most powerful leader of the German Catholic Church possessed incriminating material that should raise serious doubts about the selection of prosecution witnesses and interrogation methods in the army's trials.[30]

In November, Neuhäusler found a clever way to get around American control of the German press and radio. When the military government in Bavaria denied his request to broadcast his critique on a Munich radio station unless he modified certain statements, he refused to make any changes and instead arranged for the *Regensburger Bistumsblatt (Regensburg Bishopric*

Journal) to publish the text of his address in the form of an interview with a reporter. In the interview he recounted how he became involved with the Dachau cases, again suggesting that it was his intervention with American congressmen that resulted in stays of execution at Landsberg. As more appeals from the convicted men and lawyers poured in, he continued to press American officials, focusing his objections on "third degree methods" and the alleged use of convicted criminals as "professional witnesses." His only objective, he assured the reporter, was to convince the Americans of the necessity of halting all executions until retrials could establish the truth.[31]

Neuhäusler also took the important step of widening German press coverage of the controversy in the United States over the Malmedy trial. At the end of 1948 he made contact with the NCPW. It was Neuhäusler who arranged for one of its press releases to be translated and published verbatim on the front page of the *Muenchner Allgemeine*. Under the dramatic headline "Americans Denounce US Military Tribunals," there was a facsimile of the NCPW's letter to Neuhäusler acknowledging the archbishop's plea for assistance. A short statement from the NCPW demanded a congressional investigation into the charges of prisoner abuse, the public exposure and prosecution of those American investigators "who had abused their powers as victors and trampled justice," and the suspension of executions pending a complete judicial review of the condemned men's cases.[32]

The NCPW's statement also introduced Judge Edward Van Roden as a member of the Simpson Commission whose "official report" of prisoner abuse had been submitted to Secretary of the Army Royall but was then, according to the NCPW, suppressed. An undeterred Van Roden began giving public speeches about what he had learned in Germany, and the *Allegemeine* included the NCPW's report on one of Van Roden's Rotary Club speeches in which he described in gruesome detail the torture of prisoners in Schwäbisch Hall and blamed the Malmedy massacre on "a few criminal and sadistic German individuals."[33]

The sensational front-page story concluded with a statement by James Finucane, the NCPW officer leading the campaign against the army's trials. Under the title "Reconciliation Set Back by Years," Finucane declared that many Germans and Americans found it painful to learn that Clay had ordered executions at Landsberg to resume, adding that Cardinal Josef Frings, Archbishop Neuhäusler, and Bishop Wurm had all implored President Truman to overrule the military governor. Clay, however, had dismissed Neuhäusler's repeated pleas for retrials with the explanation that the Simpson Commission's report had addressed all the relevant questions. Despite Everett's critique and those made by others in American legal journals, the "gallows continue to operate and the American investigators, who committed atrocities in the name of the American flag, remain free and undisturbed." Since no help was to be expected from the U.S. Supreme Court and Clay had refused to intervene on behalf of the convicted Landsbergers, Finucane saw a thorough investigation of army courts by Congress and the American Bar Association as the last hope for salvaging the reputation of American justice.[34]

"Americans Denounce US Military Tribunals" presented a distorted and in large part falsified account of what had actually happened before, during, and after the Malmedy trial. But the average *Allgemeine* reader would not have known that. Rather, she or he would have learned that an American judge appointed by the U.S. secretary of the army had come to Germany, investigated the army's trials with the assistance of two of Germany's most esteemed clergymen, and concluded that suspects had been abused by American interrogators before being subjected to farcical trials. The reader would have been appalled, if not surprised, to read that the army then tried to suppress the commission's report. Those who suspected war crimes trials were nothing more than a continuation of an Allied war of revenge against the Germans would only have their suspicions confirmed by "Americans Denounce US Military Tribunals."

Horrible Tormenting and Cruelties

By the end of 1948 Johannes Neuhäusler had become the most prominent German Catholic critic of the army's trials. When it came to the press, he had acted with some restraint. This was not the case with his counterpart in the Protestant Church, Bishop Theophil Wurm. Like most Protestant clergy, Wurm welcomed the Nazi Party's assumption of power in January 1933. Though he had been drawn briefly to the Nazi-oriented German Christian movement—a faction of intensely nationalist and anti-Semitic Protestants—he soon joined a dissenting Protestant faction known as the Confessing Church.

His efforts at blocking German Christian influences in Württemberg's churches resulted in his being placed under house arrest twice in 1934, actions that led to vigils by hundreds of supporters outside his home. In addition to being a highly esteemed bishop in the Stuttgart region, he was well connected to its political and economic elite. It was likely due to the intervention of Konstantin von Neurath, then Germany's foreign minister and a member of the Swabian nobility, that Wurm was released. Thereafter he remained free to tend to his duties as bishop.[35]

Four months after Hitler's appointment as chancellor, Wurm expressed to pastors in Württemberg "our gratitude for a rescue from serious danger and our joy at the fact that the new state attacks problems regarding the health of the Volk." By "health of Volk" he revealed a basic position to which he would hold consistently throughout the prewar and wartime years: Jews and "Jewish influence" over Germany's political, cultural, and economic life had to be removed. This attitude, however, did not preclude him from objecting to the removal of "non-Aryan" Christians from the ranks of the Protestant clergy. While "no Evangelical church has denied the state the right to implement racial legislation for the purpose of maintaining the purity of the German *Volk*," he wrote to the Evangelical Church Chancellery in December 1941, he insisted that there was no scriptural justification for "the exclusion of baptized non-Aryans."[36]

Wurm wrote those lines with full knowledge that the regime was at that moment attempting to exterminate the Jews of Europe. In December 1941, he was still reluctant to take a public stand on what was happening, though he addressed a letter to Hitler the same month. In it, he expressed concern that "much has occurred that could only be of use to enemy propaganda; among this, we count the measures for the removal of the mentally ill and the increasing harshness in the treatment of non-Aryans, even those who confess the Christian faith." A year later he became bolder, writing an Interior Ministry official that "in circles not confined to confessional Christians, one is depressed by how the struggle against other races and peoples is being conducted. People returning from vacation are reporting the systematic murder of Jews and Poles in the occupied territories. Even those who years ago considered Jewry's dominance in the most diverse areas of public life to be severely detrimental, at a time when almost the entire press was philosemitic, cannot accept that one people is justified in exterminating another people." After re-

The newly elected leadership of the Evangelical Church of Germany in 1945. Bishop Theophil Wurm stands third from left (EKD Pressedienst).

ceiving a letter from Wurm just before Christmas 1943 in which the bishop wrote "we Christians perceive this policy of extermination conducted against Jewry to be a grievous injustice and an ominous one for the German people," Hans Lammers, the president of the Reich Cabinet, warned Wurm that he was putting put his life at risk.[37]

Like other Germans, Wurm feared temporal retribution for the regime's crimes. "Can we be surprised," he wrote pastors in Stuttgart in August 1943, "if we, too, now get a taste of this?!"[38] The defeat at Stalingrad in January 1943 produced a crisis of civilian morale in Germany. Against this portent of defeat on the Eastern Front was the bombing campaign of German cities by the American and British air forces, which first targeted the Rhineland's industrial centers and rolled eastward throughout 1943. Right before Wurm wrote his pastors, a series of air attacks wrought massive destruction on the port city of Hamburg. In Stuttgart, large-scale bombings had begun the previous November and continued until early 1945. On April 22, 1945, the city was occupied by French forces, having surrendered without putting up the suicidal resistance local Nazi leaders had demanded of its residents. What followed was something of a sacking, as French troops assaulted German women and looted with near impunity.[39]

In terms of its leadership, the Württemberg Protestant Church remained intact across the divide of defeat, occupation, and denazification. Despite his advanced age—he would retire as state bishop in 1948—and the material hardships of the occupation's first years, Wurm remained active in church affairs, particularly in the creation in 1948 of a federation of Protestant churches (the Evangelical Church of Germany) to represent the vast majority of German Protestants. For several years he also threw himself into opposition to denazification and advocacy for accused and convicted war criminals. Material and logistical support for Wurm's efforts would be provided by a well-funded and well-connected group of lower-level Protestant Church officials who were using a charity created during the war, the Evangelical Relief Organization *(Evangelisches Hilfswerk),* as cover for publicizing Wurm's critiques and providing aid to convicted war criminals.[40]

Control of Stuttgart was transferred to the U.S. Army in early July 1945. As they did elsewhere in other badly damaged towns and cities under their control, American officials attempted to deal with the physical destruction and simultaneously began denazification investigations. All leading Protestant church officials opposed the purges, and Wurm—whose son had been sentenced to a year's imprisonment for falsifying his military government questionnaire—was an especially outspoken critic. For William Dawson, the first regional military government director of Württemberg-Baden, the Protestant Church and Bishop Wurm quickly became one of his "most interesting problems." In his first interview with Wurm, Dawson wrote a friend, "I was convinced of the sincerity of his anti-Nazi stand but he disclosed a rather naïve attitude towards some of his clergymen and church members who were ardent Nazis. He would admit no need for any conviction of sin in many of the things that had been done." Like other Germans, Wurm's attitude was no doubt shaped by the calamitous nature of Germany's defeat. "I believe that deep in his soul," Dawson observed, "he thinks that the conquest of Germany was much worse than the continuance of the Nazi regime with all its horrors."[41]

Like Neuhäusler, Wurm had not been active in opposing the main Nuremberg trials. He did, however, appeal privately to British officials on behalf of his onetime protector and fellow member of the Swabian elite, Neurath, who had been sentenced to fifteen years' imprisonment by the IMT.[42] Like most German clergymen, Wurm had received many pleas for help from prisoners of war and convicted war criminals and their families. Other Protestant clergy also beseeched him to intercede on behalf of their congregants. Lawyers in Wuerttemberg and Bavaria representing defendants in the subsequent Nuremberg trials or those already convicted supplied him with abundant materials about those cases. The affidavits from the men convicted in the Malmedy trial also reached Wurm in the spring of 1948, most likely from legal advisers to Neuhäusler or from Evangelical Relief Organization officials.[43]

Wurm had already made his debut as a trial critic. At the end of January 1948 he initiated, and then made public, an exchange of letters with the lawyer Robert Kempner. Kempner was the lead prosecutor in the Ministries case, the longest and most controversial of the subsequent Nuremberg trials. The case involved twenty-one former high-level officials of various government ministries—most notably the Foreign Ministry—accused of multiple counts of war crimes and crimes against humanity. The chief American prosecutor, Telford Taylor, had hoped to conduct four separate trials of such functionaries but felt compelled to combine them into one case known informally as the "Wilhelmstrasse Trial," after the street in central Berlin where most of the accused had their offices.[44]

In the Ministries case, the Americans accused a segment of Germany's pre-Nazi political and economic elite of complicity in some of the regime's most serious crimes, including the Holocaust. While two prominent SS officers—Gottlob Berger and Walter Schellenberg—were among the defendants, the rest were career diplomats or members of Germany's banking and industrial managerial elite. For Wurm, these men could not possibly be guilty. Their experiences, he believed, mirrored that of the clergy: compromises, such as joining the Nazi Party, had to be made and some had allowed patriotism to temporarily blind them to the Nazis' criminality, but in the end Germany's elite—including the clergy—did what it could to curtail the worst excesses.

If the fact that men like Neurath were being prosecuted as war criminals by the IMT's successor was not offensive enough to Wurm, there was the matter of Kempner's background. Anyone with the prosecutor's job would have become the target of the accused men's supporters, but what really distinguished Kempner was the fact that he was a German émigré who had been hounded out of his position as a high-level Prussian Interior Ministry official in 1935 because of his Jewish background. Kempner fled Germany and, after arriving in the United States in 1939, served as a consultant to the Department of Justice before being brought on as an adviser to Robert Jackson, the chief prosecutor in the main Nuremberg trials. Kempner was instrumental in preparing cases against individual defendants. His knowledge of German ministerial bureaucracies and his experience with the IMT also made him the ideal choice to serve as the lead prosecutor in the Ministries case.

Wurm was especially concerned with the charges against former Foreign Ministry officials, above all Ernst von Weizsäcker, whom he knew personally. Weizsäcker, a native of Stuttgart and a scion of one Württemberg's most prominent noble families, began his career in the Foreign Ministry in 1920. By 1938 he had become its second-highest-ranking official and spent the last two years of the war as Germany's ambassador to the Vatican. The Military Tribunal charged him with seven of the eight possible counts, including crimes against peace, war crimes, and crimes against humanity. The prosecution contended, based on documentation from the Foreign Ministry, that Weizsäcker had extensive knowledge of Germany's preparations for war and also knew about the mass murder of Jews. The most incriminating piece of evidence was a note by Weizsäcker on an SS cable stating that the Foreign Ministry did not object to the deportation of thousands of French Jews to Auschwitz.[45]

In Wurm's view, the Foreign Ministry was a bastion of sanity and "one of the few offices at which men like me were still listened to," he wrote to Kempner. Wurm recalled that when he visited with Weizsäcker and Neurath, the two always struck him as "aloof" from the Nazis. As to the question of how they could possibly have attained such high positions without being committed Nazis, Wurm asserted that they "were forced now and then to participate in things and to say things" to demonstrate their "National Socialist reliability" when their real purpose was to prevent "fanatics" from controlling the nation's diplomacy. Kempner was not convinced by any of Wurm's arguments. He pointed out to the bishop that, regardless of the actions of others, Germans were in fact responsible for war crimes and had to be held accountable. He was also unimpressed by Wurm's argument that men like Weizsäcker had attempted to use their prominent positions in order to prevent the "fanatics" from running rampant. If that were true, Kempner added, then they had failed spectacularly.[46]

Like other critics of the IMT, Wurm called attention to the Nazi-Soviet nonaggression pact and the hypocrisy of blaming only Germans for starting the war, a point he had already made—albeit privately—to the IMT's president, Sir Geoffrey Lawrence.[47] In a related line of attack, he argued to Kempner that by allowing the Soviet Union to join the IMT, the British and American governments had "bowed to the compulsion of the political situation" just as "the diplomats and generals during the Hitler regime, just as numberless German professors, officials, industrialists and men in the streets did." The implication was clear—all men, however respectable and however noble their motives, were susceptible to political pressure. To single out and prosecute only Germans for displaying such a fundamentally human trait was sheer hypocrisy. In this line of reasoning, "all" diplomats and military officials lacked "moral heroism" from 1936 to 1939, the years of Hitler's diplomatic revolution in Europe. Those who had failed to stop Hitler were in part responsible for starting the war, Wurm concluded, yet now they attempted to place all of the blame on Germany.[48]

Wurm felt it necessary to explain the nature of political pressure to Kempner because, as the bishop pointed out, Kempner was "not in Germany after 1933" and thus could not possibly appreciate "the attitude of the non-Nazi" which Wurm insisted was that of the "great majority." That someone persecuted by the regime, as Kempner was, would not understand the nature of "political pressure" or could not be considered a "non-Nazi" revealed the highly constricted nature of Wurm's capacities for compassion and honesty. This limitation prevented him from thinking through the implications of the Stuttgart Declaration—which he had signed—and its acknowledgment of "infinite wrong" committed against "many peoples and countries." The undeniable fact that Germany had invaded the Soviet Union and waged a war of conquest and destruction that cost the lives of millions of innocent people would, by any reasonable standard, qualify as "infinite wrong." Yet Wurm was incapable of accepting that the Soviet Union, the nation whose peoples had endured the greatest destruction, should now be afforded the chance to seek justice against at least some of the men responsible.[49]

Given Wurm's warped view of the Nazi regime and the war, it should not be surprising that he had no interest in considering the evidence against the accused. The evidence amassed by the prosecution certainly served the purpose that Wurm and other critics of denazification and trials had demanded: that the guilt of the individual for a crime be demonstrated. Since he refused to acknowledge the validity of any prosecution evidence, however, all he could do was deny the tribunal's legitimacy or accuse it of prosecuting the defendants for making "politically wrong decisions," such as not resigning their positions in protest. For Wurm, seemingly incriminating documents were mere "camouflage" deployed by men like Weizsäcker or Hans Lammers to provide them with ideological cover as they quietly worked against the regime's criminal actions. That the defense could produce no convincing evidence of such resistance did not seem to concern him. Nonetheless, he lectured Kempner that "camouflaged" opposition was a "dangerous game," and while it was admittedly "played in vain," these people were "not criminals."[50]

Wurm's tone changed sharply after he received copies of the Malmedy case torture affidavits. These revealed to him that basic fairness was not the only matter at stake in the trials: now he considered it proven that criminal acts had been perpetrated against the accused. "Criminal methods and detestable tortures were used to extort depositions and confessions," making the verdicts nothing more than "an act of revenge which is clad in sham forms of law." He warned Kempner that now the "broad public" would question the "moral authority" of *all* trials. The documentation only reinforced Wurm's belief in the hypocrisy of trying Germans while remaining "silent on other crimes and criminals of a similar kind." Kempner brushed aside Wurm's attempt to generalize from the abuse accusations surrounding the Dachau trials to the Nuremberg trials: "The war criminals who were sentenced in Nuremberg for murder etc.—I cannot form a judgment on cases in other places—have almost without exception made no confessions at all. They were sentenced on the strength of the official German documents from the Hitler period by which they wrote their sentences themselves long ago."[51]

In his final letter to Kempner on June 5, 1948, Wurm pointed to several instances in which subsequent Nuremberg trial defendants had reported being threatened by investigators with lengthy prison terms, immediate execution, or "extradition to a foreign power." Wurm had learned from Weizsäcker's defense counsel that during one of the IMT's cases, Kempner threatened a former state secretary in the Foreign Ministry with extradition to the Soviet Union. Not surprisingly, Wurm linked the accusations of abuse in the Malmedy case with Kempner's ill-considered threat: there was a pattern of coercion and abuse in the treatment of witnesses and defendants that ran from the IMT to the subsequent Nuremberg trials to the army's trials.[52] Wurm was not the only one to attack Kempner in public. Weizsäcker's lawyers and his former colleagues in the Foreign Ministry orchestrated a series of press attacks on Kempner, replete with thinly veiled anti-Semitic references.[53]

Without warning Kempner, Wurm released their initial exchange of letters to the press, which then covered their debate extensively.[54] The dramatic appeal of the duel between the two was undeniable: it pitted multiple faces of pre-Nazi, Nazi, and postwar Germany against each other. On the one side there was Wurm, at that time Germany's most esteemed and influential Protestant clergyman and a man most Germans and Americans believed to be a bona fide anti-Nazi. Hostile to the Weimar Republic, a "Christian anti-Semite and an anti-Semitic Christian," and in fact not unsympathetic with some of the Nazi regime's aims, Wurm represented the elite stratum of Protestant Germany that perceived itself under wholesale attack in the subsequent Nuremberg trials. On the other side was Kempner, the former Prussian Interior Ministry official hounded from his position and from Germany by the Nazis because of his "non-Aryan" background and now working for the Americans as a war crimes prosecutor.[55]

The exchange with Kempner and the attention it received in the German press encouraged Wurm to capitalize on his emerging role as a prominent public critic of war crimes trials. Like Neuhäusler, he was not equipped with either a background in law or an understanding of how cases had really been investigated, prosecuted, and reviewed. Again like Neuhäusler, he relied on what the convicted men's lawyers had sent him or what he heard from the Protestant prison chaplain. Nonetheless, in the midst of his debate with Kempner, Wurm, three other bishops, and Martin Niemoeller—the entire leadership of the Evangelical Church of Germany—sent a long letter to Clay denouncing the IMT. The signatories argued that the defense had been handicapped in ways large and small vis-à-vis the prosecution, witnesses had been "interrogated under the duress of extradition to Eastern states," international law was being applied only to the vanquished, and there was no court of appeal.

Clay's response, though informed almost entirely by a blistering critique of Wurm's catalog of complaints written by another exasperated military government official, was courteous in tone, though he made clear that he found the bishops's arguments unconvincing, seeing as they were "based largely on unverified reports rather than on information within your own knowledge or supported by factual evidence." Clay also told them that he knew they were unfamiliar with the evidence against the accused, concluding that it was difficult for him to understand "how any review of the evidence of those yet to be sentenced could provide a basis for sentimental sympathy for those who brought suffering and anguish to untold millions."[56]

Undeterred, Wurm kept up the offensive in the press and in appeals to other American officials. His references to "avenging Jews," while oblique, became a more prominent part of his critique. "Until 1945, Dachau was a hell and unfortunately it remained so for some time after 1945," he wrote in a statement appearing in multiple newspapers beginning in late July. Rather than allow "neutral jurists" to investigate alleged war crimes, the Americans instead deployed those who sought to settle "personal scores" with the Nazis. And just as it was now evident to everyone "on both sides of the Atlantic ocean" that denazification was a failure, Wurm claimed that foreign opinion was for the most part coming to the same conclusion about war crimes trials. However, Wurm hinted darkly, certain unnamed "circles" who wanted to "pastoralize" Germany and destroy its industry were scheming for revenge. Here he was making an unmistakable reference to former American secretary of the treasury Henry Morgenthau's now-notorious proposal in 1944 to deprive Germany of its industrial base, a proposal that proved to be a gift to Joseph Goebbels, who made much of Morgenthau as the "Jewish angel of revenge" when the scheme became known in Germany.[57]

By August 1948 Wurm had learned of Royall's plan to dispatch the Simpson Commission to Germany. The bishop's plea to Royall was replete with the same objections made to Clay and raised by Neuhäusler. They included the same demand for a "court of appeal," meaning retrials for all war crimes cases. Wurm made another thinly veiled reference to the corrosive presence of Jewish émigrés as investigators and prosecutors. "It may have been understandable that the prosecution has been staffed chiefly with representatives of those circles who have suffered most from the National Socialist regime," he wrote Royall, adding that impartiality would have been better served had "understandable personal motives of retaliation . . . been excluded when the members of the prosecution were chosen."[58]

At the end of that month, representatives of the bishop presented their arguments and documents to the Simpson Commission. Wurm directed his emissaries to make the case for a new review of all war crimes cases in which no one with any connections to the original trials would be involved. Publicity that the very same individuals who had conducted the pretrial investigations were now involved in reviewing the verdicts and sentences, Wurm warned, had produced "a new wave of anti-Semitism" in Germany.[59] It was a remarkable claim. While it was true that War Crimes Group personnel were involved in some of the reviews of the Dachau cases, William Perl and other interrogators certainly were not. Rather, it was the convicted men, their lawyers, and prominent clergymen like Wurm who were stoking anti-Semitism in occupied Germany by blaming supposedly vengeful Jews for corrupting the pretrial investigations.

Their remonstrations had little effect on the commission's recommendations, and right after Clay ordered the resumption of executions in Landsberg, Wurm denounced the commission in an angry letter to John Foster Dulles, at that time the foreign policy adviser to Thomas Dewey, the Republican presidential candidate expected to win the upcoming election. Wurm wrote that "undeniable and proven charges can be made against the prosecution . . . to the effect that [it] has made use of illegal and even criminal methods in order to attain its ends." The bishop noted to Dulles that "quite independently from me," Archbishop Neuhäusler had arrived at the same conclusion. The letter concluded with yet another reference to vengeance-seeking Jews: "we are beginning to ask ourselves whether it is the same in your country as it was with us during the Third Reich, when clearheaded men, who were of good will, were unable to achieve their purpose against those who were profiting from certain political combinations."[60] By "us," Wurm meant those like himself, Weizsäcker, and other defendants in the Ministries case who Wurm believed had been prevented from taking meaningful steps against Nazi "excesses" by opportunists. The implication was clear: avenging Jews were taking advantage of lingering anger at Germans in the United States to settle personal scores and were thus impeding the work of those well-meaning officials who were most interested in reconciliation. The text of Wurm's letter to Dulles was published widely in the German press.[61]

A week before the *Muenchner Allgemeine*'s expose arranged by Neuhäusler appeared on December 18, the *Neue Ruhr Zeitung (New Ruhr Newspaper)*, a

British-zone paper connected to the Social Democratic Party of Germany (SPD), published a two-part attack on the army's trials titled "Justice or Revenge, That Is the Question Here!" Having procured a large quantity of "irreproachably authentic" materials about the conduct of the Nuremberg and Dachau trials from Leon Poullada, Willis Everett, and American and German lawyers representing defendants in the subsequent Nuremberg trials, the paper's editors claimed to have revealed that vengeance-driven prosecutors had deployed methods that bore a "fatal similarity" to those of the Nazis. The article reported the "fact" that most concentration camp inmates liberated by American troops were not "victims" of the Nazis, rather professional criminals, sex criminals, and other "notorious asocials," and that many of the most terrible accounts of the camps were provided by these criminals to well-meaning but gullible American officials. These very "criminals" then eagerly offered their services as "professional witnesses" in the Dachau trials in exchange for shelter, food, and extra cigarette rations.[62]

The story also reported that American investigators had meanwhile combed the country, arresting suspects and interviewing witnesses. Many of these investigators were "German emigrants, who often only emigrated to the USA in 1939 and received American citizenship. The Americans themselves described them as '39ers' and 'avenging angels.' It was these men who became the chief investigators in the concentration camp and Malmedy cases." The materials provided to the *Neue Ruhr Presse* recounted all manner of abuses: manufactured statements, "physical and spiritual abuses," and "stage shows" involving the identification of suspects by paid "witnesses." Though Wurm was not cited as a source, the front-page article was accompanied by photograph of the bishop, noting that he had appealed directly to President Truman and Clay to halt executions and review the death sentences.

Vengeance by Other Means

Despite the fact that American officials rejected their pleas for retrials, the efforts of Bishops Neuhäusler and Wurm in 1948 had not been for nothing. They used their authority to authenticate and publicize the torture allegations in Germany and, indirectly, in the United States. The credibility of their protests was bolstered by references to American officials who were pointing to severe defects in pretrial investigations and identifying "recent Americans" like Perl as the chief culprits. While public opinion surveys conducted by the military government showed generally strong support among Germans for the IMT, there is no question that attitudes—especially among Germany's political, economic, and clerical elite—hardened as the army's trials continued into 1948 and as the bulk of the subsequent Nuremberg trials took place.[63]

Neuhäusler and Wurm tapped into deep veins of anti-Semitism and intensified the willingness of Germans to perceive themselves as the victims of "Jewish revenge." It is true that neither made overtly anti-Semitic remarks in public statements. But their most vehement objections to the Dachau trials were based on their uncritical acceptance of the torture accusations, and they knew the identities of the interrogators. Wurm was particularly adept at making unmistakable allusions to those American officers seeking to "settle personal scores" and "certain circles" who had arrived in Germany to carry out Henry Morgenthau's nefarious plan to impoverish the country. Conversely, they considered confessions and the testimony of prosecution witnesses—often concentration camp survivors and other victims of the regime—to be coerced or bought and worse than worthless.

The suspicions and fears expressed in their public statements resonated powerfully among Germans in the war's immediate aftermath: namely, that war crimes trials were revenge by other means. The guns had fallen silent but retribution had continued, dressed up in the form of tribunals. Those Germans who followed the Malmedy affair in the press would have found allegations of "Jewish revenge" completely convincing. In the war's later years, many had come to expect some form of retribution for the crimes committed by them or in their name. These fears had been stoked by Nazi propaganda portraying Jews as behind the scenes manipulators of Allied governments. Joseph Goebbels had repeatedly accused Jews of conspiring to exterminate the German people by starting the war and then prolonging it. In the regime's propaganda, "angels of revenge" like Morgenthau and other Jewish American officials embodied the threat of Jewish wire-pullers behind Allied leaders. It is not difficult to see how in the war's aftermath, Germans would be convinced that "Morgenthau boys" had taken up positions throughout the occupation apparatus, where they could serve—as Wurm would later put it—as "servants of revenge."

Further, after VE Day, linking a supposed violation of justice with Jewish vengefulness could also help explain the miseries of the immediate postwar years. German civilian and former military personnel responses to U.S. Strategic Bombing Survey questions about the reasons Germany lost the war suggest a widespread belief that the Nazi regime blundered by persecuting the Jews, who consequently went abroad, convinced the Americans and British to go to war, and were now going to take their revenge on hungry and homeless Germans. The widespread awareness among Germans of the persecution and murder of European Jewry only intensified fears that men like Perl and Kempner would seek revenge.[64]

If the trauma of defeat led many Germans to perceive themselves as "innocent victims in an unfair world," as Richard Bessel characterized the sentiment, the accusation of "Jewish revenge" could serve another purpose: to demarcate the past from the present and future Germany. Opponents of war crimes trials claimed to represent two sides of Germany. One side was the best of the "old" Germany—that is, the civilized *Rechtsstaat* (constitutional state) that men like Bishop Wurm claimed most Germans always supported. The other was a new, post-Nazi democratic polity. The attempts to build on the best of the old and the new, they suggested, were being impeded by investigators like Perl and more generally by the CIC, which counted many Ritchie Boys as agents and was often referred to by Germans as the "American Gestapo." The alleged sadism of Perl, Kirschbaum, and others, they insisted with disconcerting frequency, equaled and even exceeded that of the Nazis. The attempt to equate Jews with Nazis had its origins not in postwar Soviet and East European communism or the warped imagination of the Western European New Left of the late 1960s, but in the early years of the Allied occupation of western Germany.

Clay and Judge Advocate officials in Germany devoted a great deal of time to reviewing and responding to Neuhäusler's and Wurm's petitions and public statements. Clay had agonized over every decision to reduce or confirm a sentence, refusing to make any changes unless he was convinced the evidence warranted a revision. He didn't bend under the pressures exerted by the bishops or the convicted men's lawyers. He wasn't convinced by their legal arguments and found the torture accusations ludicrous. His decision in March 1949 to reduce six of the twelve remaining death sentences to life terms was not based on his belief that the accused had not received fair trials, let alone that they had been tortured by "avenging angels." The reports of the Simpson Commission and the AJRB led him to conclude that American investigators had deployed some questionable methods, but in the end what was most important was whether the evidence against the accused presented at trial warranted the death sentence.[65]

Clay's resolve was bolstered by his advisers and War Crimes Group officers. The latter in particular were unsparing in their criticisms of Neuhäusler and Wurm. They were not fooled by the bishops' perfunctory and transparently obsequious references to the "unquestioned" guilt of some Germans. "The present smear campaign," Major Joseph Haefele wrote in late September 1948, "is obviously aimed at discrediting the program of War Crimes without regard to the question of the guilt of those who were tried and sentenced and the fate of the millions of victims of their cruelties and tortures." For Haefele, Neuhäusler was a dupe. A well-meaning dupe, perhaps, but a dupe all the same. Criminals, Haefele concluded, had succeeded in enlisting the clergy's sympathies "in order to give the smear campaign an aura of respectability."[66] His assessment of Wurm's petition to Kenneth Royall was even harsher. It was obvious to him that it "constitute[d] an unwarranted, unjustifiable and in some respects malicious attack which would hardly be tolerated by any other occupation agency and should not be tolerated by War Crimes." Wurm's editorials published in the German press in late July and early August, moreover, "obviously represents Bishop Wurm's personal opinions and opinions derived from biased sources such as convicted accused and disgruntled German attorneys" and should not appear in print.[67]

For American intelligence officials in occupied Germany, the public's perception of the trials was cause for considerable worry. In the first postwar decade, American and British intelligence operations were directed in part at monitoring the activities of German communists and in part at monitoring unrepentant Nazis seeking to foment a nationalist, antidemocratic revival. Surveillance of the far right entailed tracking the activities of individuals and groups seeking to undermine the military government or the new Federal Republic, including those advocating the release of convicted war criminals.[68]

The appearance of the Malmedy torture accusations in the form of dozens of sworn statements immediately caught the attention of the CIC. After reviewing the affidavits, an agent warned presciently in early April 1948: "Should the information contained in the [statements] be given sufficient publicity among the German population, it is bound to create the general impression that the trials were a complete farce and that a great injustice has been done. A move of this nature must, therefore, be regarded as an attempt to discredit the entire War Crimes Court, as well as the American Occupation forces as a whole." The agent recommended that the convicted men's lawyers be prohibited from publishing any of the statements.[69]

By the end of the year, the bishops' campaigns and the increasing number of references in the German press to American criticism of the Malmedy and other trials had made the situation for occupation and intelligence officers considerably more worrisome. The problem was summed up in late December by Mortimer Kollender, chief of the military government's Administration of Justice Branch. A series of stories published in the German press published in American-, British-, and French-zone German newspapers had "a most deplorable effect on German public opinion and may undo most of the efforts to impress the Germans with the fairness of American justice as practiced in Germany." Unless the military government takes steps to counter such "inaccurate and misleading" stories, the average German, "being biased against [the army's Dachau trials] from the outset, will inevitably be fortified in his antagonistic feelings." Kollender was aware that Clay had the charges investigated but argued that American authorities needed to use the German press to counteract the "smoldering propaganda . . . undermining the confidence of Germans in the fair conduct of the War Crimes tribunals."[70]

At the same time, Donald Shea, the chief of the military government's Intelligence Branch in Bavaria had initiated a "discreet investigation" into Neuhäusler's and Wurm's campaigns. Shea had become aware that Protestant church officials were planning to publish in a single volume many of the materials they had received from Landsberg prisoners and their lawyers. One of Shea's sources revealed that the funds for this publication were being provided by the church and "former Nazi groups" led by Wilhelm Karl Tengelmann, a former SS officer and general director of a major mining concern in the Ruhr region. Shea had also learned of a split between Wurm and Neuhäusler. His principal source was the lawyer Rudolf Aschenauer. Shea suggested that Wurm was "being used by a group of German ex-officers and other nationalists whose primary purpose is the embarrassment" of the military government.[71]

Unlike Haefele, Shea was convinced that Neuhäusler was "honestly worried about what he considers injustice." Because of the archbishop's stature and his concerns that attacks on the army's trials had received "disproportionate publicity," Shea offered the prospect of a deal to the archbishop: if he would agree to "go on record stating publicly that he is convinced that the trial and review authorities did everything to assure justice is done, it might be arranged to examine individual cases on the basis of [posttrial] evidence." Shea made it clear, however, that retrials were out of the question. He was confident that such posttrial "evidence" would "prove nothing," but even if it did, a few modified sentences "would be a low price indeed for Neuhäusler's public admission that [the] operation of the trials are above reproach." In Shea's view, since American authorities had "made a bid for the support and cooperation of less worthy Germans than Neuhäusler," it was worth trying to recruit him as an ally.[72]

By the middle of the month, Aschenauer was speaking with Shea as the archbishop's representative. He conveyed to Shea that Neuhäusler had no intention of participating in the planned Protestant church publication and was keeping Wurm and his circle at arm's length. The American officer became even more convinced that a quiet arrangement in which the Theater Judge Advocate's office would review certain cases in cooperation with German defense attorneys would come with multiple benefits. It would strengthen the prestige of the military government, entail "no harm" to War Crimes, and Neuhäusler would agree not to criticize the trials in public. The archbishop's evident distaste for Wurm and his circle would also make it easier for the Americans to "expose [the Wurm group's] true motives and discredit them for what they are: subversive, pro-East, anti-West." Shea considered the matter urgent, as "press and other publicity of alleged irregularities accentuated public unrest. Nationalist exploitation of this issue has great political implications."[73]

There is evidence that the Shea-Aschenauer arrangement was put into effect. Neuhäusler certainly hoped it would be. In a letter directed to Shea's office, he specifically requested that the death sentences of two men convicted by army courts be reviewed.[74] Both had their death sentences commuted. Upon submitting yet another petition on behalf of his client Joachim Peiper in early March 1949, Eugen Leer reported being given access to review board recommendations "for the first time."[75] Hans Bentz, a Munich-based journalist with close ties to right-wing Catholics in Bavaria and an informant for military government intelligence, recalled in a June 1949 report on

Aschenauer's activities that "long, top-level negotiations" had taken place and a "compromise was found" that resulted in the German Catholic Church's refusal to join with the Protestant Church in preparing a "white book" of published documents describing alleged prisoner abuse in war crimes cases.[76] Though the archbishop remained active in the campaign by the convicted men's lawyers to retry or release convicted war criminals, pointed public criticism of the Malmedy case by the archbishop did abate in early 1949.

In any case, by the summer of 1949, it was clear that multiple American intelligence arms in Germany had become intensely concerned with the publicity generated by Neuhäusler and Wurm. The CIC would become much more active in monitoring the activities of German critics as the Malmedy controversy in the United States and Germany reached its high point in 1949.

TWELVE

Lie Detectors

Interrogating American Interrogators

"It has become rather tiresome," Burton Ellis wrote a War Crimes Group official in late May 1948, "to every few weeks pick up a paper and read of some more of Everett's accusations." Over the following months, Ellis and the investigators became increasingly concerned about the proliferating stories of their alleged misconduct. Also disconcerting was what they considered an inexplicable delay in the review process and execution of the death sentences. "Could it be," Barney Crawford (one of the pretrial investigators) wrote Congressman Mike Monroney in March, "that the Commanding General of the European Theater Forces . . . thinks that Americans are no longer interested in seeing that the perpetrators of such uncalled for crimes are punished after having had a fair trial and [being] found guilty?" Such angry bewilderment was not limited to the former investigators: delayed executions prompted survivors of the massacre and fathers of the murdered GIs to write other congressmen and Secretary of the Army Kenneth Royall demanding to know why the death sentences had not been carried out.[1]

Ellis, Crawford, William Perl, Dwight Fanton, Morris Elowitz, and Raphael Shumacker all believed they had acquitted themselves effectively and professionally in Schwäbisch Hall and Dachau. Ellis welcomed Royall's decision to review the death sentences in the army's cases and he offered the War Crimes Group whatever information might be of assistance. He was worried, however, that the prosecution's side of the story might not be represented fully, given that the former investigators were at that point dispersed across the United States and Europe. Ellis remained involved with the army's trials in Dachau, serving as head of the evidence branch and then deputy chief of operations before returning to California, where he served as a Judge Advocate General Corps lawyer at Sixth Army Headquarters in San Francisco. Perl was discharged in November 1946 and worked as a business consultant in New York. Fanton, Elowitz, and Shumacker also resumed civilian careers as lawyers and businessmen. Harry Thon and Joseph Kirschbaum remained with the War Crimes Group in Germany as interpreters and investigators. Regardless, Ellis hoped, perhaps naively, that the trial record alone would go a long way toward refuting Willis Everett's charges. At the very least, he was certain it would show that most of the defendants "never saw fit to deny their confessions during the trial, which after all was the proper place to do it."[2]

When the controversy reached something of a fever pitch in early 1949, multiple U.S. congressmen introduced resolutions calling for a Senate or House investigation into the army's conduct in the Malmedy case.[3] In the spring and fall of 1949, a subcommittee of the Senate's Armed Services Committee held hearings in Washington and Munich, producing the most extensive investigation of the Malmedy massacre case to date.[4] Attacks on the Malmedy investigation and trial in the United States and Germany, however, had already incited Ellis to mobilize the investigators to defend their records. The hearings would offer them the most important forum in which they could finally correct what had become a deeply distorted account of the massacre and its aftermath.

Death Penalty for a Cold-Blooded Killer

Ellis's fears that the investigators would not be heard seemed to be realized after the Simpson Commission failed to contact a single one of them. "It was not practicable for us to have [had] the benefit of your views," an embarrassed Gordon Simpson would admit to Ellis privately in March 1949.[5] As the commission was preparing for its trip to Germany the previous summer, Fanton took the important step of informing Senator Raymond Baldwin, a thoughtful and conscientious Connecticut Republican and Fanton's law firm partner, about the case. In a long letter to the senator, at that time a member of the

Armed Services Committee, Fanton informed him that he and the other investigators were coordinating their efforts to ensure that "a complete and exhaustive investigation is made." He explained how they developed the case and insisted that "the evidence before the Court was entirely proper in every respect and that a retrial of this case is completely unwarranted."[6]

For Fanton, more was at stake than their reputations. If the case was retried without the original confessions, he argued to Baldwin, most of the convicted would be acquitted. The result would be "a gross miscarriage of justice," making "Anglo-American judicial processes and the American Army a laughing stock in the eyes of the German people" and "confirm[ing] the propaganda which is being spread by the sizable and important core of Nazism which still remains in Germany and which has always held us and our institutions in such contempt."[7] At that point, Fanton had no idea that the convicted men and their lawyers had sent batches of new sworn statements to Lucius Clay leveling accusations of systematic torture at the hands of their interrogators. Nor could he have predicted that these accusations were about to make the jump from the offices of German lawyers to German church officials and then to the Simpson Commission and the American press.

Baldwin found Fanton's concerns compelling enough to contact Royall repeatedly, urging him to give the former investigators the opportunity to be heard. While the senator's interventions with the secretary of the army had no impact on the Simpson Commission's choice of officials to consult in Germany, it did prompt Royall to ensure that the AJRB's members considered the investigators' accounts of their work in Schwäbisch Hall.[8] The AJRB had been ordered by Clay to look into Everett's charges. Its preliminary report, submitted in August 1948, concluded that there was no credible evidence of systematic prisoner abuse. Nonetheless, thanks to Royall's additional prompting, Ellis, Perl, Elowitz, Shumacker, Fanton, and Colonel Claude Mickelwait were able to submit lengthy written accounts of the entire pretrial investigation. Fanton included copies of his SOP orders and a long memorandum he wrote for Ellis in the midst of the investigation. Much of what they wrote had been brought out in the trial, but now they were given the chance to respond to Everett's charges to a review board responsible for investigating their methods.[9]

The AJRB's final report, submitted to Clay in mid-February 1949, concluded that the torture accusations were baseless, with the qualification that "undoubtedly in the heat of the moment on occasions, interrogators did use some physical force on a recalcitrant suspect." The AJRB had also reviewed some of the convicted men's affidavits assembled by Eugen Leer and concluded that they were "exaggerated far beyond anything that might have taken place, and that the individuals who may have been subjected to some physical violence were probably few in number."[10]

The final reports of the AJRB and the Simpson Commission confirmed Clay's suspicions about the torture accusations. Yet both left room for some doubt about the propriety of certain methods. Clay faced a difficult decision. Investigators in criminal cases in the United States and army interrogators in Germany were permitted to use tricks and ruses when questioning an individual suspected of committing a crime. In their responses to Everett's accusations submitted to the AJRB, the Malmedy case investigators described at length how they deployed the "psychological approach," including the use of ruses, to convince members of Battle Group Peiper to divulge the details of their operations and their involvement, if any, in war crimes. During the trial and in their affidavits, all of the interrogators denied vehemently that they had forced any suspect to confess. From their perspective, moreover, the time for the accused to have repudiated their sworn statements was during the trial, and not two years later. On the other hand, even though Clay and every review of the pretrial investigation conducted to date had dismissed the accusations of outright torture, it was possible that suspects were put under enough pressure by the interrogators' verbal techniques to make a credible claim that their statements, while not "coerced," were obtained by means that were nonetheless improper.

The problem was that the question of what constituted impropriety in interrogations remained unresolved politically and in terms of public perception. This ambiguity did not relieve Clay from the responsibility of deciding on the condemned men's fates. The negative publicity the case was generating in the United States and Germany only complicated matters. Though he had repeatedly rejected the call for retrials made by German lawyers and clergymen and was exasperated by accounts of burning matchsticks inserted under the fingernails of German prisoners, it seems probable that the pressures emanating from these sources and, not least, the American officials who found them credible, had some effect on his decisions in the twelve death sentence cases. Indeed, the twin controversies surrounding the army's handling of the Ilse Koch case and Edward Van Roden's charges led Acting

Secretary of the Army William Draper to urge Clay to include in his public announcements a detailed explanation of each decision, including references to the Simpson Commission and the AJRB's findings along with a "denial of allegations of brutality . . . not found to be substantiated." Draper also hoped the AJRB's reports and the record of the proceedings could be declassified and made available to the press.[11]

In the end, Clay took a prudent course of action. He confirmed death sentences only if enough unrepudiated, corroborated evidence remained to justify the sentence. Obliging Draper's request, he provided an explanation for each decision to the press. They were clearly difficult decisions, as Clay remained convinced that the guilty verdicts of all twelve men whose death sentences he had confirmed in 1948 were justified. As he put it in the case of Friedrich Christ, a first lieutenant in the First SS Panzer Regiment convicted for instructing the men of his company to take no prisoners and for ordering prisoners at the Baugnez crossroads to be executed:

> If the evidence which may have been obtained through improper methods is entirely excluded, there remains no direct evidence of guilt. While the general similarity in the repudiations is indicative of a concerted plan similar to the original silence of the witnesses, this cannot be proved. To my mind, Christ was a principal in these murders. I believe, as does the Judge Advocate that he was a leading participant. Circumstantially, there can be no doubt that he was present and, as an officer, took no action to prevent the crime. Knowing this, it is difficult not to approve the death penalty for this cold-blooded killer. However, to do so would be to accept the evidence which may have resulted from the improper administration of justice. Excluding this evidence in its entirety in as far as direct participation of Christ is concerned, there is no doubt that he was present and, circumstantially did nothing to prevent these murders. Thus, I have no hesitancy in approving a life sentence. It is with reluctance but with the firm aim of fairly administered justice that I commute the death sentence to life imprisonment.

As for Joachim Peiper, Clay wrote that "there is no question in my mind that [he] was, in fact, the principal in the Malmedy case." Even after excluding repudiated testimony, however, Clay believed there was enough evidence to warrant upholding the death sentence.[12]

The public release of the Simpson Commission and AJRB reports in January and February 1949, respectively, along with Clay's decisions on the twelve death sentences in March and April, only added fuel to the firestorm of public controversy over the Malmedy trial. Most press reports in the United States and Germany ignored or downplayed the major conclusions of both while emphasizing their discussions of mock trials and physical abuse. Newspaper readers possessing little or no knowledge of the investigation would be left with the impression that the army's interrogators had coerced confessions out of the suspects. Such stories had led multiple congressmen to call for an investigation, and this development pushed Royall to again order Clay to halt executions at Landsberg until any such inquiry could take place.

The Opportunity to Set the Record Straight

Ellis and the other investigators were not content to drop the matter after they had provided their statements to the AJRB. For Ellis, *Time* magazine's January 17, 1949, story, which had given such prominence to Everett's accusations without including any response from the former prosecutor, had been particularly enraging. That article, he wrote in a memorandum in mid-January requesting the army's Adjutant General's office defend its own investigators, was "pure imagination and fiction" and had "seriously prejudiced the character and professional reputation of all the officers, soldiers, and War Department civilians, male and female, who participated in the investigation and prosecution of this case" by "portray[ing] them to their relatives, friends, . . . and the general public as beasts and fiends comparable to or worse than the SS and Nazis whom they prosecuted."[13] To add insult to injury, he then learned from the army that while in Germany the Simpson Commission had not bothered to talk to a single person involved with the original investigation and prosecution.

As an active duty officer, Ellis could do little more than press the army for a response to the stories like the one in *Time* or urge former investigators now working the private sector to speak out.[14] Fanton and Elowitz, now civilians, were under no such constraints. They had made contact with the Society for the Prevention of World War III, an obscure New York–based organization supporting the postwar curtailing of German economic and military power and advocating the continuation of denazification and war crimes trials. The society, which was headed by the scholar Mark Van Doren and whose board members included the journalist William Shirer, film studio executive Darryl Zanuck, and the anti-Nazi Norwegian novelist Sigrid Undset, held a press conference in its Madison Avenue headquarters on March 3. There, Fanton and Elowitz responded to the barrage of American and German attacks on their conduct in Schwäbisch Hall. The *New York Times* reported on their statements, in which both men denied the abuse accusations. The vast bulk of newspaper coverage, however, remained focused on mock trials and physical force—and the more lurid the better.[15]

Fanton was quoted in the *Times* as welcoming a chance to give testimony in any congressional investigation "so that we may be heard fully and may have the opportunity to set the record straight." Since January several U.S. congressmen had announced—separately—that they would seek a formal investigation into the army's handling of the Malmedy case. On January 27, Senator William Langer, an isolationist North Dakota Republican with a large German American constituency and close ties to the NCPW, introduced a resolution calling for an investigation. In his statement on the floor of the Senate, he confused the Simpson Commission's final report with Van Roden's statements. Langer stated, incorrectly, that a two-man civilian board surveyed the army's trials in Germany at Royall's request and reported that "beatings and brutal kickings, knocking out teeth and breaking jaws, mock trials, solitary confinement, torture with burning splinters, posturing as priests, very limited rations, spiritual deprivations, and promises of acquittal" were used to obtain confessions, presumably in all of the army's cases.[16]

Langer also noted that the resumption of executions after the commission reported to Royall had resulted in condemnations from American and German church leaders. Cardinal Joseph Frings of Cologne, he pointed out, had warned that the executions would set the process of German-American reconciliation back by years. Like German critics, he charged that the army's courts were renegade operations that combined "American, Continental, and Russian rules" with the results "a far cry from what would be demanded by American standards." His proposed resolution called for the Committee on the Judiciary to conduct a full investigation of military courts to determine whether they have operated "in accordance with American concepts of justice."[17]

The same day Raymond Baldwin offered a similar resolution, albeit for hearings to be held by the Armed Services Committee. The wording of Baldwin's resolution was markedly different from Langer's. Baldwin had based his request on Fanton's letter to him from the previous summer, quoting long passages though neither naming Fanton nor pointing out that the two were partners in the same law firm. "I ask on behalf of these young officers," Baldwin concluded, that they be "given an opportunity to be heard before any final decisions are made in the reduction of these sentences." Unaware that Fanton and the other investigators had already submitted formal statements to the AJRB, Baldwin noted that the Simpson Commission had not taken their views into account but had consulted with Everett and a "Mr. Leer, who I understand is a German lawyer."[18]

As Langer did not object to hearings in which the investigators' side of the story would be heard, he dropped his opposition to Baldwin's resolution.[19] At the same time, another call for a formal inquiry came from a member of the House of Representatives. On March 10, Lawrence Smith, a Republican representing Milwaukee, introduced a resolution calling for the House Armed Services Committee to look into the conduct of U.S. Army officers at Dachau. Smith's language was even more prejudiced than Langer's. Like Langer, he had been informed mainly by press reports on Van Roden's accusations. Claiming that he had learned from "government reports" that "the conduct of the prosecutors and investigators engaged in these trials has been brutal beyond description" and their actions constituted "a national disgrace," Smith asked whether "the spirit of American jurisprudence or the spirit of revenge by those who have an axe to grind" was at work in the army's courts in Germany. Asserting that there was "absolute proof" that confessions were obtained by "brutal kickings," mock trials, and "kangaroo courts," he reported to the House that Perl had boasted in court that the interrogators felt compelled to use "persuasive methods" and by that Perl meant "expedients and violence." Perl and Ellis, Smith thundered, should be court-martialed. He also asked that Van Roden's *Progressive* article and an editorial from the *Christian Century* charging American interrogators with deploying methods "even the Nazi sadists never surpassed" be included with his remarks for the record.[20]

One day later, Senator Clyde Hoey, a North Carolina Democrat and chairman of the Senate Investigations Subcommittee, announced that in view of the "disturbing facts" revealed in the AJRB's report, a subcommittee consisting of himself, fellow Democratic senator James Eastland, and a junior Republican senator from Wisconsin, Joseph McCarthy, would discuss an investigation with the Armed Services and Judiciary Committees.[21] Just over two weeks later, the Armed Services Committee had prevailed and appointed the subcommittee, which would be comprised of Raymond Baldwin as chair, Wyoming Democrat Lester Hunt, and Tennessee Democrat Estes Kefauver. McCarthy was asked to join as a courtesy to the Committee on Expenditures, the members of which had taken an interest in the affair.

With the exception of McCarthy, all of the subcommittee's members were experienced politicians, if only freshman senators. Baldwin and Hunt had similar backgrounds: both were World War I veterans who had gone on to successful careers in state politics, including two terms as governors in their respective states. Kefauver and McCarthy were younger and the most junior members of the subcommittee. The former, a lawyer by profession, had been a staunch New Dealer during his five terms in the House of Representatives and had been elected to the Senate in 1948. McCarthy, also a lawyer and the only World War II veteran on the subcommittee, had been elected in 1946, but until the spring of 1949 his career in the Senate had been largely unremarkable and marred by bouts of indecorous, combative behavior toward more senior senators.[22]

McCarthy's presence on the subcommittee marked the first time he became involved in a high-profile, international political controversy. What explains his interest in the investigation? Wisconsin, for one thing, had a large German American population and his popularity in the state was flagging. For another, he had already expressed particular concern for the fate of former German soldiers imprisoned in the Soviet Union. Like numerous other Americans, and by no means only those of German descent, McCarthy's sympathies lay with the defeated Germans. Anticommunism and the Cold War division of Europe only made the need for reconciliation with the former enemy seem more urgent. The ethnic makeup of his home state, however, does not fully explain his determination to pursue the matter. A seat on a committee investigating a scandal involving alleged misconduct by U.S. Army investigators offered the publicity-hungry, impatient junior senator another chance to challenge the authority of senior senators.

There were, however, good reasons to avoid betting on the Malmedy case. McCarthy had attempted to position himself, if unconvincingly, as a strong supporter of American war veterans. Yet he risked appearing to defend a group of men convicted of massacring American prisoners of war during the Battle of the Bulge. Further, the perpetrators were not Wehrmacht veterans imprisoned in the Soviet Union four years after the war's end, but members of the Waffen SS. At least two of McCarthy's close advisers and confidants urged him to avoid becoming involved in the case. As one influential member of his staff warned him, German Americans in Wisconsin were not Nazi sympathizers.[23]

The temptation proved too great for McCarthy to resist. He believed he could dodge any accusations of sympathy for the SS by claiming—as he would do repeatedly during the hearings—to be taking a stand on principle. The Malmedy case was not only high-profile, but it seemed to him to be an open-and-shut case of abuse perpetrated by American personnel. As would become clear in the hearings' first days, McCarthy had expended very little effort in preparing himself and relied selectively on Van Roden's *Progressive* article and statements sent to his office by the NCPW, including materials from Bishops Neuhäusler and Wurm. A call from Everett may have further encouraged him to believe the army was trying to hide some very ugly business. If he did bother to read the final reports of the Simpson Commission or the AJRB, he chose to ignore their central conclusions. As would become apparent from the very start of the hearings, he had already made up his mind about the investigators' guilt.[24]

McCarthy's appointment to the subcommittee was not controversial. This was not the case with Baldwin's selection as its chair. Rumors of his appointment were particularly disconcerting for the NCPW. James Finucane, the NCPW official who had taken the lead in advocating amnesty for the convicted perpetrators, had been busy compiling a list of American and German witnesses for the subcommittee to interview. If Baldwin led the investigation, however, the effort would be wasted. "It will become a whitewash," Finucane warned the NCPW's executive board in mid-March.[25] When Baldwin was selected as chairman, the NCPW issued a statement to the press demanding that he recuse himself. The reason was the fact that Baldwin and Dwight Fanton were both partners in the same law firm. "We cannot overlook the fact," the NCPW's executive secretary, Frederick Libby, wrote Baldwin, "that you will be, in effect, acting as judge in your firm's case." This was a strange assertion to make, as Baldwin's firm had nothing to do with the investigation nor had any legal or financial stake in the allegations against the former investigators. Equally strange was Libby's claim that the Senate's investigation would be the "final court of appeal" for the thirty-nine prisoners in Landsberg then awaiting execution.[26]

To his credit, Baldwin acknowledged the perception of a conflict of interest might exist and offered to step aside if the leadership of the Armed Services Committee wished him to do so. It did not, and the senator assured Libby that the purpose of the investigation was only to "get at the facts." At the same time, he reminded Libby that "Congress is a legislative body" and not a "final court of appeal."[27] To be on the safe side, Baldwin recused himself from the hearings during Fanton's multiple appearances. In the end he was at something of a disadvantage, as Kefauver and Hunt seemed to have little interest in the inquiry. Kefauver attended few of the subcommittee's sessions in Washington and said little when he was present. Hunt became more engaged in its later stages, but offered scant support for Baldwin while McCarthy dominated its sessions.

The hearings opened on April 18. The resolution authorizing the investigation called for "a full and complete study . . . of the Army with respect to the trial of those persons responsible for the massacre of American soldiers" near Malmedy in December 1944. There was particular emphasis on the pretrial investigation, the army's conduct of the trial, and the posttrial actions that resulted in a substantial number of commuted sentences. In addition to in-person testimony, the subcommittee entered a large amount of documentary evidence into the record, starting with Everett's writ petition, Leer's February 1948 petition and its supporting documents, and the final reports of the Simpson Commission and the AJRB.[28]

Royall, appropriately enough, was the first to testify. He explained his decisions to repeatedly suspend executions at Landsberg as stemming from his response to Everett's writ petition and the interventions by members of Congress sympathetic to Everett's pleas. Despite his junior status and lack of experience with hearings of this kind, McCarthy questioned the secretary of the army aggressively. He made it clear from the first hours of the hearings that he believed the abuse accusations in the Malmedy case were established fact, and that he was confused, ill-prepared, or simply willfully ignorant as to the contents of the Simpson Commission and AJRB reports. "We have been accusing the Russians of using force, physical violence, and have accused them of using mock trials in cells in the dark of night," he told Royall, "and now we have an Army report that comes out and says we have done all the things that the Russians were ever accused of doing."

By "Army report" McCarthy meant the AJRB's final report, the conclusions of which he misstated. The accusation incited Royall to defend the army's investigators. "[They] didn't commit any atrocities in the sense you normally use the term," he told McCarthy. "They were merely seeking to establish a fact, perhaps a little too eager[ly]." Any overeagerness was justified by the fact that the suspects were "under strict orders not to talk at all." In any case, Royall did not find it surprising that the convicted men, fearful of repercussions from fellow inmates, had later repudiated their confessions.[29]

McCarthy's grilling of Royall set the tone for the hearings' first month. While Baldwin, and occasionally Hunt, were inclined to ask the witnesses concise questions and allow them to answer as they saw fit, McCarthy treated them as if they were hostile witnesses in a trial. He denigrated the qualifications and competence of nearly every witness and demonstrated little patience for any attempt to explain the complexities of the investigation, trial, and posttrial reviews. Repeatedly, he revealed that he had no idea how military courts actually worked and seemed uninterested in being informed about them. His verbal belligerence extended to his Senate colleagues, particularly Baldwin, to the point where he felt compelled (or was advised) to read a formal letter of apology to his colleague on April 21 for statements that "may have very easily been misinterpreted to mean that I was critical of your personal handling of this matter."[30]

Royall was followed by Burton Ellis. Reading from his statement to the AJRB, he explained and defended the pretrial investigation, denying that any of the accused or witnesses had ever been harmed. Ellis stressed that he had made sure the interrogators' procedures and methods were described in detail when it mattered most—during the trial. By the rules of military courts at that time, it was up to the judges to determine the value of the evidence, a determination that would take into account the means by which it was obtained.

Though McCarthy remained certain that the suspects in the Malmedy and other army cases had been abused, he also took Ellis to task for the use of mock trials. Royall, Ellis, and the other investigators did not believe the term "mock trial" was appropriate. Ellis considered it a "ceremony" and a somewhat elaborate vehicle for a ruse, the uses of which he insisted was unquestionably legitimate. As he and other witnesses would testify, the "quick process," as they preferred to call it, was used only a few times and never proved particularly effective in obtaining credible evidence, let alone full-blown confessions. Ellis conceded, however, that given the criticisms leveled at the ruse, he would not use it again. "But otherwise," he added for good measure, "I have not one thing to apologize for."[31]

Ellis could barely conceal his disdain for McCarthy's ignorance and bullying behavior. The senator's repeated conflation of the Simpson Commission report with Van Roden's *Progressive* article produced the following exchange on April 20:

McCarthy: I may not be correctly quoting from the Van Roden report, because I don't have it with me, but as I recall that report was to the effect that many accused came into court with their teeth broken out.

Ellis: Utterly ridiculous.

McCarthy: You understand that Simpson and Van Roden were two men picked, I believe by Secretary Royall—

Ellis: I do.

McCarthy: Let me finish. The President was the one that signed the order and considered that they were getting the two most competent judges in the country.

Ellis: I understand that perfectly.

McCarthy: You say that they were lying when they say the accused had teeth knocked out?

Ellis: I don't say that they were lying, but whoever told that to them was.

McCarthy: They didn't repeat that as hearsay.

Ellis: Senator McCarthy, have you seen the list of witnesses attached to that report?

McCarthy: I am asking you whether or not that part of the report is true.

Ellis: I am telling you it is not true.

McCarthy: All right.

Ellis: But, I would like to ask if you have seen the list of witnesses attached to that report.

McCarthy: I know there is a list.

Ellis: Do you know that not one of those is anyone that would know, other than hearsay knowledge?

McCarthy: I don't know that.

Ellis: That is the truth.[32]

It was during Ellis's testimony that McCarthy read into the record a letter he had just received from James Bailey, a former court reporter stationed in Schwäbisch Hall from late December 1945 until early March 1946. Bailey, who did not understand German, claimed to have taken shorthand notes through interpreters of "practically all of the so-called verbatim confessions of the prisoners." He informed McCarthy that "the methods used by these so-called interpreters to obtain these 'confessions' were such that after a period of ten weeks, I could stomach it no longer and requested my return to the United States." The letter described how the "interpreters" (by this, he meant the interrogators) operated:

> After these interpreters had "worked out" on these prisoners (some of whom were kids of 16 and 17 years of age), and softened them up and scared them into a condition where they would confess to anything, the prisoner then had a long multi-colored robe thrown over him, a black hood pulled down over his head, a rope knotted about his neck, and he was marched into a cell to be interrogated by one of the lawyers. I have been present in cells where there was only a small table with a black cloth over the top, containing a crucifix and two candles, and when the prisoner was marched up, and the black hood suddenly jerked from his head, he fainted dead away, his nose striking the concrete cell floor . . . making his face a bloody mess, and I have then seen the interpreter take his foot, push the prisoner over on his back, jerk him to his feet, and tell the American lawyer that the prisoner was faking.

Bailey insisted that the statements he took down in the cell, given by the prisoner to the "interpreter," were totally different from those presented at the trial. McCarthy's reading of Bailey's letter produced a burst of newspaper stories that gave the impression that Bailey was offering an insider's account of the army's abusive treatment of German soldiers.[33]

The letter arrived at an opportune moment for McCarthy. Even better, it was unsolicited by him. Bailey wrote the senator after having read an article in the *Pittsburgh Press* about a stay of execution for the men convicted in the Malmedy case. Yet when he did appear before the subcommittee on April 29, Bailey's testimony was hedged and unconvincing. He admitted, "I never saw anybody actually beaten by anybody, except with the possible exception of one or two occasions by this fellow Perl. . . . I saw him slap a prisoner pretty hard with his hands . . . and knee him once or twice." When McCarthy informed Bailey that "there will be testimony here to the effect that of 139 men who were sentenced to die, about 138 were irreparably damaged, being crippled for life, from being kicked or kneed in the groin" and asked him whether he had ever seen anything like that, Bailey replied "that is a gross exaggeration." He confessed that he had attended "very few" of Perl's interrogations and witnessed no mock trials.[34]

In a letter to the subcommittee's diligent and eminently fair-minded staff lawyer, Joseph Chambers, Fanton reported that Bailey had been displeased with his assignment in Schwäbisch Hall and a heavy drinker "whose difficulty in obtaining this form of stimulation . . . was also an important factor which influenced him in his desire for a return to the States." He insisted that Bailey's charges were "all false" ("His stories about brutality are false because there was none") and that Bailey never witnessed an interrogation. As he could not understand German, Fanton pointed out, he could not possibly have known whether a prisoner's statement matched what an interrogator or translator reported to him. "The most charitable thing that can be said about him," Fanton concluded, "is that he is a victim of self-delusion."[35]

Bailey's failure to deliver a credible first-person account of the abuse that McCarthy believed to be routine in Schwäbisch Hall marked the beginning of the end of the Wisconsin senator's involvement in the hearings. Ellis had already taken the important step of tracking down former American officers who had served in administrative capacities in Schwäbisch Hall, including medical personnel.[36] Neither the prosecution nor the defense had sought the testimony or physicians, wardens, or guards during the trial. Nor had the Simpson Commission or the very first review board sought out their accounts. Given the nature of the reporting on the Malmedy case in 1948 and early 1949, doing so seemed a matter of particular urgency to Ellis. He knew that guards would have had regular contact with prisoners, and physicians would certainly have been aware of mangled fingernails, broken teeth, and crushed testicles.

Fanton's Criticisms

Most prison personnel who ultimately did provide written or in-person testimony to the Senate subcommittee had not been contacted by Ellis but had been moved to speak out by stories like those appearing in *Time*. The first to testify was Dominic Scalise, who served as the provost sergeant from the fall of 1945 to March 1946, which encompassed nearly the entire period of the investigation. "There was no abuse," he told the senators on April 22. "I had nothing ever reported to me; and generally, I naturally hear about these things, floating around the prison like I did. I had quite a bit of contact personally with the SS men. They never mentioned anything about any abuses." Scalise also testified that the prisoners were well fed, that they were not kept in "solitary confinement" unless they had violated prison regulations, and that their cells were reasonably clean.[37]

Scalise's testimony was typical of that provided by every other officer who had served in Schwäbisch Hall from the end of 1945 through the early spring of 1946. Though he did not testify, Noble Johnson, the prison commander in November and December 1945, wrote Senator William Knowland (whom he thought was a member of the subcommittee) denying that any prisoners were mistreated while he was in charge of the prison. His successor, John Temple Evans, who served to May 1946, estimated that he saw every prisoner at least once per week and asserted that the accusations of brutality were totally untrue. Two supply officers also swore that prisoners were always provided with adequate food and blankets and that they had not heard of or seen any physical abuse. The sergeant of the prison guard detachment from December through February also testified that he did not receive any complaints about abusive interrogators and never saw anyone who appeared to have been maltreated.[38]

Even more important was the testimony of American medical personnel. Stunned by the accusations in the January 17 *Time* article, which Ellis had brought to his attention, Calvin Unterseher sent him a statement about his role as a Medical Corps officer in Schwäbisch Hall from January to April 1946, then testified on May 13. "I can make a flat statement," he told the senators. "Never, at any one time, were we summoned to treat a prisoner that had been mistreated in any way for any injury at all." The other orderly who served with Unterseher, Stanley Sykes, confirmed Unterseher's account in a sworn statement to the subcommittee. Sykes also recalled sitting in on several interrogations and wrote that "while the prisoners were spoken to very roughly at times, at no time did I witness any physical brutality practiced upon the prisoners."[39]

Both the nonmedical and medical personnel responded to the accusations of a German dentist, Eduard Knorr, whose affidavit asserting that he treated fifteen to twenty suspects for severe injuries to their teeth and jaws was among those prepared by Eugen Leer. Along with Friedrich Eble's accusation that interrogators had inserted matchsticks under his fingernails, Knorr's charges would be among the most frequently cited in American and German newspapers. "The only condition under which these prisoners could have had dental treatment by Dr. Knorr," Unterseher (who was a German speaker) testified, "was under the condition that I was personally there and saw to it that there was no conversation carried on aside from what was necessary for their dental care." When pressed by Joseph Chambers as to whether any of the prisoners had suffered injuries to their jaws or teeth as alleged by Knorr, Unterseher replied, "The only knowledge I have is an article in *Time* magazine."[40] A week later, the medical orderlies' superior officers, both physicians, testified and denied that any prisoners had complained about or been treated for the kinds of injuries they were alleged to have sustained.[41] John Evans also testified that Knorr had never treated any prisoner for the injuries some claimed to have sustained. "I observed much of [Knorr's] work and he appeared to be a first-class dentist," Evans told the subcommittee on May 6. "On none of these patients did I see any evidence of recent violence."[42]

Fanton and Van Roden—witnesses representing the two opposing sides of the controversy—testified on May 4 and 5. In Van Roden's first appearance, he stated that it was his "personal" and "professional" opinion that the original sworn statements of the accused were not given voluntarily by them and that all members of the Simpson Commission felt they were "unreliable as testimony." When pressed by McCarthy about "evidence" that most of the prisoners under death sentence in Landsberg had been "crippled" after being "kicked in the testicles," Van Roden admitted that newspaper and magazine reports on this subject had been "exaggerated." It would be under questioning by Baldwin and Hunt that Van Roden's lack of credibility was made completely apparent, if only to those present in the hearing room. When Baldwin asked Van Roden what evidence he had to support his statements about "beatings and brutal kickings," Van Roden admitted that "the only evidence I can recall was what the person who came before us talked to us about, and the petitions that were filed, and I suppose Colonel Everett . . . spoke to us and told us what he knew." The affidavit from Knorr was the only evidence of broken teeth and jaws he could recall. When Hunt asked him about the article in the *Progressive,* Van Roden replied that he had not written the article and then perjured himself by claiming to not have known what a "byline" was. Van Roden was in fact fully aware that the *Progressive* article was to be ghostwritten by James Finucane of the NCPW and then published under the judge's name.[43]

Van Roden returned the following day and Hunt continued to press him on the fact that the Simpson Commission had no interest in speaking with the investigators or Burton Ellis. "I think apparently from your testimony," Hunt declared, "you were interested in only one side of the case." Van Roden proceeded to contradict himself, stating that the investigators were not available but insisting that "we have not got the facts from one side or another." McCarthy, who remained hopelessly confused about the work of the Simpson Commission and the AJRB, insisted that the commission interviewed "a preponderance" of the prosecution staff. In his final appearance before the subcommittee on June 3, Van Roden admitted that he had not spoken with a single person who had seen any physical abuse in Schwäbisch Hall. All he could do was repeat that he had been convinced while in Germany "that these things had taken place."[44]

Fanton's lengthy testimony on May 5 provided another in-depth explanation of the pretrial investigation and a rather critical assessment of the army's handling of the controversy. Like Ellis, Fanton read a version of his review board report, denying mistreatment and defending the "quick process." Fanton considered the term "mock trial" to be a misnomer, and dismissed Everett's description of the technique in his writ petition as "read[ing] like the flights of fancy associated with an Orson Welles dramatization rather than the carefully considered and solemnly sworn-to statements one would expect to find in a petition . . . addressed to our highest court." He denounced the Simpson Commission for ignoring the investigators and Schwäbisch Hall personnel and criticized the AJRB for considering Knorr's affidavit without bothering to corroborate it with American medical officers who served the prisoners.[45]

But it would be Van Roden who would draw Fanton's most severe reproach. "If a thorough investigation had been insisted upon by the Army," he told the senators, "Judge Van Roden would not have written the completely false account of the use of brutality and other improper methods to extort confessions which appeared in the *Progressive* and would have not have taken the rostrum so many times to shock uninformed audiences with similar recitals. The conduct of this man who as a judge must have known that his charges were based on extravagant allegations unsupported by proof, and who must have known that these charges would be seriously received by all who heard them, is indefensible and should have been denounced long ago."[46]

McCarthy had proclaimed Fanton to be the single most important witness in the hearings and that he planned to spend "many hours" questioning him. But he said little to Fanton on May 5. In his more extensive questioning a week later, McCarthy was unusually considerate, though he questioned the witness repeatedly about aspects the trial, which Fanton did not attend and thus could not speak to credibly. By that point in the hearings it was becoming apparent that the case, so to speak, against the investigators was in tatters. Fanton, Ellis, and Elowitz had explained the procedures of the pretrial investigation in considerable detail, and the first of six personnel who had served in Schwäbisch Hall had testified that the accusations of prisoner abuse were baseless. John Raymond and Gordon Simpson, the respective heads of the AJRB and Simpson Commission, also testified and denied that prisoners had been tortured.

Other witnesses McCarthy hoped would substantiate the accusations, such as James Bailey, did not do so. Nor did John Dwinell, the former defense attorney in the Malmedy trial and Everett's principal American ally. Dwinell remained adamant that the defense was at a severe disadvantage from the start, given that it had too little time to prepare and because the court's procedures, in his view, limited its ability to challenge the prosecution's evidence. "It was a hopeless task. It was a hopeless case," he told the subcommittee. "Psychologically you could tell that from the trying of the case." His language was more restrained when it came to the abuse accusations and he would not confirm the torture claims during his two days of testimony. "There were varying degrees of brutality, and varying degrees of duress," he told the subcommittee, adding that all the accused "complained generally about mistreatment in one form or another. In some instances we gave it little weight, and said, 'We have not time to bother about that; we have not got time to get any witnesses on that score, and let us forget about it.'" When Baldwin asked him whether he had seen any outward signs of defendants being physically abused—recall that McCarthy had stated that nearly every one had walked into the courtroom with most of their teeth knocked out—Dwinell could only reply, "They did not," adding that none of the men he represented ever complained about being kicked in the testicles.[47]

You Cannot Fool the Lie Detector

McCarthy would not depart, however, before smearing the reputations of the German-born Jewish investigators whose work had been so important to the Malmedy and most other war crimes trials. It was during Ellis's testimony that he first raised the issue of the backgrounds of some of the interrogators. Clearly, he had no idea that several had been Jewish refugees from Nazi Germany. The temptation to suggest that they had been motivated by personal animosity to abuse those who had formerly persecuted them only increased as he was overwhelmed by testimony from Ellis, Fanton, Elowitz, and the former prison personnel. When James Bailey, for instance, did not prove to be as important a witness as McCarthy had hoped, he made an explicit connection between the backgrounds of Perl and Kirschbaum and the abuse charges: "As of today [April 29], as we look over that trial, we do know this, that the men who are getting confessions upon which the convictions were based did intensely hate the German people as a race." Later that day, he accused the prosecution of "hiring" "men whose wives were in concentration camps, men who had every reason to dislike the German race" and then "giv[ing] them complete charge of the job of getting confessions." In questioning Gordon Simpson, McCarthy used the term "vengeance team" to describe the investigators, interpreters, and interrogators. His interest only grew when Van Roden recounted hearing the term "39ers" for the first time during the Simpson Commission's visit to Germany.[48]

Yet the unexpected testimony of two "39ers" disrupted the new trajectory of McCarthy's attack. Kurt Teil, a German Jewish émigré hired as an interpreter and investigator after the war, testified that during a brief visit to Schwäbisch Hall in early 1946, he learned that Thon and Perl had a reputation for believing that effective interrogation required the use of physical force. Teil had contacted McCarthy's office at the end of April and written a letter claiming to have seen a hooded, bloody prisoner lying unconscious on the floor of an interrogation room. In his appearance before the subcommittee on May 11, he testified that Thon showed him the man and remarked, " 'He just got out of interrogation and probably got roughed up a bit.' " However, Teil never claimed to have seen anybody harmed (and in his testimony denied that he had seen any blood). Though he believed that a few German-born interrogators had been unable to restrain themselves, he defended the "39ers" in general and Ellis in particular, whom he insisted was "strongly opposed to the use of any physical violence" and issued repeated warnings to investigators that "no physical violence was to be used under any circumstances."[49]

No more helpful to McCarthy was Herbert Strong, another German-born Jewish émigré and a member of the defense team during the Malmedy trial. Strong believed some of the suspects had been mistreated, though "probably not so often as the defendants claim. Probably primarily by the Polish guards . . . I remember very often when I asked the accused who mistreated them, the answer was the 'Poles.' " When asked why the defense never sought prison medical personnel to testify at the trial, Strong replied, "For the simple reason that all the mistreatments about which we received complaints had occurred in Schwäbisch Hall and not in Dachau, and that all of this so-called mistreatment was of a nature which ordinarily would not have left any prominent damage." Strong knew nothing of the German dentist Knorr, who claimed he had treated suspects for knocked out teeth and broken jaws, and recalled knowing nothing about such injuries.[50]

Strong, of course, still believed that the defense was hamstrung against the prosecution in the Malmedy case. But he would not denounce the army's trials as corrupt and driven by a desire for vengeance. He had defended Germans accused of murdering downed American fliers in trials preceding the Malmedy case and found the fairness of the proceedings "exemplary." Like Teil he defended the "39ers," stating that "I, personally, despite all unpleasant accusations and innuendos to which the former Germans who were members of the occupation forces have been subjected, consider it a privilege to have been able to work for the War Department." Forgetting or ignoring his repeated derogatory, on-record references to "39ers" over the previous two weeks, Strong's testimony moved McCarthy to proclaim, "I have always felt there was no foundation" behind the charge that "non-Aryans who suffered persecution in Germany and were forced to leave Germany have carried a feeling of vengeance toward the whole German race."[51]

Teil and Strong had poked substantial holes in McCarthy's blanket assertions that "39ers" possessed an uncontrollable hatred for the "German race." McCarthy hoped he might be able to get what he believed to be the truth from the one alleged bad apple in the bunch: William Perl. Perl testified for the better part of four days—longer than any other witness—and much of the time was taken up in series of lengthy verbal duals with McCarthy.

Perl began his testimony by describing his background at length: his education in psychology and law, his eight years working for one of the largest law firms in Vienna during which he handled many criminal cases, his journey to the United States, and his training and experience as an interrogator. He had weeks to prepare for his appearances, and had brought with him copies of documents from his interrogations, including original copies of the suspects's confessions written in their hands and some of the hand-drawn maps they provided the investigators. Certainly, Perl was not the hate-filled, thuggish rogue agent of McCarthy's imagination. The diminutive, balding former army interrogator remained composed and in control of his responses, and his loquaciousness drove McCarthy to distraction. Over the course of his testimony, Perl explained in considerable detail every important aspect of the pretrial investigation and denied that he or the other interrogators resorted to any form of coercion.

As in his many appearances on the stand in the trial and in his long affidavit to the AJRB, he never denied using ruses on the suspects. He also defended the "quick process" as a legitimate, though not terribly useful, method. Its purpose, Perl explained, was to convey to the suspect that he was being subjected to "a very formal and very important interrogation," hence the cloth-covered table, candles, and crucifix. He pointed out that he had adapted a pretrial examination procedure from continental European legal systems and assumed that his subjects would find it familiar and not totally disorienting, though generating some level of uncertainty on the part of the suspect was critical to the ruse's success.[52]

Perl's refusal to use the term "mock trial" notwithstanding, it was not unreasonable to conclude that the suspect might have assumed he was being "tried." Yet for the ruse to be effective, the interrogators believed it was necessary to be unclear as to their roles in the "ceremony," which might include a version of a good cop / bad cop routine. For McCarthy and other critics of the investigation, if a suspect thought he was in fact being tried, then he had been subjected to a form of interrogation that broke the boundaries of the acceptable and more likely than not confessed falsely. What the boundaries should have been was not anything McCarthy was able or willing to define. For Perl, Ellis, Fanton, and the other interrogators, however, it was one among several legitimate forms of extracting information. The chasm between the two views on the matter would not be bridged during or after the hearings.[53]

A few hours into the first day of Perl's testimony, McCarthy made a last-ditch effort to salvage his failed attempt to expose alleged "American atrocities" in Germany. The only way to resolve the matter definitively, he asserted, was to subject Perl to a lie detector test. "I think you are lying," McCarthy told him. "I do not think you can fool the lie detector. You may be able to fool us. I have been told you are very, very smart. I know you are a psychologist and psychiatrist and work at it. I have been told I can get nothing from you in cross-examination, and I think that is true. I am convinced you cannot fool the lie detector." Perl agreed on the spot, though he thought the idea was wrong-headed and counterproductive. "I believe we would make a laughingstock out of the whole thing for the whole world," he told McCarthy, adding that "the importance of machines in America is known too much, maybe, and evaluated even too highly." In any case, if the subcommittee had that much faith in the device, Perl argued, then "we should have started with it."[54]

Baldwin was skeptical from the start. He remarked that basic fairness would require the convicted men who swore that they had been abused to submit to testing, an idea McCarthy considered "excellent." But this suggestion was not a serious one, and after reminding McCarthy that the subcommittee's purpose was to investigate the army's procedures and not to serve as an appeals court, he made it clear that his preference was to "proceed in the normal way of finding out what did happen as much as we can from those who actually participated." His reservations provoked McCarthy to accuse the committee of being afraid of the facts and attempting to "whitewash" the army. A week later, Baldwin announced that, with the backing of Hunt and Kefauver, no lie detector would be used.[55]

Along with this setback, Perl's testimony was the last straw for McCarthy. That he resorted to such a stunt as a lie detector test should not be surprising. Perl's lengthy descriptions of how he conducted his interrogations led McCarthy to complain repeatedly that the hearings might drag on for months. The four days during which Perl appeared were broken only by testimony from Calvin Unterseher, the first of several American medical officers who served in Schwäbisch Hall to testify that no prisoner had been abused in the ways they had claimed, and Raphael Shumacker, who provided the same explanation of the investigators' methods as Ellis, Fanton, Elowitz, and Perl before him.

On May 20, McCarthy read out a statement of resignation written for both Baldwin and the press. He accused Ellis of "prostitut[ing] and pervert[ing] justice before the world" and Fanton of promising immunity to members of Battle Group Peiper in exchange for providing testimony against the accused. As for the "refugees" hired by the army as interrogators, they "had every reason to thoroughly dislike members of the German troops" and were charged with "brutalities greater than any we have ever accused either the Russians or Hitler Germany of employing." For McCarthy, Baldwin's refusal to allow the use of lie detectors made one thing clear: "this subcommittee not only has no desire to obtain the truth but is conducting a deliberate attempt to avoid the facts and effect a whitewash of the Army officers involved." His press release included the extraordinary claim that "testimony" and "documentary evidence" revealed that the accused German soldiers "were subject to beatings and physical violence in such forms as only could be devised by warped minds. They were subjected to sham trials, to mock hangings; and families were deprived of rations—all of which the prosecution justified as being necessary to create the right psychological atmosphere in which to obtain confessions." Baldwin's response expressed regret that the Wisconsin senator had "lost his temper and with it . . . sound impartial judgment," and pointed out what had been obvious from the start: that McCarthy had made up his mind before the subcommittee had completed its work.[56]

The hearings continued for another two weeks, though the dramatic high point had been reached with McCarthy's departure. The pattern established in April and May held: American officials with firsthand or at least very close knowledge of the pretrial investigation, trial, and posttrial reviews insisted the torture accusations were false and defended the integrity of the court and the review process. James Finucane of the NCPW gave mawkish testimony. While admitting that "everything I have to say about the United States atrocities that took place against unarmed Germans is hearsay," he made the perverse claim that "just as we were concluding the Nuremberg trials with charges of crimes against peace, crimes against humanity, and war crimes, we were beginning to commit the same crimes ourselves, through our agents in Germany. . . . Certainly it is a crime against humanity for the Americans to run a concentration camp like Schwäbisch Hall or Landsberg." The convicted men should go free, Finucane asserted, as "the days have been vivid with terror and wretched with loneliness for these soldiers now in jail for the fourth year. Let them go home. Let them return to their families and friends." An unimpressed Baldwin told Finucane, "You have judged this case already while this committee is still in the process of taking testimony."[57]

The most important American official who did not testify was Willis Everett. He had been debilitated by a heart attack in March and his doctor had forbidden him from appearing before the subcommittee. He was, however, strong enough to be interviewed in his Atlanta office by Joseph Chambers on October 4, after the hearings had concluded but just in time for his deposition to be included in the subcommittee's final report. Everett stuck to his previous criticisms of the pretrial investigation and the trial, though he refrained from commenting on the posttrial affidavits submitted by the convicted men to Leer in early 1948. Similar to his acquaintance Van Roden's testimony, the best Everett could muster was "there was funny business going on with the prosecution at Schwäbisch Hall. I couldn't say that I believe that this defendant was telling the truth when he made his initial statement, but I do state with certainty that on account of this original pattern without the benefit of collaboration among themselves that there was enough smoke coming out of Schwäbisch Hall to make a reasonable person apprehensive of whether it was possible that all these things could have happened. Whether they did happen or not, I can't say." He denied ever telling Ellis right before the trial that four defendants had lied about being abused, though Everett did in fact believe this at the time. For Everett, what mattered most in the end was the "cloud of doubt" that remained hanging over the pretrial investigation and trial. Such a situation that, he believed, made a retrial necessary.[58]

Whatever doubts Everett harbored about the veracity of his former clients' posttrial affidavits, he certainly shared McCarthy's opinion that the subcommittee whitewashed the army's conduct in the Malmedy case. For Everett, the "whitewash" was more evidence that vengeance-seeking Jews had, at least for the time being, prevailed over his efforts to call the army to account for its misdeeds. In a February 1950 letter to Finucane, he noticed that Ellis—who had provided the subcommittee with copies of his private correspondence with Perl, Thon, and other investigators—had a habit of closing letters with "yours in all the bonds." Everett wondered what "blood bonds . . . Ellis had with Harry Thon, 'the thug'?" In any case, he wrote to Finucane that "someday God, who is more powerful even that those bloodthirsty and vengeful wrongdoers whose race tendencies will over-shadow, will take them to task."[59]

A Striking Conflict of Evidence

A heavy legislative workload prevented the senators from holding hearings in Munich until early September. These lasted a total of six days, during which the committee heard testimony from more American investigators and several Germans, including two of the most important lawyers representing the convicted men and two former members of Battle Group Peiper. The four former investigators—Harry Thon, Joseph Kirschbaum, Frank Steiner, and Bruno Jacob had played relatively minor roles in the investigation and, unsurprisingly, their testimony added little of significance to that of the others.

An intriguing aspect of the subcommittee's investigation in Germany was the rather anemic or absent testimonies of several Germans who had invested a great deal of effort to discrediting the trial. Both Rudolf Aschenauer and Eugen Leer gave brief and opaque testimony. While Aschenauer represented Neuhäusler's views to the American senators, the Evangelical Church dispatched Bishop Hans Meiser's secretary to deliver more documents to the senators but did not give him authority to testify. Undoubtedly, the awkwardness of simultaneous translation was a deterrent to lengthy testimony and discussion. It may also be that Leer and Aschenauer saw little value in presenting their already well-known case to the subcommittee, which at that point did not include McCarthy, the one person they believed to be supportive of their position. In any case, they understood that the subcommittee was in Germany to investigate and had no authority to revise any sentences.

The testimonies of several other Germans, however, was far more revealing. The dentist Eduard Knorr had died, so the senators interviewed Maria Geiger, an assistant to Knorr who confirmed that American personnel were always present when he treated prisoners and that Knorr told her about cases in which he had treated patients for a broken jaw and knocked out teeth. She could recall only one instance in which she saw a patient who had just lost several teeth. No records existed of Knorr's visits to Schwäbisch Hall, Geiger told the senators, as Knorr had them destroyed. Following his death, two German lawyers approached her about preparing an affidavit for Leer, and the transcript of Geiger's testimony suggests strongly that they had influenced the wording of her statement.[60]

Dietrich Schnell, a former German Army paratrooper and prisoner in Schwäbisch Hall who had sent Leer an affidavit in January 1948 swearing he had assisted in the treatment of prisoners for injuries received during

The Baldwin subcommittee visiting the Malmedy massacre memorial site, August–September 1949. Estes Kefauver and Raymond Baldwin stand to the right of the crucifix, Lester Hunt stands to the left (NARA).

interrogations, was interviewed multiple times by Chambers. Schnell recalled watching Perl conduct an interrogation in which he shouted at the subject repeatedly, " 'You lying pig!' " before "hitting him in the face and kicking him." In a dramatic flourish, Schnell added, "I often heard shrieks and sometimes cries of pain during the night. On various occasions these cries were heard even by people who lived in the private houses adjoining the prison."[61] Schnell swore that he heard Arvid Freimuth call out, "They extorted perjury from me! I want to die!" the night before he hanged himself in his cell. When Chambers questioned him in Munich, however, Schnell denied ever seeing any prisoner being mistreated, admitting "the mistreatments I have not seen. I have only heard, and there seen the results [on] such individuals." Schnell's credibility collapsed once American investigators took him to Schwäbisch Hall, where they figured out that he could not have seen nor heard the things he had sworn to in person or in writing. They also learned that he telephoned Leer immediately after being questioned by Chambers, despite insisting that he had had no contact with any German lawyers involved with the case.[62]

Leer had suggested the committee interview Rolf Reiser, a former second lieutenant and First Panzer Regiment battalion adjutant whose conviction had been overturned. Unbeknownst to the senators and Chambers, Reiser had been instrumental in seeking out new "witnesses" for Leer. Reiser was one of the few battle group veterans who did not claim to have been physically abused. In his meeting with Chambers in Munich, he provided a lengthy description of how a "quick process" conducted by Perl worked. Reiser's account contradicted Perl's assertions that it was a simple ruse applied only to suspects the interrogators considered unintelligent. Reiser resisted signing a statement until Perl, after fourteen days of questioning, wore him down. Chambers was skeptical, telling Reiser, "I have been marveling at your memory." Horst Vollprecht's testimony most likely struck Chambers as even less credible. Vollprecht had testified as a defense witness at the trial and now insisted that Morris Elowitz had alternately threatened him and promised him a light sentence, before Joseph Kirschbaum spat at him, called him a "pig," and "beat me in my face, left and right, with his fist." The only other Waffen SS veteran to testify was Friedrich Eble, who stuck to his now infamous claim that Perl or Kirschbaum had inserted sharpened matchsticks under his fingernails and stabbed him in the arm.[63]

More significant for the committee's final report was what took place before, during, and after the senators' visit to Munich. First, there was the question of the suspects' medical records from their internment in Schwäbisch Hall. During the hearings in Washington, Baldwin noted that he found it strange that no testimony by any medical personnel was offered at the trial, particularly since the defense objected to the introduction of the sworn statements on the grounds they had been obtained through various forms of duress, including "beatings."[64] Two physicians and three medical orderlies all testified that no prisoners had suffered injuries consistent with those reported by the convicted men, Knorr, or Schnell. After attempts to locate medical records from Schwäbisch Hall failed, the subcommittee decided to go a step further: those prisoners who claimed to have suffered the most serious injuries would be examined by a team of two American physicians and a dentist.[65]

Beginning on August 31, the team spent ten days examining fifty-nine men convicted in the Malmedy case. Eleven denied that they had been mistreated in Schwäbisch Hall, while thirty-five reported mistreatment, though no physical evidence remained of the alleged abuse. That left thirteen who asserted that there was such evidence of their ordeal. Among that group, nine told the team that their teeth or jaws had been damaged (though only one reported being treated by a civilian German dentist). Of the thirteen, the team concluded that "three of these, on examination, had conditions which definitely were not due to physical maltreatment. The remaining ten showed physical findings which might have resulted from trauma. However, none of these ten prisoners showed evidence of acts of severe physical violence. . . . The evidence of physical maltreatment found in the examination of these 59 prisoners is relatively minimal. When these findings are compared with the allegations of physical maltreatment in the prisoners' histories there is a striking conflict of evidence."[66]

The evidence in the physicians' report was not conclusive. Physical injuries that might have been inflicted upon a suspect during an interrogation in early 1946 might well have healed in the intervening years. More serious injuries could also have been war-related. Their report, nonetheless, went a long way in confirming the senators' suspicions that the accusations of extreme forms of abuse were baseless.

For good measure, Lester Hunt questioned eight of the convicted men in Landsberg on September 6, including Dietrich and Peiper. Hunt asked pointed questions about each man's claims of beatings and mistreatments and why more did not take the stand at the trial to repudiate their sworn statements. Valentin Bersin, who alleged he had four teeth knocked out, told Hunt that he had never received dental treatment in Schwäbisch Hall. Hubert Huber had also accused interrogators of abusing him, but told Hunt that he now made "no claim with reference to any injury." There were other contradictions. Several indicated that unnamed lawyers solicited posttrial affidavits from them, while others insisted that the convicted men themselves had written the statements without prompting from "Dr. Leer or anyone else," as Fritz Kraemer put it to the senator. The ever-cagey Peiper hinted that he knew the torture claims were false. "It is not necessary to treat a man with violence to get a confession from him," he told Hunt, as "psychological tricks [are] for some men more effective." As for the reason why more defendants did not take the stand, six told Hunt that their lawyers advised them not to do so. Like the medical reports, Hunt's short interviews did not disprove the torture accusations conclusively, though his visit to Landsberg reinforced the strong suspicion that at least some of the convicted men had concocted their stories, most likely with the guidance of Leer and other lawyers.[67]

The second important development involved American counterintelligence operations in Germany. As we have seen, by late 1948 intelligence and other occupation officials had become intensely concerned about the activities of German lawyers and Bishops Neuhäusler and Wurm. Criticism of the subsequent Nuremberg and army trials—and especially the Malmedy case—by German church leaders in 1948 and early 1949 led the subcommittee to dispatch Joseph Chambers to meet with the commanding officer of a regional CIC detachment. Chambers wanted whatever information was available regarding any "organized effort underway to discredit War Crimes Trials, the Occupation, and Military Government in the eyes of the German people using [the] Malmedy case as a basis." If such a campaign was underway, he wanted to know what group was behind it, and "is there any indication of joined forces of Nazi[s] and Communist[s]?"[68] In particular, Chambers was interested in intelligence on Aschenauer's activities, as the German lawyer had become active in representing some of the convicted Malmedy case men and was particularly close to Neuhäusler. He had also served as an informal go-between for the bishop in negotiations with American military government intelligence officials in Bavaria and as an unpaid informant for the CIC on the activities of the postwar German far right.

Initial CIC reports answered Chambers's main question in the affirmative. "A number of former ex-Nazis, particularly high-ranking ones are financing and supporting campaigns against the Malmedy Case," one agent reported.[69] It was also clear that both churches were providing some financial and institutional support to lay advocates of the convicted men such as Aschenauer.[70] CIC agents considered Neuhäusler's main motivation to "see justice done." There was no question that he was a nationalist, but CIC sources suggested that he was not interested in aiding ex-Nazi elements. Bishop Wurm's activities were another matter. "It is questionable," CIC agent Willard Johnson reported in mid-September, "that the Wurm group in Stuttgart is campaigning primarily for the promotion of justice. The primary goal of this group appears to be a propaganda angle to promote their nationalistic purposes." Sources suggested that the aging but still enormously influential Protestant bishop was being "used by rightist elements in the Stuttgart area."[71] In Bavaria, the CIC learned that the Evangelical Relief Organization was using some of its funds, as its business manager told a Special Agent, "to pay for the defense of former Nazis and war criminals as well as people being brought before [local denazification tribunals] because of their former NSDAP activities."[72] Through the use of informants, wire taps, and mail intercepts, the CIC would learn a good deal more about the "organized effort" on behalf of Dietrich, Peiper, and other battle group veterans still imprisoned in Landsberg.

A Dead Pigeon Except for the Smell

The subcommittee's final report came to the same conclusion as every other investigation into the Malmedy case: the accused received a reasonably fair trial and had not been tortured or otherwise coerced into signing false confessions. Baldwin, Hunt, and Kefauver were convinced that conditions of confinement in Schwäbisch Hall, including the provision of medical care, were adequate and humane. On the crucial subject of torture, the subcommittee had considered accusations leveled before and during the trial, the affidavits assembled by Leer, and all the testimony given in the hearings. The senators were particularly impressed by the testimony of former Schwäbisch

Hall personnel and the reports submitted by the team of physicians. "There is little or no evidence," they concluded, "that there was physical mistreatment by members of the interrogation team. . . . The preponderance of evidence is all to the contrary and there are too many discrepancies which appear in the allegations made concerning such physical mistreatment." The senators did concede, however, that in some cases a suspect was slapped, struck, or shoved, but if these things did occur, they "were the irresponsible act[s] of an individual in the heat of anger" and "definitely not a general or condoned practice." They also found no significant problems with the use of tricks and ruses, concluding that "it would seem that the bulk of the success of this interrogation stemmed from the ability to confuse and deceive a group of persons who had taken an opportunity to prepare their stories in advance."[73]

In other areas, however, the senators' conclusions were more ambiguous. Despite their limited use and the fact that no physical violence appeared to be involved, mock trials were a "grave mistake," if only because their use "has been exploited to such a degree by various persons that American authorities have leaned over backwards in reviewing any cases affected by mock trials," with the unfortunate result that "many sentences have been commuted that otherwise might not have been changed."[74] The evidence regarding promises of acquittal was "very conflicting," and the senators found Fanton's guidelines on the matter to be unclear. The courts, and certainly not investigators, should have the sole authority to make any such deals with suspects. The subcommittee also concluded the army's court in Dachau was constituted properly and the posttrial reviews were, for the most part, adequate (it considered Clay's "thoroughness" particularly praiseworthy). It further found the participation of John Dwinell in one of the early trial reviews was improper and the Simpson Commission's work completely one-sided. Qualified support was offered for Everett's long-standing contention that the defense did not have adequate time to prepare its case. The senators—Baldwin and Kefauver were both lawyers by profession—also questioned the Malmedy court's refusal to agree to the defense's request for severance.

The matter of personnel was another area of concern. The lack of enough qualified investigators, lawyers, and interrogators was a problem recognized by War Crimes Group personnel from the start. Additionally, the senators pointed out that the lack of experience among most of the American defense lawyers resulted in mistakes that, while not fatal to their clients' cases, could have been avoided had more seasoned lawyers been made available.

The harshest criticism, however, was reserved for Van Roden and the NCPW. "Those citizens of the United States who have accepted and published these allegations as truth," the final report asserted, "without attempting to secure verification of the facts, have done their country a great disservice." Repeating the accusations of an individual like Friedrich Eble as fact not only "caused considerable anxiety in the minds of some Americans" but damaged American authority in occupied Germany, where the accusations were accepted as factual because of the "cloak of authority" given to them by Van Roden and the NCPW. As the most important American conduit for those Germans seeking to undermine the credibility of all war crimes trials, the NCPW had succeeded in getting the allegations of abuse "accepted as fact" and its activities "have been most damaging to the interests of our country, and to the cause of peace."[75]

The results of the CIC's first investigations had to be presented carefully, and not only because the senators could not report the details of its classified findings to the public. Outright criticism of two powerful and well-connected German clergymen would not have been wise. Hence, they commended the clergy's sincerity in "assist[ing] their parishioners during a time of uncertainty and trouble" while noting that there were "strong reasons to believe that groups within Germany are taking advantage of the understandable efforts of the church and the defense attorneys to . . . discredit the American occupation forces." In this connection, the senators took the opportunity to call attention to the significance of the transatlantic network of the like-minded that had formed between "many of the [German] figures involved in this situation" and the NCPW. It was through this network that "most of the allegations made in this case have become accepted as fact," with the result being a decline in American prestige in occupied Germany.[76]

The committee's most significant failure was its unwillingness to defend the service of German-born Jews as investigators and interrogators. It was unfortunate, read the findings on personnel, "that more native-born, trained American citizens were not available. . . . The natural resentment that exists within a conquered nation was aggravated by the fact that so many of the persons handling these matters were former citizens of that country." The subcommittee recommended that the State and Defense Departments "employ no civilians on military-government work who have not been American citizens for at least ten years" and that "military personnel engaged in war crimes work should meet the same citizenship requirements." The language of its final report was a less stridently worded version of McCarthy's accusations of allegedly hate-filled "39ers."[77]

The final report of the Baldwin subcommittee did not whitewash the army. It was as an impartial investigation into the Malmedy massacre trial controversy as anyone could have reasonably expected. Stories along the lines of "American Atrocities in Germany" no longer appeared in American newspapers and magazines. The Malmedy affair, Clio Straight wrote to Ellis on August 9, had reached the "high water mark," as "no more damning accusations could be made as to the operation." This is not to say the case was henceforth uncontroversial, especially in Germany. Straight also predicted, accurately, that the new German government would "be the source of lots more pressure and propaganda."[78] Positions on both sides of the issue had hardened. Those Americans or Germans whose minds were made up about the Malmedy case were unlikely to swayed by a new round of sensational newspaper stories or yet another official American investigation, however impartial.

Certainly, the investigators felt vindicated. "We wanted a fair and impartial hearing," Burton Ellis wrote Dwight Fanton on May 21, and once McCarthy departed, "the hearing will be fair."[79] For a time, Ellis was intent on bringing lawsuits against Edward Van Roden, the NCPW, and the *Progressive*. That publication's chastened editor—who had taken to referring to Van Roden as "Van Rodent"—at least offered Ellis the opportunity to write a rebuttal to the discredited ghostwritten article that had caused so many problems.[80]

"The Malmedy case," Ellis wrote William Perl in mid-November, 1949, "is a dead pigeon except for the smell and it will smell unto eternity."[81] Ellis was responding to Perl's concerns that the Malmedy case was going to be retried. That was out of the question, Ellis assured him, and he was right. More accurate was the subcommittee's prediction that a "general amnesty program"—a political, rather than a legal, solution to what was becoming an intractable problem in a changing diplomatic context—would result in the release of most imprisoned German war criminals. The lingering odor of the Malmedy affair would, however, pervade the final debates over the fate of the convicted men.

THIRTEEN

Red Jackets

Releasing the Prisoners

On December 22, 1956, two guards opened the door to Joachim Peiper's cell in Landsberg prison and informed him that he was to be released immediately. Peiper was allegedly so stunned that he stared wordlessly at the guards as the unexpected news sunk in. While Lucius Clay's successor as commander in chief of EUCOM, General Thomas Handy, had commuted his death sentence to life imprisonment in early 1951 and a clemency board approved a further reduction four years later, Peiper believed he might never be released. His requests for parole had been denied repeatedly and he had barely evaded being prosecuted by a West German court for having ordered the execution of four young Waffen SS recruits in Belgium a month before D-Day. Yet to his surprise and the delight of many of his former comrades, his parole application was approved on December 21. He left Landsberg the next day, having spent nearly eleven years incarcerated by the Americans. He moved into an apartment in Stuttgart, where he began working for the Porsche automotive firm.[1]

With the release of Hubert Huber a month later, every one of the men convicted in the Malmedy trial had been freed. Like Peiper, Huber had been a "red jacket," the informal designation for prisoners under death sentences that for most Germans became synonymous with victor's justice. They were among hundreds of German war criminals that exited West German and European jails in the same period, their sentences commuted or parole requests approved.[2] The fact that the release of most of them coincided with the creation of the Federal Republic of Germany (FRG) and a hardening of Europe's division makes it tempting to conclude that the Cold War was solely responsible for a short-circuiting of the judicial reckoning with Nazi crimes that took place in the immediate postwar years. A closer look at the German amnesty network's activities following the conclusion of the Baldwin subcommittee's investigation, the internal deliberations of the clemency boards, and the political and diplomatic situation in the FRG in the early 1950s suggests a more complex explanation.

Congratulating the Morgenthau Clique

The release in early 1949 of the Simpson Commission's and the AJRB's final reports provoked a new round of attacks in the German press.[3] Not surprisingly, the most outspoken German critics were not swayed by the evidence presented to the Baldwin subcommittee in the fall. "The happenings in Schwäbisch Hall simply cannot be denied," Bishop Wurm wrote in a statement for the NCPW following the publication of the subcommittee's final report in October. Wurm had already expressed regret that McCarthy had left the subcommittee and issued an unmistakable accusation of Jewish revenge, this time by appropriating the language of the subcommittee's recommendations: "How tempting it is for the investigators to do everything in their power to make their misdeeds appear as innocent as possible, misdeeds through which they abused their newly-acquired American civic rights." With a memorably dramatic flourish, Wurm added, "Never will the people of Schwäbisch Hall, who in the night heard the cries of pain of the tortured beyond the prison walls, be made to believe that these investigators were servants of justice and not servants of revenge." The latter formulation was reprinted for American readers of the *Christian Century*.[4]

Wurm also derided the subcommittee's fear that nationalists might be colluding with pro-Soviet elements in Germany with the hope of uniting German and Russian power against the West. Even some very well-informed CIC agents thought this particular accusation against Wurm was patently absurd. For the bishop, however, vengeful Jews were behind the charge. "One can only congratulate the Morgenthau clique," he was quoted in multiple newspapers in mid-October, "that it has two such boogie men at its disposal to scare the children of the USA." Not surprisingly, Wurm backed the recommendation of a citizenship requirement for war crimes personnel, warning that "the disastrous role played by people who have only been American citizens for a few years . . . will become clear one day to the American people."[5]

Bishop Neuhäusler remained less strident in his comments to the press. A priest close to the bishop admitted quietly to Joseph Chambers that Neuhäusler "was a little too much of an advocate at times, did not weigh the matters from the legal or judicial point of view and was perhaps . . . a little intemperate in the way he proceeded."[6] Neuhäusler remained keenly interested in the Nuremberg and Dachau cases, however, and the fate of the convicted men in Landsberg made him even more convinced that vengeful Jews were responsible for derailing American justice in Dachau.

In August he received a long report from Jost Schneider, a Waffen SS veteran imprisoned by the U.S. Army in Dachau. From the fall of 1945 to the end of 1947, Schneider worked on the trials as a record keeper and translator. In the fall of 1946 he wrote, "the Jews entered everywhere" and viewed the trials as a "means of revenge against the Germans." If any happened to serve the defendants, Schneider believed they did so only to subvert an effective legal defense. In particular, he blamed German Jewish investigators for holding "stage shows"—which he admitted he never witnessed personally—conducted by "a Jewish American of Austrian origin," meaning Joseph Kirschbaum. He also reported being told that Kirschbaum offered witnesses cigarettes and alcohol and encouraged them to verbally abuse and identify suspects, falsely, as concentration camp personnel. Schneider allowed that it was understandable that men like Kirschbaum "had a hostile, even hateful, attitude toward people whom they supposed to be involved in these persecutions and murders," but this fact should have precluded them from working on the trials, "where justice, and not revenge, was to be served."[7]

Though he insisted that Schneider's account was totally reliable and hoped that the subcommittee would interview him in Munich, Neuhäusler was nervous about being associated with its conspiratorial anti-Semitism. So rather than use it to make thinly veiled public references to a "Morgenthau clique" or "servants of revenge," he forwarded the statement to the NCPW with the request that the material be handled with care. "When the author explains that it was a Jew who did this and that or gave this or that testimony," he argued to the NCPW, Schneider was not expressing anti-Jewish sentiments. Rather, he was "clarifying and almost excusing what [was] done, since it was the Jews who suffered most terribly under Nazism and especially in concentration camps and therefore were naturally particularly interested in the punishment of the offenders."[8]

NCPW officials assured the bishop that they would be discreet. They had the document translated and then sent it to Baldwin, McCarthy, and Chambers. By that point, however, there was nothing new to say on the matter of Jewish American interrogators in Nuremberg or Dachau. At most, Schneider's account would have bolstered existing suspicions among even well-meaning American officials like Baldwin or Chambers that men like Kirschbaum and Perl, while in most ways eminently qualified as investigators, were prone to excessive zeal or that their presence intensified "the natural resentment that exists within a conquered nation."[9]

Whether quoting clergymen or not, the German press in the American zone was almost uniformly critical of the hearings. True to form, commentary in multiple newspapers focused on only those elements that supported the abuse accusations, especially those given by German sources testifying in Munich. References to the NCPW and individual Americans also appeared, albeit with less frequency. McCarthy was presented as a crusader for truth and justice—his citing of Winston Churchill's warning that "grass may grow on the battlefield but never under the gallows" during a rant against Baldwin on the Senate floor in July was quoted frequently.[10] Willis Everett's contribution to exposing the supposed truth was not forgotten. During the hearings in Munich, Franz Josef Schöningh, the cofounder of the *Süddeutsche Zeitung (South German Newspaper)* and during the war an enthusiastic participant in the evacuation of Jews from Tarnopol to the ghettos, visited with Everett in Atlanta. In a fawning, sentimental profile, Schöningh called Everett a "Michael Kohlhaas in Atlanta," a reference to the doomed horse trader in Heinrich von Kleist's famous novella. The tribute moved Peiper to write Everett, expressing his admiration for Everett's "gallant struggle for fair play" and bemoaning the "ocean of tendenciously [*sic*] slanders in the waves of which a certain group is trying to drown the remnants of an old culture . . . these hyenas of the battlefield are citizens of very recent origin and by far no representatives of your great nation."[11] Gratitude extended beyond Waffen SS veterans and ex-Nazi journalists. In 1958 a West German consular official presented Everett with a check for $5,000 on behalf of his government to compensate him for his allegedly selfless efforts on behalf of his former clients.[12]

Exceptional among German newspapers was *Die Neue Zeitung (The New Newspaper),* a publication overseen by American authorities and staffed by Germans, many of them returning émigrés. It was the only major paper to offer anything like an accurate summary of the hearings or to publish a defense of the pretrial investigation by any of the interrogators. William Perl authored the article. He began by pointing out that the incident at the Baugnez crossroads—the Malmedy massacre proper—was only one of many war crimes committed by the men of Battle Group Peiper on orders from Sepp Dietrich, who had received them from Hitler. Perl described the cases against several of the defendants and informed readers that the army had had the earliest abuse accusations investigated by Edward Carpenter and Paul Guth. He also noted that during the trial only ten defendants took the stand to deny their sworn statements. The U.S. Army, he assured the paper's readers, had not attempted to conceal anything. Rather, it was the irresponsible actions of Judge Edward Van Roden that resulted in the widely publicized accounts of horrific abuses in Schwäbisch Hall.[13]

The editors included another critique by Bishop Wurm on the same page, and Perl's article provoked Rudolf Aschenauer to respond in a Munich newspaper two weeks later. Aschenauer avoided linking Perl's past to his defense of the prosecution's case. As with other German press accounts of the hearings, he cited selectively from the subcommittee's final report. He summarized Dietrich Schnell's accusations, for instance, without noting that Joseph Chambers had discredited Schnell's accounts of what he supposedly witnessed in Schwäbisch Hall. Despite Aschenauer's stated intention not to smear Perl personally, he called attention to James Bailey's and Kurt Teil's testimonies that Perl had bragged to them about the effectiveness of "third degree interrogations" and that he had struck prisoners. In the end, however, Aschenauer could not resist pandering to his readers' "good common sense" when it came to Perl: "Is it probable, and in conformity with the general experience in life, that during an interrogation which supposedly was conducted without any moral and physical duress, the accused would voluntarily incriminate themselves in crimes which lack any factual basis[?]" or was it more likely that such admissions were extracted by force?[14]

In short, there was next to nothing in German newspaper coverage to dislodge the belief among Germans that the Malmedy trial was nothing more than the imposition of victor's justice. By September, however, the emphasis in mainstream press coverage was shifting from sensational stories of gruesome tortures to "tricks and ruses," especially "mock trials" and mock executions. Yet there was never any doubt expressed that the suspected men had been subjected to a wide range of physical and psychological abuses and pressures. Germans following accounts of the hearings in the press would read confirmations from American and German sources of what Bishops Wurm and Neuhäusler had been saying for months. That stories about permanently damaged jaws and testicles no longer appeared reflected the simple fact that they had lost their shock value.[15] What Germans did not read about, of course, was the abundant testimony and documentation that indicated respected figures like Wurm and Neuhäusler had been, willingly or not, misled.

More important was the tectonic shift in Germany's political situation taking place during the hearings in Washington and Munich that saw the end of the occupation and the creation of the FRG. Having failed to embarrass the Americans into overturning the sentences, German amnesty advocates would now turn to other forms of pressuring the new government to intercede with the Americans on behalf of the convicted men in Landsberg.

Quieter Help

The wartime Allies had not agreed on Germany's political future when the war ended in May 1945. Within a few months, however, they had settled on a framework for the occupation and a general vision of the near-term future. Beyond the loss of Alsace-Lorraine in the west and a large amount of territory on its eastern border, Germany would not be dismembered. Political division seemed a sure way to keep the embers of German nationalism smoldering at a time when Allied governments were determined to stamp them out, so they agreed to oversee the creation of a unified nation state with a decentralized political structure. During the occupation period, the Allies would carry out "the four d's": denazification, democratization, demilitarization, and decartelization. Some $20 billion in reparations would be paid by Germany to the victors and victims of the Nazi regime, with half slated for the Soviet Union (which it eventually received). Though each nation was responsible for managing the affairs of its zone of occupation, including a portion of Berlin, Allied officials would coordinate the implementation of their broad agreements through a Berlin-based Control Council.

It became clear very quickly that Allied cooperation on nearly every major aspect of the occupation would be impossible. Soviet intransigence, the slow pace of recovery, housing and food shortages, the burden of reparations payments, and an unusually cold "hunger" winter in 1946–1947 pushed the Western Allies to unify the administration of their three zones by 1949, in the process issuing a new currency to contain rampant inflation and eliminate a massive black market. The Soviets responded in kind, and in an effort to forestall the creation of two German states, attempted to block American, British, and French access to Berlin. By supplying the three western zones by air for nearly a year, the Americans and British demonstrated their resolve to hold out in that city. The Berlin Airlift handed Stalin a humiliating diplomatic defeat and catalyzed the creation of the FRG in the fall of 1949.

Military occupation and the unraveling of the wartime alliance did not preclude the revival of German political life, which had begun almost immediately after VE Day. All four occupying powers authorized the reestablishment of political parties by the end of 1945. In the Western zone, three were of the greatest significance for Germany's political future. The old SPD was reformed under the leadership of Kurt Schumacher, the fiercely anti-Nazi and anticommunist socialist who had spent a decade imprisoned in Dachau. The prewar centrist, free market–oriented liberal parties emerged as the right-of-center Free Democrats. The dominant party through the remainder of the occupation years and through the 1950s was the moderate conservative Christian Democratic Union (CDU) and its Bavarian-based sister party, the Christian Socialist Union (CSU), which appealed mainly to middle-class Catholics and Protestants, including many former Nazis. Smaller parties proliferated, mainly on the far right. However, their ability to impede parliamentary politics was limited by the efforts of the major parties to appeal to as broad an electoral base as possible and, not least, by a provision in an electoral law that required a party to win at least 5 percent of total votes cast to win seats in the national parliament, the Bundestag.[16]

The dominant politician in the republic's first decade was Konrad Adenauer. Known to Germans as "the Old Man"—he was seventy when he became the head of the CDU in the British occupation zone—Adenauer was determined to oversee the establishment of a stable parliamentary democracy underpinned by a social-market economic system and close ties to

Western Europe and the United States. Unlike the Social Democrats and some on the far right, he rejected the idea that Germany should chart a political course independent of both the liberal democratic, capitalist West and the Russian-dominated, communist East. For Adenauer, this was a recipe for dangerous revanchism. Fortunately, postwar American, British, and French leaders backed his agenda—their support was critical—and by the mid-1950s, the FRG had become stable democracy, a cornerstone of the Western European economic integration project, and, by 1955, a member of the North Atlantic Treaty Organization.

None of this came easily. There were formidable obstacles in Adenauer's path from the beginning, one of the most significant being the unresolved fate of convicted war criminals. Like most Germans, Adenauer wanted to make a clean break with the past. He understood, however, that while National Socialism had been discredited as a viable political challenger to democratic socialism, liberal democracy, or communism, the attitudes of Germans did not change overnight after VE Day. A sullen, self-pitying resentfulness pervaded Germany in the early occupation years, with most Germans convinced that they were the principal victims of twelve years of Nazi Party rule and a massively destructive war. For the pragmatic Adenauer, this situation produced a political calculation regarding the presence of the past in postwar Germany: creating a functioning parliamentary democracy required a clean break with the Nazi past and silence about the extent of the regime's crimes. In practical terms, this meant an end to denazification and war crimes trials, the two most widely despised vehicles for confronting Germans with the ugly realities of their recent history, and a comprehensive solution to the entire "war criminals problem."[17]

The last vestiges of denazification were the first to be done away with by the Bundestag. Responsibility for denazification had been handed over to local German tribunals in the Western zones three years earlier, and both the Bundestag and Bundesrat (the legislative body representing the FRG's states), moved immediately to end all denazification proceedings and pass an amnesty law that affected nearly eight hundred thousand people serving sentences or paying fines imposed by denazification courts. The restoration of voting rights and pensions and the lifting of employment bans for civil servants who had lost their positions in the purges followed shortly after.[18] Determining the fate of those convicted in Allied war crimes trials was a more complicated matter. Public opposition to the subsequent Nuremberg trials and zonal military tribunals had been very strong, and after the creation of the FRG, political parties and voters found it increasingly intolerable that the Western allies refused to release the convicted men or transfer all authority to deal with the matter to the new German state.

Adenauer did not disagree, but his ability to maneuver was constricted by two factors. One involved the makeup of his governing coalition, which was comprised of the CDU / CSU, the Free Democrats, and the far-right German Party. As an entirely right-of-center coalition, it was more vulnerable to the pull of far-right elements in and outside its ranks. Even on the left, there was a newly assertive nationalism that could threaten the coalition's support among more moderate voters. The Communists and Social Democrats, while remaining bitter enemies, both advocated their own versions of a unified and neutral socialist German state and rejected Adenauer's pro-Western foreign policy and social-market economic program.[19] The second was the fact that the new state was not entirely sovereign. The military governors in the three Western zones were replaced in 1949 by an Allied High Commission (AHC), represented by an American, British, and French civilian high commissioner. As a condition for Allied recognition of the new state, the AHC had to give its approval to all laws passed by the Bundestag, and each high commissioner had jurisdiction over war criminals imprisoned in his nation's former occupation zone.

The first American commissioner, the former assistant secretary of war and World Bank president John J. McCloy, was committed to West Germany's rapid economic recovery and its integration with the West. He held both projects to be essential to constructing a bulwark against the Soviet Union and channeling German power in the right directions. McCloy was generally optimistic that the FRG would succeed as a democracy living at peace with its neighbors. Though he was well aware that nationalist and anti-Jewish sentiment was intensifying—including on the unrepentant far right—he rejected what he considered overblown reports in the American press warning of West Germany's impending "renazification."[20]

On the matter of war criminals, however, he was not as accommodating as Adenauer and most Germans wanted. As one of the architects of the IMT, he was committed to the integrity of that enterprise, and not least because he believed that it was essential that Germans acknowledge the regime's responsibility for the war and the extent of its crimes. McCloy made it clear from the start of his tenure as high commissioner that he would not support a program of general clemency. He also declared "general attacks on the soundness of the sentences" to be "improper."[21] That McCloy's jurisdiction was limited to the subsequent Nuremberg trial cases further complicated matters for amnesty advocates. Those cases tried by the army were the responsibility of Clay's successor as commander in chief of EUCOM, General Thomas Handy. He and his successors likewise rejected of any kind of general amnesty.

The most sensitive issue was the execution of outstanding death sentences. In his last months as military governor, Clay tried to avoid handing over what had become one of his most intractable problems to McCloy and Handy. At the end of March, he sent what he admitted was a "ghoulish" request to Tracy Voorhees, the assistant secretary of the army: that Royall's order to stay executions in the Nuremberg and Dachau cases be lifted. "I would not like to have a mass execution," he told Voorhees, "and yet I do want to free my successor from this thankless task." Noting what he called their "difference in status" (a reference to the forthcoming congressional investigation), Clay excluded the six remaining Malmedy death sentences from his request.[22] The remaining Landsberg prisoners wearing the red jacket were not executed, however, and McCloy and Handy inherited the problem.

As soon as they arrived in Germany both officials were presented with the amnesty lobby's well-rehearsed arguments along with some new ones suited to Cold War conditions and the desire of the FRG's political leadership to achieve complete independence. With the outbreak of the Korean War in the summer of 1950, the question of a West German contribution to the collective defense of Western Europe became an urgent one. It would entail the creation of a new German army and rearmament, a seemingly risky prospect to Americans, Europeans, and even many Germans only five years after VE Day. It quickly became clear, however, that there would be powerful opposition among Wehrmacht and Waffen SS veterans to the creation of a new army unless prisoners in Landsberg, Wittlich, and Werl were released.[23]

Adenauer did not hesitate to use both popular domestic opposition to rearmament and the American, British, and French desire to see a new West German army embedded in a collective European defense force as leverage to pressure the Allies to release all convicted war criminals and grant the FRG full sovereignty. The Cold War and the question of rearmament comprised only one dimension of the war criminals problem. Also at stake was the restoration of national honor. Most Germans believed individual and collective honor had not been lost in complicity with a murderous dictatorship, but during the war of revenge by the Allies and the punitive occupation that followed.

The basic arguments made by German amnesty advocates did not change fundamentally after 1949. Their approaches to resolving the war criminal problem, however, did evolve. In contrast to the situation facing the beleaguered Clay, McCloy and Handy did not face a flood of sensational American and German newspapers stories, stacks of appeals from ex-Nazi lawyers, or constant and intemperate pleas from influential church leaders. Moreover, the controversy had passed its high point in the United States. More significant than any rehashing of old charges of torture and tricks was the creation of the Central Bureau for Legal Defense, an office housed within the FRG's Ministry of Justice devoted to advocating for the release of all Germans imprisoned anywhere as war criminals. Its first head was Hans Gawlik, a former Nazi Party member and defense counsel in multiple Nuremberg cases.

At the same time, the network of amnesty groups expanded, and some of its members became enmeshed with the new Central Bureau for Legal Defense. The network continued to keep the public informed about the fate of imprisoned war criminals and the injustices they allegedly suffered. Unconvinced by the findings of the Baldwin subcommittee, they accepted the torture accusations as established fact—an "open secret" in the United States and Germany. They also continued to provide various forms of aid to prisoners (or those recently released) and assisted the West German political establishment—mainly via its close connections to the Central Bureau for Legal Defense—with keeping pressure on the Western Allies, especially the Americans. In effect, the basic position of the amnesty lobby became the official one of the West German government.

The fate of the Protestant Church's long-planned "white book" on war crimes trials illustrates the nature of this evolving strategy. In 1948 clergy in both churches threatened to make materials about conditions in Schwäbisch Hall, Dachau, and other Allied prisoner enclosures public with the hope of embarrassing the Americans into retrying certain cases. This was not a bluff. Evangelical Church leaders began assembling the materials in the summer of 1948. To be included were statements by both churches opposing the trials, letters exchanged between Bishop Wurm and Lucius Clay, the bishop's widely publicized debate with Robert Kempner, the text of an American judge's dissenting opinion in the Ministries case, and hundreds of documents from German lawyers, witnesses, and defendants alleging improper procedures and abuses in various prisoner enclosures. Among the last were the entire text of Dietrich Schnell's affidavit and a few excerpts from the convicted Malmedy defendants' 1948 statements describing threats and beatings administered by Perl, Harry Thon, and Raphael Shumacker.[24]

While it included several statements from Catholic bishops, the German Catholic Church did not cosponsor the project. In its final form, the compendium was solely a Protestant Church effort. The introduction to the nearly two-hundred-page "Memorandum" bore the signatures of Wurm, Martin Niemoeller, and the Stuttgart-based prelate Karl Hartenstein. Its final recommendation was that all prisoners in Landsberg be paroled while their cases were reviewed by judges not connected to any of the trials.

Whatever the original intentions, the memorandum was not made widely available to the public. CIC agents had been aware from the start that the document was in the making and it is doubtful that occupation officials would have allowed its publication in Germany. By 1949 a more targeted and circumspect approach seemed appropriate. The documents were translated into English (the costs were covered by lawyers for IG Farben) and one thousand numbered, bound copies were printed. One was delivered to McCloy in late February 1950. Given the anodyne title *Memorandum of the Evangelical Church in Germany on the Question of War Crimes Trials before American Military Courts,* it is doubtful the compendium had any influence on him or any American official of significance. Much of the documentation had either previously been reported in the press or otherwise been made public. Its recommendations had no chance of being approved by the high commissioners.

More helpful in some ways was the ongoing advocacy of the amnesty network. As its constituent organizations were riddled with informants, CIC detachments were able to track its activities closely. In addition to the Evangelical Relief Organization, several other church-backed prisoners' aid organizations formed part of the network. One was actually called "Quiet Help for Prisoners of War and Interned Persons," the leadership of which included Helene Elisabeth Princess von Isenburg (known as the "Mother of the Landsbergers"), Neuhäusler, Wurm, General SS colonel and Einsatzgruppe veteran Dr. Wilhelm Spengler, and the lawyer (and CIC informant) Heinrich Malz. Rudolf Aschenauer handled its legal affairs. As CIC agents learned quickly, some of these groups were infiltrated or effectively controlled by ex-SS officers. One such organization, also fronted by a member of the old nobility, struck one CIC agent as indistinguishable from a newly formed Waffen SS veterans' organization.[25] Groups like "Quiet Help" were most useful for keeping the public's attention focused on the plight of the prisoners. The organization's regular plaintive missives from the "Mother of the Landsbergers" no doubt pulled at the heartstrings of newspaper readers and donors, as did her well-publicized visits to the prison.[26]

By 1949, Waffen SS veterans already had a good deal of experience operating quietly. From the start of the occupation, they had practiced low-key forms of opposition to trials in or outside Germany. Their exploits—real, farcical, or fictitious—to hide or aid the escape from Europe of wanted war criminals have tended to overshadow more quotidian kinds of assistance provided to their imprisoned comrades and their families. On the question of a West German contribution to a European defense alliance, however, Waffen SS veterans became more organized and vocal. Just as Wehrmacht veterans formed organizations to represent their interests and demands, one of which was the release of convicted war criminals as a precondition for any such contribution, Waffen SS veterans did the same. Like Wehrmacht veterans, they were intent on restoring the collective "honor" of the organization, which its members believed had been lost not in the commission of war crimes but by defeat, occupation, denazification, and war crimes trials.

Because of the connection many Americans and Europeans (but fewer Germans) made between the Waffen and the General SS, along with the IMT's designation of the entire SS as a criminal organization, Waffen SS veterans had additional hurdles to overcome. Wehrmacht veterans, as we have seen, had distanced themselves from the Waffen SS during the Nuremberg trials. A law passed by the Bundestag in the early 1950s that restored state pensions to those dismissed from their positions during the postwar occupation excluded most Waffen SS veterans. Hundreds remained imprisoned in and outside West Germany, including most of the men convicted in the Malmedy case. The challenge for veterans was to convince the new West German political establishment and the Western Allies that Waffen SS soldiers had fought for their country honorably, were now in full support of the new FRG, and were prepared to contribute to its future defense. The price was the release of their imprisoned comrades and the state's recognition of their status as former civil servants eligible for pensions.[27]

To these ends, ex-Waffen SS officers forged hundreds of local veterans groups into a national organization, giving it the innocuous-sounding name "Mutual Aid Society" (Hilfsgemeinschaft auf Gegenseitigkeit, or HIAG). According to the first iteration of its official publication, HIAG had nearly four hundred local chapters in West Germany by the fall of 1951.[28] Convincing West Germany's political leadership of the Waffen SS's supposedly honorable wartime service and respectable future intentions was not difficult. All political parties wanted to court veterans' votes and were attuned to the sensitivity of the war crimes issue. It certainly helped that a few well-known Wehrmacht officers, most notably General Heinz Guderian, publicly and privately supported their former Waffen SS comrades. The leaders of the major parties soon embraced the position of Waffen SS veterans articulated at the IMT: that they had served their country honorably and had had nothing to do with the General SS or the Einsatzgruppen.[29]

Convincing the American, British, and French governments of its benign patriotic intentions was another matter. Lingering hostility toward the SS was difficult to overcome, particularly among U.S. Army officers serving in EUCOM. The fact that the fate of the Malmedy convicts would be decided by an army general and not the civilian high commissioner may explain why HIAG did not undertake a strong public push for amnesty in that case. By 1956, however, the point was moot, as nearly every one of the convicted men had been paroled by a mixed American, British, French, and West German clemency board. In the intervening years, however, HIAG continued to aid the Malmedy convicted by supporting organizations like "Quiet Help" and raising funds for prisoners, assisting their families, and arranging jobs for the recently released.[30]

The energetic and enigmatic Rudolf Aschenauer remained the lawyer most directly engaged with the convicted men in the Malmedy case. By 1949 he represented most of them as they applied for sentence commutations and parole. He had established several church-funded legal aid offices in Munich and Nuremberg and churned out a steady stream of pamphlets on the case. These were no more than tedious rehashings of the abuse accusations and the alleged fatal flaws in the trial and the posttrial reviews, though now updated with critiques of the Baldwin subcommittee. Some were translated into English, most likely with the assistance of two neo-Nazis, the Anglo-American publicist H. Keith Thompson and Francis Parker Yockey, a former civilian employee of the U.S. War Crimes Group who worked briefly in its posttrial review section. Aschenauer was also a valuable informant for the CIC on the activities of amnesty advocates and the far right until EUCOM ordered its counterintelligence wing to cut ties with him for fear that, should his cooperation be revealed, it might appear that the army was interfering in the legal representation of German prisoners. Aschenauer's connections to counterintelligence did not end there, as he also became an informant for the West German Federal Office for the Protection of the Constitution, the rough equivalent to the American Federal Bureau of Investigation (FBI). Though there is no question that he was an unreconstructed National Socialist and an apologist for the worst crimes of the Nazis, it seems he was also driven by a desire to promote himself as a well-connected attorney, which he did in fact become.[31]

Most emblematic of the transition to what Norbert Frei and Kerstin von Lingen have characterized as the "politicization of the war crimes issue" was the formation of the Heidelberg Jurists Circle in the spring of 1949. Its membership included lawyers and legal scholars, most of them ex-Nazi Party members, mid-level clergymen, Bundestag delegates, and West German federal and state court officials. It was created to serve as a quasi-official coordinating body that would draw on the considerable experience many of its members had with the Nuremberg and Dachau trials and in the activities of the amnesty network. Georg Froeschmann and Aschenauer were both active in the circle, as was Hans Gawlik. Its members, of course, continued to deny the legal legitimacy of Allied courts and accepted the abuse accusations in the Malmedy case as factual, but they were determined to take a more pragmatic approach to securing the release of prisoners in Landsberg, Wittlich, and Werl. Hence, some of the more outspoken proponents of a general amnesty, along with the publicity-seeking Princess Isenburg, were excluded from the group's roster. Early on, the circle's leaders had agreed to avoid a "battle in the press," though some of its members would advocate for publicizing its criticisms of Allied resistance to releasing prisoners.[32] Reaching out to sympathetic American organizations became a lower priority. The NCPW was estimated, correctly, by the circle's leadership as being totally without influence in Washington. Future lobbying in the United States would have to be done with precision and be directed only at those that mattered.

Those officials who mattered most, of course, were in Germany. The positions, prestige, and connections of the circle gave its members access to Adenauer, the Central Bureau for Legal Defense, important Bundestag committees, and to American officials, especially McCloy and EUCOM commanders. The circle's pragmatic orientation did not prevent it from indulging in a degree of fear mongering by warning Adenauer and the Americans that if the war criminals problem was not resolved quickly, the far right would be the political beneficiaries. As evidence that Adenauer and the Allies were playing with fire, the circle's leaders pointed to the electoral success of the neo-Nazi Socialist Imperial Party in Lower Saxony state elections in May 1951, which they claimed resulted from popular frustration over the unresolved war criminals problem. Along with Allied resistance to any general clemency scheme, the circle's eventual advocacy of a permanent American-German sentence modification board likely influenced the equally pragmatic Adenauer to embrace the idea in the course of 1952.[33]

The Lesser of Two Evils

A modification board, rather than an appeals court or a general amnesty, became the compromise solution to the war criminal problem in West Germany. The issue had become a highly unwelcome impediment to full West German political sovereignty alongside economic and military interdependence with the West. Though convinced that the verdicts were justified and adamantly opposed to a blanket clemency, McCloy did concede that some sentences were "too severe." He was receptive, then, to reviewing and reducing sentences in individual cases. The vehicle for sentence modification would be a permanent review board along the lines of one created in late 1949 by EUCOM.[34] The AHC was not far behind, and in March 1950, McCloy created the Advisory Board on Clemency for War Criminals.

This compromise solution did not at first appease most German critics, and throughout the remainder of the year the pressure on McCloy and Handy to lift the remaining Landsberg death sentences intensified. In the ugliest episode of the months leading up to his decision on the cases under his jurisdiction, McCloy and his family—including his children—received death threats and had to be protected by bodyguards. German officials also made a final effort to convince General Handy to lift the thirteen death sentences left from the army's Dachau trials. A state secretary in the Justice Ministry met with him for over an hour on January 10, insisting that it was unproven that a war crime had been committed near Malmedy and warning the unimpressed American general that approving executions would endanger the existence of the FRG.[35]

One of the more even-tempered and thoughtful assessments of the situation at that moment was contained in an intelligence assessment written by the German Jewish émigré occupation officer Erich Isenstead. The report, which reached Handy's desk in late December, urged the commander in chief not to approve the condemned men's executions. A little over a week before their decisions were announced, former Wehrmacht general Leo Geyr von Schweppenburg met with Isenstead and other American intelligence officers in Munich. The former Waffen SS general Paul Hausser had asked Schweppenburg to appeal to the Americans to overturn the death sentences, especially in the case of Joachim Peiper. Schweppenburg refrained from any commentary on the legal aspects of the Malmedy trial, but felt duty bound to warn the Americans that Peiper's execution "would make it extremely difficult to overcome the already existing great differences among former German soldiers over a German contribution to a European western defense." He pointed out that Peiper was not only regarded very highly among Waffen SS veterans but also among those of the Wehrmacht as a "competent and decent officer and soldier."[36]

The meeting concluded on a cordial note, as Isenstead had promised to convey Schweppenburg's position to higher authorities. Isenstead implored Handy to consider the political implications of his decision on the death sentences. The continued incarceration of former German soldiers—Wehrmacht or Waffen SS—in Landsberg "constitutes one of the greatest stumbling blocks for a real understanding of the United States' desire for a German contribution toward a western defense," with the "treatment of the war crimes prisoners . . . [as] perhaps the one issue on which a national solidarity could be achieved in Germany against the United States, if another press campaign would be instituted by the Germans." Isenstead was convinced that a negative decision on the commutation of death sentences would produce another war of words over every aspect of the trials, and he believed it was particularly important to lift the death sentences in the Malmedy case.

That trial, he wrote, "has been under too much fire both by Americans and Germans and enough doubt has been raised, even in the minds of people who cannot by any stretch of the imagination be accused of condoning Nazi atrocities, that no such execution delayed years after the verdicts have been pronounced would lend itself to a reasonable defense." Those Germans, he added, who had been willing to cooperate with the United States would be put under a great deal of pressure to become less cooperative. Isenstead was aware that there would be negative repercussions should Handy lift the death sentences, but doing so would represent the "lesser of two evils."[37]

McCloy and Handy announced their decisions on January 31, 1951. McCloy commuted ten death sentences and confirmed those of SS Lieutenant General Oswald Pohl and four Einsatzgruppen officers for whom "no mitigating circumstances whatsoever have been found." Handy spared the lives of all but two notoriously brutal concentration camp guards. Regarding the Malmedy cases, he blamed the "continuous and organized flood of accusations and statements made to discredit the trial and repeated reviews and studies requested by and on behalf of the prisoners" for the long delay in the execution of the sentences. Like his predecessor Clay, he remained adamant that the convicted men were guilty. He was willing to allow, however, that the fluid conditions of battle in the opening days of a desperate counteroffensive should be considered a mitigating factor in considering sentence modification. Adenauer's office was supportive, though cautiously so and with reservations. Responses by the leaders of West Germany's mainstream parties were generally favorable. Bundestag president Hermann Ehlers praised McCloy's decision, as did the influential SPD delegate Carlo Schmid, though the latter considered it "regrettable" that Handy "could not go further" on the Malmedy sentences.[38]

Following this moment of high drama, both boards operated separately until the summer of 1953, when they merged into the Interim Mixed Parole and Clemency Board (hereafter "interim board"), which now included German representatives nominated by the West German government. When it was established in August, 31 individuals convicted in the subsequent Nuremberg trials and 281 convicted in the army's Dachau trials remained in Landsberg. Of the 74 men convicted in the Malmedy trial, 13 had been released in 1948 following the reversal of their original sentences. One had died of natural causes that year. During the period when the EUCOM War Crimes Modification Board worked independently, 19 were released. Thirty were paroled during the years in which the interim board was in operation (nine in the month of December 1953 alone). In 1955 the interim board became the Mixed Parole and Clemency Board, now expanded to include American, British, French, and West German representatives. The mixed board would be responsible for the final ten Malmedy trial cases.[39]

The records of the boards' deliberations reveal that they did not rubber-stamp prisoner applications for parole and clemency. EUCOM officials were often reluctant to recommend sentence reductions when the evidence against the defendants seemed very strong, while civilian lawyers and State Department officials advising or serving on the boards tended toward leniency. The latter had fewer professional and emotional connections to the cases. More important, they were convinced that the interrogators' had coerced confessions from the accused. Everyone familiar with the Malmedy case, as one

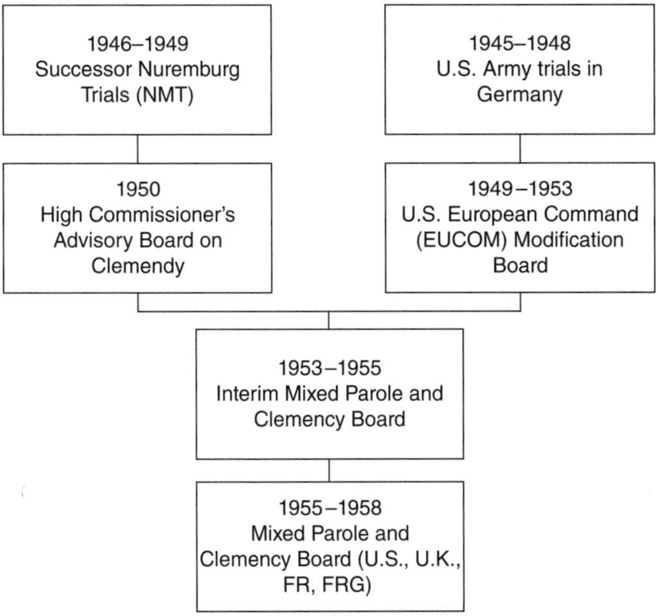

War crimes trials (U.S.) and sentence modification boards in Germany, 1946–1958.

civilian adviser to EUCOM's board put it in May 1951, knows "that the method of obtaining the confessions in this case carries an odium and stigma that in common parlance 'stinks'" and that the prosecution's case would not have stood a chance in an American civil court.[40]

The fate of Theodor Rauh's case was typical. Rauh was a corporal in the Eleventh Panzer Grenadier Company convicted of participating in the execution of seven or eight American prisoners in La Gleize. Statements of other participants indicated that they had used their captives as target practice. Though sentenced to death at the trial, his youth and low rank led Clay to commute the sentence to a life term two years later. In May 1951, the EUCOM modification board reviewed Rauh's case. The three civilian lawyers advising the board based their recommendation to reduce Rauh's sentence to time already served on a highly selective review of the posttrial controversy. The advisers emphasized Rauh's plea for mitigation, in which he denied committing any crimes, and the entire text of his February 1948 affidavit in which he claimed that Harry Thon, William Perl, and Joseph Kirschbaum threatened, insulted, and physically abused him before Perl wrote out his "confession." They also noted that defense counsel John Dwinell testified in 1949 that during the trial one of the members of the court told him that all the accused were going to be convicted. That the court found seventy-four defendants guilty after deliberating for a little over two hours struck the reviewers as confirmation of Dwinell's testimony. Also significant to them was the recommendation of the first review board in February 1948—on which Dwinnel served as the principal adviser—that Rauh's guilty verdict be overturned.[41]

Most revealing was the reviewers' commentary on the backgrounds of the interrogators. They pointed to the February 1948 recommendation as evidence that the "so-called confessions were creations of the investigation team." To this they added, "It is futile to discuss the weight to be attached to these pre-trial statements in view of the unprecedented circumstances under which three over-zealous investigators, two of whom because of Hitler became refugees, contrived by despicable ruses and abuse to obtain confessions." The reviewers also pointed out that "various boards" had found "some truth" in the abuse accusations.[42]

Similar references to vengeful Jewish interrogators pervade the civilian advisers' recommendations to the EUCOM modification board in 1950 and 1951. In the case of Kurt Sickel, a First SS Panzer Regiment surgeon, the advisers did not doubt that he had in fact ordered Otto Wichmann to shoot a debilitated American prisoner, but that the language of Wichmann's confession "was one of Lieutenant Perl's many creations." As in other cases, the reviewers found Wichmann's posttrial repudiations of his sworn statement more convincing than his original confession, as Perl had a "known reputation" for invention.[43]

EUCOM officials, however, were reluctant to support sentence reductions on these grounds. In Rauh's case, the chief of the Judge Advocate Division's War Crimes Branch agreed with the civilian advisers, but the modification board officers making the formal recommendation to the commander in chief voted to commute Rauh's sentence to fifteen years. General Handy would only agree to twenty. In late 1953, at which point parole and clemency decisions had been taken up by a mixed American and German board, the two German members requested more information from the Judge Advocate's office about the shootings at La Gleize, indicating that they did not believe any prisoners had been killed there. Given that they were closely connected to the West German amnesty lobby, it should not be surprising that they based their request verbatim on a petition submitted by Rudolf Aschenauer on Rauh's behalf.[44]

Once again, Judge Advocate Division officials defended the integrity of the original investigation, replying that it had been demonstrated beyond a reasonable doubt that American prisoners had been shot in La Gleize. For good measure, the responsible officer added that since Rauh had not authorized Aschenauer to represent him or advocate on his behalf, it was clear that "some person or persons . . . in some undisclosed manner" had attempted to influence the board's German members. Such skepticism did not, however, prevent the same official from supporting the prisoner's application for parole, as Rauh was fit for work and his record in Landsberg was excellent. He was paroled in February 1954. Three years later, the mixed board unanimously voted to reduce his sentence to time served.[45]

A few cases remained much more delicate and contentious. The two highest-visibility and most problematic were those of Sepp Dietrich and Joachim Peiper. Dietrich had received a life sentence at the trial, which Clay reconfirmed in 1948. Three years later, the EUCOM modification board recommended that Handy reduce his sentence to twenty years. True to form, the civilian advisers, referring to "over-zealous [refugee] investigators," had suggested a reduction to time served. The head of the War Crimes Branch concurred on the grounds that there was not enough credible evidence to support the charge that Dietrich had given preoffensive orders that prisoners of war and civilians were to be killed. Both the civilian advisers and the War Crimes Branch chief believed that any order to kill prisoners originated within Peiper's regiment.[46]

Handy approved a reduction in Dietrich's life sentence to twenty years in August. His release under parole was impeded after CIC agents intercepted several copies of a seven-page essay about the Malmedy case Dietrich was trying to send Dietrich Ziemssen, one of the more active Waffen SS veterans working to discredit the Malmedy trial in Germany. The essay was written from the perspective of a fictional unnamed visitor to Landsberg who had just spoken with a prisoner, also unnamed, "involved in the Malmedy case." The visitor leaves the prison convinced that it was "the duty and responsibility of every respectable German" to demand, and if necessary "force," the release of the convicted men. What followed was an account of the Malmedy affair that offers intriguing insight into Dietrich's mind-set in the early 1950s. With "the Moloch [Hitler] in his dying convulsions," he wrote, a desperate counteroffensive had been ordered, and the tanks of his army were charged with breaking through to the Meuse River. When the spearhead encountered an American convoy near Malmedy, a firefight ensued. Though most of the GIs panicked, a "Lt. Lary" took charge and "attempt[ed] a heroic defense" and the outgunned Americans suffered heavy casualties. No American prisoners had been intentionally killed. The ensuing trial was a farce and the forty-three death sentences a "violation of justice," with false confessions forced out of the defendants by German émigrés who had returned to Germany as "zealous defenders of the Morgenthau Plan" and who "played the part of 100% Americans." Nearly two pages were taken up with a quotation from Joseph McCarthy's May 20 statement to the Baldwin subcommittee. At the end of the essay, the author admonished the German people not to forget that in 1945 "they were collectively [blamed] for the concentration camp[s] despite the fact that the little man in the street knew nothing about them" and that now, as the nation wrestled with the question of rearmament, "the victims of demilitarization are still in jail."[47]

Dietrich timed the writing of the essay to influence upcoming national elections. "The idea is to have it published in numerous German newspapers . . . since we hope that something will be done for us before the elections," he told Ziemssen. He also warned Ziemssen to be careful, "as this is going out illegally." When confronted by American officials about the article, Dietrich admitted his responsibility and attempted to justify his actions with reference to his stature among Waffen SS veterans, who expected him to do something to pressure Adenauer's government to help the Malmedy case prisoners. Dietrich was not disciplined, and the prison director understood that given his desire to be released, the incident would serve to discourage any future rule breaking. The parole board nonetheless denied two applications submitted over the following months, with the Judge Advocate Division officers citing Dietrich's "background and history as an unscrupulous and aggressive opportunist" and that the article he attempted to smuggle out of Landsberg revealed his hostility to the United States and the FRG. Not least, as Judge Advocate officials held him responsible for issuing orders to kill prisoners of war and civilians, he should not be released while his former subordinates remained incarcerated. Edwin Plitt, a career diplomat and head of the interim board, disagreed, having been convinced that Dietrich now "fully realizes that National Socialism was wrong" and wants nothing to do with unrepentant comrades.[48]

Officers in the Judge Advocate Division remained unconvinced, however, and urged the EUCOM commander in chief at that moment, General Anthony McAuliffe, to deny Dietrich's request. That McAuliffe sided with the Judge Advocate should not be surprising. During the Battle of the Bulge, he had briefly taken command of the 101st Airborne Division and led the defense of Bastogne, which had been encircled by numerically superior German forces. Holding Bastogne made McAuliffe's reputation, as did his one word reply—" 'Nuts' "—to a German demand that he surrender.[49] While he was willing to approve the requests of other Battle Group Peiper veterans, the release of Dietrich was too great a symbolic step to take.

Dietrich finally prevailed once the mixed board had taken over jurisdiction of the Landsberg cases and he was paroled in October 1955. As long as its decision on a prisoner's request was unanimous, the mixed board's recommendation was binding on the state that imposed the original sentence, so there was no more possibility that a EUCOM commander in chief with a longer memory could impede the clearing out of Landsberg prison. Army officials did, however, lodge two protests following the decision, and Dietrich's release generated considerable press commentary in the United States, revealing that the Malmedy massacre story as formulated in the aftermath of the Baugnez encounter still resonated powerfully in some quarters. The commander of the Veterans of Foreign Wars was quoted in the *New York Times* as being "shocked beyond words" and that it was a "tragedy that in the short span of ten years United States authorities have forgotten the violent deeds of one of Hitler's most vicious killers."[50] In a letter to the *Times,* William Clark, a former military government and AHC legal officer, denounced the mixed board for "making a clean sweep of the inhabitants of Landsberg" and the U.S. State Department for bowing to political expediency. Clark's letter provoked a response from Willis Everett and Herbert Strong, who insisted that there was never any convincing evidence presented at the trial that Dietrich was guilty and that the U.S. Senate had "exposed the un-American pretrial methods used by the prosecution." The two former defense attorneys added that it was time "to forget, as far as humanly possible, all the terrible things which happened" and to "overcome the war hatred of 1941 and . . . allow the wounds to heal."[51]

The criticism voiced in some American press reports unnerved West German Foreign Ministry officials, prompting the mixed board to assure the ministry that its future decisions would not be swayed by any outside pressures. The removal in January of the mixed board's compliant American representative, Edwin Plitt, only heightened suspicions among Germans working to secure the release of the remaining prisoners that "powerful forces" were trying to sabotage their desired clean sweep. This was not the case, however, and releases continued after what was most likely considered a decent interval of a few months following Dietrich's parole.[52]

The old SS general would soon return to Landsberg, however. Less than a year after being paroled, a Bavarian state court sentenced him to nineteen months' imprisonment for his involvement in the June 1934 purge of the Sturmabteilung (the "Night of the Long Knives"). A heart condition won him early release but did not prevent him from becoming an energetic HIAG activist. Plitt and other members of the interim board had misjudged Dietrich. His funeral in 1966 was attended by some six thousand SS veterans, among them Joachim Peiper.[53]

One last well-known and controversial case from the Malmedy trial remained to be resolved: that of Peiper's. Once again, Judge Advocate officers were reluctant to support sentence reductions and parole applications. In its May 1954 recommendation, for instance, Colonel E. H. Snodgrass argued that "the commission of the atrocities which formed the basis of the charge and particulars, are traceable to the energy and ruthlessness of Peiper more than any other person." Further, Peiper seemed unrepentant. In this case, the interim board, at that time still under Plitt's leadership, took a tough line and denied further clemency in December, despite Peiper's excellent record as a prisoner. In a reversal three months later, however, Plitt recommended a reduction in Peiper's sentence to thirty-two years on the grounds of his "apparent acceptance of responsibility for his actions" and "the possibility that Peiper's guilt may also have stemmed to a considerable degree from the desperate situation in which his command became involved and not altogether from criminal intent." As evidence in support of the latter claim, Plitt pointed to Hal McCown's trial testimony about Peiper's behavior in La Gleize. McAuliffe denied this request, Peiper's third.[54]

The stalemate was broken by the mixed board, as it was in other cases, though it would take another two years before his final parole request was approved. Initially, the American representative, Robert Upton (who had replaced Plitt on the interim board and served on the mixed board) remained convinced that Peiper bore a large degree of responsibility for the crimes committed by the men under his command. Since the vote was not unanimous, the EUCOM commander in chief was not required to give his approval, and he backed Upton. By the summer, the West German Foreign Ministry quietly requested an explanation from the State Department. Within a few months, the Judge Advocate Division was willing to support Peiper's parole plan, which restricted his movements to the Stuttgart area (where his future employer, Porsche, was based) and required twice-monthly written reports to his parole officer.[55]

Peiper's release did not produce a strongly negative response in the American press, as had Dietrich's a year earlier. Newspaper coverage was perfunctory, though many reports made reference to Senator Estes Kefauver's warning that freeing Peiper would "destroy any hope we might have that the proper punishment of war criminals would deter similar atrocities in the future." The State Department deferred to the authority of the mixed board. A U.S. Army Headquarters spokesman remarked "we're only jailers."[56] Also quiet was the West German press. By the end of 1956, the battle to win the release of nearly every prominent former Wehrmacht and Waffen SS officer along with former officials in the Third Reich's ministries and the heads of major industrial concerns had been won.

Men such as Peiper—to say nothing of a young ex-enlisted man like Theodor Rauh—who were not members of Germany's pre-Nazi political and economic elite were useful to the mainstream amnesty lobby as symbols of

Allied vengeance by other means, but only while they were imprisoned. Peiper's Waffen SS comrades, however, had not forgotten him during or after his imprisonment. In Landsberg, he received letters, visits, and packages from veterans, who also maintained close contact with his wife, Sigurd. His job with Porsche was arranged by SS veterans—the company in those years was a kind of way station for integrating former Nazis into the booming West German private sector. He maintained regular contact with some of his comrades, though never took an active role in HIAG.

A good measure of reserve was in order in the 1960s, as West German courts became more active in prosecuting former members of the SS in particular, and Peiper had been more than an ordinary soldier. As one of Himmler's adjutants, he knew some of the men who would be indicted. After learning the residents of Boves in Italy, where Peiper's men had massacred civilians in 1943, had built a memorial and identified his unit by name, Peiper and a handful of former comrades invented and coordinated stories about the incident, just as they had done in the earliest days of their postwar confinement. Though Peiper would not be extradited to Italy, he narrowly avoided being tried in a West German court for the Boves massacre and for his role in the deportation of Italian Jews to Auschwitz.[57]

Outside the relatively protective confines of West Germany in these years, however, were those who would neither forget nor forgive. After leaving Porsche, Peiper bought a small house outside Traves, a village in the Franche-Comte region of eastern France. Beginning in 1972, he attempted to live there full time and as quietly as possible. The past caught up with him two years later, when a local tradesman and former member of the French Resistance learned he was living in the area. On the night of July 13–14, 1976, after weeks of thinly veiled anonymous warnings, newspaper articles announcing his presence, and various low-level threats, a group of assailants set fire to Peiper's house while he was at home alone. He was killed, perhaps by gunfire or as a result of the fire. No one has ever been charged in the attack.[58] Peiper's fate, however, was not at all typical of the other men convicted in the Malmedy massacre trial. Some, notably Dietrich, would remain active with HIAG and otherwise contribute to maintaining the myth of the honorable and persecuted Waffen SS. Most of the others would live out their lives quietly, convinced they had never committed any crimes.

Conclusion

Massacres, American Interrogators, and Postwar Memory

In the American mythology of World War II, the Battle of the Bulge remains the "greatest generation" 's greatest battlefield triumph. "An ever famous American victory," as Winston Churchill would call it in the House of Commons. Triumph was accompanied by tragedy. Underestimating German capabilities in late 1944, the Americans had not fortified defenses in the Ardennes. The initial success of the German counterattack was also the result of the most disastrous intelligence failure in American history. The price of these mistakes and the battle that produced victory was steep: in terms of casualties, the Bulge was the costliest ever fought by American forces. And it's often overlooked that Belgian civilians paid a heavy price for their country's final liberation. Some three thousand men, women, and children were killed in the fighting and thousands more displaced in the middle of winter.

The Malmedy massacre retains a prominent place in this accounting of failure and hard-won victory, and no history of the entire battle is complete without a dramatic retelling of the crossroads encounter. The apologetic account of the massacre, investigation, and trial has also enjoyed a long afterlife. Its durability suggests that it is not always the winners who get to write history.

The postwar amnesty campaign was a transatlantic effort, with Germans and Americans feeding off each other's denunciations of the investigation, trial, and posttrial reviews. Similarly, the perpetuation of the apologetic narrative has been fueled by a selective assessment of German and American sources. Memoirs by Waffen SS veterans and the willingness of many of them to speak to those they believed would be sympathetic became an important source of misinformation for gullible historians, Waffen SS fetishists, and neo-Nazis well into the 1990s.[1] The prolific British Army veteran and military historian Charles Whiting, author of several accounts of the Ardennes counteroffensive and the Malmedy massacre, relied heavily on the input of SS veterans—including Joachim Peiper—who saw him, rightly, as useful tool to perpetuate the apologetic narrative for English-language readers. Like others, Whiting also made selective use of the trial record and the transcript of the subcommittee hearings. He even went so far as to credit Joseph McCarthy with saving the lives of the remaining red jackets in Landsberg.[2]

Another influential historian to draw selectively on German and American sources was John Toland, who not only corresponded with Peiper, Sepp Dietrich, and Otto Skorzeny, but also with Willis Everett and Hal McCown. To Burton Ellis's considerable irritation, Toland did not seek out any of the prosecutors. While Toland, like Whiting, did not go so far as to deny that a massacre of American prisoners had taken place at the Baugnez crossroads, both authors invariably excoriated the investigation, trial, and the refusal of the U.S. Army to rectify an obvious miscarriage of justice. Toland later corresponded with Ellis, who ultimately expressed admiration for his book on the Bulge. The historian accepted Ellis's suggestion that future editions of his book include the sentence "The allegation that the trial was 'a poor advertisement of American justice' is denied by the chief prosecutor of that trial and the [Senate] subcommittee's findings do not conclude that any such activities existed."[3]

Access to Waffen SS veterans and a selective reading of sources only partly explains the apologetic narrative's durability. Also important has been changing international contexts. The Cold War reshaped collective memory of the war in West Germany, Britain, and the United States in a way that encouraged a romanticizing of the German war on the Eastern Front. In the postwar decades, works of history, movies, and television documentaries portrayed members of the Wehrmacht—and to a lesser extent the Waffen SS—as ordinary soldiers battling the vast "Asiatic hordes" of the Red Army. This popular genre of historical representation, of course, de-emphasized or simply ignored war crimes and crimes against humanity.[4]

The significance of changing contexts and the willingness of historians to be influenced by access to ex-Wehrmacht or Waffen SS officers is best illustrated by the American historian James Weingartner's influential 1979 account of the Malmedy massacre and trial, *Crossroads of Death*. The book was neither a sentimental account of heroic GIs martyred in the Ardennes nor an uncritical restatement of the most extreme apologetics promoted by the amnesty lobby and Waffen SS veterans. Written in a post–Vietnam War and post–My Lai massacre trial context, *Crossroads of Death* reflected a deep skepticism about the applicability of law to warfare and its aftermath.[5]

Nonetheless, *Crossroads of Death* reinforced the apologetic narrative. Weingartner could not hide his admiration for Peiper, with whom he corresponded and whose death prevented a planned in-person interview. That Peiper shared Weingartner's doubts about the ability of the law to constrain war's inherent savagery or mete out justice fairly is suggested in a letter he wrote the young American historian in 1976: "[My] battalion attacked Russian villages like cavalry units: from multiple directions at full throttle with all guns blazing. The thatched roofed houses always burned, increasing the panic. By the way: would you see a moral difference whether you burned houses with a flamethrower from 50 meters or a blow torch from 30 centimeters? Or whether you shoot civilians from 50 meters distance with a machine gun or from 50 meters height from a helicopter? It is but total hypocrisy to condone war and condemn its mechanisms. Clean war, clean hands—there is no such thing!"[6]

Unlike other historians, Weingartner had also sought out Burton Ellis, who was impressed by the extent of his research, though expressed exasperation at what he felt was a one-sided presentation of the affair. "It beats the hell out of me," he wrote Weingartner in March 1977, "why everyone tries so hard to show that the prosecution were [*sic*] insidious, underhanded, unethical, immoral and God knows what monsters, that unfairly convicted a group of whiskerless Sunday school boys. What motivates you authors? I think that my staff did a hell of a great job. We didn't have available the information that the researchers have today, not even a small part of it, but still we came up with the hard evidence that satisfied the trial court that they were all guilty."[7]

Weingartner did not agree, and *Crossroads of Death* attempts to make the case that the army failed to determine responsibility for the shootings at Baugnez and other crimes. The author did not deny that American prisoners were killed at the crossroads, though he doubts whether significant numbers were killed elsewhere, especially at La Gleize. For Weingartner, the twin problems were the pretrial investigation and the trial. Though he did not examine the investigation closely, he dismissed its findings as not credible. He held the army's court in particularly low regard for its willingness to accept as evidence the defendants' sworn statements, which he considered "so transparently worthless that [their] introduction suggested either contempt for the intelligence of the bench or confidence that any prosecution evidence, no matter how lacking in substance, would weigh in the scales against the defendants."[8]

Weingartner's general outlook on the investigation and trial tracked closely with that of Peiper's: namely, that no one would ever know what really happened at that tiny crossroads village. Like Peiper, he was convinced the investigators never found out, and their attempt to build a case against the suspects was a shameful farce. In the book's conclusion, Weingartner quotes Peiper's interview with Senator Lester Hunt in Landsberg approvingly: "It is not necessary to treat a man with violence to get a confession from him. . . . There are other possibilities especially after a complete breakdown of a nation and a lost war. That is the story of Schwäbisch Hall, the lost war and the hopeless situation of men who came from the front and who had been heroes of the country and who were now subject to Polish guards." Their only duty in such circumstances, Peiper insisted, was to "cover their subordinates."[9]

Since the publication of *Crossroads of Death,* the apologetic narrative has remained entrenched among Anglo-American historians writing about the Battle of the Bulge and the Malmedy massacre. A 1994 account by the British historian Trevor Dupuy purporting to offer "an objective and balanced assessment of the Malmedy Incident [*sic*]" was—absurdly—based on Edward Van Roden's speeches, Hal McCown's account of his captivity in La Gleize, the writings of the ex-Waffen SS officer Ralf Tiemann, and Weingartner's dismissal of the prosecution's evidence as "transparently worthless." Like every other recent general history of the Bulge, the author accepts that elements of Battle Group Peiper massacred American prisoners at Baugnez. But as far as bringing the perpetrators to justice, the U.S. Army resorted to "punishing German soldiers who had been coerced into confessions that no person in his right mind would make without coercion." As for those responsible for the supposed coercion, "they were hardly less cold-blooded than the Germans who committed murder." Though Dupuy thought Peiper bore a degree of responsibility for the behavior of the forces under his command, he and his coauthors "are prepared to give [him] the benefit of the doubt and accept the unquestioned evidence of his soldierly performance as commander of [Battle Group] Peiper."[10]

More recent assessments of the Malmedy massacre and affair continue to perpetuate the narrative. American writer Rick Atkinson, in his 2013 Pulitzer Prize-winning account of the war's last year in the West, *Guns at Last Light,* writes in his summary of postwar trials that in the Malmedy case "confessions had been coerced, by threats to defendants' relatives, physical force, and other wrongful inducements." British historian Peter Caddick-Adams concedes in his 2014 history of the Bulge that the men of Battle Group Peiper brought the mode of warfare they had practiced on the Eastern Front to Belgium, as "they knew no other way," but concludes that posttrial investigations revealed that interrogators and prosecutors "overstepped the mark by conducting mock trials, using false death sentences, beatings and abuse to extort confessions."[11]

The cornerstone of the apologetic narrative—the torture accusations—took on something of a new life in the aftermath of 9/11 and the American invasions of Afghanistan and Iraq. Following the revelations that American soldiers, CIA officers, and private military contractors abused prisoners and systematically tortured suspected terrorists, it was difficult for some to resist the temptation to draw a connection between Schwäbisch Hall and Guantanamo Bay. A spate of American, British, and German television documentaries were churned out, the most revealing of the lot being a 2005 German production titled *"No Grass Grows over Gallows": U.S. Torture Justice from the Malmedy Trial to Abu Ghraib.* The ninety-minute documentary is a near-perfect recapitulation of the apologetic narrative. The running commentary of Franz Seidler, an emeritus professor at the Bundeswehr's equivalent of the U.S. Army War College and a right-wing publicist, provides only the appearance of scholarly respectability. Seidler's assessment of the massacre at Baugnez was taken almost verbatim from Dietrich Ziemssen's 1957 booklet: that the Americans prisoners were shot while attempting to take up arms again against their captors or while trying to escape.[12]

But the program's real attraction is the appearance of a handful of the defendants. Hans Siptrott, who was accused of ordering Georg Fleps to begin shooting at the prisoners, confirms Seidler's description of the Baugnez encounter. Most sensational is their accounts of being tortured at Schwäbisch Hall. "Even though decades have passed," the narrator proclaims, "those who were tortured have remained silent until today. Only after the media recently reported on U.S. torture in Iraqi prisons . . . were the last living eyewitnesses willing to break the silence." Their testimony now, he claims, proved that American interrogation practices had remained unchanged from Schwäbisch Hall to Abu Ghraib. Siptrott, Rolf Reiser, and Paul Ochmann—they had certainly not "remained silent" since 1946—run through the familiar list of torments. Indeed, the similarities between their on-camera accounts to the torture affidavits from 1948 is striking. Reiser's lies are particularly egregious. He had not been among those who wrote affidavits for Eugen Leer in 1948 and never otherwise claimed to have been tortured. But in 2005 he borrows Friedrich Eble's story and informs viewers that, among other cruelties, the Americans had shoved sharpened matchsticks under his and his fellow suspects' fingernails and set them alight.

William Perl, Harry Thon, and Raphael Shumacker are identified repeatedly as the "principal torturers." Why, the narrator asks, were they never prosecuted for their crimes against the suspects? Here the documentary makes its only significant departure from the apologetic narrative: there is no mention of Perl's background as a German Jewish émigré. Instead, the historian Alfred de Zayas, another commentator, proposes a novel interpretation, one fully in line with the producers' intention to link Schwäbisch Hall with Abu Ghraib. De Zayas argues that the interrogators' misdeeds were in fact exposed in the late 1940s, but the U.S. government's unwillingness to hold them accountable sent the unmistakable message to the army and the new CIA that torture would be tolerated and torturers protected.

Such comparisons are misleading, to say the least. World War II appears now to represent an exceptional moment in the history of American military interrogation training and practice. In the U.S.-Philippine War (1899–1902), the torture of Filipinos by American forces was widespread—water boarding was a specialty—and soon after investigated by a U.S. Senate standing committee. During World War II, by contrast, the War Department created a special facility—Camp Ritchie—to train interrogators in noncoercive methods of interrogation. There is no evidence that in the North African, European, or Pacific theaters American interrogators relied on systematic forms of physical and psychological pressure to obtain information from combatants or civilians. Nor is there convincing evidence that they did so in war crimes investigations after the war. A reversion to brutality would originate during the early years of the Cold War, when the American military and the CIA developed coercive and supposedly scientifically informed interrogation methods. It would take the attacks of 9/11 to bring about their legal justification by the U.S. Justice Department.[13]

In this context, the Malmedy affair should encourage us to look more closely at the record of wartime and postwar interrogation practices. The memoirs of a few American interrogators who operated in Afghanistan and Iraq and denounced abusive methods are highly illuminating. The interrogator writing as Matthew Alexander, for instance, has recounted how the same methods deployed by interrogators during and after World War II produced the intelligence that allowed U.S. forces to locate and kill Abu Musab al Zarqawi, the head of Al Qaeda in Iraq and the founder of the Islamic State of Iraq and Syria, in 2006. Interestingly, Alexander refers repeatedly to nonviolent interrogation methods—humane treatment, familiarity with the enemy's language and culture, demonstrations of empathy, tricks and ruses—as the "new methods." They were only "new" in that they departed from the regimes of systematic brutality developed after World War II. Alexander showed how such brutality was not only inhumane but useless as a method of intelligence gathering, a conclusion also reached by the Senate Select Committee on Intelligence's 2014 final report on the CIA's interrogation program.[14]

Earlier that year, I received an email from a local television news program in Jena, Germany. One of the men convicted in the Malmedy trial, Herr G., a resident of the town and likely the last living defendant, had contacted the station. I was told that he wanted, at the end of his life, to say something about his experiences as a nineteen-year-old private in Battle Group Peiper and as a defendant in the trial. Accused of participating in the execution of American prisoners in La Gleize, he received a life sentence. Three codefendants named him as part of the execution detail, and he had confessed to committing the crime. After the trial, Herr G. claimed that he had been pressured by an unnamed interrogator to write in a sworn statement that a superior officer had ordered him to shoot and that "I was stupid enough to write that I shot." Unlike many of his comrades, he did not later swear to being physically abused, only subjected to various verbal threats and promises of immunity allegedly made by Harry Thon. In March 1948, convinced that the evidence was not strong enough to convict a very young soldier who was almost certainly put under enormous pressure to comply with a superior officer's order, Lucius Clay overturned the verdict. He was released from Landsberg on April 10, along with twelve other former comrades whose verdicts the military governor had overturned for the same reasons.

The program's producer wanted to know more about Herr G's case. She told me that he not only remained adamant that the execution in La Gleize never took place, but that American interrogators resorted to mock executions and other forms of "psychic torture" to secure confessions from the suspects. Though not present at the Baugnez crossroads massacre, he insisted to her that the American soldiers who had surrendered there had attempted to run for cover and were thereby shot by their captors. A tragedy for sure, but not a war crime. For my part, the segment's producer wanted to know whether any of his claims were true. Would I be willing to be interviewed, certainly not with the aim of revealing Herr G. to be either a liar or a victim, but to provide a historian's perspective on the alleged incidents in La Gleize and Schwäbisch Hall?

I agreed, and in a Skype interview I summarized the argument of this book. I suggested that some of Herr G.'s claims were possibly not true. At the very least they reflected the long-standing apologetic account of the Malmedy affair, which seemed to me to be the important thing to stress. The creation and perpetuation of self-serving myths about the past remains one of the most powerful cultural and political forces in the modern world. Gone unchallenged, such myths harden hearts and impede dialog and reconciliation between individuals, communities, and entire nations. They block the flow of honest and open-ended argument about the past and its significance to the present. Understanding the relationship between conflict and memory—individual and collective—will always be difficult and inconclusive. The point is to keep having the arguments.

NOTES

ACKNOWLEDGMENTS

INDEX

Notes

Abbreviations

AHC	Allied High Commission
AJRB	Administration of Justice Review Board
AMP	Cardinal Aloisius Muench Papers, American Catholic History Research Center and University Archives, Catholic University of America
BAK	Bundesarchiv Koblenz, Koblenz, Germany
CDU	Christian Democratic Union (West Germany)
CIA	Central Intelligence Agency
CIC	U.S. Army Counter Intelligence Corps
CSU	Christian Socialist Union (West Germany)
DP	William Dowdell Denson Papers, Yale University Library, Manuscripts and Archives
ELA	Evangelisches Landesarchiv, Stuttgart, Germany
EP	Burton French Ellis Papers, University of Idaho, Special Collections and Archives
ETHINT	European Theater Historical Interrogation reports
EUCOM	United States European Command
FBI	Federal Bureau of Investigation
FRG	Federal Republic of Germany (West Germany)
HIAG	Hilfsgemeinschaft auf Gegenseitigkeit (Mutual Aid Society)
HIG	High Value Detainee Interrogation Group

IfZ	Institut fuer Zeitgeschichte, Munich, Germany
IMT	International Military Tribunal
IPW	Interrogator Prisoner of War
IRR	Investigatory Records Repository
MITC	Military Intelligence Training Center
MMIH	*Malmedy Massacre Investigation, Hearings before a Subcommittee of the Committee on Armed Services, United States Senate, Eighty-First Congress, First Session, Pursuant to S. Res. 42* (Washington, DC: U.S. Government Printing Office, 1949)
MP	military policeman
NARA	National Archives and Records Administration, Washington, DC, and College Park, Maryland, U.S.
NCO	noncommissioned officer
NCPW	National Council for Prevention of War
NCPWR	National Council for Prevention of War Records, Swarthmore College Peace Collection, Swarthmore College
OMGUS	Office of Military Government, United States
OMGWB	Office of Military Government Wuerttemberg-Baden
OWI	Office of War Information
PP	William R. Perl Papers, Special Collections Research Center, Gelman Library, George Washington University
RG	Record Group
SHAEF	Supreme Headquarters Allied Expeditionary Force
SOP	standard operating procedure
SPD	Social Democratic Party (West Germany)
SPW	Schützenpanzerwagen (armored personnel carrier)
SS	Schutzstaffel
USAEUR	Records of the United States Army in Europe
USFET	United States Forces European Theater
WCC 6–24	*Records of U.S. Army War Crimes Trials in Europe, United States of America v. Valentin Bersin, et al., War Crimes Case 6–24, May 16–July 18, 1946* (Washington, DC: National Archives, 1946)

Introduction

1. Christopher Dillon, *Dachau and the SS: A Schooling in Violence* (New York: Oxford University Press, 2015); and Harold Marcuse, *Legacies of Dachau: The Uses and Abuses of a Concentration Camp, 1933–2001* (New York: Cambridge University Press, 2001).
2. On this lesser-known category of war crimes trials, see Lisa Yavnai, "U.S. Army War Crimes Trials in Germany, 1945–1947," in Patricia Heberer and Jürgen Mat-

thäus, eds., *Atrocities on Trial: Historical Perspectives on the Politics of Prosecuting War Crimes* (Lincoln: University of Nebraska Press, 2008), 49–74.

3. The most influential English-language account of the incident, trial, and post-trial controversy has been James Weingartner's *Crossroads of Death: The Story of the Malmedy Massacre and Trial* (Berkeley: University of California Press, 1979). See also his *A Peculiar Crusade: Willis M. Everett and the Malmedy Massacre* (New York: New York University Press, 2000).

4. See the essays in David A. Messenger and Katrin Paehler, eds., *A Nazi Past: Recasting German Identity in Postwar Europe* (Lexington: University Press of Kentucky, 2015), and in Norbert Frei et al., *Karrieren im Zwielicht: Hitlers Eliten nach 1945* (Frankfurt: Campus Sachbuch, 2001). On high politics, see Philipp Gassert, *Kurt Georg Kiesinger 1904–1988: Kanzler zwischen den Zeiten* (Stuttgart: DVA, 2006). On the Wehrmacht and postwar memory, see Omer Bartov, *Germany's War and the Holocaust: Disputed Histories* (Ithaca, NY: Cornell University Press, 2003). On the West German foreign ministry, see Eckart Conze, Norbert Frei, Peter Hayes, and Moshe Zimmermann, *Das Amt und die Vergangenheit: Deutsche Diplomaten im Dritten Reich und in der Bundesrepublik* (Munich: Karl Blessing, 2010). On industrial and business elites, see S. Jonathan Wiesen, *West German Industry and the Challenge of the Nazi Past, 1945–1955* (Chapel Hill: University of North Carolina Press, 2001); Norbert Frei, Ralf Ahrens, Jörg Osterloh, and Tim Schanetzky, *Flick: Der Konzern, Die Familie, Die Macht* (Munich: Karl Blessing, 2009); and Lutz Hachmeister, *Schleyer: Eine deutsche Geschichte* (Munich: Beck, 2004). On medicine, see Ernst Klee, *Was sie taten, was sie wurden: Ärzte, Juristen und andere Beteiligte am Kranken- und Judenmord* (Frankfurt: Fischer Taschenbuch, 2004). On the press, see Lutz Hachmeister, *Die Herren Journalisten: Die Elite der deutsche Presse nach 1945* (Munich: Beck, 2001). On universities, see Steven P. Remy, *The Heidelberg Myth: The Nazification and Denazification of a German University* (Cambridge, MA: Harvard University Press, 2003). On the debate over the 1933 Reichstag fire after 1945, see Benjamin C. Hett, *Burning the Reichstag: An Inquiry into the Third Reich's Enduring Mystery* (New York: Oxford University Press, 2014). On the churches, see Matthew Hockenos, *A Church Divided: German Protestants Confront the Nazi Past* (Indianapolis: Indiana University Press, 2004). On the work of German historians, see Nicholas Berg, *The Holocaust and the West German Historians: Historical Interpretation and Autobiographical Memory* (Madison: University of Wisconsin Press, 2015).

5. An exception is Kerstin von Lingen's important study of Luftwaffe General Albert Kesselring, in which she shows how a concerted effort by German, American, and British sympathizers in the late 1940s and early 1950s led to his release from prison in October 1952. *Kesselring's Last Battle: War Crimes Trials and Cold War Politics, 1945–1960* (Lawrence: University Press of Kansas, 2009).

1. The Commitments of a Bad Reputation

1. Charles Whiting, *Ghost Front: The Ardennes before the Battle of the Bulge* (Cambridge, MA: Da Capo Press, 2002). On Honsfeld's capture, see Don Smart, "Terror at Honsfeld," *World War II* 16 (2001): 50; and Charles MacDonald, *A Time for Trumpets: The Untold Story of the Battle of the Bulge* (New York: HarperCollins, 1985), 199–205.
2. Sworn statements by Charles O. Huttoe, August 3, 1945, and John Dluski, September 18, 1945, in *Records of U.S. Army War Crimes Trials in Europe, United States of America v. Valentin Bersin, et al., War Crimes Case 6–24, May 16–July 18, 1946* (Washington, DC: National Archives, 1946) (hereafter WCC 6–24).
3. Williamson Murray and Allan R. Millet, *A War to Be Won: Fighting the Second World War* (Cambridge, MA: Harvard University Press, 2000), 395–483.
4. On planning the offensive, see Peter Caddick-Adams, *Snow and Steel: The Battle of the Bulge, 1944–1945* (New York: Oxford University Press, 2014).
5. Quoted in Walther Hofer, ed., *Der Nationalsozialismus: Dokumente 1933–1945* (Frankfurt: Fischer Bücherei, 1965), 110.
6. Bernd Wegner, *The Waffen-SS: Organization, Ideology, and Function* (New York: Basil Blackwell, 1990).
7. George Stein, *The Waffen SS: Hitler's Elite Guard at War, 1939–45* (Ithaca, NY: Cornell University Press, 1966); Heinz Höhne, *The Order of the Death's Head: The Story of Hitler's SS* (New York: Coward-McCann, 1970); and James Weingartner, *Hitler's Guard: The Story of the Leibstandarte Adolf Hitler, 1933–1945* (Carbondale: Southern Illinois University Press, 1974), and his *Crossroads of Death*.
8. Jan Erik Schulte, Peter Lieb, and Bernd Wegner, eds., *Die Waffen-SS: Neue Forschungen* (Paderborn: Ferdinand Schöningh, 2014); and Sönke Neitzel and Harald Welzer, *Soldaten: On Fighting, Killing, and Dying: The Secret World War II Transcripts of German POWs* (New York: Alfred A. Knopf, 2012), 290–316.
9. Richard Breitman, "Hitler and Genghis Khan," *Journal of Contemporary History* 25 (1990): 337–351.
10. Quoted in Richard J. Evans, *The Third Reich at War* (New York: Penguin, 2009), 11.
11. Terry Goldsworthy, *Valhalla's Warriors: A History of the Waffen SS on the Eastern Front, 1941–1945* (Indianapolis, IN: Dog Ear, 2007); and Martin Cüppers, *Wegbereiter der Shoah: Die Waffen-SS, der Kommandostab Reichsführer-SS und die Judenvernichtung, 1939–1945* (Darmstadt: Primus, 2011).
12. Peter Lieb, *Konventioneller oder NS-Weltanschauungskrieg? Kriegsführung und Partisanenbekämpfung in Frankreich, 1943/4* (Munich: Oldenbourg, 2007); and Stephen Hart, "Indoctrinated Nazi Teenaged Warriors: The Fanaticism of the 12th SS Panzer Division Hitlerjugend in Normandy, 1944," in Matthew Hughes and

Gaynor Johnson, eds., *Fanaticism and Conflict in the Modern Age* (London: Frank Cass, 2005), 81–100.

13. Jens Westemeier, *Himmlers Krieger: Joachim Peiper und die Waffen-SS in Krieg und Nachkriegszeit* (Paderborn: Ferdinand Schöningh, 2014), 163. On the Wormhoudt massacre, see Adrian Weale, *Army of Evil: A History of the SS* (New York: NAL Caliber, 2010), 251–254. On Le Paradis, see Charles Sydnor, *Soldiers of Destruction: The SS Death's Head Division, 1933–1945* (Princeton, NJ: Princeton University Press, 1977), 106–107. On the massacre of African prisoners, see Raffael Scheck, *Hitler's African Victims: The German Army Massacres of Black French Soldiers in 1940* (Cambridge: Cambridge University Press, 2006).
14. Paulo Pezzino, *Memory and Massacre: Revisiting Sant'Anna di Stazzema* (New York: Palgrave Macmillan, 2012); Carlo Gentile, *Wehrmacht und Waffen-SS im Partisanenkrieg* (Paderborn: Ferdinand Schöningh, 2012); and Kerstin von Lingen, *Kesselring's Last Battle: War Crimes Trials and Cold War Politics, 1945–1960* (Lawrence: University Press of Kansas, 2009).
15. Howard Margolian, *Conduct Unbecoming: The Story of the Murder of Canadian Prisoners of War in Normandy* (Toronto: University of Toronto Press, 1998). On the Graignes massacre, see Peter Lieb, "'Rücksichtlos ohne Pause angreifen, dabei ritterlich bleiben': Eskalation und Ermordung von Kriegsgefangenen an der Westfront 1944," in Sönke Neitzel and Daniel Hohrath, eds., *Kriegsgruel: Die Entgrenzung der Gewalt in kriegerischen Konflikten vom Mittelalter bis ins 20. Jahrhundert* (Paderborn: Schöningh, 2008), 344–345. For Oradour, see Jean-Jacques Fouche, *Massacre at Oradour, France 1944: Coming to Grips with Terror* (DeKalb: Northern Illinois University Press, 2005). On the German retreat from Belgium, see William I. Hitchcock, *The Bitter Road to Freedom: The Human Cost of Allied Victory in World War II Europe* (New York: Free Press, 2008), 62–64.
16. Quoted in Neitzel and Welzer, *Soldaten*, 312.
17. Though the portion of the surviving transcript of this address, given in Bad Nauheim on December 12, 1944, does not include a reference to "spreading terror," Sepp Dietrich and Hermann Priess both certified to American interrogators that Hitler used this language at this meeting. Helmut Heiber and David M. Glantz, eds., *Hitler and His Generals: Military Conferences 1942–1945: The First Complete Stenographic Record of the Military Situation Conferences, from Stalingrad to Berlin* (New York: Enigma Books, 2003); and Josef Dietrich and Hermann Priess sworn statements, April 11 and 16, 1946, respectively, WCC 6–24.
18. Quoted in Danny S. Parker, *Fatal Crossroads: The Untold Story of the Malmedy Massacre at the Battle of the Bulge* (Philadelphia: Da Capo Press, 2012), 290; and the sworn statements of Franz Sievers and Erich Rumpf, February 27 and March 22, 1946, respectively, WCC 6–24.
19. Westemeier, *Himmlers Krieger*, 130–136.

20. Caddick-Adams, *Snow and Steel,* 235.
21. Westemeier, *Himmlers Krieger,* 81.
22. Ibid., 46–155; and Richard Breitman, *The Architect of Genocide: Himmler and the Final Solution* (New York: Knopf, 1991), 95, 168. Peiper admitted at his trial that he accompanied Himmler "on an inspection where the first gassing experiments on living [subjects] were conducted." Cross-examination of Joachim Peiper, June 22, 1946, WCC 6–24.
23. Quoted in Parker, *Fatal Crossroads,* 290.
24. Westemeier, *Himmlers Krieger,* 223–254.
25. Ibid., 242.
26. Oswald Siegmund, *Meine Ehre Heisst Treue: Von der Leibstandarte ins Landsberger Gefängnis* (Essen: Heitz & Höffkes, 1992), 54.
27. Sworn statement by Paul Zwigart, February 11, 1946, WCC 6–24.
28. Peiper quoted in Gordon Williamson, *Loyalty Is My Honor* (Osceola, WI: Motorbooks International, 1995), 156.
29. Westemeier, *Himmlers Krieger,* 254–267.
30. Ibid., 267–273.
31. Ibid., 294.
32. Ibid., 313, 317. Westemeier notes that Peiper appeared jaundiced and speculates he may have been suffering from a hepatitis infection.
33. Sworn statement by Joachim Peiper, March 21, 1946, WCC 6–24.
34. Quoted in Weingartner, *Hitler's Guard,* 120.
35. Whiting, *Ghost Front,* 184.
36. On the initial delays, see Weingartner, *Hitler's Guard,* 126–127; and Peter Schrivjers, *The Unknown Dead: Civilians in the Battle of the Bulge* (Lexington: University Press of Kentucky, 2005).
37. Sworn statements of Marcel Boltz and Siegfried Jäckel, March 21 and 1, 1946, respectively, in WCC 6–24.
38. For a detailed account of the Baugnez encounter, see Parker, *Fatal Crossroads.*
39. The autopsy reports are in WCC 6–24.
40. This figure is based on autopsies conducted from January to April 1945. For a summary, see Parker, *Fatal Crossroads,* 255–60.
41. American investigators learned of a coordinated effort by former battle group members imprisoned by the Americans to blame Poetschke for ordering the Baugnez shootings. Memorandum, Dwight Fanton to Burton Ellis, February 19, 1946, U.S. National Archives and Records Administration (hereafter NARA) Record Group (hereafter RG) 549, Records of the U.S. Army in Europe (hereafter USAEUR), War Crimes Branch, Case Files, Cases Tried 1945–1959 (6–24), box 5. Gerhard Schlaich, a private in First Panzer Regiment's Seventh Company, told American investigators that "the rumor [in the Zuffenhausen prisoner of war

camp] was that Peiper gave the order to shoot the American prisoners of war." But other accounts identify Poetschke. Screening Results, November 24 to 29, 1945, and December 10 to 19, 1945, in Burton French Ellis Papers, 1903–2000, University of Idaho, Special Collections and Archives (hereafter EP), box 9, folder 110.

42. Sworn statement by Paul Ochmann, March 29, 1946, and testimonies of Maria Lochen and Anna Willens, May 29 and 31, 1946, respectively, all in WCC 6–24. More details on Ligneuville are in a report by Clyde Walker and John Barnett to the Chief of the War Crimes Branch, March 18, 1945, NARA RG 153, Records of the Office of the Judge Advocate General, War Crimes Branch, Case Files (6–24), box 71. Also MacDonald, *Time for Trumpets,* 229–230.
43. Quoted in Schrivjers, *Unknown Dead,* 40.
44. Ibid., 52; and Danny S. Parker, *To Win the Winter Sky: The Air War over the Ardennes, 1944–1945* (Conshohocken, PA: Combined Books, 1994).
45. Schrivjers, *Unknown Dead,* 42, 48. Testimony of Maria Tombeux and Antoine Colinet, May 31, 1946, WCC 6–24; and "More About Your Enemy," First U.S. Army Periodic Report No. 204 [January 1945], NARA RG 153, Records of the Office of the Judge Advocate General, War Crimes Branch, Case Files (6–24), box 72. Hans Hillig, a sergeant in First SS Panzer Division's Headquarters Company, confessed on March 8, 1946, to "shooting down women with babies in their arms at Stavelot." Burton Ellis to Dee Ellis, March 8, 1946, EP, box 8, folder 91.
46. Schrivjers, *Unknown Dead,* 54.
47. Ibid., 50.
48. On Wanne and Petit-Spay, see ibid., 57–58, and 50, respectively, and trial testimony of Zelie Hemroulle, Joseph Brecht, and Edmund Engelbert, all on June 3, 1946, in WCC 6–24.
49. Erich Rumpf and Rolf Reiser, sworn statements, March 22 and March 20, 1946, respectively, WCC 6–24. Hans Hennecke, a sergeant in the First Company of the First SS Panzer Regiment, claimed that Reiser was one of the officers who ordered American prisoners in La Gleize executed. Hans Hennecke, sworn statement, March 13, 1946, WCC 6–24.
50. Hal D. McCown, "Observations of an American Field Officer Who Escaped from the 1st SS Panzer Division 'Adolf Hitler' " [December 1944–January 1945], NARA RG 153, Records of the Office of the Judge Advocate General, War Crimes Branch, Case Files (6–24), box 72.
51. Statement of Russell H. Heginbotham, August 1945, NARA RG 549, USAEUR, War Crimes Branch, Case Files, Cases Tried 1945–1959 (6–24), box 41.
52. Quoted in Jens Westemeier, *Joachim Peiper: A Biography of Himmler's SS Commander* (Atglen, PA: Schiffer Military History, 2007), 119–120.
53. On this point, see Weale, *Army of Evil.*

54. Another pattern of Waffen SS leadership not unique to Peiper; see Sydnor, *Soldiers of Destruction,* 278.
55. William Perl, undated notes [February–March 1946], "Rumpf's Description of Personalities," NARA RG 549, USAEUR, War Crimes Branch, Case Files, Cases Tried 1945–1959 (6–24), box 32.
56. A comparison with one of Peiper's military mentors, SS General Paul Hausser, is again instructive; see Sydnor, *Soldiers of Destruction,* 278. It may also be the case that Peiper's reputation among his competitors as well-connected to Himmler made him more prone to recklessness as a means of demonstrating that he was more than a "political big-shot."
57. Norman Ohler, *Blitzed: Drugs in Nazi Germany* (London: Allen Lane, 2016).

2. Now It Comes Home to Us

1. Memorandum to Col. Hall, June 10, 1945, NARA RG 549, USAEUR, War Crimes Branch, Case Files, Cases Tried 1945–1959 (6–24), box 22.
2. Outgoing Classified Message, October 29, 1945, NARA RG 319, Records of the U.S. Army Staff, Assistant Chief of Staff, G-2, box 32.
3. Testimony of 1st Lt. Virgil T. Lary, December 18, 1944, NARA RG 153, Records of the Office of the Judge Advocate General, War Crimes Branch, Cases Files (6–24), box 7. Also see Danny S. Parker, *Fatal Crossroads: The Untold Story of the Malmedy Massacre at the Battle of the Bulge* (Philadelphia: Da Capo Press, 2012), 181–228, 256–259.
4. See Howard Margolian, *Conduct Unbecoming: The Story of the Murder of Canadian Prisoners of War in Normandy* (Toronto: University of Toronto Press, 1998); Jean-Jacques Fouche, *Massacre at Oradour, France 1944: Coming to Grips with Terror* (DeKalb: Northern Illinois University Press, 2005); and Stephen Hart, "Indoctrinated Nazi Teenaged Warriors: The Fanaticism of the 12th SS Panzer Division Hitlerjugend in Normandy, 1944," in Matthew Hughes and Gaynor Johnson, eds., *Fanaticism and Conflict in the Modern Age* (London: Frank Cass, 2005), 89.
5. Quoted in John T. Greenwood, ed., *Normandy to Victory: The War Diary of Courtney H. Hodges and the First U.S. Army* (Lexington: University Press of Kentucky, 2008), 217.
6. Tom Yarbrough, "Story of Slaughter by Germans Fires First Army to Vengeance," *Racine Journal Times,* December 20, 1944; and "Nazi Murder of 100 Yanks Is Confirmed," *Washington Post,* December 21, 1944.
7. William Boehme to Raymond Baldwin, May 1, 1949, NARA RG 46, Records of the U.S. Senate, 81st Congress, Committee on Armed Services, War Crimes Investigations, box 139. For accounts of similar reactions, see Antony Beevor, *Ardennes 1944: The Battle of the Bulge* (New York: Viking, 2015); Gerald F. Linderman, *The World within War: America's Combat Experience in World War II* (New

York: Free Press, 1997), 138–139; and William I. Hitchcock, *The Bitter Road to Freedom: The Human Cost of Allied Victory in World War II Europe* (New York: Free Press, 2008), 78–80.

8. Quoted in Hugh M. Cole, *The Ardennes: The Battle of the Bulge* (Washington, DC: Office of the Chief of Military History, Department of the Army, 1965), 264.
9. Rick Atkinson, *Guns at Last Light: The War in Western Europe* (New York: Henry Holt, 2013). American soldiers were not alone in retaliating against SS forces following reports of summary executions of prisoners of war. The massacre of Canadian soldiers near Caen the previous summer by elements of the Hitler Youth Division had provoked a similar wave of retaliatory killings. See Margolian, *Conduct Unbecoming.*
10. Forrest Pogue, *Pogue's War: Diaries of a WW II Combat Historian* (Lexington: University Press of Kentucky, 2001), 296–298.
11. Peter Caddick-Adams, *Snow and Steel: The Battle of the Bulge, 1944–1945* (New York: Oxford University Press, 2014), 361–367.
12. See Max Hastings, *Armageddon: The Battle for Germany, 1944–1945* (New York: Alfred A. Knopf, 2004), 209–210; Linderman, *World within War,* 90–142; and Jürgen Zarusky, "'That Is Not the American Way of Fighting': Die Erschiessungen gefangener SS-Leute bei der Befreiung des KZ Dachau," *Dachauer Hefte* 13 (1997): 27–55.
13. Andrew Mollo, "Dachau: The Webling Incident," *After the Battle* 27 (1980): 30–33.
14. "Brutal Germans," in *Abilene Reporter-News,* and "German Tank Force," in *Washington Evening Star,* both December 18, 1944.
15. Hal Boyle, "German Tank Force Pours Fire into 150 Unarmed Americans," *Washington Evening Star,* December 18, 1944.
16. "Captured Americans Shot in Open Field by Germans," *New York Times,* December 18, 1944.
17. "Yanks, Crying in Rage, Tell How Nazis Killed Wounded," *Stars and Stripes,* and "Nazis Massacre Captive Yanks in Belgium, Survivors Report," *Washington Post,* both December 18, 1944.
18. "Murder," *Time,* December 25, 1944.
19. Wallace Perry, untitled editorial, *Las Cruces Sun-News,* December 21, 1944.
20. Lee Carson, "Brutal Nazi Massacre Spurs Yanks," *Long Beach Independent,* December 21, 1945.
21. See, for example, the International News Service dispatch, published as "Belgian Women, Children Found Slaughtered, U.S. Army Announces. Massacre Occurs Where Nazis Tried Vainly for Breakthrough; Crime Part of 'Master Plan,'" *Albuquerque Journal,* December 27, 1944.
22. Headquarters Communications Zone, European Theater of Operations, US Army, Paris to War Department, January 26, 1945, NARA RG 153, Records of the Office of the Judge Advocate General, War Crimes Branch, Case Files (6–24), box 70.

23. "More about Your Enemy," First U.S. Army Periodic Report No. 204 [January 1945], NARA RG 153, Records of the Office of the Judge Advocate General, War Crimes Branch, Case Files (6–24), box 72; "Yank Prisoners Ordered Slain, Nazi PWs Say," *Stars and Stripes,* January 17, 1945; and Hal Boyle, "Slaughter of 100 Belgians Is Revealed. Men, Women, and Children Clubbed, Shot to Death by Nazis," *The Evening Independent* (Massillon, Ohio), January 2, 1945.
24. See, for example, Ed Cunningham, "Survivors of Malmedy Massacre of War Prisoners Recount Tales of Nazi Brutality," *Lima News,* January 31, 1945; and "Hutchinson Soldier Tells of Escape from Massacre," *Hutchinson News Herald,* February 4, 1945.
25. The remains of twelve more American soldiers would be located and identified over the next four months. Scott T. Glass, "Mortuary Affairs Operations at Malmedy—Lessons Learned from a Historic Tragedy," *Quartermaster Professional Bulletin* (1997): 25–32.
26. Hal Boyle, "Yanks Find Slain Mates at Five Points, Field of Dead," *Manitowoc Herald-Times,* January 16, 1945. Also Russell Jones, "Bodies of Murdered Yanks Discovered in Malmedy Snow," *Stars and Stripes,* January 16, 1945; and "Slain U.S. Captives Found in Belgium," *New York Times,* January 14, 1945.
27. "Murder in the Snow," *Life,* February 5, 1945, 26–27. *Life* first broke this barrier in its September 20, 1943, issue with the publication of George Strock's photograph of three U.S. Marines killed in New Guinea.
28. George H. Roeder Jr., *The Censored War: American Visual Experience during World War Two* (New Haven, CT: Yale University Press, 1993), 39.
29. Michaela Hönicke Moore, *Know Your Enemy: The American Debate on Nazism, 1933–1945* (New York: Cambridge University Press, 2010).
30. Edward Stettinius to the American Legation in Bern, December 29, 1944, NARA RG 153, Records of the Office of the Judge Advocate General, War Crimes Branch, Case Files (6–24), box 70.
31. S. P. MacKenzie, "The Treatment of Prisoners of War in World War II," *Journal of Modern History* 66 (1994): 487–520.
32. Testimony of Alfred Jodl, June 3, 1946, in *Trial of the Major War Criminals before the International Military Tribunal: Proceedings Volumes (The Blue Set),* vol. 15 (Nuremberg: IMT, 1948), available at http://avalon.law.yale.edu/imt/06-03-46.asp#jodl. During questioning by American investigators in November 1945, Gerhard Ellhoff, a radio operator in a Waffen SS panzer signals battalion, recalled reading a teletype dated December 23, 1944, and "signed by Hitler" inquiring as to who had committed the Baugnez massacre. EP, box 9, folder 110.
33. *Malmedy Massacre Investigation, Hearings before a Subcommittee of the Committee on Armed Services, United States Senate, Eighty-First Congress, First Session, Pursuant to S. Res.* 42 (Washington, DC: U.S. Government Printing Office, 1949) (hereafter MMIH), 271.

34. American Legation in Bern to Stettinius, April 17, 1945, NARA RG 153, Records of the Office of the Judge Advocate General, War Crimes Branch, Case Files (6–24), box 70. Quotes in Alfred M. de Zayas, *The Wehrmacht War Crimes Bureau, 1939–1945* (Lincoln: University of Nebraska Press, 1989), 118, 119.
35. "German Defends War Brutalities," *Baltimore Sun,* February 10, 1945.
36. Statement of Rolf Roland Reiser, January 3, 1946, NARA RG 549, USAEUR, War Crimes Branch, Case Files, Cases Tried 1945–1949 (6–24); and MMIH, 1477.
37. "Declaration of German Atrocities," *Foreign Relations of the United States: Diplomatic Papers, 1943, General* (Washington: U.S. Government Printing Office, 1963), 1:768–769.
38. Ibid., and Richard Overy, *Interrogations: The Nazi Elite in Allied Hands, 1945* (New York: Viking, 2001), 6.
39. Bradley F. Smith, *The Road to Nuremberg* (New York: Basic, 1981). Quote on 51.
40. Telford Taylor, *The Anatomy of the Nuremberg Trials: A Personal Memoir* (New York: Alfred A. Knopf, 1992), 41–42.
41. Quoted in Bradley F. Smith, *The American Road to Nuremberg: The Documentary Record 1944–1945* (Stanford, CA: Hoover Institution Press, 1982), 26.
42. Henry L. Stimson and James Forrestal to the Secretary of State, November 11, 1944, in *Foreign Relations of the United States: Diplomatic Papers, 1944, General* (Washington, DC: U.S. Government Printing Office, 1966), 1:1392.
43. On the organization of the War Crimes Group, see Lt. Col. Clio E. Straight, Report of the Deputy Judge Advocate for War Crimes, U.S. European Command (hereafter EUCOM), June 1944 to July 1948, NARA RG 549, USAEUR, War Crimes Branch, Case Files, Cases Tried 1945–1959 (6–24), box 13 (hereafter "Straight report"). In December 1945, the Allied Control Council, the four-nation body created to oversee the occupation of Germany, issued Law No. 10, which authorized each member state (the Soviet Union, Great Britain, the United States, and France) to conduct war crimes trials in its occupation zone. Control Council Law No. 10, Punishment of Persons Guilty of War Crimes, Crimes against Peace and against Humanity, December 20, 1945. Available at http://avalon.law.yale.edu/imt/imt10.asp.
44. Smith, *American Road to Nuremberg,* 58–61.
45. Quoted in Earl F. Ziemke, *The U.S. Army in the Occupation of Germany* (Washington, DC: Center of Military History, U.S. Army, 1975), 171. The directive excluded high-level Nazi Party and German military figures, who were to be tried by the IMT.

3. Like a Division Reunion

1. Carl Levin, "Nine the Nazis Failed to Slay Turn Up at Massacre Memorial," *New York Herald Tribune,* July 23, 1945.

2. On the costs of Belgium's liberation, see William I. Hitchcock, *The Bitter Road to Freedom: The Human Cost of Allied Victory in World War II Europe* (New York: Free Press, 2008), 60–97.
3. Straight report, 1–6. On Fanton's and Shumacker's backgrounds see MMIH, 270, 476–477, and 803.
4. William R. Perl, *Operation Action: Rescue from the Holocaust* (New York: F. Ungar, 1983); and Yehuda Bauer, *Jews for Sale? Nazi-Jewish Negotiations, 1933–1945* (New Haven, CT: Yale University Press, 1994).
5. "History of Military Intelligence Training at Camp Ritchie, Maryland, Supplement for the Period 1 January 1945–15 October 1945, Volumes I–II," NARA RG 319, Records of the U.S. Army Staff, Assistant Chief of Staff, G-2, Historical Studies and Related Records of G-2 Components, 1918–1959, box 27. See also Christian Bauer and Rebecca Göpfert, *Die Ritchie Boys: Deutsche Emigranten beim US Geheimdienst* (Hamburg: Hoffmann & Campe, 2005).
6. Walter Hasenclever, *Ihr werdet Deutschland nicht wiedererkennen: Erinnerungen* (Köln: Kiepenheuer & Witsch, 1975), 41–42.
7. Quoted in Ralph Hockley, *Freedom Is Not Free* (Indianapolis, IN: Brockton, 2001), 111.
8. Daily Bulletin, MITC, for November 13, 1942, NARA RG 319, Records of the U.S. Army Staff, Assistant Chief of Staff, G-2, Historical Studies and Related Records of G-2 Components, 1918–1959, box 2; and Bauer and Göpfert, *Die Ritchie Boys,* 55.
9. Quoted in Hockley, *Freedom Is Not Free,* 57. I am grateful to my late colleague Hans Trefousse for sharing this and other memories from his days as a Ritchie Boy.
10. Bauer and Göpfert, *Die Ritchie Boys,* 56.
11. MMIH, 609–612.
12. "History of Military Intelligence Training at Camp Ritchie"; and Vernon Walters, *Silent Missions* (Garden City, NY: Doubleday, 1978), 19.
13. General Board, U.S. Forces, European Theater, "The Military Intelligence Service in the European Theater of Operations," Study No. 12 (1945) (Wilmington, DE: Scholarly Resources, 1985), 28–29; and Office of the Assistant Chief of Staff, G-2, to the Assistant Chief of Staff, G-2 of Armies, Corps and Divisions of Twelfth Army Group, May 31, 1945, reprinted in U.S. Army, *12th Army Group, Report of Operations (Final After Action Report), G-2 Section,* parts I–IV, vol. 3 (U.S. Army, 1945), 119, 138, 139–140.
14. Walter Laqueur, *Generation Exodus: The Fate of Young Jewish Refugees from Nazi Germany* (Hanover, NH: Brandeis University Press, 2001). In addition to Perl, Rolf Wartenberg, the chief interrogator in the Einsatzgruppen case, was a Ritchie Boy, as was Paul Guth, the lead interrogator in the Mauthausen concentration camp case. On Wartenberg's and Guth's roles in these cases, see Hilary Earl, *The Nuremberg SS-Einsatzgruppen Trial: Atrocity, Law, and History* (New York: Cambridge

University Press, 2009); and Tomaz Jardim, *The Mauthausen Trial: American Military Justice in Germany* (Cambridge, MA: Harvard University Press, 2012), respectively. See also Richard W. Sonnenfeldt, *Witness to Nuremberg: The Many Lives of the Man Who Translated at the Nazi War Trials* (New York: Arcade, 2006).

15. MMIH, 613.
16. Internal Route Slip, Headquarters, U.S. Forces European Theater, Subject: SS Lt. Col. Peiper, October 1, 1945, NARA RG 319, Records of the U.S. Army, Assistant to the Chief of Staff, G-3 Intelligence, box 369.
17. Jens Westemeier, *Himmlers Krieger: Joachim Peiper und die Waffen-SS in Krieg und Nachkriegszeit* (Paderborn: Ferdinand Schöningh, 2014), 356–371.
18. Gallagher's report was published in newspapers across the country, including *Stars and Stripes*. "SS Colonel, Malmedy Murderer, Captured," *Stars and Stripes*, August 20, 1945.
19. Preliminary Intelligence Report, August 24, 1945, Headquarters, Third U.S. Army Intelligence Center, NARA RG 153, Records of the Office of the Judge Advocate General, War Crimes Branch, Case Files (6–24), box 71.
20. European Theater Historical Interrogation report (hereafter ETHINT report) 10 (1945), in Donald S. Detweiler, Charles Burton Burdick, and Jürgen Rohwer, eds., *World War II German Military Studies: A Collection of 213 Special Reports on the Second World War Prepared by Former Officers of the Wehrmacht for the United States Army* (New York: Garland, 1979).
21. Joshua Greene interview with Paul Guth, William Dowdell Denson Papers, Yale University Library, Manuscripts and Archives (hereafter DP), series V, box 45.
22. Burton Ellis to Dee Ellis, September 30, 1945, EP, box 8, folder 89.
23. Internal Route Slip, Headquarters U.S. Forces European Theater, Subject: SS Lt. Col. Peiper, October 1, 1945, NARA RG 319, Records of the U.S. Army, Records of the Assistant Chief of Staff, G-3 Intelligence, box 369.
24. ETHINT report 10.
25. The War Department had prohibited trials before the end of hostilities for fear of inciting reprisals against Allied prisoners of war. In August 1944, Eisenhower issued orders that suspected war criminals be arrested and that Standing Courts of Inquiry make preliminary investigations.
26. "Report of the Supreme Headquarters Allied Expeditionary Force Court of Inquiry re Shooting of Allied Prisoners of War by the German Armed Forces near Malmedy, Liege, Belgium, 17 December 1944," NARA RG 153, Records of the Office of the Judge Advocate General, War Crimes Branch, Case Files (6–24), box 70.
27. Statement of 1st Lt. Benone [*sic*] Junker, January 19, 1945, NARA RG 549, USAEUR, War Crimes Branch, Case Files, Cases Tried 1945–1959 (6–24), box 42.
28. Testimony of Generaloberst Josef (Sepp) Dietrich, July 31, 1945, ibid., box 31.

29. Statement of Josef Diefenthal, November 14, 1945, ibid., box 39.
30. Joshua Greene, *Justice at Dachau: The Trials of an American Prosecutor* (New York: Broadway Books, 2003); and Jardim, *Mauthausen Trial.*
31. Headquarters Third US Army and Eastern Military District, Instructions to Screening Personnel, October 22, 1945, NARA RG 319, Records of the U.S. Army, Investigatory Records Repository (hereafter IRR) Impersonal Name File ZA021038 (Malmedy Massacre), box 34.
32. Affidavit of Raphael Shumacker, November 9, 1948. NARA RG 549, USAEUR, War Crimes Branch, Case Files, Cases Tried 1945–1959 (6–24), box 5.
33. Burton Ellis to Dee Ellis, November 2, 1945, EP, box 8, folder 89.
34. William Perl recalled that "some of the weaker links in the chain admitted that an order from . . . Peiper had been passed to charge a certain Major Poetschke with the order for the shooting at the crossroads." William Perl statement, November 15, 1948, NARA RG 549, USAEUR, War Crimes Branch, Case Files, Cases Tried 1945–1959 (6–24), box 5.
35. Otto Wichmann, sworn statement, January 23, 1946, WCC 6–24. Other prisoners told interrogators of a coordinated effort at Zuffenhausen to place the blame on Poetschke. Dwight Fanton to Burton Ellis, February 19, 1946, NARA RG 549, USAEUR War Crimes Branch, Case Files, Cases Tried 1945–1959 (6–24), box 5.
36. Wichmann sworn statement.
37. Morris Elowitz's screening results, mid-to-late November 1945, EP, box 9, folder 110.

4. The Psychological Approach

1. SOP No. 1, December 5, 1945, and SOP No. 2, February 7, 1946, both in NARA RG 549, USAEUR, War Crimes Branch, Case Files, Cases Tried 1945–1959 (6–24), box 5.
2. MMIH, 329, 365.
3. U.S. Army, Theater Judge Advocate's Office, War Crimes Branch, European Theater of Operations, "Suggestions to Investigators of War Crimes," April 18 and October 29, 1945, in Straight report, 141–152.
4. Ibid. Ironically, a pioneer of the psychological approach was the Luftwaffe interrogator Hanns Scharff, whose noncoercive approach to questioning captured American airmen during the war proved highly productive. It's unclear whether Fanton, Perl, and the other Malmedy case investigators knew about Scharff. See Raymond F. Toliver, *The Interrogator: The Story of Hanns Joachim Scharff, Master Interrogator of the Luftwaffe* (Atglen, PA: Schiffer, 1997).
5. Raphael Shumacker affidavit, November 9, 1948, NARA RG 549, USAEUR, War Crimes Branch, Case Files, cases tried 1945–1959 (6–24), box 5.

6. SOP No. 2, December 14, 1945, EP, box 9, folder 110, and SOP No. 4, February 7, 1946, NARA RG 549, USAEUR, War Crimes Branch, Case Files, Cases Tried 1945–1959 (6–24), box 5.
7. The most detailed descriptions of the "quick process" are in the affidavits of William Perl, Burton Ellis, Raphael Shumacker, and Dwight Fanton, NARA RG 549, USAEUR, War Crimes Branch, Case Files, Cases Tried 1945–1959 (6–24), box 5.
8. MMIH, 722–724.
9. Of the forty-nine defendants who signed statements in early 1948 claiming various forms of abuse in Schwäbisch Hall, twelve claimed they had been subjected to "mock trials." "Analysis of Affidavits of Defendants" [n.d.], NARA RG 46, Records of the U.S. Senate, 81st Congressional Committee on Armed Services, War Crimes Investigations, box 141.
10. SOP No. 4, NARA RG 549, USAEUR, War Crimes Branch, Case Files, Cases Tried 1945–1959 (6–24), box 5.
11. Tomaz Jardim, *The Mauthausen Trial: American Military Justice in Germany* (Cambridge, MA: Harvard University Press, 2012).
12. Burton Ellis to Dee Ellis, March 5, 1946, EP, box 8, folder 89.
13. William Perl to Charles Goosby; and Perl to Danny S. Parker, January 6 and March 7, 1997, respectively, William R. Perl Papers, 1925–1998, Special Collections Research Center, Gelman Library, George Washington University (hereafter PP).
14. Shumacker affidavit. Also see Ellis, Elowitz, Perl, and Fanton affidavits; and Burton Ellis to Dee Ellis, March 8, 1946, in EP, box 8, folder 89.
15. Shumacker affidavit.
16. Preliminary screening results, December 10 to 19, 1945, EP, box 9, folder 110.
17. Perl described his interrogations of Christ at length in his testimony before the Senate subcommittee on May 13, 1949. See MMIH, 614–625.
18. Perl affidavit, November 15, 1948, and Friedrich Christ, sworn statement, December 17, 1945, WCC 6–24.
19. Rolf Ritzer, Roman Clotten, and Paul Zwigart sworn statements, March 13, March 22, and February 11, 1946, respectively, ibid.
20. Georg Fleps and Hans Siptrott, sworn statements, January 5 and January 7, 1946, respectively, ibid.
21. Interrogation transcript, Siegfried Jäckel, February 15, 1946, NARA RG 549, USAEUR, War Crimes Branch, Case Files, Cases Tried 1945–1959 (6–24), box 38.
22. Affidavit of Siegfried Jäckel, March 1, 1946, WCC 6–24.
23. In addition to Jäckel's affidavit, see the sworn statements of Gustav Sprenger, February 27 and March 15, 1946, and that of Heinz Hofmann, March 6, 1946, all in ibid.
24. Burton Ellis to Dee Ellis, February 12 and 17, 1946, EP, box 8, folder 89.
25. Interview with Col. Burton Ellis, Retired, U.S. Army Military History Institute, Senior Officer Oral History Program (Project 1988-MSP), 1988.

26. Burton Ellis to Dee Ellis, February 19 and 21, 1946, EP, box 8, folder 89.
27. Burton Ellis to Dee Ellis, March 22, 1946, ibid.
28. On Byrne's investigation in Belgium, see MMIH, 373–403. Burton Ellis to Dee Ellis, April 7, 1946, EP, box 8, folder 89.
29. Joachim Peiper, sworn statement, March 21, 1946, WCC 6–24.
30. Ibid.; and statements of Hans Hennecke and Rolf Reiser, March 13 and 20, 1946, respectively.
31. Hans Hillig and Joachim Peiper sworn statements, March 15 and March 26, 1946, respectively, ibid.
32. Peiper sworn statement, March 26.
33. Military Government Charge Sheet, Dachau, Germany, April 11, 1946, NARA RG 549, War Crimes Branch, Case Files, Cases Tried 1945–1959 (6–24), box 13.
34. Joachim Peiper and Sepp Dietrich sworn statements, March 21 and March 22, 1946, respectively, WCC 6–24; and Burton Ellis to Dee Ellis, March 22, 1946, EP, box 8, folder 89.
35. Fritz Kraemer and Hermann Priess sworn statements, April 10 and April 16, 1946, respectively, WCC 6–24.
36. See the interrogation transcripts in NARA RG 549, USAEUR, War Crimes Branch, Case Files, Cases Tried 1945–1959 (6–24), especially boxes 31, 33, 36, 37, 38, 39, 41, and 44.

5. Nazi Method Boys

1. Burton Ellis to Dee Ellis, February 19, 21, 25, March 12, 18, 22, and April 2, 1946, all in EP, box 8, folder 89.
2. James J. Weingartner, *A Peculiar Crusade: Willis M. Everett and the Malmedy Massacre* (New York: New York University Press, 2000), 1–38.
3. Ibid., 39–43.
4. Ibid., 46.
5. For Strong's testimony and Everett's deposition, see MMIH, 571–608 and 1555–1570, respectively. See also Weingartner, *Peculiar Crusade,* 42–43.
6. "Personal Data of Accused for Information of Defense Counsel" [n.d.], EP, box 9, folder 112.
7. MMIH, 883–896, 948.
8. Ibid., 943–948, quote on 945.
9. Ibid., 1561.
10. Burton Ellis to Deputy Theater Judge Advocate, War Crimes Branch, July 29, 1946, NARA RG 549, USAEUR, War Crimes Branch, Case Files, Cases Tried 1945–1959 (6–24), individual case files, boxes 42–70 (hereafter "USAEUR Case Files") (Hennecke, Hans).

11. Ellis claimed in 1948 that Carpenter told him that "four of the accused had admitted to him that their accusations of violence and beatings were only made 'to get out from under' their confessions and were not true." Ellis affidavit.
12. MMIH, 945–946; and Joshua Greene interview with Paul Guth, DP.
13. Statement of Lt. Col. Charles J. Perry, March 6, 1947, MMIH, 935–936. Testifying in his own defense at the trial on June 21, Peiper claimed he was he was "beaten" while hooded and presumed that his assailant was a "Pole" or "Poles." When asked by John Dwinell whether he was beaten in Schwäbisch Hall more than once, Peiper replied, "No, only on this one occasion." WCC 6–24, 1893.
14. MMIH, 931–932. Having learned about Perry's Senate subcommittee testimony about his conversations with Peiper and Junker, Junker prepared an affidavit denying the accuracy of Perry's account. Benoni Junker affidavit, November 9, 1949, USAEUR Case Files (Peiper, Joachim).
15. MMIH, 948.
16. Interrogation of Willy Schäfer at Landsberg prison, February 6, 1947, EP, box 4, folder 112.
17. MMIH, 1170–1172.
18. Tomaz Jardim, *The Mauthausen Trial: American Military Justice in Germany* (Cambridge, MA: Harvard University Press, 2012), 162–167.
19. MMIH, 947.

6. A Monstrous Slaughter Machine

1. Burton Ellis to Dee Ellis, May 6, 1946, EP, box 8, folder 89; and Interview with Col. Burton Ellis, Retired, U.S. Army Military History Institute, Senior Officer Oral History Program (Project 1988-MSP), 1988, p. 69.
2. On Nuremberg, see Telford Taylor, *The Anatomy of the Nuremberg Trials: A Personal Memoir* (New York: Alfred A. Knopf, 1992). On the subsequent Nuremberg trials, see Kevin Jon Heller, *The Nuremberg Military Tribunals and the Origins of International Criminal Law* (Oxford: Oxford University Press, 2001); Valerie Hébert, *Hitler's Generals on Trial: The Last War Crimes Tribunal at Nuremberg* (Lawrence: University Press of Kansas, 2010); Hilary Earl, *The Nuremberg SS-Einsatzgruppen Trial: Atrocity, Law, and History* (New York: Cambridge University Press, 2009); and Eckart Conze, Norbert Frei, Peter Hayes, and Moshe Zimmermann, *Das Amt und die Vergangenheit: Deutsche Diplomaten im Dritten Reich und in der Bundesrepublik* (Munich: Blessing, 2010).
3. Straight report. Over 95,000 Germans and Austrians were tried and convicted of crimes related to the war and Nazi Germany's occupation of, or collaboration with, various European nations. Most cases were tried in Eastern Europe. A total of 8,812 Germans and Austrians were tried by the four wartime Allied nations in

Germany. Devin O. Pendas, "Seeking Justice, Finding Law: Nazi Trials in Postwar Europe," *Journal of Modern History* 81 (2009): 347–368.

4. Patricia Heberer, "The American Military Commission Trials of 1945," in Nathan Stolzfus and Henry Friedlander, eds., *Nazi Crimes and the Law* (Washington, DC: German Historical Institute, 2008), 43–62.
5. John Fabian Witt, *Lincoln's Code: The Laws of War in American History* (New York: Free Press, 2012); and Peter Maguire, *Law and War: An American Story* (New York: Columbia University Press, 2001).
6. Quoted in Witt, *Lincoln's Code,* 383.
7. The exception was the trial of Curt Bruns by a military commission on April 7, 1945, one month before the end of the war in Europe. Bruns, a Wehrmacht captain, was convicted of executing two members of an American Interrogation Prisoner of War team, both Jewish and most likely Ritchie Boys.
8. On the Belsen trial, see John Cramer, *Belsen Trial 1945: der Lüneburger Prozess gegen Wachpersonal der Konzentrationslager Auschwitz und Bergen-Belsen* (Göttingen: Wallstein, 2011). On Yamashita's case, see Richard L. Lael, *The Yamashita Precedent: War Crimes and Command Responsibility* (Wilmington, DE: Scholarly Resources, 1982).
9. Quoted in Straight report, 52.
10. There were two types of courts: General and Intermediate Special Military Government Courts. The former could impose any sentence, including death, while the latter could impose sentences of up to ten years only.
11. See Straight report, 52–70.
12. Leon Jaworski, *After Fifteen Years* (Houston: Gulf, 1961); and MMIH, 572.
13. John Dower, *Embracing Defeat: Japan in the Wake of World War II* (New York: W. W. Norton, 1999), 461.
14. James J. Weingartner, *A Peculiar Crusade: Willis M. Everett and the Malmedy Massacre* (New York: New York University Press, 2000), 53.
15. Burton Ellis to Dee Ellis, April 23, 1946, EP, box 8, folder 89.
16. Hillig's statement to investigator Gerald Coates is in ibid., box 9, folder 110. For Wichmann's statement to the same investigator, see Gerald Coates to Burton Ellis, September 19, 1947, ibid., box 4, folder 122.
17. WCC 6–24, 23–31.
18. Ibid., 7–26.
19. Ibid., 26–28.
20. Ibid., 76.
21. Ibid., 77–78.
22. Ibid., 89.
23. Ibid., 92–100.
24. Ibid.

25. Ibid., 100.
26. Ibid., 101–102.
27. Ibid., 91–488.
28. On the taking of statements, see ibid., 157.
29. Ibid., 112.
30. Ibid., 575–576.
31. Ibid., 701.
32. Ibid., 406–539, 911–918, 966–978, 987–1000, 1015–1036, 1076–1103, 1128–1147, 1179–1207, 1256–1262, 1406–1408, 1506–1530.
33. Ibid., 856.
34. Weingartner, *Peculiar Crusade,* 68–74. In 1977 Ellis confirmed to Weingartner that he never had any interest in or intention of taking the district attorney job. Burton Ellis to James Weingartner, March 17, 1977, EP, box 4, folder 47.
35. The headlines are from the *New York Times-Herald,* May 24, 1946; *Washington Star,* May 23, 1946; and the *New York Times,* May 30, 1946, respectively.
36. *Washington Post,* May 23, 1946.

7. Entirely a Heat of Battle Case

1. "150 Nazi Armed Vehicles Burn as 800 of Foe Flee La Gleize Trap," *New York Times,* December 27, 1944; Hal D. McCown, "Observations of an American Field Officer Who Escaped from the 1st SS Panzer Division 'Adolf Hitler,'" December 1944–January 1945, NARA RG 153, Records of the Office of the Judge Advocate General, War Crimes Branch, Case Files (6–24), box 72; and James J. Weingartner, *A Peculiar Crusade: Willis M. Everett and the Malmedy Massacre* (New York: New York University Press, 2000), 78.
2. WCC 6–24, 1580–1628.
3. Ibid., 1815–1853.
4. In testimony before the U.S. Senate subcommittee investigating the Malmedy case, Rosenfeld stated, "I did not like McCown's testimony. That wasn't a question of a lawyer sitting on a bench evaluating his testimony. That was a question of one soldier who had been in combat evaluating another soldier who had been in combat. . . . All the other members of the court agreed with me, unanimously. . . . McCown and Peiper were entirely too friendly those nights they spent together. Peiper, with 600 of his men, were able to escape the trap when he was completely surrounded, and when he escaped McCown was with him . . . when they got to a certain stage in their march out of La Gleize, McCown simply walked off and Peiper went in another direction with his some 600 men." MMIH, 1429.
5. Weingartner, *Peculiar Crusade,* 75–106.

6. Statements by Prisoner SS Standartenfuehrer Joachim Peiper, September 15, 1945, USAEUR Case Files (Peiper, Joachim).
7. WCC 6–24, 1885–2045.
8. Ibid., 1886–1892.
9. Ibid., 1888–1889.
10. Ibid., 1889.
11. Ibid., 2045.
12. Ibid., 1899–1902.
13. Ibid., 1902–1966.
14. Ibid., 1921, 1924, 1929.
15. Ibid., 1931, 1934.
16. Ibid., 1938, 1943.
17. Ibid., 1958–1959.
18. Ibid., 2031–2032.
19. Sworn statement of Gottlob Berger, May 27, 1946, NARA RG 549, USAEUR, War Crimes Branch, Case Files, Cases Tried 1945–1959 (6–24), box 37.
20. WCC 6–24, 1765–1769.
21. Ibid., 2024–25.
22. Quoted in Weingartner, *Peculiar Crusade,* 98.
23. WCC 6–24, 2125.
24. Ibid., 2136, 2132.
25. Ibid., 2180–2187.
26. Ibid., 2226–2228, 2230–2232.
27. Ibid., 2350, 2353.
28. Ibid., 2439–2440. Motzheim had in fact confessed to executing a prisoner outside Honsfeld.
29. Ibid., 2471–2472. Former First Pioneer Battalion corporal Ernst Goldschmidt's testimony departed from the pattern set by the other six defendants who took the stand. Goldschmidt, whose company commander was Sievers, was one of the few defendants to have denied in his sworn statement that he ever received any orders to shoot prisoners or participated in any executions, despite the fact that the investigators placed him at the Baugnez crossroads at the time of the massacre and in mid-February, 1946, Fanton had asserted to Ellis that Goldschmidt had admitted to having administered coups de grace. His sworn statement, signed on February 28, contains no such admission. By the end of the investigation, several of Goldschmidt's former comrades had identified him as having executed prisoners at Baugnez and La Gleize. On the stand, however, he simply repeated his denials and insisted that his former comrades' accusations were pure inventions. Ibid., 2398–2434.
30. Ibid., 2379.

31. Ibid., 3209–3250.
32. Ibid., 3002–3070.
33. Ibid., 3194.
34. Ibid., 3207.
35. Ibid., 3206.
36. Ibid., 3251–3268.
37. Peiper quoted in Weingartner, *Peculiar Crusade,* 106; and Recommendation for Change in the Method of Execution of Convicted "Malmedy" Defendants, July 18, 1946, NARA RG 549, USAEUR, War Crimes Branch, Case Files, Cases Tried 1945–1959 (6–24), box 13.
38. Melissa B. Russano, "The Psychology of Interrogations and False Confessions: Research and Recommendations," *Canadian Journal of Police and Security Services* 1 (2003): 53–64.

8. Other Battlefields

1. Those convicted by the IMT were imprisoned in Spandau prison in Berlin, while the British used a prison in Werl and the French a facility in Wittlich for the individuals convicted in their respective zonal trials.
2. "Appeal for 43 Nazis in Malmedy Massacre Reported on Way Here," *Washington Star,* January 25, 1947.
3. Quoted in James J. Weingartner, *A Peculiar Crusade: Willis M. Everett and the Malmedy Massacre* (New York: New York University Press, 2000), 109.
4. Everett petition, Evangelisches Landesarchiv, Stuttgart (hereafter ELA), Nachlass Theophil Wurm, 320 (hereafter Papers of Theophil Wurm).
5. Willis Everett to Fritz Kraemer, September 1948, ibid.
6. While investigating another case in the fall of 1946, Lt. Col. Charles Perry recalled that Everett told him that the Malmedy court was a "travesty" and that "as a Georgian and a 'rebel' he considered War Crimes Group as a whole to be derelict in its handling of Germans accused of war crimes." Charles J. Perry to Burton Ellis, January 31, 1947, EP, box 9, folder 112.
7. Weingartner, *Peculiar Crusade,* 88, 110, 115.
8. For an account of the debacle on the American side, see Michael Beschloss, *The Conquerors: Roosevelt, Truman and the Destruction of Hitler's Germany, 1941–1945* (New York: Simon & Schuster, 2002). On its propaganda value to Goebbels, see Jeffrey Herf, *The Jewish Enemy: Nazi Propaganda during World War II and the Holocaust* (Cambridge, MA: Harvard University Press, 2006).
9. Directive to SCAEF Regarding the Military Government of Germany in the Period Immediately Following the Cessation of Organized Resistance (Post-Defeat), September 22, 1944, *Foreign Relations of the United States: Diplomatic*

Papers. Conferences at Malta and Yalta, 1945 (Washington, DC: United States Government Printing Office, 1955), 153.

10. Steven P. Remy, *The Heidelberg Myth: The Nazification and Denazification of a German University* (Cambridge, MA: Harvard University Press, 2003); Joseph Bendersky, *The Jewish Threat: Anti-Semitic Politics of the U.S. Army* (New York: Basic Books, 2008); and Suzanne Brown-Fleming, "The Worst Enemies of a Better Germany: Postwar Antisemitism among Catholic Clergy and U.S. Occupation Forces," *Holocaust and Genocide Studies* 18 (2004): 379–401.
11. For a description of the counterintelligence activities of one Camp Ritchie–trained CIC agent, Henry Kissinger, see Niall Ferguson, *Kissinger: 1923–1968: The Idealist* (New York: Penguin, 2015). See also Richard Breitman and Norman Goda, *Hitler's Shadow: Nazi War Criminals, U.S. Intelligence, and the Cold War* (Damascus, MD: Pennyhill, 2014), esp. "The CIC and Right-Wing Shadow Politics."
12. See, for example, the series of articles by the German Jewish émigré writer and Ritchie Boy Stefan Heym: " 'I Am Only a Little Man': That's the Alibi of the German Prisoner When He Is Charged with Sharing the Guilt of the Nazis. 'I Am Only a Little Man, I Am Only a Little Man' "; "The Germans Hear A New Master's Voice: Americans Must Give Orders to Win the Respect of a Spineless People Who Know No Law except Force"; and "But the Hitler Legend Isn't Dead: It Lives and Grows Stronger in Germany Today, and It Can Be Killed Only By a Realistic Policy of Education," *New York Times*, September 10, 1944, December 3, 1944, and January 20, 1946, respectively.
13. On the "unwritten rule" at Nuremberg and Dachau, see Donald Bloxham, *Genocide on Trial: War Crimes Trials and the Formation of Holocaust History and Memory* (New York: Oxford University Press 2003), 63–69; and Lisa Yavnai, "Military Justice: The U.S. Army War Crimes Trials in Germany, 1944–1947" (PhD dissertation, London School of Economics, 2007), 204–205. On Jewish prosecution witnesses in the Mauthausen trial, see Tomaz Jardim, *The Mauthausen Trial: American Military Justice in Germany* (Cambridge, MA: Harvard University Press, 2012), 141–145.
14. Warren Magee to Pope Pius XII [n.d., but most likely written in early 1948], Cardinal Aloisius Muench Papers, American Catholic History Research Center and University Archives, Catholic University of America (hereafter AMP), box 58, folder 3. Pius would award Magee with a papal gold medal for his work on the trials.
15. Willis Everett to Theater Judge Advocate, February 28, 1947, NARA RG 549, USAEUR, War Crimes Branch, Case Files, Cases Tried 1945–1959 (6–24), box 10.
16. Willis Everett to Aloisius Muench, October 26, 1948, AMP, box 58, folder 4. Edwin Hartrich, "Army Clamps Ban on Rumors SS Defendants Were Beaten," *New York Herald-Tribune*, January 24, 1946. See also "Appeal for 43 Nazis in Malmedy Mas-

sacre Reported on Way Here"; and "Malmedy Plea Stirs Capital," *Stars and Stripes,* January 27, 1947.

17. Edwin Hartrich, "Malmedy Confessions Called Forced from German Soldiers," *New York Herald-Tribune,* February 1, 1947.
18. Willis Everett to Cecil F. Hubbert, June 17, 1947, NARA RG 153, Records of the Office of the Judge Advocate General, War Crimes Branch, Case Files (6–24), box 71.
19. Willis Everett to Lucius Clay, January 10, 1948. NARA RG 549, USAEUR, War Crimes Branch, Case Files, Cases Tried 1945–1959 (6–24), box 10.
20. *Congressional Record, Proceedings and Debates of the 80th Congress, First Session,* vol. 93, no. 154 (Washington, DC: U.S. Government Printing Office, 1947), 11052.
21. Quoted in William Bosch, *Judgment on Nuremberg: American Attitudes toward the Major War Crimes Trials* (Chapel Hill: University of North Carolina Press, 1970), 82–83.
22. Hal Foust, "Nazi Trial Judge Rips 'Injustice,'" *Chicago Daily Tribune,* February 23, 1948. A day later, the *Hamburger Allgemeine Zeitung* translated and published Wennerstrum's remarks.
23. Quoted in H. A. Hauxhurst, Owen Cunningham, Charles F. Wennerstrum, and James T. Brand, "Forum on War Crimes Trials," *Proceedings of the Section of International and Comparative Law,* September 6–7, 1948, 41–42.
24. Willis Everett to Col. E. H. Young, March 15, 1948, NARA RG 549, USAEUR, War Crimes Branch, Case Files, Cases Tried 1945–1959 (6–24), box 10.
25. Quoted in Weingartner, *Peculiar Crusade,* 144.
26. Sally Rose Hayett to Henry Luce, January 14, 1949, NARA RG 153, Records of the Office of the Judge Advocate General, War Crimes Branch, Case Files (6–24), box 73.
27. Wade Fleischer to Colonel Decker, March 19, 1947; Wade Fleischer to Acting Judge Advocate, March 21, 1947; and Claude Mickelwait to Clarence Huebner, March 26, 1947, all in NARA RG 549, USAEUR, War Crimes Branch, Case Files, Cases Tried 1945–1959 (6–24), box 10; and Huebner to Everett, March 27, 1947, NARA RG 153, Records of the Office of the Judge Advocate General, War Crimes Branch, Case Files (6–24), box 71.
28. The striking detainees' petition is reproduced in *Memorandum by the Evangelical Church in Germany* (Stuttgart, 1949).
29. Clio Straight, "Mistreatment of Detainees at Dachau," September 2, 1947; James Harbaugh, "Conference at Munich on 6 and 7 September 1947 with Colonel Straight Respecting Alleged Irregularities in the Operation at Dachau and Other Matters," September 17, 1947; and Straight to Harbaugh, "Alleged Mistreatment of Detainees in War Crimes Enclosure," October 5, 1947, all in NARA RG 153, Records of the Office of the Judge Advocate General, War Crimes Branch, Case

Files (6–24), box 75. See also Straight's testimony on the matter in MMIH, 1065–1068.

30. Straight, "Mistreatment of Detainees at Dachau."
31. Reports of Major Paul Foster, September 30 and October 2, 1947, NARA RG 153, Records of the Office of the Judge Advocate General, War Crimes Branch, Case Files (6–24), box 75.
32. Ibid.
33. Joshua Greene, *Justice at Dachau: The Trials of an American Prosecutor* (New York: Broadway, 2003), 55–64; and Jardim, *Mauthausen Trial*, 90–94.
34. Straight, "Mistreatment of Detainees at Dachau"; Straight to Harbaugh, October 5, 1947; and "Conference at Munich on 6 and 7 September 1947." Also see Tom Bower, *The Pledge Betrayed: America and Britain and the Denazification of Post-War Germany* (Garden City, NY: Doubleday, 1981), 251–254. On Everett's shifting views of Kirschbaum, see Willis Everett to Aloisius Muench, October 26, 1948, AMP, box 58, folder 4. Everett's letter of recommendation for Kirschbaum is reprinted in MMIH, 1305.
35. Straight report, 4, 71–72.

9. The Sword of Public Opinion

1. *Review and Recommendations of the Deputy Judge Advocate for War Crimes, United States v. Valentin Bersin et al., Case No. 6–24*, October 20, 1947 (publisher not identified), 33–36, 51–52, 76, 92–93, 99–101, 112–113, 139–141, 151–153. A copy of the report is in NARA RG 549, USAEUR, War Crimes Branch, Case Files, Cases Tried 1945–1959 (6–24), box 4.
2. Ibid., 43–162.
3. MMIH, 1063, 1064.
4. *Review and Recommendations*, 61.
5. In his Senate subcommittee testimony, Dwinell claimed that he had been ordered by unnamed superior officers to present the defense's case to the board aggressively. Harbaugh, who assigned him as an adviser, denied giving him such orders. MMIH, 447, 1165.
6. James Weingartner, *Crossroads of Death: The Story of the Malmedy Massacre and Trial* (Berkeley: University of California Press, 1979), 180–185; and James Harbaugh to Lucius Clay, March 8, 1948, NARA RG 549, USAEUR, War Crimes Branch, Case Files, Cases Tried 1945–1959 (6–24), box 4.
7. Harbaugh to Clay, March 8, 1948.
8. Quoted in Tom Bower, *The Pledge Betrayed: America and Britain and the Denazification of Post-War Germany* (Garden City, NY: Doubleday, 1981), 256.
9. Petition for Writ of Habeas Corpus, Willis M. Everett Jr. on behalf of Valentin Bersin et al., Petitioner vs. Harry S. Truman, James V. Forrestal, Kenneth G.

Royall, Omar M. Bradley, and Thomas C. Clark, Respondents, May 1948, reprinted in MMIH, 1181–1190.

10. In late January 1949, Everett appealed to President Truman to appoint an "agent" to represent Everett's case to the Court and asked U.S. attorney general Thomas Clark to appoint "a suitable counsel or advocate to present this matter to the International Court of Justice." Willis Everett to Thomas C. Clark, January 24, 1949, NARA RG 549, USAEUR, War Crimes Branch, Case Files, Cases Tried 1945–1959 (6–24), box 10.
11. *Washington Post,* April 30, 1948.
12. The Analysis Branch of the U.S. Army's Public Information Division tracked Malmedy case-related editorial opinion in American newspapers closely. For the *Tribune*'s editorial and others critical commentary, see "The Judicial Processes Concerning the Malmedy War Criminals: Digest of Editorial and Column Opinion, 22 May 1946–27 January 1949," January 27, 1949, NARA RG 153, Records of the Office of the Judge Advocate General, War Crimes Branch, Case Files (6–24), box 72.
13. Jean Edward Smith, ed., *The Papers of General Lucius D. Clay: Germany, 1945–1949* (Bloomington: Indiana University Press, 1974), 742–743; and Bower, *Pledge Betrayed,* 257–262.
14. Edward Young, Memorandum for Record, June 25, 1948, NARA RG 153, Records of the Office of the Judge Advocate General, War Crimes Branch, Case Files (6–24), box 72.
15. Report of Proceedings of Administration of Justice Review Board, August 20 1948, ibid., box 95.
16. Memorandum for the Secretary of the Army, September 14, 1948, ibid., Records Related to the Simpson Commission Report.
17. Only Howard Bresee, chief of the War Crimes Group Trial Branch during the trial, submitted a short memorandum to Simpson denying the defendants had been abused and asserting they received a fair trial. Bresee to Gordon Simpson, August 12, 1948, EP, box 4, folder 122.
18. James Weingartner, *A Peculiar Crusade: Willis M. Everett and the Malmedy Massacre* (New York: New York University Press, 2000), 163–166.
19. As he recalled in a contribution to a volume of commentary by former American military personnel criticizing war crimes trials collected by the Anglo-American neo-Nazi H. Keith Thompson, "Colonel Peiper . . . [was] obliged to spend years in confinement for doing for their country exactly what every good and loyal officer of the American Army did for his country." Quoted in H. Keith Thompson and Henry Strutz, eds., *Doenitz at Nuremberg, A Reappraisal: War Crimes and the Military Professional* (New York: Amber, 1976), 66. The book was republished in 1983 by the Institute for Historical Review.

20. NARA RG 153, Records of the Office of the Judge Advocate General, War Crimes Branch, Case Files (6–24), Records Related to the Simpson Commission Report.
21. James Harbaugh to Lucius Clay, November 3, 1948, NARA RG 549, USAEUR, War Crimes Branch, War Crimes Branch Case Files, Cases Tried 1945–1959 (6–24), box 20. On Clay's desire to see a clemency board established, see Clay to William Draper, May 26, 1948, in Smith, *Papers of General Lucius D. Clay*, 659.
22. For a summary of the controversy, see Valerie Hébert, *Hitler's Generals on Trial: The Last War Crimes Tribunal at Nuremberg* (Lawrence: University Press of Kansas, 2010), 48–51.
23. "Leniency for Nazi Arouses Germany," *New York Times*, September 18, 1948.
24. John O'Donnell, "Capitol Stuff," *Daily News* (New York), October 4, 1948.
25. "The Trial of Ilse Koch: Former Counsel in War Crimes Cases Says Assembly-Line Techniques Flouted Principals of Justice," *Washington Evening Star*, October 2, 1948.
26. Burton Ellis, marginal notes to Weingartner, *Crossroads of Death*, EP, box 126a.
27. "Dachau Sentence Prober Tells of 3d Degree Use," *Washington Times Herald*, October 9, 1948; "Van Roden Raps War Trial Setup," *Philadelphia Bulletin*, October 9, 1948; and "Third Degree Charged in Nazis' Trials," *Stars and Stripes* (European ed.), October 10, 1948.
28. Notes on Talk by Judge A. [*sic*] Leroy Van Roden Given at Luncheon of Federal Court Attorneys, December 8, 1948, National Council for Prevention of War Records, 1921–1975, Swarthmore College Peace Collection, Swarthmore College (hereafter NCPWR), series F, box 397.
29. NCPW Press Release, December 18, 1948, NARA RG 319, Records of the U.S. Army Staff, Office of the Chief Legislative Liaison, Congressional Investigations Division, War Crimes Trials, Correspondence, 1948–1951, box 91.
30. Edward van Roden to James Finucane, December 18, 1948, NARA RG 46, Records of the U.S. Senate, 81st Congress, Committee on Armed Services, War Crimes Investigations, box 141.
31. "Appeal for Action against U.S. Investigators," *Christian Century*, January 5, 1949, 5–6.
32. Morris Rubin to James Finucane, January 5, 1949; and Finucane to Rubin, January 6, both in NCPWR, series F, box 398.
33. Edward L. Van Roden, "American Atrocities in Germany," *Progressive*, February 1949, 21–22.
34. Walter H. Waggoner, "Army Board Urges Commutation for 12 in the Malmedy Massacre," *New York Times*, January 7, 1949; Howard Kennedy, "Lenity Asked on Malmedy," *Stars and Stripes*, January 8, 1949; "3-Man Board Criticizes Army for Reducing German Sentences" (United Press), *Evening Observer* (New York), January 8, 1949, "Leniency Advised for Doomed Nazis" (Associated Press), *Press-*

Telegram (California), January 7, 1949; and "Clemency Asked for 29 Germans" (International News Service), *Independent* (California), January 7, 1949.

35. Edward Van Roden to James Finucane, February 3, 1949, NCPWR, series F, box 398.
36. Frank A. Hall to A. J. Muench, March 28, 1949, AMP, box 58, folder 51.
37. "Texas Judge Says Nazi Trials Fair" (Associated Press), *Wichita Daily Times*, March 19, 1949.
38. *Chicago Daily Tribune*, February 13, 14, 15, and 17, 1949.
39. Freda Utley, *The High Cost of Vengeance: How Our German Policy Is Leading Us to Bankruptcy and War* (Chicago: Henry Regnery, 1949), 195. The book was published in German as *Kostspielige Rache* ("Costly Revenge") in 1951 by the H. H. Nölke publishing house in Hamburg.
40. Willis Everett to Frederic M. Miller, September 4, 1948, AMP, box 58, folder 4.
41. Weingartner, *Peculiar Crusade*, 247.

10. The Daring Fists of Lieutenant Perl

1. Sworn statement, Otto Eble, July 13, 1947, NARA RG 153, Records of the Office of the Judge Advocate General, War Crimes Branch, Case Files (6–24), box 72.
2. John O'Donnell, "Capitol Stuff," *Daily News* (New York), February 8, 1949; Judge Advocate General to Lucius Clay, March 14, 1949, NARA RG 549, USAEUR, War Crimes Branch, Case Files, Cases Tried 1945–1959 (6–24), box 41.
3. James Costello to Wade Fleischer, March 22, 1949, ibid.
4. Wade Fleischer, memorandum for the record, June 24, 1949, ibid.
5. Interrogation of Erwin Sennhausen [Friedrich Eble], May 19, 1948, ibid.; and Wade Fleischer, Memorandum to Armed Services Subcommittee, June 24, 1949, MMIH, 1597–1598.
6. MMIH, 1628.
7. Wade Fleischer, Memorandum for Judge Advocate Files, April 5, 1949, NARA RG 549, USAEUR, War Crimes Branch, Case Files, Cases Tried 1945–1959 (6–24), box 44.
8. MMIH, 1513–1523.
9. Lucius Clay to Judge Advocate General, March 16, 1949, NARA RG 549, USAEUR, War Crimes Branch, Case Files, Cases Tried 1945–1959 (6–24), box 44.
10. Hans Korte, "Sternenbanner in Landsberg eingeholt," *Deutsche Soldaten Zeitung*, June 1958.
11. Nuremberg Trial Proceedings, September 30, 1946, in *Trial of the Major War Criminals before the International Military Tribunal: Proceedings Volumes (The Blue Set)*, vol. 22 (Nuremberg: IMT, 1948), available at http://avalon.law.yale.edu/imt/09-30-46.asp.

12. Ibid.
13. The Oradour case, tried in France in 1954, also involved only former Waffen SS members. Of the 21 tried, 14 were French nationals. The trial sparked a severe political crisis in France as it laid bare the ugly realities of collaboration. See Sarah Farmer, *Martyred Village: Commemorating the 1944 Massacre at Oradour-sur-Glane* (Berkeley: University of California Press, 2000).
14. Quoted in Jan Erik Schulte, "The SS as the 'Alibi of a Nation'? Narrative Continuities from the Nuremberg Trials to the 1960s," in Kim C. Priemel and Alexa Stiller, eds., *Reassessing the Nuremberg Military Tribunals: Transitional Justice, Trial Narratives, and Historiography* (New York: Berghahn, 2012), 134–160, quote on 136.
15. Sönke Neitzel and Harald Welzer, *Soldaten: On Fighting, Killing, and Dying: The Secret World War II Transcripts of German POWs* (New York: Alfred A. Knopf, 2012), 303–316.
16. Valerie Hébert, *Hitler's Generals on Trial: The Last War Crimes Tribunal at Nuremberg* (Lawrence: University Press of Kansas, 2010); and Kerstin von Lingen, "Hitler's Military Elite in Italy and the Question of 'Decent War,'" in David A. Messenger and Katrin Paehler, eds., *A Nazi Past: Recasting German Identity in Postwar Europe* (Lexington: University Press of Kentucky, 2015), 169–199.
17. Testimony of Robert Brill, August 5, 1946, in *Trial of the Major War Criminals before the International Military Tribunal: Proceedings Volumes (The Blue Set),* vol. 20 (Nuremberg: IMT, 1948), available at http://avalon.law.yale.edu/imt/08-05-46.asp.
18. Telford Taylor, *The Anatomy of the Nuremberg Trials: A Personal Memoir* (New York: Alfred A. Knopf, 1992), 513. Eleven Waffen SS veterans ranging in rank from private to general testified for the defense before the IMT.
19. Jens Westemeier, *Himmlers Krieger: Joachim Peiper und die Waffen-SS in Krieg und Nachkriegszeit* (Paderborn: Ferdinand Schöningh, 2014), 412–413.
20. Schulte, "SS as the 'Alibi of a Nation'?"
21. "Analysis of Affidavits of Defendants" [n.d.], NARA RG 46, Records of the U.S. Senate, 81st Congress, Committee on Armed Services, War Crimes Investigations, box 141.
22. Records Officer's Summary of the Case, USAEUR Case Files (Zwigart, Paul).
23. Affidavit, Paul Zwigart, February, 1948, ELA, Papers of Theophil Wurm, 321.
24. MMIH, 928, 931–932.
25. Junker's January 19, 1948, statement is reprinted in ibid., 929.
26. Sworn statement, Joachim Peiper, February 11, 1948, NARA RG 549, USAEUR, War Crimes Branch, Case Files, Cases Tried 1945–1959 (6–24), box 14. Peiper elaborated on this statement in June. Affidavit, June 5, 1948, Institut fuer Zeitgeschichte (hereafter IfZ) (OMGUS file), Signatur 2 / 135–3 / 6–12.
27. Most of the men who wrote out final statements before their executions held fast to their innocence. See Katharina Von Kellenbach, *The Mark of Cain: Guilt and*

Denial in the Post-War Lives of Nazi Perpetrators (New York: Oxford University Press, 2013).

28. Ibid.; and Westemeier, *Himmlers Krieger,* 423.
29. Claude J. Kramer, "Conditions at Landsberg War Crimes Prison," October 20, 1949, NARA RG 319, Records of the U.S. Army, IRR Impersonal Name File ZA021038 (Malmedy Massacre), box 34.
30. Westemeier, *Himmlers Krieger,* 430.
31. Ibid., 444. One source of the abuse stories may have been rumors about the maltreatment of prisoners in two secret British military prisons and interrogation centers in and near London—the "London Cage" and Camp 020—and in Bad Nenndorf, Germany, in the British occupation zone. The British journalist Ian Cobain has revealed that suspected British traitors and, later, German prisoners and suspected Soviet spies were subjected to some of the abuses described by the Landsbergers in their affidavits. It is possible that information about the treatment of prisoners—many of them members of the SS—in Camp 020 and Bad Nenndorf reached the Landsbergers and their lawyers and may have served as the basis of their tales of torture in Schwäbisch Hall. See Ian Cobain, *A Secret History of Torture* (Berkeley, CA: Counterpoint, 2012), 1–75.
32. MMIH, 1433.
33. Westemeier, *Himmlers Krieger,* 439; and MMIH, 1494.
34. Quoted in Westemeier, *Himmlers Krieger,* 440.
35. Gerald Coates to Burton Ellis, September 19, 1947, EP, box 9, folder 122.
36. Memorandum for the Officer in Charge, Counter Intelligence Corps Region 1, 970th Counter Intelligence Corps Detachment, April 12 and 30, 1948, NARA RG 319, Records of the U.S. Army, Records of the Office of the Assistant Chief of Staff, G-3 Intelligence, box 369.
37. Agent Report, Activities at Landsberg War Crimes Prison No. 1, September 26, 1949, NARA RG 319, Records of the U.S. Army, Records of the Army Staff, Assistant Chief of Staff G-2, box 32; and Col. C. C. Fenn to Joseph W. Chambers, May 19, 1949, NARA RG 319, Records of the U.S. Army, Army Staff, Office of the Chief Legislative Liaison, Congressional Investigations Division, War Crimes Trials, Correspondence, 1948–1951, box 95. Eckardt later boasted of his "interventions" to officials of the NCPW. See his May 26, 1949, statement to the NCPW, NCPWR, series F, box 397.
38. Karl Morgenschweis, "'Fuer Wahrheit und Gerechtigkeit': Das Bekenntnis des Monsignore Morgenschweis," *Der Freiwillige* 18–19 (1972–1973). Eckardt and Morgenschweis were not atypical in their sympathies or in their willingness to transmit prisoner statements to their superiors. See Ronald Webster, "'Opposing Victors' Justice': German Protestant Churchmen and Convicted War Criminals in Western Europe after 1945," *Holocaust and Genocide Studies* 15 (2001): 47–69.

39. Eugen Leer to War Crimes Group, Post Trial Section, February 1, 1948; and Recommendations concerning Petition for Clemency Filed by Dr. Eugen Leer, April 1, 1948, both in NARA RG 153, Records of the Office of the Judge Advocate General, War Crimes Branch, Case Files (6–24), box 86.
40. Ibid.
41. Edgar L. Jones, "One War Is Enough," *Atlantic Monthly,* February 1946.
42. Affidavit of Dr. Knorr, May 29, 1948, ELA, Papers of Theophil Wurm, 321.
43. Richard A. Wolfe to Office of Military Government for Bavaria Legal Division, August 10, 1948, NARA RG 549, USAEUR, Judge Advocate Division, War Crimes Branch, Records Related to Georg Froeschmann.
44. Interrogation of War Criminals at War Criminal Prison No. 1, Landsberg, Germany, May 31, 1949, NARA RG 549, USAEUR, Judge Advocate Division, War Crimes Branch, Records Related to Post-Trial Activities 1945–1957, box 10.
45. Georg Froeschmann to Lucius Clay, July 30 and October 8, 1948, Bundesarchiv Koblenz (hereafter BAK), B305 / 131.
46. Ibid.
47. "The Trial of Ilse Koch: Former Counsel in War Crimes Cases Says Assembly-Line Techniques Flouted Principals of Justice," *Washington Evening Star,* October 2, 1948.
48. Froeschmann to John J. McCloy, September 1, 1949, NARA RG 549, USAEUR, Judge Advocate Division, War Crimes Branch, Records Related to Georg Froeschmann.
49. Judge Advocate, EUCOM, to Lucius Clay, October 27, 1948, ibid.
50. James L. Harbaugh to Lucius Clay, May 20, 1948, NARA RG 153, Records of the Office of the Judge Advocate General, War Crimes Branch, Case Files (6–24), box 86.
51. Summary of allegations [n.d.], NARA RG 549, USAEUR, War Crimes, Case Files, Cases Tried 1945–1959 (6–24), box 5.

11. Avenging Angels

1. Quoted in Norbert Frei, *Adenauer's Germany and the Nazi Past: The Politics of Amnesty and Integration,* trans. Joel Golb (New York: Columbia University Press, 2002), 347 fn. 39.
2. Ernst Klee, *Persilscheine und Falsche Pässe: Wie die Kirchen den Nazis halfen* (Frankfurt: Fischer Taschenbuch, 1991); and Gerald Steinacher, *Nazis on the Run: How Hitler's Henchmen Fled Justice* (New York: Oxford University Press, 2011).
3. Theophil Wurm to Robert M. W. Kempner, May 5, 1948, reprinted in *Memorandum by the Evangelical Church in Germany* (Stuttgart, 1949), 29.
4. William Perl to Burton Ellis, March 31, 1949, PP.

5. Hans Korte, "Sternenbanner in Landsberg eingeholt," *Deutsche Soldaten Zeitung,* June 1958.
6. Richard Steigmann-Gall, *The Holy Reich: Nazi Conceptions of Christianity, 1919–1945* (New York: Cambridge University Press, 2003); Georg Denzler, *Widerstand ist nicht das richtige Wort: katholische Priester, Bischöfe und Theologen im Dritten Reich* (Zurich: Pendo, 2003); and Matthew Hockenos, *A Church Divided: German Protestants Confront the Nazi Past* (Bloomington: Indiana University Press, 2004).
7. On the August 1945 Fulda statement, see Michael Phayer, *The Catholic Church and the Holocaust, 1930–1965* (Bloomington: Indiana University Press, 2000), 134–138. On the Stuttgart declaration, see Katharina Von Kellenbach, *The Mark of Cain: Guilt and Denial in the Post-War Lives of Nazi Perpetrators* (New York: Oxford University Press, 2013), 51–55.
8. Phayer, *Catholic Church and the Holocaust,* 138.
9. Von Kellenbach, *Mark of Cain,* 52–55.
10. Klaus von Eickstedt, *Christus unter Internierten* (Neuendettelsau: Freimund, 1948), available at http://www.moosburg.org/info/stalag/christus3.html.
11. Frederick Taylor, *Exorcising Hitler: The Occupation and Denazification of Germany* (New York: Bloomsbury, 2011).
12. William E. Griffith, "Denazification in the United States Zone of Germany," *Annals of the American Academy* 267 (1950): 68–76.
13. William Dawson to G. Herbert Smith, September 7, 1945, NARA RG 260, Office of Military Government Württemberg-Baden (hereafter OMGWB), Records of Headquarters, General Records, 1945–1949, box 1.
14. Quoted in Artur Straeter, "Denazification," *Annals of the American Academy of Political and Social Science* 260 (1948): 43–52, at 43.
15. Frederic Spotts, *The Churches and Politics in Germany* (Middletown, CT: Wesleyan University Press, 1973), 89–116.
16. "Bishop Is Angered by Hunt for Nazis," *New York Times,* July 28, 1948.
17. Quoted in Spotts, *Churches and Politics in Germany,* 105.
18. Frei, *Adenauer's Germany,* 98–102.
19. Günter Lewy, *The Catholic Church and Nazi Germany* (New York: McGraw-Hill, 1964).
20. Johannes Neuhäusler to Francis Case, John Vorys, Charles Vursell, Overton Brooks, and Ed Cox, March 23, 1948, NARA RG 549, USAEUR, Judge Advocate Division, War Crimes Branch, Records Related to Post-Trial Activities 1945–1957, box 11.
21. Ibid.
22. Francis Case to Johannes Neuhäusler, April 19, 1948, AMP, box 58, folder 10; and Francis Case to Kenneth Royall, April 19, 1948, NARA RG 153, Records of the Office of the Judge Advocate General, War Crimes Branch, Case Files (6–24), box 101.

23. "Umstrittene Prozessführung in Nuernberg und Dachau. Einer Erklärung von Weihbischof Dr. Neuhäusler," CND Pressedienst, May 22, 1948; and "Durch Misshandlung erpresst? Weihbischof Dr. Neuhäusler zum Malmedy-Prozess," *Allgemeine Zeitung* (Mainz), May 25, 1948.
24. Johannes Neuhäusler to Robert Murphy, July 22, 1948, NARA RG 549, USAEUR, Judge Advocate Division, War Crimes Branch, Case Files, Cases Tried 1945–1959 (6–24), box 21.
25. "Petition of the German Bishops (Catholic) concerning the Nuremberg and Dachau Trials," August 26, 1948, copy in NCPWR, series F.
26. Johannes Neuhäusler to the American Military Government in Germany, August 23, 1948, NARA RG 153, Records of the Office of the Judge Advocate General, War Crimes Branch, Case Files (6–24), box 101.
27. Robert Gellately, *Backing Hitler: Consent and Coercion in Nazi Germany* (New York: Oxford University Press, 2001).
28. Memorandum to Chief of the War Crimes Branch, EUCOM, September 22, 1948, NARA RG 549, USAEUR, Judge Advocate Division, War Crimes Branch, Case Files, Cases Tried 1945–1959 (6–24), box 20.
29. Ibid.
30. "Umstrittene Dachauer Urteile: Stellungnahme des Muenchner Weihbischofs" and "110 Hinrichtungen in Landsberg angeordnet," both in *Muenchner Allgemeine,* October 24, 1948.
31. *Regensburger Bistumsblatt,* November 14, 1948; and Agent Report, Malmedy Case (U.S. Senate Sub-Committee Investigation), Re: Rudolf Aschenauer, Bishop Johannes Neuhäusler and Bishop Theophil Wurm, September 15, 1949, NARA RG 319, Records of the U.S. Army, IRR Impersonal Name File ZA021038 (Malmedy Massacre), box 34.
32. "Amerikaner klagen US-Militärtribunale an," *Muenchner Allgemeine,* December 18, 1948.
33. Ibid.; and "Schwerste Vorwürfe gegen den Malmedy Prozess," *Muenchner Allgemeine,* October 30, 1948.
34. "Schwerste Vorwürfe gegen den Malmedy Prozess."
35. Wolfgang Gerlach, *And the Witnesses Were Silent: The Confessing Church and the Persecution of the Jews* (Lincoln: University of Nebraska Press, 2000).
36. Quoted in ibid., 195.
37. Ibid., 199–201, 204–205.
38. Ibid., 203.
39. Ian Kershaw, *The End: The Defiance and Destruction of Hitler's Germany, 1944–1945* (New York: Penguin, 2011), 299–300.
40. Headquarters, Counter Intelligence Corps Region I, 66th Counter Intelligence Corps Detachment, U.S. Army Europe, Subject: Hilfswerk der Evangelischen

Kirchen Deutschlands (Welfare Organization of the Protestant Churches in Germany), November 29, 1949, NARA RG 319, Records of the U.S. Army, IRR Impersonal Name File Entry ZZ-6 (Hilfswerk der Evangelischen Kirchen), box 8.

41. William Dawson to Ralph W. Stockman, October 1, 1945, NARA RG 260, OMGWB, Records of Headquarters, General Records, 1945–1949, box 1.
42. Norman Goda, *Tales from Spandau: Nazi Criminals and the Cold War* (New York: Cambridge University Press, 2007), 77.
43. CIC Region 1, 66th CIC Detachment, Agent Report (Subject: Wurm, Theophil [Doctor of Divinity]), December 9, 1949, NARA RG 319, Records of the U.S. Army, IRR Impersonal Name File ZA021038 (Malmedy Massacre), box 34.
44. The exchange is reproduced in *Memorandum by the Evangelical Church in Germany,* 26–32.
45. Eckart Conze, Norbert Frei, Peter Hayes, and Moshe Zimmermann, *Das Amt und die Vergangenheit: Deutsche Diplomaten im Dritten Reich und in der Bundesrepublik* (Munich: Karl Blessing, 2010), 375–439.
46. Theophil Wurm to Robert M. W. Kempner, January 29, 1948; and Kempner to Wurm, February 9, March 16, and March 23, 1948, reprinted in *Memorandum by the Evangelical Church,* 26, 27–28.
47. Frei, *Adenauer's Germany,* 99.
48. Theophil Wurm to Robert M. W. Kempner, January 29 and February 19, 1948, both reprinted in *Memorandum by the Evangelical Church,* 26–27.
49. Theophil Wurm to Robert M. W. Kempner, February 19, 1948, ibid., 26–27.
50. Theophil Wurm to Robert M. W. Kempner, March 30, 1948, ibid., 28–29.
51. Theophil Wurm to Robert M. W. Kempner, May 5 and 15, 1948, ibid., 29, 30.
52. Theophil Wurm to Robert M. W. Kempner, June 5, ibid., 30–32. The relevant exchange between Kempner and the state secretary, Friedrich Gaus, is reprinted on 92–98.
53. The campaign against Kempner is summarized in Conze et al., *Das Amt,* 428–433.
54. "Urteil oder Racheakt? Landesbischof Wurm gegen Nuernberger Gerichtsmethoden," *Allgemeine Zeitung,* May 15, 1948; "Schwere Anschuldigungen Dr. Wurms gegen die Nuernberger Gerichte," *Stuttgarter Zeitung,* May 15, 1948; "Kempner antwortet Bischof Wurm: Keine erpressten Geständnisse in Nuernberg," *Allgemeine Zeitung,* May 18, 1948; "Eine Diskussion um Nuernberg: Landesbischof Wurms schwere Beschuldigungen—Kempners Antwort," *Stuttgarter Zeitung,* May 19, 1948; "Erklärung Wurms zu dem Brief an Kempner: Der Landesbischof nimmt Stellung zu seinen schweren Beschuldigungen," *Stuttgarter Nachrichtendienst,* May 22, 1948; "Bischof Wurm ergänzt seine Vorwürfe," *Neue Zeitung,* May 23, 1948; "Dr. Kempner antwortet Bischof Wurm," *Neue Zeitung,* June 6, 1948; "Streit Wurm-Kempner geht weiter," *Flensburger Tageblatt,* June 19, 1948; and Richard Tüngel, "Der angeklagte Ankläger," *Die Zeit,* June 17, 1948.

55. Dirk Pöppmann, "The Trials of Robert Kempner: From Stateless Immigrant to Prosecutor of the Foreign Office," in Kim C. Priemel and Alexa Stiller, eds., *Reassessing the Nuremberg Military Tribunals: Transitional Justice, Trial Narratives, and Historiography* (New York: Berghahn, 2012), 23–46.
56. Theophil Wurm et al. to Lucius Clay, May 20, 1948; and Clay to Wurm, June 19, 1948, both in NARA RG 549, USAEUR, Judge Advocate Division, War Crimes Branch, Records Related to Post-Trial Activities 1945–1957, box 9. Portions of Clay's response were published in the German press. See, for example, "Clay antwortet den Bischöfen: Rechte der Nuernberger Angeklagten werden gewahrt," *Neue Zeitung*, July 1, 1948. Clay's June 19 letter was informed by a long letter to him by Charles LaFollette, director of OMGWB. LaFollette to Clay, June 8, 1948, IfZ, MF 260 (OMGUS file), Signatur AG49 / 75 / 3.
57. Theophil Wurm, "Achtung von dem Menschenleben," *Schwäbische Zeitung*, July 27, 1948; and Theophil Wurm, "Nuernberg und Dachau," *Flensburger Tageblatt*, August 7, 1948. On Goebbels and Henry Morgenthau's "plan," see Jeffrey Herf, *The Jewish Enemy: Nazi Propaganda during World War II and the Holocaust* (Cambridge, MA: Harvard University Press, 2008), 252–263.
58. Theophil Wurm et al. to Kenneth Royall, August 1948, ELA, Nachlass Theophil Wurm, 291.
59. Quoted in Frei, *Adenauer's Germany*, 111.
60. Theophil Wurm to John Foster Dulles, October 18, 1948, NARA RG 549, USAEUR, Judge Advocate Division, War Crimes Branch, Records Related to Post-Trial Activities 1945–1957, box 10.
61. For example, *Der Tagesspiegel*, October 22, 1948; "Wurms Ansicht zu den Dachauer Todesurteilen," *Nouvelles de France*, October 22, 1948; and "Landesbischof Wurm an J. F. Dulles," *Union*, November 7, 1948.
62. "Recht oder Rache, das ist hier die Frage!" and "Wer von Verbrechen weiss und dennoch schweigt . . . ," *Neue Ruhr Zeitung*, December 11 and 13, 1948, respectively.
63. Anna J. Merritt and Richard L. Merritt, *Public Opinion in Occupied Germany: The OMGUS Surveys, 1945–1949* (Urbana: University of Illinois Press, 1970), 33–35.
64. William I. Hitchcock, *The Bitter Road to Freedom: The Human Cost of Allied Victory in World War II Europe* (New York: Free Press, 2008), 200.
65. Clay's decisions in the twelve cases are reprinted in MMIH, 1602–1615. "Final Report of Proceedings of Administration of Justice Review Board," February 14, 1949, NARA RG 153, Records of the Office of the Judge Advocate General, War Crimes Branch, Case Files (6–24), box 95.
66. Joseph L. Haefele to Chief of the War Crimes Branch, EUCOM, September 22, 1948, NARA RG 549, USAEUR, War Crimes Branch, Case Files, Cases Tried 1945–1959 (6–24), box 20.

67. Joseph L. Haefele, Allegations in the Bishop of Wurm [*sic*] file, September 4, 1948, NARA RG 549, USAEUR, Judge Advocate Division, War Crimes Branch, Records Related to Post-Trial Activities 1945–1957, box 9.
68. On the postwar German right, see Kurt Tauber, *Beyond Eagle and Swastika: German Nationalism after 1945* (Middletown, CT: Wesleyan University Press, 1967). See also Thomas Boghardt, "America's Secret Vanguard: US Army Intelligence Operations in Germany, 1944–1947," *Studies in Intelligence* 57 (2013): 1–14.
69. Memorandum for the Officer in Charge (Subject: Interrogations for Malmedy Trials), 970th CIC Detachment, April 2, 1948, IfZ, MF 260 (OMGUS file), Signatur 7 / 20–1 / 27.
70. Mortimer Kollender to Colonel Raymond, December 21, 1948, ibid., Signatur 17 / 217–2 / 9.
71. Donald T. Shea to Assistant Land Director, December 9 and 17, 1948 and January 1 1949, ibid., Signatur 10 / 88–2 / 7.
72. Shea to Assistant Land Director, December 9, 1948, ibid.
73. Ibid.
74. Johannes Neuhäusler to Paul Moeller, January 11, 1949, ibid.
75. Memorandum for the Senate Armed Services Committee, Subject: Rudolf Aschenauer, August 4, 1949, NARA RG 46, 81st Congressional Committee on Armed Services, War Crimes Investigations, box 141. Leer's testimony is in MMIH, 1436.
76. Hans Bentz, "Rudolf Aschenauer," June 13, 1949, NARA RG 319, Records of the U.S. Army, Office of the Chief of Staff for Intelligence (G-2), IRR Personal Name File XE260416 (Aschenauer, Rudolf), vol. 4, folder 3.

12. Lie Detectors

1. Burton Ellis to Cecil Hubbert, May 25, 1948; and H. Barney Crawford to Mike Monroney, March 30, 1948. Also see James B. Rosenfeld (the father of George Rosenfeld, who was among those murdered at the Baugnez crossroads) to Ralph Gamble, June 1, 1948, all in NARA RG 153, Records of the Office of the Judge Advocate General, War Crimes Branch, Case Files (6–24), box 72.
2. Burton Ellis to Cecil Hubbert, May 25, 1948.
3. Department of the Army, Public Information Division, Analysis Branch, "The Judicial Processes concerning the Malmedy War Criminals: Digest of Editorial and Column Opinion, 22 May 1946–27 January 1949," ibid.
4. It would be the second such congressional inquiry into allegations that American interrogators had resorted to torture, the first being an investigation, held in 1902, into the army's record in the Philippine War. See Henry F. Graff, ed., *American Imperialism and the Philippine Insurrection: Testimony Taken from Hearings*

on Affairs in the Philippine Islands before the Senate Committee on the Philippines, 1902 (Boston: Little, Brown, 1969).

5. Gordon Simpson to Burton Ellis, March 29, 1949, EP, box 4, folder 118.
6. Dwight Fanton to Raymond Baldwin, July 13, 1948, PP.
7. Ibid.
8. Raymond Baldwin to Kenneth Royall, September 28, 1948, NARA RG 319, Records of the U.S. Army Staff, Office of the Chief Legislative Liaison, Congressional Investigations Division, War Crimes Trials, Correspondence 1948–1951, box 91; and Memorandum, War Department Special Staff to Burton Ellis, October 6, 1948, EP, box 9, folder 118.
9. Statements of Barney Crawford, November 9, 1948; Claude Mickelwait, October 22, 1948; Burton Ellis, October 27, 1948; Raphael Shumacker, November 8, 1948; Morris Elowitz, November 10, 1948; William Perl, November 15, 1948; Dwight Fanton, October 20 and November 3, 1948; all in NARA RG 549, USAEUR, War Crimes Branch, Case Files, Cases Tried 1945–1959 (6–24), box 5.
10. "Final Report of Proceedings of Administration of Justice Review Board," February 14, 1949, NARA RG 153, Records of the Office of the Judge Advocate General, War Crimes Branch, Case Files (6–24), box 95.
11. William Draper to Lucius Clay, February 11, 1949, NARA RG 153, Records of the Office of the Judge Advocate General, War Crimes Branch, Case Files (6–24), box 72.
12. Clay's decisions are reprinted in MMIH, 1602–1615.
13. Burton F. Ellis to Adjutant General, Department of the Army, January 17, 1949, PP.
14. On February 3 Ellis wrote Senator Homer Capeheart of Indiana, an old acquaintance, pleading with him to support Raymond Baldwin's resolution calling for a Senate investigation into the Malmedy case that would "give the investigation and prosecution staff the opportunity to be heard." Ellis to Homer Capeheart, February 3, 1949, NARA RG 153, Records of the Office of the Judge Advocate General, War Crimes Branch, Case Files (6–24), box 72.
15. Society for the Prevention of World War III, Inc., News Release, March 4, 1949, Columbia University Libraries, Archival Collections, Society for the Prevention of World War III Records, 1945–1972; and "Two U.S. Investigators Disavow Abuse of Germans in Malmedy," *New York Times*, March 5, 1949.
16. Investigation of Administration of Military Justice, January 27, 1949, *Congressional Record* 95, no. 12 (1949).
17. Ibid.
18. Ibid.
19. Ibid.
20. Speech of the Honorable Lawrence H. Smith of Wisconsin, March 10, 1949, copy in NARA RG 319, Records of the U.S. Army Staff, Office of the Chief Legislative

Liaison, Congressional Investigations Division, War Crimes Trials, Correspondence 1948–1951, box 94. "Appeal for Action against U.S. Investigators," *Christian Century,* January 5, 1949. By "government reports," Smith meant the Administration of Justice Review Board. "Congressman Asks Probe of Malmedy '3d-Degree Tactics,'" *Stars and Stripes,* March 12, 1949.

21. Committee on Expenditures in the Executive Departments, Senate Investigations Committee, Press Release, March 11, 1949, copy in NCPWR, series F, box 937.
22. On McCarthy's involvement, see Thomas C. Reeves, *The Life and Times of Joe McCarthy: A Biography* (New York: Stein and Day, 1982); and David M. Oshinsky, *A Conspiracy So Immense: The World of Joe McCarthy* (New York: Free Press, 1983).
23. Reeves, *Life and Times of Joe McCarthy,* 162.
24. Ibid., 168–169.
25. Minutes of Executive Board Meeting, March 16, 1949, NCPWR, series F, box 397; and Finucane to Willis Everett, April 4, 1949, ibid., series F, Correspondence with Willis M. Everett.
26. Frederick J. Libby to Raymond Baldwin, April 7, 1949, ibid., series I, Literature Produced, 1949.
27. Raymond Baldwin to Frederick Libby, April 14, 1949, ibid.
28. MMIH, 2, 9.
29. Ibid., 11, 16, 13.
30. Ibid., 98.
31. Ibid., 47, 67.
32. Ibid., 59.
33. James J. Bailey to Joseph McCarthy, April 18, 1949, NARA RG 319, Records of the U.S. Army Staff, Office of the Chief Legislative Liaison, Congressional Investigations Division, War Crimes Trials, Correspondence 1948–1951, box 95, reprinted in MMIH, 53–54.
34. MMIH, 167, 175, 176.
35. Dwight Fanton to Joseph Chambers, April 22, 1949, NARA RG 46, Records of the U.S. Senate, 81st Congress, Committee on Armed Services, War Crimes Investigations, box 139. Morris Elowitz also denied that Bailey had ever witnessed an interrogation. MMIH, 138–139.
36. Burton Ellis to John Evans, March 29, 1949, ibid., 343–345; and John W. King to Burton Ellis, April 4, 1949, EP, box 9, folder 121; Calvin Unterseher to Ellis, April 16, 1949; and Jack Plano to Ellis, April 18, 1949; both in EP, box 9, folder 122.
37. MMIH, 112–131.
38. Noble Johnson to William Knowland, April 9, 1949, NARA RG 46, Records of the U.S. Senate, 81st Congress, Committee on Armed Services, War Crimes Investigations, box 139; and MMIH 322–371, 555–571. Viggo Gruy, a former first lieutenant and company executive officer assigned to the battalion responsible for

overseeing Schwäbisch Hall prison in November and December, 1945, sent Ellis a sworn statement asserting the prisoners were provided with blankets, heated cells, and adequate rations, and denying that any of them had been physically abused. Statement of Viggo K. Gruy, April 11, 1949, EP, box 9, folder 121. Also see statement of Arnold F. W. Frank, April 19, 1949, ibid., box 9, folder 122.

39. Calvin Unterseher to Burton Ellis, April 16, 1949, ibid., box 9, folder 122. Unterseher's testimony, MMIH, 640–654, and Stanley B. Sykes statement, April 21, 1949, EP, box 9, folder 122.

40. MMIH, 643, 644.

41. Testimony of Max Karan and John Ricker, ibid., 844–881. Gerard Gert, an OMGUS Civil Affairs Division investigator was dispatched to interview Knorr, but was unable to as Knorr was incapacitated following surgery to amputate one of his legs. Gert did speak with two Germans who had been employed at the prison during the investigation who claimed never to have seen any injured prisoners and recalled that the prisoners "ate better than we did. They received tobacco, white bread, chocolate etc., things which the public on the outside did not have." Statement of Gerard M. Gert, April 24, 1949, EP, box 9, folder 121.

42. MMIH, 321–348.

43. Ibid., 233, 250, 251.

44. Ibid., 307, 1087.

45. Ibid., 276.

46. Ibid., 281.

47. Ibid., 433, 430, 431.

48. Ibid., 30, 170–173, 179, 188, 201, 239.

49. Ibid., 548–549. McCarthy's announcement of Teil's call to his office marked the low point of the hearings for Burton Ellis. "This is worst blow yet," he wrote to Harry Thon on April 29. Thon replied by cable from Germany that Teil was "definitely not telling the truth" and was never in Schwäbisch Hall. Ellis speculated that the unconscious man Teil claimed to have seen was Gustav Neve, who, following his interrogation by Raphael Shumacker, fainted after being hooded for return to his cell. Ellis to Thon, April 29, 1949, NARA RG 46, Records of the U.S. Senate, 81st Congress, Committee on Armed Services, War Crimes Investigations, box 141; and Harry Thon to Burton Ellis, May 4, 1949, EP, box 9, folder 118.

50. MMIH, 600, 577–578, 601.

51. Ibid., 572, 608.

52. Ibid., 722–724.

53. Perl's testimony is in ibid., 609–640, 658–690, 695–754, and 759–791.

54. Ibid., 631.

55. Ibid., 632, 634, 793.

56. Ibid., 837–844.

57. Ibid., 951, 959.

58. Ibid., 1555–1570.

59. Willis Everett to James Finucane, February 22, 1950, NCPWR, series F, box 397.

60. MMIH, 1523–1527.

61. Affidavit of Dietrich Schnell, January 10, 1948, NARA RG 549, USAEUR, War Crimes Branch, Case Files, Cases Tried 1945–1959 (6–24), box 44.

62. MMIH, 1528–1544; and *Malmedy Massacre Investigation: Report of Subcommittee of the Committee on Armed Services, United States Senate, Eighty-First Congress, First Session, Pursuant to S. Res. 42* (Washington, DC: U.S. Government Printing Office, 1949) (hereafter "MMI Report"), 12–14.

63. Reiser's, Vollprecht's, and Eble's testimonies are in MMIH, 1469–1499, 1499–1511, and 1513–1523, respectively.

64. To Baldwin's question, "Did you yourself ever think of pressing that medical side of this thing?," John Dwinell had replied simply, "I did not." MMIH, 432.

65. Edward Young to Col. C. C. Fenn, July 12, 1949; and Fenn to Joseph Chambers, August 12, 1949, both in NARA RG 46, Records of the U.S. Senate, 81st Congress, Committee on Armed Services, War Crimes Investigations, box 139.

66. Summary Report on the Medical Examination of the Malmedy Prisoners, August–September 1949, ibid., box 148; and the testimony of the three officers, all in MMIH, 1545–1552.

67. MMIH, 1630–1639.

68. Aaron Bank, CO, Headquarters Region IV, 7070th Counter Intelligence Corps Group to CO, 7979 CIC Group, EUCOM, August 31, 1949, NARA RG 319, Records of the U.S. Army, Office of the Chief of Staff for Intelligence (G-2), IRR Personal Name File XE260416 (Aschenauer, Rudolf), vol. 4, folder 3.

69. Agent Report, 7970th CIC Group, Region I, September 16, 1949, NARA RG 319, Records of the U.S. Army, IRR Impersonal Name File ZA021038 (Malmedy Massacre).

70. Hans G. Bentz, "Rudolf Aschenauer," June 13, 1949, NARA RG 319, Records of the U.S. Army, Office of the Chief of Staff for Intelligence (G-2), IRR Personal Name File XE260416 (Aschenauer, Rudolf), vol. 4, folder 3.

71. Aaron Bank, "Malmedy Case (U.S. Senate Sub-Committee Investigation), Re: Rudolph Aschenauer, Bishop Johannes Neuhaeusler, and Bishop Theophil Wurm," September 15, 1949, ibid., vol. 4, folder 2.

72. Agent Report, Evangelisches Hilfswerk in Bavaria, November 30, 1949, NARA RG 319, Records of the U.S. Army, IRR Impersonal Name File Entry ZZ-6 (Hilfswerk der Evangelischen Kirchen), box 8.

73. MMI Report, 16, 19.

74. Ibid., 8.

75. Ibid., 14, 34.

76. Ibid., 32–34.
77. Ibid., 31–32, 34. Six months after the final report's release, Undersecretary of State James Webb, speaking on behalf of the secretary of state, wrote Senate Armed Services Committee chairman Millard Tydings and defended the service records of German-born personnel in Germany. Webb conveyed a recommendation of a five-year citizenship requirement. James Webb to Millard Tydings, April 18, 1950, NARA RG 153, Records of the Office of the Judge Advocate General, War Crimes Branch, Case Files (6–24), box 86.
78. Clio Straight to Burton Ellis, EP, box 4, folder 120.
79. Burton Ellis to Dwight Fanton, May 21, 1949, NARA RG 46, Records of the U.S. Senate, 81st Congress, Committee on Armed Services, War Crimes Investigations, box 141.
80. Morris Rubin to James Finucane, June 10, 1949, NCPWR, series F, box 397; and Rubin to Ellis, EP, box 9, folder 119.
81. William Perl to Burton Ellis, November 13, 1949; and Ellis to Perl, November 17, 1949, both in EP, box 4, folder 120.

13. Red Jackets

1. Danny S. Parker, *Hitler's Warrior: The Life and Wars of SS Colonel Jochen Peiper* (Cambridge, MA: Da Capo, 2014), 200; and Jens Westemeier, *Himmlers Krieger: Joachim Peiper und die Waffen-SS in Krieg und Nachkriegszeit* (Paderborn: Ferdinand Schöningh, 2014), 496–515.
2. In April 1950 there were a total of 1,315 convicted war criminals in Landsberg, Werl, and Wittlich prisons. By August 1952, that number had fallen to 575. Three years later, 95 remained in all three prisons. All were freed by 1958. Figures from Frank M. Buscher, *The U.S. War Crimes Trial Program in Germany, 1946–1955* (New York: Greenwood, 1989), 171–174.
3. For example, "'Todesstrafen zu weitgehend': USA-Kommission empfiehlt Begnadigung," *Die Welt,* January 8, 1949; and "Mittelalterliche Methoden," *Süddeutsche Zeitung,* March 8, 1949.
4. Theophil Wurm, "The Demands of Justice," October 26, 1949, NCPWR, Misc., series H; NCPW Press Release, June 1, 1949, ibid., series F, box 397; and "German Bishops on War Crimes Trials," *Christian Century,* June 15, 1949.
5. See Headquarters, Counter Intelligence Corps Region I, 66th Counter Intelligence Corps Detachment, U.S. Army Europe, Subject: Hilfswerk der Evagelischen Kirchen Deutschlands (Welfare Organization of the Protestant Churches in Germany), November 29, 1949, NARA RG 319, Records of the U.S. Army, IRR Impersonal Name File Entry ZZ-6 (Hilfswerk der Evangelischen Kirchen), box 8; *Süddeutsche Zeitung,* October 19, 1949; *Stuttgarter Zeitung,* October 19, 1949; *Neuer*

Kurier (Nuremberg), October 20, 1949; *Die Neue Zeitung,* October 27, 1949; and Wurm, "Demands of Justice."

6. Joseph Chambers, Notes on a Meeting with Father Zeiger, August 21, 1949, NARA RG 319, Records of the U.S. Army, Army Staff Office, Chief Legislative Liaison, Congressional Investigations Division, War Crimes Trials, Correspondence 1948–1951, box 96.
7. "The Dachau 'War Crimes Trials': An Eye-Witness Account" [summer 1949], NCPWR, series F, box 398.
8. Ibid.
9. Johannes Neuhäusler to NCPW, July 20, 1949; Frederick J. Libby to Raymond Baldwin, August 25, 1949; and Joseph Chambers, memorandum [n.d.], all in NARA RG 46, Records of the U.S. Senate, 81st Congress, Committee on Armed Services, War Crimes Investigations, box 141; and Libby to Neuhäusler, August 26, 1949, NCPWR, series F, box 397.
10. The CIC monitored German press coverage. For a summary see 66th CIC Detachment, "Malmedy Case (U.S. Senate Sub-Committee Investigation), Re: German News Response to Rebuttal by 'American National Council for the [*sic*] Prevention of War,'" December 14, 1949, NARA RG 319, Records of the U.S. Army Staff, Assistant Chief of Staff, G-2, box 32.
11. Franz Josef Schöningh, "A Michael Kohlhaas in Atlanta," *Süddeutsche Zeitung,* September 8, 1949; Peiper quoted in James Weingartner, *A Peculiar Crusade: Willis M. Everett and the Malmedy Massacre* (New York: New York University Press, 2000), 200.
12. Westemeier, *Himmlers Krieger,* 502–503; and Weingartner, *Peculiar Crusade,* 219–220.
13. "Untersuchungsergebnis der US-Senatskommission: Verfahren gegen die deutschen Angeklagten war fair"; and William Perl, "Die Verbrechen von Malmedy wurden begangen," both in *Die Neue Zeitung,* October 27, 1949.
14. Rudolf Aschenauer, "Um Recht oder Unrecht im Malmedy-Prozess: Hat die Wahrheit verschiedene Gesichter?," *Muenchner Merkur,* November 11, 1949.
15. The U.S. Army and the CIC remained wary of the possibility of another wave of torture exposés. In December 1949, CIC agents became aware of rumors emanating from within the CIC that Perl had shot a German prisoner at the Fifteenth Army Interrogation Center Prison in Rheinbach in May or June 1945. The rumor—never substantiated—became a matter of some concern as intelligence officials knew what would happen should it become public in West Germany: "Incomplete information in regards to the . . . incident may cause German leaders to renew their investigation of the Malmedy case with continued vigor." 66th CIC Detachment, "Malmedy Case (U.S. Senate Sub-Committee Investigation), Re: German News Response to Rebuttal by 'American National Council for the [*sic*]

Prevention of War." Also see Aaron Bank to Headquarters, 66th CIC Detachment, Attn: Mr. Coopman, December 14, 1949, NARA RG 319, Records of the U.S. Army, Records of Army Staff, Assistant Chief of Staff, G-2, box 32, and Memorandum, Director, FBI, May 7, 1951, copy in PP.

16. Anthony Glees, *Reinventing Germany: German Political Development since 1945* (London: Bloomsbury Academic, 1996).

17. On this subject, see Norbert Frei, *Adenauer's Germany and the Nazi Past: The Politics of Amnesty and Integration,* trans. Joel Golb (New York: Columbia University Press, 2002); and Jeffrey Herf, *Divided Memory: The Nazi Past in the Two Germanys* (Cambridge, MA: Harvard University Press, 1999). Adenauer described his position and outlined a comprehensive solution in an April, 1951 letter to the pope. Konrad Adenauer to Pope Pius XII, April 10, 1951, BAK B141 / 9576.

18. Frei, *Adenauer's Germany,* 5–91.

19. The re-formed Communist Party of Germany *(Kommunistische Partei Deutschlands)* in the Western occupation zones managed to secure seats in the Bundestag in the first national elections in 1949 but then lost what little popular support it had. The FRG's Federal Constitutional Court banned the party in 1956. See Eric D. Weitz, *Creating German Communism, 1890–1990: From Popular Protest to Socialist State* (Princeton, NJ: Princeton University Press, 1997).

20. Thomas Alan Schwartz, *America's Germany: John J. McCloy and the Federal Republic of Germany* (Cambridge, MA: Harvard University Press, 1991). On "renazification" fears, see Norbert Frei, "'Vergangenheitsbewaeltigung' or 'Renazification'? The American Perspective on Germany's Confrontation with the Nazi Past in the Early Years of the Adenauer Era," in Michael Ermarth, ed., *America and the Shaping of West Germany Society, 1945–1955* (Providence, RI: Berg, 1993), 47–59.

21. Quoted in Frei, *Adenauer's Germany,* 126.

22. Lucius Clay to Tracy Voorhees, March 29, 1949, in Jean Edward Smith, ed., *The Papers of General Lucius D. Clay: Germany, 1945–1949* (Bloomington: Indiana University Press, 1974), 1062.

23. On Wehrmacht veterans and convicted war criminals, see Jay Lockenour, *Soldiers as Citizens: Former Wehrmacht Officers in the Federal Republic of Germany, 1945–1955* (Lincoln: University of Nebraska Press, 2001). On Waffen SS veterans, see Karsten Wilke, *Die "Hilfsgemeinschaft auf Gegenseitigkeit" (HIAG) 1950–1990. Veteranen der Waffen-SS in der Bundesrepublik* (Paderborn: Verlag Ferdinand Schöningh, 2011).

24. Drafts of the "Memorandum" are archived in the Evangelisches Zentralarchiv, Berlin, B2 / 261. On the creation of the "Memorandum," see Frei, *Adenauer's Germany,* 123–126; Ernst Klee, *Persilscheine und Falsche Pässe: Wie die Kirchen den Nazis halfen* (Frankfurt: Fischer Taschenbuch, 1991), 87–93; and Katharina Von Kellenbach, *The Mark of Cain: Guilt and Denial in the Post-War Lives of Nazi Perpetrators* (New York: Oxford University Press, 2013), 55–61.

25. Agent Report, 66th CIC Detachment, Subject: Die Bruderschaft, July 20, 1951; and Summary of Information, 66th CIC Detachment, Subject: Hilfswerk der Hilfenden Haende, November 27, 1951, both in NARA RG 319, Records of the U.S. Army, IRR Impersonal Name Files XE306114 (Helping Hands).
26. For example, "Meine liebe Prinzessin," *Der Spiegel*, January 31, 1951.
27. Karsten Wilke, "Die Truppenkamaradschaften der Waffen SS 1950–1990: Organisationsgeschichte, Entwicklung und innerer Zusammenhalt," in Jan Erik Schulte, Peter Lieb, and Bernd Wegner, eds., *Die Waffen-SS: Neue Forschungen* (Paderborn: Ferdinand Schöningh, 2014), 421–435; and Frei, *Adenauer's Germany*, 41–66.
28. David Clay Large, "Reckoning without the Past: The HIAG of the Waffen-SS and the Politics of Rehabilitation in the Bonn Republic, 1950–1961," *Journal of Modern History* 59 (1987): 79–113, esp. 82.
29. Westemeier, *Himmlers Krieger*, 467–471.
30. Hans Korte praised HIAG by name for its contributions to freeing the remaining Landsberg prisoners. See his "Sternenbanner in Landsberg eingeholt," *Deutsche Soldaten Zeitung*, June 1958.
31. See, for example, Rudolf Aschenauer, *Um Recht und Wahrheit im Malmedy-Fall. Eine Stellungsnahme zum Bericht eines Untersuchungsausschusses des amerikanische Senats in Sachen Malmedy-Prozess* (Munich: Val. Hoefling, 1950), in English translation as *Truth or "Clever Strategy" in the Case of Malmedy? A Critical Analysis of the "Baldwin Report"* (Munich: Val. Hoefling, 1950); Jerome S. Legge Jr., "Resisting a War Crimes Trial: The Malmedy Massacre, the German Churches, and the U.S. Army Counter Intelligence Corps," *Holocaust and Genocide Studies* 26 (2012): 229–260. Also see Kevin Coogan's excellent study of the postwar American far right, *Dreamer of the Day: Francis Parker Yockey and the Postwar Fascist International* (Brooklyn, NY: Autonomedia, 1999). I'm grateful to Benjamin C. Hett for information about Aschenauer's connection to the Federal Office for the Protection of the Constitution.
32. "Niederschrift ueber die Besprechung am 21. Januar 1950 in Heidelberg," January 30, 1950, BAK B305 / 132. The circle debated the wisdom of reviving a publicity campaign in September 1951. See "Protokoll der Sitzung des Heidelberg Juristenkreis am 17. September 1951 in Heidelberg," ibid., B305 / 61. See also Frei, *Adenauer's Germany*, 121–123.
33. For a concise summary of the circle's activities, see Buscher, *U.S. War Crimes Trial Program in Germany*, 101–105.
34. The creation of a modification board—comprised solely of American personnel—had been recommended by Lucius Clay in the spring of 1948 and supported by the Simpson Commission. Army officials initiated a study of the idea in July 1949. See Memorandum for the Record, Subject: Recommendations of

Clemency Committee concerning War Crimes Clemency Program, July 18, 1949, NARA RG 549, USAEUR, Judge Advocate Division, War Crimes Branch, Records Related to General Administration.

35. Frei, *Adenauer's Germany*, 159. The German theologian Helmut Thielicke made a similar argument in an editorial published in the *Frankfurter Allgemeine Zeitung* on January 25.
36. Office of Land Commissioner for Bavaria, Intelligence Division, War Crimes Prisoner[s] at Landsberg, December 27, 1950, USAEUR Case Files (Peiper, Joachim).
37. Ibid.
38. Jack Raymond, "21 Nazi Criminals Saved from Death"; and "German Reaction Cautious on Nazis," both in the *New York Times*, February 1, 1951. On McCloy's decisions, see Schwartz, *America's Germany*, 157–175. For Handy's decision, see "General Handy Announces Decision in War Crimes Capital Case," Headquarters, EUCOM, Public Information Division, EUCOM Release No. 51–91, January 31, 1951.
39. John Mendelsohn, "War Crimes Trials and Clemency in Germany and Japan," in Robert Wolfe, ed., *Americans as Proconsuls: United States Military Government in Germany and Japan, 1944–1952* (Carbondale: Southern Illinois University Press, 1984), 226–259.
40. Dissenting opinion, Harry D. Pritchard, Review of the War Crimes Branch, Judge Advocate Division, May 4, 1951, USAEUR Case Files (Ochmann, Paul).
41. Review of the War Crimes Branch, Judge Advocate Division, May 17, 1951, USAEUR Case Files (Rauh, Theodor).
42. Ibid.
43. Review of the War Crimes Branch, Judge Advocate Division, April 18, 1951, USAEUR Case Files (Sickel, Kurt).
44. The relevant documents and correspondence are in Review of the War Crimes Branch, Judge Advocate Division, April 18, 1951, USAEUR Case Files (Rauh, Theodor).
45. Ibid.
46. Review of the War Crimes Branch, Judge Advocate Division, April 17, 1951; and Chief of the War Crimes Branch to EUCOM War Crimes Modification Board, May 1, 1951, in USAEUR Case Files (Dietrich, Josef [Sepp]).
47. Ibid.
48. Ibid.
49. Peter Caddick-Adams, *Snow and Steel: The Battle of the Bulge, 1944–1945* (New York: Oxford University Press, 2014), ch. 28.
50. Quoted in the *New York Times*, October 25, 1955.
51. Review of the War Crimes Branch, Judge Advocate Division, April 17, 1951, USAEUR Case Files (Dietrich, Josef [Sepp]). Clark's and the Everett-Strong letters to the *Times* were published on January 5 and 19, 1956, respectively.

52. *New York Times,* January 26, 1956; and Westemeier, *Himmlers Krieger,* 502.
53. Parker, *Hitler's Warrior,* 216.
54. USAEUR Case Files (Peiper, Joachim).
55. Ibid.
56. "Malmedy Col Wins Release," *Stars and Stripes,* December 23, 1956; and Westemeier, *Himmlers Krieger,* 508–509.
57. Westemeier, *Himmlers Krieger,* 257–267.
58. Ibid., 612–618.

Conclusion

1. For example, Dietrich Ziemssen's 1952 booklet, *Der Malmedy-Prozess: Ein Bericht auf Grund dokumentarischer Unterlagen und eigenen Erlebens* (Munich: Deschler, 1952) was reissued in 1981 by the Institute for Historical Review as *The Malmedy Trial: A Report Based on Documentary Sources and Personal Experience* (Torrence, CA: Institute for Historical Review, 1981); Paul Hausser, *Waffen-SS im Einsatz* (Göttingen: Plesse, 1953), and his *Sodaten wie andere auch: Der Weg der Waffen-SS* (Osnabrück: Munin, 1966); and Kurt Meyer, *Grenadiere* (Munich: Schild, 1957).
2. Charles Whiting, *Massacre at Malmedy: The Story of Jochen Peiper's Battle Group Ardennes, December, 1944* (London: Leo Cooper, 1971).
3. John Toland, *Battle: The Story of the Bulge* (New York: Random House, 1959); Burton Ellis to John Toland, March 16, 1977; and Toland to Robert Loomis, with attached note to Ellis, May 31, 1977, all in EP, box 4, folder 47. The U.S. Army's official history, published in 1965, based its account of the battle group's actions on Peiper's interviews with army historians in 1945 and the trial transcript. The author accepts that Dietrich gave an order to spread a "wave of terror" and that the men of Battle Group Peiper killed hundreds of Americans and Belgians. Why it was that Peiper's battle group alone that committed atrocities in the Ardennes could, the author speculated, be attributed to Peiper's experiences in Russia or the fact that since his unit was spearheading the German attack on the northern shoulder, it was "in a position to carry out the orders for the 'wave of terror' tactic." The account does not discuss the posttrial controversy. See Hugh M. Cole, *The Ardennes: The Battle of the Bulge* (Washington, DC: Office of the Chief of Military History, Department of the Army, 1965), 260–264. In *A Time for Trumpets,* Cole's protégé, the historian and Bulge veteran Charles MacDonald, gives a similar account of events, augmented with personal anecdotes from the American, German, and Belgian eyewitnesses with whom MacDonald had corresponded. He devotes a brief epilogue to summarizing the posttrial controversy, expressing mild skepticism about the torture accusations. MacDonald, *Time for Trumpets,* 197–244, 430–465, 620–623.

4. Ronald Smelser and Edward J. Davies II, *The Myth of the Eastern Front: The Nazi-Soviet War in American Popular Culture* (New York: Cambridge University Press, 2008).
5. Weingartner's skepticism was expressed more forcefully in two later works, *A Peculiar Crusade: Willis M. Everett and the Malmedy Massacre* (New York: New York University Press, 2000); and *Americans, Germans, and War Crimes Justice: Law, Memory, and "The Good War"* (Santa Barbara, CA: Praeger, 2011).
6. Quoted in Jens Westemeier, *Himmlers Krieger: Joachim Peiper und die Waffen-SS in Krieg und Nachkriegszeit* (Paderborn: Ferdinand Schöningh, 2014), 240.
7. Burton Ellis to James Weingartner, March 17, 1977, EP, box 4, folder 47. MacDonald praised Weingartner's account as "careful, detailed, and scholarly," though added "Professor Weingartner is kinder to the defendants than one who lay on the ground that dreadful day." See MacDonald, *Time for Trumpets*, 681.
8. James Weingartner, *Crossroads of Death: The Story of the Malmedy Massacre and Trial* (Berkeley: University of California Press, 1979), 148.
9. Ibid., 252–253; and MMIH, 1637.
10. Trevor Dupuy, *Hitler's Last Gamble: The Battle of the Bulge, December 1944–January 1945* (New York: HarperCollins, 1994), 366–367 and 487–497.
11. Rick Atkinson, *Guns at Last Light: The War in Western Europe* (New York: Henry Holt, 2013), 634–635; and Peter Caddick-Adams, *Snow and Steel: The Battle of the Bulge, 1944–1945* (New York: Oxford University Press, 2014), 237, 710. Antony Beevor avoids the temptation to perpetuate the apologetic narrative in his *Ardennes 1944: The Battle of the Bulge* (New York: Viking, 2015).
12. Alistair McGill and Michael Friedrich Vogt, *"Über Galgen wächst kein Gras": US-Folterjustiz vom Malmedyprozess bis Abu Ghraib* (Gescher: Polar Film & Medien GmbH, 2005), DVD. An earlier American example is "Malmedy Massacre," a 1993 episode of the History Channel series *Our Century*. The program's writers and most of the commentators do not deny the massacre of American prisoners by Peiper's men, but do offer the viewer a perfect summary of the apologetic narrative.
13. For an introduction to the subject, see Alfred W. McCoy, *Torture and Impunity: The U.S. Doctrine of Coercive Interrogation* (Madison: University of Wisconsin Press, 2012). See also Mark Danner, *Torture and Truth: America, Abu Ghraib, and the War on Terror* (New York: New York Review Books, 2012); Jane Mayer, *The Dark Side: The Inside Story of How the War on Terror Turned into a War on American Ideals* (New York: Anchor, 2009); and Seymour M. Hersh, *Chain of Command: The Road from 9/11 to Abu Ghraib* (New York: HarperCollins, 2004).
14. See Matthew Alexander and John R. Bruning, *How to Break a Terrorist: The U.S. Interrogators Who Used Brains, Not Brutality, to Take Down the Deadliest Man in Iraq* (New York: Free Press, 2008); Tony Lagouranis and Allen Mikaelian, *Fear Up*

Harsh: An Army's Interrogator's Dark Journey through Iraq (New York: NAL Caliber, 2007); and Chris Mackey and Greg Miller, *The Interrogators: Task Force 500 and America's Secret War against Al Qaeda* (New York: Back Bay, 2004). In 2009 U.S. president Barack Obama authorized the creation of the High Value Detainee Interrogation Group (HIG), a joint project of the Defense Department, CIA, and FBI. HIG's purpose is to develop and deploy noncoercive human intelligence-gathering techniques informed by current research (some of it funded by HIG) on interrogation methods. Results of some of this research suggest the "psychological approach" used in the Malmedy investigation—especially lengthy questioning by well-informed interrogators who do not resort to bullying and abusive behavior—may have reduced the chances of producing false confessions. See, for example, the special issue of *Applied Cognitive Psychology* 28 (2014), "Information Gathering in Law Enforcement and Intelligence Settings: Advancing Theory and Practice."

Acknowledgments

Writing a book is an intensely rewarding, not infrequently frustrating, and humbling experience. I am grateful to many people and institutions for their interest, support, criticism, and encouragement. It is a privilege to once again be able to contribute to Harvard University Press's distinguished body of scholarship addressing the relationship between war, memory, and the contemporary world, and I thank Kathleen McDermott for her interest in this project. Thanks also to Katrina Vassallo, Melody Negron, and Paul Vincent for their assistance in preparing the manuscript. The research phase would not have been possible without support from the Deutscher Akademischer Austauschdienst and the PSC CUNY–Research Foundation of the City University of New York. I thank my Brooklyn College colleagues David Troyansky and Christopher Ebert for their encouragement and, not least, patience. Thanks also to Miriam Deutsch and Nick Irons at Brooklyn College for their help with some of the images. I'm grateful to my CUNY colleague Benjamin C. Hett for his encouragement and comments, and Jens Westemeier was most generous in sharing his vast knowledge of the Waffen SS. Richard Remy's comments on the early chapters were extremely helpful.

It was an honor to be hosted by Norbert Frei, to whom all historians interested in the relationship between war, memory, and politics are indebted, at his seminar at the Friedrich-Schiller-Universität Jena. I presented portions of this book at various stages of its development to Professor Frei's seminar, the German Studies Association, the Columbia Seminar on Twentieth Century Politics and Society, the Modern Germany Workshop at Temple University, the New York Military History Affairs Symposium, Ohio University's Contemporary History

Institute, and the Jewish Studies Association, and I'm grateful for the questions and feedback.

This book could not have been written without the assistance of archivists and librarians at the U.S. National Archives, the Bundesarchiv in Koblenz, the Evangelisches Zentralarchiv in Berlin, the Evangelisches Landesarchiv in Stuttgart, the Politisches Archiv at the Auswärtiges Amt in Berlin, the Wiener Library in London, and the archives and special collections divisions at Columbia University, the Catholic University of America, the George Washington University, the University of Idaho, and Swarthmore College.

Family and friends provided constant encouragement and support. I thank Richard and Delores Remy and Sharon Remy-Williams. I owe a particular debt of gratitude to William and Susan Koppes, who hosted me in their home during my multiple visits to the National Archives. Their hospitality and generosity made my trips to College Park as enjoyable as they were productive.

Above all, I thank April Henning. Her interest in and enthusiasm for this project was unflagging, and her close reading and critique of every chapter was invaluable. This book is for her.

Index